Perspectives on Southern Africa

Crown and Charter

CECIL RHODES

Crown and Charter

The Early Years of the
British South Africa Company

John S. Galbraith

UNIVERSITY OF CALIFORNIA PRESS
BERKELEY LOS ANGELES LONDON

UNIVERSITY OF CALIFORNIA PRESS
BERKELEY AND LOS ANGELES, CALIFORNIA
UNIVERSITY OF CALIFORNIA PRESS, LTD.
LONDON, ENGLAND
COPYRIGHT © 1974, BY
THE REGENTS OF THE UNIVERSITY OF CALIFORNIA
ISBN: 0-520-02693-4
LIBRARY OF CONGRESS CATALOG CARD NUMBER: 73-93050
PRINTED IN THE UNITED STATES OF AMERICA

TO LAURA

Contents

Illustrations

Preface

THE BRITISH SOUTH AFRICA COMPANY IN ITS EARLY YEARS
has usually been considered to be the corporate extension of the
drive and ambition of Cecil John Rhodes. This assumption has
considerable justification. Rhodes became the most powerful
force in the company. He did so both by his own dynamism and
by the quiescence of his fellow directors. His dominance was
also made possible by the unwillingness of the imperial government to exercise those controls over the operation of the company which were incorporated in the charter. Various rationali-
zations were offered for this abdication of authority, but two
factors were fundamental—recognition that responsibility might
require expenditure and an increasing timidity in the face of
Rhodes's aggressiveness.

As both managing director of the company and prime minister of the Cape, Rhodes was able to exercise great power. He
could usually rely upon the support of the London board for
his actions, and his majority in the House of Assembly was so
strong that he had little cause to be concerned over parliamentary opposition. Absence of restraint fed his arrogance. Unvarying success made him reckless and led him to the folly of the
Jameson Raid. Many writers have taken this line. Their focus,
however, has been on the drama of the raid and the consequent
fall from grace of Rhodes. But the events of December 1895
were long foreshadowed. Rhodes had previously contemplated
similar actions against the Ndebele and the Portuguese.

This book will devote considerable attention to Rhodes. But
though Rhodes was a great force, the policies of the company
were not solely of his making. I will attempt to describe the

environment within which the company operated, the interrelationships between Rhodes and the London board, and the interplay between the company's directors and the imperial government.

The intrusion of the British South Africa Company into Central Africa can be viewed as merely an episode of European expansion. But the British South Africa Company had distinctive attributes. No other chartered company appealed so strongly to the cupidity of the gamblers in the stock exchange. None attracted such widespread admiration or condemnation. And no other company had a Rhodes.

In evaluating the early years of the company, the writer is beset with a strong temptation to moralize. Noble professions and amoral actions stimulate such a response. In few other enterprises of the era is the contrast more striking. The British South Africa Company was avowedly dedicated to the advancement of Livingstone's Christianity, Commerce, and Civilization. But the concerns of the directors had little relationship to noble objectives. Some were businessmen interested in business ends and were not less ethical than most in pursuing them. Some were not above using questionable means to promote those ends. Rhodes professed devotion to the advancement of "Anglo-Saxondom," but he demonstrated devotion to the advancement of self, and his methods were those most appropriate for his purposes, without great concern for ethical considerations.

Harry Truman observed with the pithiness characteristic of his Missouri background, "When they're shouting the loudest in the Amen corner, go out and lock the smoke-house door." His cynical view was not entirely justified. Idealism can be sincere, though it also provides a comely cloak to mask the most venal of motives. The leadership of the South Africa Company during the period treated here cannot be indicted en bloc for hypocrisy. The directors undoubtedly believed that they served a great cause. They all had scant regard for the rights of Africans, but in this respect they did not differ from most of their contemporaries in England and Europe. Most leaders of British society believed that the world should be developed by those most capable of doing so. They had no doubt that people of European lineage, in particular the British, were peculiarly fitted to carry out that responsibility. Some thought Africans and Asians had potentialities which in time would enable them to rise to the level of Europeans; some maintained that the intellectual gap was hereditary; but there was little argument that for the present at least, civilization and progress must be advanced primarily by Europeans. The humanitarians of the Aborigines Protection Society did not dissent from this conclusion. Their concern was that the trusteeship be genuine, rather than a rationalization for exploitation and enslavement. The staff of the Colonial Office was influenced by such considerations; some were actively sympathetic to the peoples over whom they ruled. Their actions in support of these principles, however, were feeble and ineffective.

The dynamism of Rhodes was encouraged by the passivity of those who had a responsibility to control him. With two or three exceptions, the company's directors devoted little energy to supervision of the company's policies. They had neither the will nor the desire to restrain Rhodes so long as he appeared to be successful. The staff of the Colonial Office were privately critical of Rhodes, but these strictures were not evident in policy. Their inaction contributed to the dramatic consequences associated with the actions of Rhodes.

In the preparation of this study I have received advice from my former colleague Terence Ranger, now at Manchester; Leonard M. Thompson, Yale University; John E. Flint, Dalhousie University; and Lewis H. Gann, Senior Fellow, Hoover Institution on War, Revolution, and Peace. Professor George Shepperson of the University of Edinburgh generously shared with me his materials on the African Lakes Company and gave me other valuable assistance. My research assistants, W. Max Smith and Phillip A. Kennedy, have been a great help. I appreciate the assistance of the staffs of the National Archives of Rhodesia, Public Record Office, and the curators of the Grey Papers at the University of Durham. I acknowledge the courtesy of the Public Record Office in permitting me to reproduce the company map of Central Africa and the cartoon by Edward Fairfield. My thanks go to Susan V. Welling for an excellent job of editing. And, as always, I acknowledge the multifarious assistance of my wife.

I

Prelude to the Charter

The Contest for the Southern Interior, 1884–1885

FEW MEN HAVE BEEN SO SUCCESSFUL IN CREATING THEIR own immortality as did Cecil Rhodes; his assessment of himself endures seventy years after his death. Both admirers and detractors concede that he pursued great dreams. His alleged last words—"so little done, so much to do"—are still quoted and requoted as epitomizing the drive of his life. No matter that his actual valedictory may have been the far more poignant "turn me over, Jack." The hero must depart life as he lived it! Rhodes continues to dominate the thoughts of writers who are drawn to late nineteenth-century southern Africa. The power struggles of that day are the stuff of great drama, and Rhodes, the dynamo driven by cosmic ambition, makes a perfect antithesis to Kruger, the immovable object who stood in his way. This personalization of the great issues of the day, however, lends itself to gross oversimplification. The turmoil of southern Africa was deeply affected by Rhodes; it was not created by him nor did he determine its character. He did not set the diamond mines in Kimberley or the gold mines in the Witwatersrand; he did not create the legend of Ophir which was to contribute to the end of the Ndebele independence. Nor did he single-handedly create the British South Africa Company.

Rhodes performed in the major role, but the general character of the play was determined by the interactions of men in Europe and Africa with forces generated by economic impulses, power drives, and illusions as to the wealth of Africa. All of these elements were involved in the movement to the north which swept over the Ndebele, the Shona, and other peoples of the African interior.

Advocates of expansion in Africa often had all the zeal of religious fanatics. One of the most ardent, Harry Johnston, eloquently expressed their creed. In August 1888, writing in the guise of "an African Explorer," Johnston laid out a blueprint for readers of the *Times* on Great Britain's policy in Africa. His line was, predictably, expansionist. He conceded that other European powers had "legitimate" interests in Africa—Italy had a "natural heritage" in Tripoli, and France its "established rights" in Algeria and Tunis. The latecomer, Germany, had pegged out claims which must be accepted with good grace, but her irruption into Africa was a testament to the languidness of the British government in defending the "rights" of its traders. A new era had arrived with the "scramble for Africa"; protectionist states sought to erect barriers against British commerce; the imperial government to ensure "a fair field and no favour" must "extend our direct political influence over a large part of Africa."[1]

Johnston's indictment was directed not only against the imperial government. The ineffectiveness of the British response, he maintained, was attributable not only to Whitehall but to the lack of cohesiveness of the British Empire. Each self-governing colony was concerned only with its own environment and was indifferent to the rest of the world. This combination of indolence at the center and parochialism on the periphery had enabled the anti-imperialists in Britain to frustrate the advancement of Greater Britain. In Southern Africa, Germany had thereby been able to gain a foothold and the Boers of the Transvaal, who might have been rendered innocuous by the British acquisition of Delagoa Bay, had become a threat. Even feeble Portugal was able to challenge British interests in the interior of

1. The *Times*, August 22, 1888. Roland Oliver, *Sir Harry Johnston and the Scramble for Africa*, pp. 140–141, calls this article "perhaps the ablest . . . piece of argument that Johnston ever wrote," perhaps "the clearest surviving exposition of Salisbury's African policy," with Johnston's own flavor. That it was a reflection of Salisbury's policy is doubtful; that it was one of Johnston's ablest statements is unquestionable.

southern Africa because there was no consensus either in London or in Cape Town as to what those interests were.

This condemnation and exhortation were based on an assumption that there were great stakes to be won by energetic action, that in the interior of Africa was a treasure house awaiting exploitation. The exact location of this wealth and its precise nature were a matter of conjecture; that it was there was an article of faith of the cult of Africa. Zealots like Johnston pressed for action to secure these riches for Britain. The area around the Great Lakes exerted a particular fascination. Otherwise cautious men were captivated by the prospects of the region, prospects that were not less alluring by being undetermined.

Most Afro-maniacs were youthful, reckless of life, lacking in capital, and literally irresponsible. They sought to convert others who had the means to realize their dreams, but the great men of commerce and politics remained agnostics. Whitehall and Downing Street conceded that West Africa in particular had some commercial value and might have more. British merchants established on the Niger delta and elsewhere should receive governmental protection to carry on their trade without interruption by African or European rivals, but state intervention should be minimal and preferably all expenses should be defrayed by the mercantile interests who benefited. Caution in assuming responsibility or expense characterized the policy of the imperial government, whether the party in power was Liberal or Conservative.[2]

These strictures applied not only to the tropics but to those parts of Africa that were universally acknowledged to be significant, the areas adjacent to the routes to India. Egypt was important because of Suez, and the Cape was still valuable from its

2. Before the arrival of Germany, France was the main source of concern among the European powers. French discrimination against British trade was a major source of complaint. In 1883 T. V. Lister noted, "Were the French really as liberal as they proposed to be in their Colonial policy it is probable that no one in the country wd grudge them the honour of establishing markets for British Trade on the pestilential coasts of West Africa." Memo by Lister, November 16, 1883, F.O. 84/1655, Public Record Office (hereafter P.R.O.).

position on the alternative life line and on one of the great commercial routes of British shipping. Indeed, in strictly mercantile
terms the Cape route exceeded in value that through the canal.[3]
Policy toward both Egypt and the Cape had to be geared to the
need for protection of the sea lanes. Strategic considerations required securing the bases that controlled the routes to India.
But Gladstone and other statesmen refused to accept the corollary that possession of the coast implied involvement in the interior, particularly when the hinterlands were such apparently
worthless wastes as the Sudan and the Transvaal, inhabited by
such troublesome peoples as the Mahdi's dervishes or Kruger's
Boers. British policy in southern Africa had vacillated over the
years between the "forward school" and the advocates of retirement and retrenchment.[4] The latter were in the ascendant in the
Gladstone government of 1880 to 1885. Carnarvon's federation
schemes had brought humiliation and failure. Gladstone's colleagues were determined not to become involved in adventures
that produced only negative dividends—hostility of both settlers
and Africans, and endless expense.

The Pretoria Convention of 1881, like that at Sand River almost thirty years before, represented a "realistic" assessment of
the limits of British interests and responsibilities. Not only was
the Transvaal restored to quasi-independence but Britain withdrew from substantive involvement in the affairs of African
peoples in the environs of the republic. A British military force
which had been stationed in Kuruman, in Bechuanaland, was

---

3. In December 1887 Captain C. E. Darwin estimated the value of the
three main maritime routes leaving England as follows:

	Annual Value
(1) To Cape and South America	£131,600,000
(2) To United States and Canada	119,100,000
(3) Through Suez Canal	47,000,000

The routes to the Cape and South America bifurcated at the Cape
Verde Islands. Memo., C. E. Darwin, Captain, R.E., F.O. 84/1916,
P.R.O. The trade to South America was approximately double that to
South Africa. Ronald Robinson and John Gallagher, *Africa and the
Victorians*, 6 n.
4. There is a very perceptive memorandum in confidential print by
Edward Fairfield, August 4, 1885, describing the vacillations of British
policy in South Africa during the previous half century. See C.O.
879/23/304, P.R.O.

recalled despite the efforts of the missionary John Mackenzie and the administrator of Griqualand West, Colonel William Owen Lanyon, to retain the force and to assert imperial authority at least to the Molopo River. The borders of the Transvaal were defined to leave open the so-called "missionary road" to the interior, but the British government was not prepared to assert direct influence by proclaiming the African areas west of the Transvaal to be under British protection. Instead it relied on treaty proscriptions against the republic's expansion to the west. The results were predictable. "Private citizens" from the Transvaal and British subjects from Griqualand West became involved in the quarrels of the peoples of Bechuanaland, and in 1882 Transvaal burghers, avowedly acting independently of Pretoria, proclaimed the establishment of two new republics, Stellaland and Goshen, which lay across the road to the north. Both "republics" were the product of the intervention of Transvaal burghers in the quarrels of African and colored chiefs, from which they derived claims to land either from their "ally," their "enemy" or both. Stellaland, centered on Vryburg, came into being as a result of burgher support of the colored leader Taaibosch Massouw against the Tlhaping chief Mankurwane. Goshen, whose "capital" was a farm called Rooi Grond, was the prize for supporting the Ratlou-Rolong chief Moswete against Montshiwa, a chief of the Tshidi-Rolong.[5] In both cases the settlers were intent on securing valid titles to land they had won or seized; but the leaders of Goshen were more extreme in their determination not to accept the intervention of British authority, whether imperial or colonial.

This unofficial imperialism might have continued without protest from London had not politicians in Cape Colony been aroused by the prospect of their hinterland being closed. The imperial government might not respond to an importunate missionary like Mackenzie, but it did pay attention to representations from a self-governing colony. The concerns of the Cape government and of the high commissioner, Sir Hercules Robinson, were reflected in clauses in the London convention of 1884

5. Leonard Thompson, "The Subjection of African Chiefdoms, 1870–1898," in *The Oxford History of South Africa*, eds. Monica Wilson and Leonard Thompson, 2:272–273.

by which the Transvaal government not only agreed to respect a boundary that kept open the road north but promised to prevent its citizens from encroaching beyond that line. Among the members of the Cape Assembly who had been most exercised by Transvaal expansion was Cecil Rhodes, a recently elected representative from a district of Griqualand West, who had already made his fortune in diamonds and now turned his energies and his wealth to the expansionist career with which posterity identifies him. In one of the debates in the assembly, Rhodes made a statement that is frequently cited as evidence of his unremitting zeal for northward expansion: "You are dealing with a question upon the proper treatment of which depends the whole future of the Colony. I look upon this Bechuanaland territory as the Suez Canal of the trade of the country, the key of its road to the interior."[6]

Rhodes's ambitions for Cape expansion were unquestioned. Many of his colleagues shared his enthusiasm, but there remained the question of who should accept the responsibilities and expense of governing the territory to the west of the Transvaal. The Cape government of Sir Thomas Scanlen of which Rhodes was a member favored the establishment of a British protectorate; the imperial government expressed a willingness to accommodate provided the colony made a substantial monetary contribution. Scanlen gave his pledge that he would support such a subsidy, but his personal endorsement meant nothing without a vote by the assembly. On his return to Cape Town the prime minister encountered opposition within his own cabinet to the colony's making a financial contribution. Shortly thereafter the Scanlen government fell and that of his successor, Sir Thomas Upington, refused to honor the pledge and instead advocated the annexation to Cape Colony of Bechuanaland to the Molopo River. With regard to the north, Upington's party was divided, some being willing to accept the westward expansion of the Transvaal, provided there were guarantees of free transit by Cape traders through the territory. The Afrikaner Bond led by J. H. Hofmeyr, a powerful factor in the assembly, went even further. Hofmeyr not only advocated acceptance of

6. Speech, August 16, 1883, quoted in F. Verschoyle (Vindex), *Cecil Rhodes, His Political Life and Speeches 1881–1900*, p. 62.

Transvaal expansion north of the Molopo but opposed Cape annexation south of the line on the basis that it would promote a quarrel with the Transvaal.[7]

Internal conflicts in Cape Colony and ambivalence in London contributed to an impasse which further exacerbated the problem. The sacrificial victim was John Mackenzie. The imperial government, on the strength of Scanlen's commitments, had appointed Mackenzie in April 1884 as deputy commissioner in Bechuanaland to assert imperial authority, to resolve the problems created by the occupation of African lands by whites, and to restore order in the area. Mackenzie, with little money or power at his disposal, did remarkably well. He induced some of the settlers of Stellaland as well as the dominant African chiefs in southern Bechuanaland, Mankurwane and Montshiwa, to accept a British protectorate. But Mackenzie did not have the continuing support of the high commissioner, Sir Hercules Robinson, who allowed Cecil Rhodes to undercut Mackenzie and in effect made Rhodes his principal source for information on Bechuanaland. The result was the resignation of Mackenzie and the appointment of Rhodes to replace him. Rhodes was even less able to deal with the "wild men" of Goshen than his predecessor had been. Disorder continued west of the Transvaal border, and President Kruger in September 1884 decided to end it by taking Goshen under his protection.

Mackenzie had been sent to carry out large objects with small resources. He had attempted to do so by involving the prestige and power of Britain even though the power was not in evidence and the prestige was blighted in the aftermath of Majuba. He might have performed the feat had he enjoyed the backing of the representative of the imperial presence in South Africa, the high commissioner. But Robinson's failure to support his representative was fatal to Mackenzie's hopes. Instead, Robinson accepted untrue or unverified reports from Rhodes and in effect became an accessory of the "colonial" party against an imperial protectorate. Robinson's cooperation with Rhodes

7. See excerpt from Hofmeyr's speech in John Mackenzie, *Austral Africa, Losing It or Ruling It*, 1:398. Mackenzie's book, though written as a defense of his conduct, contains a great deal of useful information on the Bechuanaland controversy.

in 1884 was the first evidence of a partnership that would continue over the years and would have a significant effect on the course of South African history. It was also an illustration of how a policy formed in London could be subverted by the actions of the imperial representative on the spot.

One month before Kruger moved on Goshen, Germany announced a protectorate over the coast of South West Africa. Again the event was attributable in large part to the characteristics of British imperial policy and of the relations between the home government and the self-governing colonies. "Imperial policy" was not the province of any department. The Colonial Office dealt primarily with existing colonies; it could not make decisions with regard to additional imperial responsibilities. The Foreign Office was centrally concerned in issues involving relations with other European states; but it could not make commitments that entailed additional responsibility and expense, as was invariably the case. Such decisions were matters for the cabinet, which usually acted cautiously and with a healthy regard for parliamentary strictures against expenditures in overseas areas. Where the interests of a self-governing colony were affected, its government must, of course, be consulted. All of these elements were involved in the British reaction to Bismarck's inquiry about British claims in South West Africa and to the imbroglio that followed. His first approach in February 1883 was couched in terms that encouraged the disinclination of Whitehall to act. The chancellor appeared to be inviting Britain to assume responsibility for Angra Pequeña and the protection of German subjects who had established an insignificant commercial operation in that area. The Foreign Office, assuming that Bismarck continued to be averse to undertaking overseas responsibilities, would have disclaimed any British interests in the area but was deterred by the Colonial Office which sought to ascertain from the government of Cape Colony what South African interests would be involved. The result was long delay and temporizing responses. In November the Foreign Office stated that while Britain had no sovereign rights in South West Africa, it had responsibilities to British subjects in the area which gave it a special position against any other European power. A German request for a more precise statement went unanswered for six months. Bismarck's annoyance, whatever his motivations may have been, was abundantly justified.[8]

The delay was occasioned primarily by the familiar problem that Cape Colony's pretensions were greater than its willingness to accept responsibility. The colonial government was eager to have the coast annexed as British territory but at British, not colonial expense. Furthermore, the Scanlen cabinet, at this time still in office, was too involved with ministerial changes and other domestic problems to become exercised about the issue of South West Africa. The treasurer in the cabinet that failed to recognize the danger of the German intrusion into the environs of the colony was Cecil Rhodes.

Rhodes thus shared in the responsibility for the inaction that led to Germany's annexation of Damaraland and Namaqualand. It was the only time in his life that he would be subject to indictment for such indifference.

Bismarck's intervention in South West Africa and elsewhere produced consternation in Whitehall. Confident assumptions which had been accepted over many years were now exposed as bankrupt. Bismarck had acted in an un-Bismarckian way. The assessment of his motives became a matter of great urgency in the cabinet and among its advisers. Sir Percy Anderson, rapidly emerging as the Foreign Office's African expert, noted to his counterpart in the Colonial Office: "This mine that Bismarck has sprung makes us pause to know what is coming next. The affair was deliberate and it can be looked on in no other light than as a direct act of hostility: first while Busch was playing with Bobsy[9] about a compromise, came the announcement of the taking of the whole."[10]

8. There is a considerable amount of literature on the background of the German acquisition of South West Africa. Still of value is William O. Aydelotte, *Bismarck and British Colonial Policy. The Problem of South West Africa.* See also Henry Ashby Turner, "Bismarck's Imperialist Venture: Anti-British in Origin?" in *Britain and Germany in Africa,* eds. Prosser Gifford and William Roger Louis (New Haven, 1967), pp. 47–82.

9. The reference is to Dr. Busch of the German Foreign Office and to Robert Meade of the British Colonial Office who had discussions in Berlin in 1884 with regard to German interests in overseas areas.

10. Anderson to Lister, private, December 20, 1884, PRO 30/29/195, P.R.O.

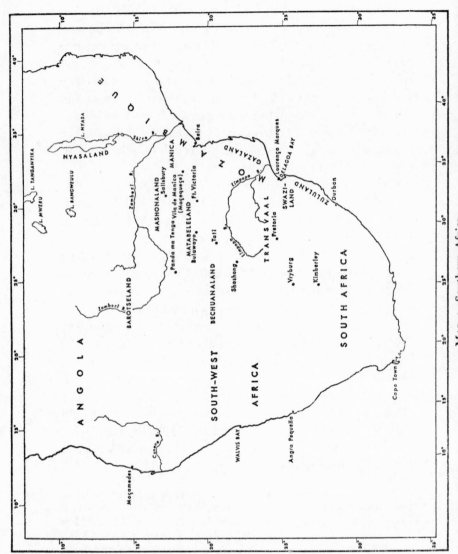

MAP 1. Southern Africa

Members of the Gladstone cabinet thought, or professed to think, that Bismarck's abrupt change was a gambit for electioneering purposes.[11] But beneath this nervous mutual reassurance was a nagging doubt. Perhaps his actions manifested a shift in German foreign policy which might be threatening to Britain both at home and overseas. This possibility led to a reassessment of the British position with regard to those areas of southern Africa not yet claimed by any European power. If Germany had ambitions to use its position in South West Africa as a base for expansion into the interior, and perhaps to link up with the Transvaal, this required Britain to take immediate action. The Transvaal in this pre-gold mining era was at worst a minor annoyance but a German-Transvaal alliance shutting off the interior could not be regarded so lightly. Sir Robert Meade, the government's principal negotiator on Anglo-German issues, warned Granville that "it is impossible to exaggerate the importance of preventing the German government joining hands with the Transvaal," [12] and a previously lethargic cabinet moved with unaccustomed speed to prevent that eventuality.

Before Germany entered the scene the position of the Gladstone government had been that there were no imperial interests of any significance to the north of the Transvaal. By the London Convention of 1884 the boundaries of the Transvaal were defined, but the republic was interdicted from concluding treaties with African peoples only on the east and west. There evidently was an unwritten understanding that Britain would not interfere if the Transvaal were to extend its influence with the peoples to the north.[13] But the conjunction of German action in South West Africa and Kruger's announcement of pro-

11. The new British representative in Berlin, Sir Edward Malet, offered this hypothesis which was seized upon by cabinet members. Malet to Granville, October 23, 1884, very confidential, enclosure in F.O. to C.O., October 30, 1884, C.O. 537/124B, P.R.O. Even before Malet wrote the letter, this line was being suggested. Gladstone to Granville, September 9, 1884, PRO 30/29/29a, P.R.O., printed in Agatha Ramm, *The Political Correspondence of Mr. Gladstone and Lord Granville, 1876–1886*, 2:230–232.

12. Meade to Granville, private, December 20, 1884, PRO 30/29/147, P.R.O.

13. See notes on dispatch, High Commissioner to C.O., May 6, 1885, C.O. 417/5, P.R.O.

tection over Goshen produced a new British initiative in the territories both to the west and to the north of the Transvaal. Fear of further German expansion was an important factor in the decision in November 1884 to dispatch a force of 5,000 men under the command of Sir Charles Warren to assert British authority in Bechuanaland and to wipe out the filibustering republic of Goshen. Warren accomplished his mission without bloodshed, but the fact that the British government had been willing to risk war and to commit itself to an expenditure of £1,500,000 was impressive evidence of imperial concern. Reports of German activity on the southeast coast added to the sense of urgency. August Einwald, avowedly acting on behalf of the same Franz Lüderitz whose claim was the basis for German action in South West Africa, was engaged in the later half of 1884 in expeditions in the southeast into Zululand and Tongaland. In November he announced that he had acquired from Dinizulu the rights to St. Lucia Bay and to 60,000 acres of adjacent land, and he publicized his intention to seek concessions from Tonga chiefs. Eventually, he announced, he hoped to be the agent by which a trade route was opened across the continent to Angra Pequeña.[14] This time there was no hesitation on the part of the British government—a warship was dispatched immediately and the flag hoisted over the only harbor between Durban and Delagoa Bay which could be used to provide access to the Transvaal.[15] Bismarck was not prepared to press German claims to the point of a major confrontation and agreed to accept concessions in the Cameroons as the price for acquiescence in the British action.

Within a few months the position of the majority of the Gladstone cabinet had shifted dramatically. Gladstone himself remained opposed to Britain's joining the scramble. But even he was irritated at the bluster and blackmail that had characterized Bismarck's tactics,[16] and most of his colleagues not only

14. Lister to Malet, secret, December 22, 1884, F.O. 244/384; Malet to Granville, December 30, 1884, F.O. 244/383, both in P.R.O.
15. Granville to Malet, February 25, 1885, F.O. 244/391, P.R.O.
16. Gladstone to Granville, private, January 29, 1885; same to same, January 31, 1885, both in Ramm, *Political Correspondence*, 2:329, 331. Gladstone was emphatic that he would not be bullied either by

shared his anger but demanded urgent measures to frustrate Germany's intentions. They were not certain precisely what these intentions were, but they were inclined to believe the worst. When the German minister to the Vatican was reported to have indiscreetly dropped the intelligence that his government desired to possess Delagoa Bay, the Foreign Minister, Lord Granville, immediately called for action to ensure the reversion of the bay to Britain should Portugal decide to relinquish it.[17] As Sir Charles Dilke told Count Herbert Bismarck, while the British government might not be willing to annex new territories in the neighborhood of Cape Colony, it would strongly oppose their being appropriated by any foreign power.[18] Southern Africa must remain a British sphere of influence. This position was the basis for the announcement in March 1885 of a British protectorate over Bechuanaland to 22° south latitude and 20° east longitude, thus interposing a British band between the Transvaal and German South West Africa.[19]

These various moves effectively eliminated whatever threat there was from Germany,[20] though disturbing rumors continued to circulate of German ambitions to link up South West Africa with the German sphere in East Africa through Matabeleland and Mashonaland and the Great Lakes.[21] But as had been the

---

Cape Colony or by Bismarck into taking a line not in accordance with British interests.

17. Note by Granville on Malet to Granville, December 27, 1884, PRO 30/29/179, P.R.O.

18. Herbert Bismarck to Bismarck, March 7, 1885, in E. T. S. Dugdale, ed., *German Diplomatic Documents, 1871–1914*, 1:192.

19. This decision was communicated to Germany in February 1885. Granville to Malet, February 4, 1885, F.O. 244/399, P.R.O.

20. Fears of German expansion were largely unjustified. The German government was not prepared to commit the necessary resources, and private money was not available. Lüderitz's experience in South West Africa, where he spent most of his fortune, did not encourage other investors. Oskar Hintrager, *Südwestafrika in der deutschen Zeit* (Munich, 1955), p. 16.

21. Edward Maund alleged that he had been approached by Count Montgelas for information on the suitability of Matabeleland and Mashonaland as a field of German colonization. Typescript, "How Matabeleland Narrowly Escaped Being German," 1928. That there was some basis for Maund's statement, at least so far as Montgelas was concerned, is indicated by a draft letter, Maund to Montgelas, private,

case with previous British advances into the interior of southern Africa, these measures had little to do with the problem of effective government. Announcements of protectorates might keep out other European powers; a demonstration in force might deter the burghers of the Transvaal; but these actions were essentially preventive rather than positive. Britain did not acquire these territories with any plan or philosophy of administration. Whatever their differences regarding the extension of political influence, imperial statesmen were agreed that the British taxpayer must not be required to foot the bill. The feeling of sympathy for "backward" peoples was genuine enough; significant elements in British society could still be outraged at reports of brutality and oppression; but humanitarianism alone could not dictate policy. The plight of Mankurwane and Montshiwa had not produced the Warren expedition, and concern for the future of their peoples was not the primary motive for the announcement of the Crown Colony of Bechuanaland. Bechuanaland became British because of the area's relations to the north and its adjacency to the Transvaal. But Britain expected to transfer responsibility to Cape Colony at the earliest possible time. In the protectorate to the north, between the Molopo River and the twenty-second parallel, the imperial government was also committed to minimum responsibility, and hoped as soon as possible to shift to other hands what little powers it was prepared to assume. The government of Cape Colony, on the other hand, was not anxious to accept the burdens that Downing Street wished to transfer. It had recently felt compelled to transfer Basutoland to imperial control after the disastrous and expensive Gun War, and its financial condition was not robust.

Rhodes and his ally Hofmeyr won applause by attacks on the bogey of "the Imperial Factor," those meddling functionaries from Britain who exacerbated problems in southern Africa by intrusions into societies they did not understand. But the picture they drew bore little relationship to reality. The imperial presence in South Africa in 1885 was represented by two officials

---

December, 1885. Both these documents are in the Maund Papers, Afr. S 229 (4), Rhodes House, Oxford. But Montgelas was an Austrian, not a German, and his connection, if any, with the German government is not clear.

with diametrically opposed views on the desirable policy in the interior. Sir Charles Warren, to some extent influenced by Mackenzie, advocated powerful assertion of imperial rule over the British sphere, and perhaps beyond into the Ndebele country. He would have established a Crown Colony and accepted grants of land proffered by Kgama and other chiefs north of the Molopo which he would have assigned only to settlers of British origin; Boers would be excluded. By this energetic line he would at the same time protect the interests of the African peoples of the new dominion, "redress the balance" between Britons and Boers, and eliminate any threat of German expansion into Central Africa. This was an ambitious undertaking based upon an overoptimistic assessment of the land and climate of the area, and would have required a considerable imperial expenditure for civil and military purposes. Furthermore, Warren's grants from Kgama would have involved acceptance of land in dispute between Kgama and Lobengula, thus embroiling the British with the Ndebele.[22] Warren's proposed policy was directly contrary to that of the Gladstone ministry which had sent him out; the hesitation of the government to reject the plan was based far more on a disinclination to repudiate him than on the merits of his ideas.

The other imperial presence in South Africa, the governor and high commissioner, Sir Hercules Robinson, emphatically opposed Warren's plan, contending that it would cost Britain £300,000 a year in military and civil expenditures,[23] and the eventual decision of the imperial government supported Robinson in his argument for minimal administration. The imperial factor against which Rhodes raged was thus an officer who had frustrated Rhodes in his attempted land settlement in Stellaland but whose recommendations for the government of Bechuanaland were rejected by the imperial government. The high commissioner who advocated minimal responsibilities, on the other hand, evoked no indignation from Rhodes. Rhodes, in

22. Telegram, Robinson to Derby, May 27, 1885. C. 4588, 1885; telegram, Warren to Stanley, July 27, 1885, and notes thereto, C.O. 417/6, P.R.O. Confidential Print, "Bechuanaland Affairs," July 15, 1885, C.O. 806/247, P.R.O.
23. Confidential print, "Bechuanaland Affairs," July 15, 1885, C.O. 806/247, P.R.O.

sum, was not directing his fire against the imperial government but rather against those who threatened to thwart his own ambitions, whether these opponents resided in London, in Cape Town, or in Pretoria.

Rhodes by the mid-1880s had committed himself to the north, but a north with which he himself would be identified rather than the little men who were involved with policy in Britain and Cape Colony. Though Rhodes had entered politics in 1880 and became prime minister of the Cape a decade later, he was no more a conventional politician than he was a conventional businessman. The limitations imposed on governments by the representative process were repugnant to his being. Governments responsible to the parliamentary process he saw as inherently weak, unworthy of the greatness of the people whom they were elected to lead. The destiny of the Anglo-Saxons could not be realized by the agency of governments; the necessary force and fire must be provided by men eager to devote their lives, their energy, and their money to the mission. Rhodes by the mid-1880s, if not earlier, had concluded that he must provide the dynamism of which the Scanlens and the Upingtons were incapable.

Rhodes

The life of Cecil Rhodes continues to fascinate. Some portray him as a selfless idealist devoted to the expansion of the British Empire; others, as a man corrupted by power, a megalomaniac who rationalized his crimes against humanity by parroting clichés from the Social Darwinism popular in the British society of his day. Kipling eulogized him as

> Dreamer devout by vision led
> Beyond our reach or guess.[24]

His architect, Sir Herbert Baker, described Rhodes as a man who concentrated his thoughts and energies into the realization of a noble vision, who cared little for recognition: "I want the power, let him who will have the peacock's feathers."[25] But, as

24. Herbert Baker, *Cecil Rhodes by His Architect*, p. 7.
25. *Ibid.*, pp. 112–113.

Baker recognized, Rhodes was not beyond vanity. When a country was named for him, he confessed that "I find I am human and should like to be living after my death still perhaps if that name is coupled with the object of England everywhere and united the name may convey the discovery of an idea which ultimately leads to the cessation of all wars and one language throughout the world. . . ."[26] Rhodes thus identified his life with the advancement of a great humanitarian cause. His severest critics acknowledged his achievements, but branded them as crimes against humanity. Olive Schreiner's *Trooper Peter Halket* was a condemnation of Rhodes and all that he represented. Mark Twain thought he should have been hanged,[27] and G. K. Chesterton sought to demolish the myth of Rhodes's idealism:

> . . . what was wrong with Rhodes was not that, like Cromwell or Hildebrand, he made huge mistakes, nor even that he committed these crimes and errors in order to spread certain ideas. And when one asked for the ideas they could not be found. Cromwell stood for Calvinism, Hildebrand for Catholicism, but Rhodes had no principles whatever to give to the world. He had only a hasty but elaborate machinery for spreading the principles that he hadn't got. What he called his ideals were the dregs of a Darwinism which had already grown not only stagnant, but poisonous. That the fittest must survive and that any one like himself must be the fittest, that the weakest must go to the wall, and that any one he could not understand must be the weakest; that was the philosophy which he lumberingly believed through life, like many another agnostic old bachelor of the Victorian era. All his views on religion . . . were simply the stalest ideas of his time.
> . . . he spread no ideas that any cockney clerk in Streatham could not have spread for him. But it was exactly because he had no ideas to spread that he invoked slaughter, violated justice, and ruined republics to spread them.[28]

Chesterton overstated his indictment as admirers overstated Rhodes's virtues. Most writers, including those who are critical, describe Rhodes as a man with a lifelong passion to expand the British Empire. Some have maintained that he saved central Africa for Britain. A committee of the imperial government de-

---

26. Rhodes to Stead, strictly private, August 19, 1891, RH 1/1/1, National Archives of Rhodesia (hereafter N.A.R.).
27. Mark Twain, *Following the Equator*, 2:378.
28. G. K. Chesterton, *A Miscellany of Men*, p. 204.

clared in 1918: "If it had not been for the enterprise, courage, and resources of Cecil Rhodes, the Territory which is now Northern and Southern Rhodesia would not have been secured for the Empire but would have fallen into alien hands."[29]

This assertion cannot be disproved, but there was little likelihood of the kingdom of the Ndebele being appropriated by any foreign power even if Rhodes had not been involved, since the imperial government had made it clear that the area was a British sphere of influence.

Rhodes's "lifelong passion" is also suspect. His conversion to the religion of empire did not come in a flash of revelation. He himself maintained that he had been devoted to the creed since the age of twenty-four, and he could cite a draft of his ideas written at that time to prove his dedication. His admirers and he himself believed that like Saul of Tarsus he experienced a conversion which dominated his whole adult life. Precisely when Rhodes became the apostle of empire, however, has remained uncertain. In addition to his musings at the age of twenty-four, Rhodes frequently cited his debt to John Ruskin. The two did share a commitment to great ideals and a contempt for mediocrity and materialism. But where Ruskin preached, Rhodes acted. While Ruskin wrote of truth, Rhodes saw truth or falsity only in their relation to great ends in which he was the prime mover. Those who obstructed the object must be pushed aside or "squared"; this to Rhodes served the ultimate morality.

Few men whose careers are so well documented are enveloped in so much myth as is Cecil Rhodes. Rhodes was not a thinker; he was a doer. He appropriated the ideas of others rather than conceiving ideas himself. He did not originate the idea of Cape to Cairo,[30] and his views on the survival of the fittest were hardly

29. *First Report of a Committee appointed by the Secretary of State for the Colonies to consider certain questions relating to Rhodesia.* Cmd. 1273, 1921.

30. Sir Harry Johnston attributed the origin of "Cape to Cairo" to Sir Edwin Arnold in 1876, but a similar expression was used in 1875 by H. B. T. Strangway in connection with a telegraph. Albert Grey, the future fourth Earl, refers to a Cape to Cairo telegraph in a notebook of 1878 in the Durham Archives. Johnston took the credit for introducing the idea to Rhodes. See Lois A. C. Raphael, *The Cape-to-Cairo Dream.* Sir Charles Metcalfe claimed credit for the idea of a

distinctive from the spirit of Social Darwinism which pervaded the British society of his day. Rhodes did not live for principles. He lived for the exercise of power, and he was not fastidious in his methods. In the last years of his life, Rhodes frequently engaged in reflection on the meaning of life. He professed admiration for, among others, Marcus Aurelius, and the high idealism that had infused his life. But Rhodes during his rise to power was no follower of Aurelian principles.

The assertion that Rhodes lived for power does not contradict the fact that he believed that in so doing he served a great cause —the expansion of the British Empire through his instrumentality. That he appropriated ideas from others did not lessen the intensity of his commitment. That his British Empire differed greatly from that of Lord Salisbury did not affect the sincerity with which he proclaimed his dedication to expansion. This passion in Rhodes is incontestable, however it may be explained. And the great energy that he expended in pursuit of his aims affected the character of central and southern Africa.

Rhodes used much of his personal fortune in the advancement of his great ambition. He understood the relationship of money and power. Many writers have stated that he cared nothing for money except as a means to power. His biographies are replete with anecdotes of his having had no money in his pockets, of his love of life on the veld, of the primitive shacks with which he was content and in one of which he died. The implication is that this Spartan life and unconsciousness of money made Rhodes unique among men of wealth. In fact, his life style was not so unlike that of many other rich men. Money was and is the means to power; its possessor can use it to command other men. Rhodes indeed repeatedly emphasized that money was power. As he sat with Hans Sauer, looking at the great cavity of the Kimberley mine, Sauer asked, "What do you see here?" and "with a slow sweep of his hand, Rhodes answered the single word: 'Power.' "[31] But, say Rhodes's admirers of his day and since, Rhodes cared nothing for self; he used power only

---

Cape to Cairo railway. Notes by Basil Williams, s. 134, Rhodes Papers, Rhodes House.

31. James Percy Fitzpatrick, *South African Memories*, p. 85.

as a means to advance great ends. Flora Shaw, normally a woman of probity and good judgment, was entranced. Just before the Jameson Raid she wrote:

> . . . I have met now most of the English public men of my day but the impression conveyed to me by Mr. Rhodes is one of unselfishness of aim greater and more complete than I have ever recognized before. He appears to me to seek nothing for himself. He cares neither for money, nor place, nor power, except in so far as they are a necessity for the accomplishment of the national ideal for which he lives.[32]

The euphoria of Miss Shaw was a testament to the remarkable charm that Rhodes exercised on both men and women. Even his most severe critics confessed to a reluctant admiration, a feeling that he was made of finer stuff than those with whom he associated in his imperial schemes. Henry Labouchere, who violently attacked Rhodes's practices, admitted that he liked the man. The British South Africa Company he considered the most scandalous fraud on the public since the South Sea Bubble,[33] but he thought that Rhodes had deceived himself in good faith, unlike the hypocrites who served him. The actions were detestable, but yet there was something about their author which was most attractive.[34]

Though there have been many biographies of Rhodes, the nature of the appeal that made him the idol of so many remains elusive. He was generally acknowledged to be a poor speaker. His voice was thin and high pitched, and sometimes rose to a falsetto when he became excited. His speeches in cold print do not suggest that he had great aptitude as an orator. He gave little of himself to those around him. Even toward Dr. Jameson, who was as close to him as anyone, he was reserved in his expressions of personal affection. Yet he evoked powerful emotional responses from others. One of the elements of Rhodes's appeal to his admirers and to many of his detractors was that he was not a "money grubber."[35] He was a man dominated by a mission to win vast territories and great resources for the British Empire

32. Margery Perham, *Lugard, The Years of Adventure, 1858–1898.*
33. Algar L. Thorold, *The Life of Henry Labouchere,* p. 393.
34. Hesketh Pearson, *Labby,* p. 273.
35. *Truth,* February 20, 1896.

and prepared to use his energies and fortune to that end. These attributes had great appeal for the late-Victorian upper class. Some called him an Elizabethan come to life; in fact his achievements realized the dreams and aspirations of many of his contemporaries. In an age when doubts had begun to intrude as to the permanence of British supremacy, the exploits of Rhodes were a reassurance that the great days were not yet over. He asserted the superiority of Britons, and he extended the empire at no cost to the British taxpayer. That he and his associates in Africa advanced these great purposes at the expense of Africans produced little reaction. Humanitarians sometimes protested the methods, but few questioned the avowed objective. One eulogist wrote, at Rhodes's death, that his aims were "the embodiment of an ideal towards which all that is best in Anglo-Saxondom is working."[36] Whether or not he represented the "best," he most certainly was admired by Britons of all classes as were few other men of his day. His appearance at stockholders' meetings always produced great crowds who listened in awe and admiration as the great man expatiated on the bright future of the new estates he had won for the British Empire, and in their adulation were transported from the cold world of balance sheets and nondividends.

The mythology surrounding Rhodes invested him with qualities of idealism and selflessness. But self-realization was central to his life as with other men. The specific means of ego satisfaction varied—Barney Barnato sought to use his wealth for the social recognition and prestige that his Jewish Limehouse antecedents denied him; J. B. Robinson gloried in the power that he was able to exercise in the Witwatersrand; Rhodes realized himself through empire. Sir Alfred Milner perceptively noted that "men are ruled by their foibles, and Rhodes' foible is size."[37] Rhodes succeeded in deluding himself, as he convinced others, that his cause was Britain when in fact his cause was Rhodes.

After the Jameson Raid, Rhodes's associates sought to explain his involvement in the fiasco—the effects of a fall from a horse,[38]

36. *St. James's Gazette*, April 10, 1902.
37. Baker, *Cecil Rhodes*, p. 91.
38. He had a serious fall from a horse in 1891.

over-reliance on a trusted subordinate, or a preoccupation with imminent death which affected his usual judgment. But the characteristics he displayed in 1895 he had exhibited long before. Rhodes's life had been a series of demonstrations that the prize was to the daring; he had succeeded over and over again where prudent men had failed. He was convinced that he would have ousted the Portuguese from South East Africa had it not been for "dynastic twaddle";[39] he had occupied Mashonaland against the warning of "prudent" men that the Ndebele would annihilate the pioneering column; throughout his life he had been a gambler who always won. Unvarying success and its attendant power made him more and more arrogant, and his humanity shriveled. In 1886 he had interrupted negotiations in the gold fields to rush to the side of his dying young secretary, Neville Pickering. But such a display of sentiment was unique; Rhodes's comment on his return from the cemetery was more characteristic of the man: "Well, I must go on with my work. After all, a thing like this is only a big detail . . . only a big detail . . . a big detail."[40]

After Pickering, there were other young subordinates, all male. Though he did not betray the emotional attachment to them he had displayed toward Pickering, he expected from them a degree of loyalty and commitment far beyond that of the usual business relationship. Those who succumbed to the love of a woman to the extent of a decision to get married could expect damnation and perpetual exile from their employer. The involvement of Rhodes with young men and his avoidance of the company of women has led to speculations about his "homosexuality." This line of inquiry is not particularly helpful to an understanding of Rhodes's imperialism. There seems to be no evidence that "homosexuals" have stronger power drives than "heterosexuals," and "homosexual" is a word with different shades of meaning. That Rhodes almost certainly never had sexual relations with a woman does not imply a corollary that he had such relations with a man. Rhodes's passion was the exercise of power, from this he derived his gratification.

39. The phrase is used by Edward Maund in his "Reminiscences," September 16, 1925, Afr. s 229 (4). Rhodes House.
40. Felix Gross, *Rhodes of Africa*, p. 129.

The sweetness of adulation involved another element which became increasingly evident as power corroded his nature. Men were judged by their relationship to his ambitions. Those who served well were rewarded; those who thwarted him he tried to destroy. He was "the God in the Car":

> Some will catch the golden shower
> Some will neath the car be caught
> Priests may call their god—a power
> Victims call him—Juggernaut.[41]

Such a man was dangerous in the South African environment of the late nineteenth century, for there was no effective countervailing force. When Rhodes was made a privy councillor in the New Year's honors of 1895 one editor observed, "It has been well said that Rhodes has been making Imperial history on a large scale for many years."[42] He did so by a combination of his own energy and others' default. Before the Jameson Raid he dominated Cape politics; he determined the policies of the British South Africa Company with no check by the directors; and Whitehall and Downing Street were loath to restrain him so long as his impetuosity did not embroil the government in serious international complications. These negative controls were completely inadequate to contain a Rhodes. Officials on Downing Street recognized that he was a dangerous force. Two months before the Jameson Raid, Edward Fairfield of the Colonial Office observed: "He [Rhodes] both repels and attracts by his grasping policy. He is often compared to Napoleon, & Napoleon felt he always had to be doing something, until at last he got land at S. Helena."[43]

Rhodes's ruination was a product of his own recklessness and the laxity of controls exerted on him by those who were responsible for imperial policy and for the management of the British South Africa Company. The considerations that led Salisbury to restrain Rhodes's movements against the Portuguese did not operate in the Transvaal; they did not apply to the Ndebele or to the Shona.

41. *South Africa*, September 7, 1895.
42. *Ibid.*, January 5, 1895.
43. Note by Fairfield, n.d., on BSAC to Fairfield, October 10, 1895, C.O. 417/60, P.R.O.

The Ndebele and the Europeans

The kingdom of the Ndebele was marked for demise even if there had been no Rhodes. In the 1880s any African people in the possession of riches or reputed riches was destined for early European domination; the question was not whether but when and by whom. But without the involvement of Rhodes, the process of European expansion into central Africa might have been substantially different.

Long before the advent of Rhodes the rulers of the Ndebele had become aware of the threat of European migration to the continuing independence of their state. In 1835 an official expedition from Cape Colony under the command of Dr. Andrew Smith had visited Mzilikazi, who was sufficiently convinced of the importance of good relationships with the British that he sent a senior induna to Cape Town to affix his mark to a treaty of friendship with Governor Benjamin D'Urban. The agreement, however, had no effect in restraining the voortrekkers who first collided with Mzilikazi in the same year. Menaced by both Boers and Zulus, the Ndebele chief sought isolation on the high veld between the Zambezi and the Limpopo.[44] His vigilance and the awesome reputation of his people deterred European adventurers, but even before his death events had occurred which foreshadowed the end of Ndebele independence. Mzilikazi and his successor could control elephant hunters; they could not withstand a gold rush. In the last years of the Ndebele state, David Carnegie, one of the missionaries who for many years had been trying without success to convert the Ndebele to Christianity, wrote that "gold and the gospel are fighting for the mastery, and I fear gold will win."[45] In fact there was no contest. The Gospel had no relationship to events in Matabeleland in the 1880s and 1890s. The Ndebele could not be converted into disciples of the Victorian morality espoused by the evangelists. The gold seekers used that morality as justification for the destruction of the Ndebele state and the dispossession of Africans from their lands and their consignment to the role

44. Edward C. Tabler, *The Far Interior*, p. 197.
45. Constance E. Fripp and V. W. Hiller, eds., *Gold and the Gospel in Mashonaland*, p. v.

of an industrial and agricultural proletariat. This process they called civilization. Most whites both in South Africa and in Britain believed Europeans should have the right to exploit lands in Africa which the Africans themselves had not developed. At a meeting of the London Chamber of Commerce in May 1888, at which John Mackenzie was the principal speaker, Joseph Chamberlain expressed baldly a sentiment that less direct contemporaries clothed in idealistic language:

> ... so far as the unoccupied territories between our present colonial possessions and the Zambesi are concerned, they are hardly practically to be said to be in the possession of any nation. The tribes and Chiefs that exercise domination in them cannot possibly occupy the land or develop its capacity, and it is as certain as destiny that, sooner or later, these countries will afford an outlet for European enterprise and European colonisation. . . .[46]

The noted hunter Frederick C. Selous referred to "the good old rule, the simple plan, that they should take who have the power and they should keep who can."[47] He had in mind the possible ousting of the Portuguese from their African possessions, but the principle applied with even greater force to the Ndebele and other African peoples. An essential part of the justification for British intervention was the accepted picture of the tyrannical African chief who terrorized not only his enemies but his own people, living in fear of the whims of a despot who might, if the mood struck him, order the death of any of his subjects, or even of hundreds of them. Shaka represented the apotheosis of the African tyrant; his Zulus feared him more than death itself; and they in turn terrorized other peoples over vast areas of South Africa. Britain by breaking the Zulu power had liberated other Africans and the Zulus themselves. So ran the accepted line. And, of course, the Ndebele of Mzilikazi and Lobengula were Zulus, with essentially the same characteristics as the parent people from whom they had fled. They were irreclaimable savages who lived for war, "who knew no power but a stern unbending will, and no punishment but mutilation or

---

46. Pamphlet, "Austral Africa" (London, 1888). Copy in Grey Papers, 184/6, University of Durham.
47. Frederick C. Selous, *Travel and Adventure in South East Africa*, p. 324.

death."[48] The missionaries blamed the failure of the efforts at
conversion on the character of the Ndebele state and welcomed
the prospect of its destruction as opening the way to the Gospel.
But the whites accorded the Ndebele a grudging respect; they
were brutal but they had the manly virtue of courage. The
Shona people, on the other hand, were despised. Like the
Ndebele, Europeans looked down upon the Shona as contemptible cowards who accepted vassalage rather than risk their lives
against the Ndebele impis. Bishop Knight-Bruce reported that
"Mashona" was a nickname given by the Ndebele which meant
"tripe-cleaners" and that they were also called "old women";
he did not indicate his dissent from either designation.[49]

The stereotype of Ndebele wolves and Shona sheep was almost universally accepted, but Europeans found it difficult to
fit Lobengula into the role of the cunning, bloodthirsty tyrant.
Even John S. Moffat, who considered Lobengula as deceitful as
many Europeans,[50] admitted that the Ndebele chief exhibited
impressive qualities of statesmanship[51] (perhaps Moffat regarded deceit and statesmanship as akin). Moffat saw Lobengula
as a prisoner of circumstances rather than a free agent. The
chief's desire to be honest was increasingly subject to the play
of forces that threatened to destroy him. On the one side he had
to contend with white men, many of whom were unscrupulous.
Sometimes he felt it desirable to conclude agreements with
them. But if the anger of his people was aroused, he might find
it necessary to deny what he had done.[52] Moffat's assessment had
considerable justification. Lobengula unquestionably had great
ability and shrewd perception but he contended against an in-
soluble dilemma. His people, particularly the younger war-

48. Ralph Williams, *How I Became a Governor* (London, 1913), p.
94.
49. G. W. H. Knight-Bruce, *Memories of Mashonaland*, pp. 16–17.
The exact meaning of the word "Shona" is uncertain, though it apparently was used by the Ndebele in a derogatory sense. See Hilda Kuper,
"The Shona," in Hilda Kuper, A. J. B. Hughes, and J. van Velsen,
The Shona and the Ndebele of Southern Rhodesia, p. 9.
50. Robert U. Moffat, *John Smith Moffat*, p. 241.
51. Moffat to ———, September 11, 1888, in Moffat, *ibid.*, 220.
52. Moffat to Leask, November 28, 1888, LE 2/1/1, N.A.R.

riors, believed that they could defeat the Boers or the British and were impatient to be unleashed against the whites. Lobengula knew better, but he had to maintain control over his turbulent warriors.

Contrary to Moffat, most Europeans who dealt with Lobengula considered him scrupulously honorable in his dealings with them. Edward A. Maund, who advanced his own career by deceiving Lobengula, wrote long after the chief's death that "traders found him honest, and many of his acts showed him a staunch friend."[53] "Old Lo Ben" commanded respect even from those who sought to dispossess him of his kingdom. They acknowledged his intelligence and his dignity. Furthermore, in his native attire he looked the part of a great chief. Estimates of his height varied from approximately five feet, ten inches to well over six feet. In his mature years he became immensely corpulent (perhaps as much as 280 pounds), but all observers commented upon the dignity of his bearing. Those who saw him stalk before his regiments with a majestic, deliberate gait were much impressed.[54] But he was still, after all, "a savage"; and, while his going might be poignant, it was necessary. When Lobengula appealed to the British high commissioner against the South Africa Company's occupation of Mashonaland, he was not only told that Her Majesty's government could do nothing on his behalf but was rebuked for addressing a representative of the great queen without the deference appropriate from an inferior to a superior.[55]

Europeans appraised Lobengula and the peoples who inhabited Matabeleland and Mashonaland by European standards, and, naturally, found them sadly deficient. There was little inclination to inquire as to the bases for "savage" customs and practices which, it was generally accepted, must give way to more progressive European mores. African societies had significance to Europeans in terms of European interests. A chief could

53. E. A. Maund, "Lo Bengula," in Leo Weinthal, ed., *The Story of the Cape to Cairo Railway & River Route*, 4 vols. (London, 1921–1923), 1:401.

54. *Ibid.*, p. 395.

55. Loch to Lobengula, October 31, 1891, S 1428/17/9, N.A.R.

be described as a proud, intelligent ruler when he was useful
and as a dipsomaniac tyrant when he became an obstruction.
The Europeans who visited Matabeleland and Mashonaland
were, with few exceptions, uninterested in analysis of African
institutions. They saw gold and land; the missionaries saw
souls to be saved. But they did not seek to understand the con-
geries of complex societies that inhabited the area, and their
misconceptions were long perpetuated by so-called scholarly
writers.

The accepted myth of the 1890s was that the Ndebele lived
by war and exterminated or enslaved other African societies
who came within their reach. The destructive power of the
Ndebele was well documented, but whites generally overrated
Ndebele military capabilities and underrated the resistance of
other peoples.[56] Europeans assumed that the Shona people had
been demoralized by the raids of the Ndebele and had been reduced to abject servitude by the conquerors who exacted tribute
from them whenever it suited their fancy.[57] The myth was perpetuated in part because of lack of knowledge of the true facts,
in part because it was convenient. The Shona were indeed dis-
united. What central authority there had been prior to the
arrival of the Ndebele had disappeared and had been succeeded
by many independent chieftainships of widely varying size and
power. Some succumbed to the Ndebele to the extent of becoming vassals; some occasionally paid tribute, some fought so successfully that the Ndebele left them alone, and others were outside the range of effective Ndebele power.[58]

At the time when Europeans appeared upon the scene, the
relative power of the Shona and the Ndebele was shifting toward the Shona. In the last years of the nineteenth century the
Shona from the sale of gold and ivory and from work in the
diamond mines were acquiring guns in sufficient quantities to
make them formidable adversaries to the Ndebele, and in their

56. Lewis H. Gann, *A History of Southern Rhodesia*, p. 37.
57. Terence O. Ranger, *Revolt in Southern Rhodesia*, pp. 2ff.
58. D. N. Beach, "The Adendorff Trek in Shona History," Henderson
Seminar Paper No. 14, University of Rhodesia, October 2, 1971, 6–7.
For a discussion of the oral tradition of the Shona with regard to their
relationship with the Ndebele in this period, see Lawrence Vambe,
An Ill-Fated People, pp. 57–73.

own hilly redoubts many Shona people were more than a match for the Ndebele.[59]

Despite the growing power of the Shona, however, that of the Ndebele was undeniably impressive, particularly at short range from its nucleus. The bulk of the kingdom was concentrated within a radius of less than 40 miles from the capital of Bulawayo, thereby facilitating communication and execution of the royal commands. Estimates of the size of the population varied considerably. One visitor in 1868 guessed that there were between 300,000 and 400,000 Ndebele, of whom ten percent were warriors. This was probably a considerable exaggeration. Most white observers agreed that in the 1880s the population was in excess of 100,000, with an army of between 15,000 and 20,000.[60] This was indeed a formidable force. But the Ndebele were ill equipped to fight Europeans, particularly mounted men. Edward Maund estimated in 1885 that Lobengula had collected between 600 and 800 breech-loading rifles and carbines and about 6,000 or 7,000 rounds of ammunition.[61] These arms were subsequently augmented, but the stabbing assegai remained the primary weapon of the Ndebele impi. Nor were the Ndebele invincible against other Africans. The further from the nucleus of Ndebele power, the greater was the resistance, and Ndebele raiding parties were by no means uniformly successful. The British South Africa Company initially maintained to its advantage that its rights to exploit the territory derived from the title it had received from Lobengula and that the local chiefs were his vassals. This assumption, so convenient in 1889, was modified in 1893 when the Matabele War altered the company's interest.

European impressions of the discipline of the Ndebele nation

59. This theme is developed in a paper by David N. Beach, "The Shona and Ndebele power," delivered at a workshop in Gaberones, September 3–8, 1973. Dr. Beach is engaged in a revisionist study of Shona history.
60. Duncan McIntosh, *South Africa*, p. 189; Richard Brown, "Aspects of the Scramble for Matabeleland," in *The Zambesian Past*, eds. Eric Stokes and Richard Brown, pp. 64–65. The missionary David Carnegie estimated 17,000 warriors with several thousand auxiliaries, "King Lobengula and his Military System," CA 3/1/1, N.A.R.
61. A. J. B. Hughes, *Kin, Caste and Nation among the Rhodesian Ndebele*, p. 9.

were closer to reality. The Ndebele were a tightly knit people
whose cohesion derived from their institution of royalty. Mzilikazi had successfully formed the diverse peoples who were
brought under his rule into a highly stratified caste society
which accepted the king as the source of all authority. During
the last years of Mzilikazi the traditional discipline of the
Ndebele had begun to weaken, and the conflict within the
society over the succession, which resulted in a civil war in 1870,
left continuing divisions among the Ndebele after Lobengula
established himself as king. Lobengula actively uprooted all
signs of dissidence as they appeared. But when the advance of
the whites presented him with new and grave problems, Lobengula was by no means secure upon his throne. Lobengula, like
his father, recognized that a war with the whites would likely
end in an Ndebele defeat, and he attempted to avoid it. By a
pacific, temporizing policy, however, he risked a challenge to his
leadership from his own impis. Caught between the contradictions of white objectives and the nature of Ndebele society, he
sought to minimize the impact of the whites without bringing
on a war with either the Transvaal or the British. His statesmanship was intelligent; that the cause was hopeless made his fate
more poignant.

In the early days of the Ndebele occupation the whites who
sought entry into the trans-Limpopo country were usually elephant hunters or traders who in themselves posed no threat to
the Ndebele kingdom. Mzilikazi's concern was not with these
few outriders from the south but with the hundreds who might
follow them. He was well aware of the land hunger of the
burghers of the Transvaal, and the high veld inhabited by the
Ndebele was attractive country for herders and pastoralists. His
policy of isolation remained absolute until 1853, when he relaxed it under pressure. By a treaty of that year with the Transvaal, he not only promised to cooperate in stopping gun-running but agreed to admit and to protect hunters and travelers,
provided they received his prior approval and journeyed by a
prescribed route.[62]

This concession opened the interior to hunters who slaughtered huge numbers of elephants for their tusks, and other game

62. Tabler, *The Far Interior*, p. 197.

for the exhilaration of the kill. The ecstasies of Selous and other hunters in their descriptions of their prowess provide an interesting commentary on nineteenth-century masculine psychology. But, perhaps more important, the ivory trade in which both Europeans and Africans became involved brought Africans into dependent relations with the European economy. The Ndebele and other peoples began to acquire guns, blankets, tools, and other commodities, for which they paid at first in ivory and later by their labor in the diamond mines of Kimberley.[63]

The advent of the hunters and the traders thus brought the first erosion of the self-sufficiency of the Ndebele economy; but their direct impact on the society was minor. Some abused their privileges; some were cheats; but the vast majority lived on good terms with the Africans in a community of mutual trust and mutual interest. The threat of this advance guard of the Europeans was not from the hunters and traders themselves, but from the fact that they were an advance guard. They not only traded, but they observed, and some reported what they saw in terms that excited the avarice of others whose objectives were incompatible with the independence of the Ndebele society.

By the 1860s Matabeleland was being widely advertised as the Land of Ophir, studded with vast gold deposits barely exploited by ancient miners. An early source of this bedazzling myth was Carl Mauch. Traveling first in company with Henry Hartley, a pioneer hunter, and later by himself, Mauch saw much of Matabeleland and Mashonaland and wrote reports in which imagination sometimes dominated observation. In 1867, after inspecting with Hartley two allegedly rich fields later to be known as Tati and Hartley Hills, Mauch reported in a letter published in a Transvaal paper, "how the vast extent and beauty of these goldfields are such that at a particular point I stood as it were transfixed, riveted to the place, struck with amazement and wonder at the sight and for a few minutes was unable to use the hammer." This heady rhetoric also was evident in a book of his travels published in 1874.[64]

Mauch's reconnoiterings of gold deposits were conducted

63. Gann, *Southern Rhodesia*, pp. 46–47.
64. *Ibid.*, pp. 50–51.

under the pretense of innocent travel, for Mzilikazi strictly prohibited gold mining in any of the territories over which he
claimed dominion, and Mauch did not dare to remove any
specimens from the country. But in the interregnum between
Mzilikazi's death in 1868 and the installation of Lobengula in
1870 many prospecting parties sought to take advantage of the
confusion in Matabeleland to search for gold, principally in the
area between the Shashi and Ramaquabane rivers, which came
to be known as the Tati district. Most of them returned with no
gold, their capital exhausted, but still retaining the illusion that
somewhere in the area there were fabulously rich deposits. Most
of the gold seekers had little capital and less experience. Among
them was the Durban Gold Mining Company formed by ten
members of the local volunteer artillery who contributed a total
of £250 toward an expedition which returned empty handed.[65]
But some substantial capitalists also were attracted. A London
group in 1868 formed the London and Limpopo Mining Company, and sent out a party under Sir John Swinburne and Captain Lionel Levert which reached Tati in April 1869.[66] Another
London company formed about the same time, the South Africa
Gold Fields Exploration Company, employed Thomas Baines,
an artist-traveler whose paintings of South African scenes would
later make him famous, to lead a gold-seeking expedition which
established claims in the western part of Matabeleland in the
Hartley Hills area.[67] Neither of these ventures was successful.
Most of Swinburne's miners, disappointed in not finding gold,
departed for the diamond diggings to the south.[68] Swinburne
was unable to get sufficient financial support to work the mines
and make the annual payments to Lobengula, and he had to
abandon his concession,[69] which Lobengula in 1880 assigned to
the Northern Light Gold Mining Company, formed by some of
the miners who had left for the diamond fields a decade earlier
and now returned with money and mining machinery. One of
them was Daniel Francis, a New Zealander for whom Francis-

65. McIntosh, *South Africa*, pp. 5, 115, 135, 190.
66. Thomas Baines, *The Gold Regions of South Eastern Africa*, p. 3.
67. Memo of Thomas Baines, September 4, 1871, HO 1/3/4, N.A.R.
68. "Tati Concession," information in N.A.R.
69. Swinburne to Knutsford, December 18, 1888, C.O. 417/26, P.R.O.

town was named.[70] This company's rights were eventually acquired by the Tati concession, which engaged in profitable mining operations. Baines's London backers, on the other hand, through a combination of incompetence and inadequate capital, did not provide the necessary equipment to work his concession and he died in 1875 still a poor man.[71] But both of these bankrupt companies had value in their rights if not in their gold. Swinburne, a member of Parliament, was later able to blackmail the promoters of the British South Africa Company into payments for his dormant rights, on pain of his contesting the validity of their concession. Baines acquired for his company a verbal concession from Lobengula granting mining rights in western Matabeleland extending from the Gwelo River north almost one hundred miles to the Hunyani River west of modern Salisbury,[72] and this concession was also bought by the chartered company's founders to bolster their position.

Lobengula's willingness to authorize mining concessions was a departure from the strict prohibitions enforced by his father. The reversal reflected a change both in times and in the security of the royal power. One possible reason for the altered position was that the ivory trade from which the king derived revenue was on the decline, and the money which might be gained from concessions was a means of replacing these lost funds. The Ndebele king's treasury was a source of patronage which strengthened the loyalty of his supporters and bolstered his position against dissident elements in his kingdom. But another consideration was undoubtedly the security of the kingdom against the increasing number of concession hunters who were entering the country. Lobengula, plagued by the influx of goldseekers into the Tati area, found it expedient to make an arrangement with one of the more substantial companies, which he hoped would help to secure British endorsement of his rights against the claims of the Ngwato and of the Transvaal.

During the 1870s and early 1880s Lobengula's delaying action succeeded. The concessionaires found no Ophir. Uniformly un-

70. "Tati Concession," information in N.A.R.
71. J. P. R. Wallis, ed., *The Northern Goldfields Diaries of Thomas Baines*, 1:xvii–xviii.
72. Memo of Thomas Baines, September 4, 1871, HO 1/3/4, N.A.R.

favorable reports from the gold-bearing areas discouraged speculators from risking their capital; mining fever in the 1870s was centered in Kimberley, and in the mid–1880s on the Witwatersrand. Matabeleland thus enjoyed a brief remission from the onslaught of the gold seekers. Even during this period of relative quiet, however, there were indications that it would not long remain outside the sphere of white interest. One evidence of the opening of a new era was the mission of Alexander Bailie to Matabeleland in 1876. Bailie, a land surveyor, was employed by the Cape Colony administration in Griqualand West, the district of the diamond mines, to travel to Matabeleland with the objects of promoting friendly relations with Lobengula and inquiring into the possibility of employing Ndebele to come to work in the mines.[73]

Lobengula responded favorably to the proposal to supply labor, and provided the first contingent of workers to be dispatched from Matabeleland to the diamond mines, but he expressed no desire for the extension of British influence into his kingdom. Sir Bartle Frere, governor of the Cape and high commissioner for South Africa between 1877 and 1880, was a strong advocate of the extension of British influence into the interior. He had been selected by Lord Carnarvon, the colonial secretary, to advance the federation of the various European dominated entities—republics and colonies—in a single government under the British flag. This responsibility he accepted with enthusiasm, for he was a dedicated imperialist, a believer in the manifest destiny of Britain as an agent of civilization. Frere's experience in India had strengthened this conviction, and the Indian pattern affected his policy toward African peoples on the frontiers of white settlement. The Indian government had established the resident system with native states, and Frere desired to promote the extension of British influence in a similar manner with Africans. In 1878 he dispatched a mission to Lobengula under the leadership of Captain Robert Patterson

73. J. R. Merriman, Chief Clerk, Colonial Secretariat, Kimberley, to Bailie, June 21, 1876, BA 10/1/1, N.A.R. Gann, *Southern Rhodesia*, pp. 60–61. Bailie had been instructed to be extremely circumspect and to confine his mission to investigation and to inquiry into the possibility of getting labor.

with the object of establishing friendly relations with the Ndebele king. Patterson saw Lobengula, with no definite results, and then set out on a journey to Victoria Falls during which he and his companions died.[74] No further embassies were sent by Frere. His hopes to advance the residential system were shattered by the outbreak of violence among the Gcaleka and Ngquika Xhosa in 1877–1878, followed by the Zulu War of 1879. Frere with some justice was held responsible for precipitating a war that opened with the disaster of Isandhlwana and contributed to unseating the Disraeli government. He was recalled. His successor, Sir Hercules Robinson, was understandably more cautious, and the "forward policy" was temporarily discredited by the revolt of the Transvaal and the British humiliation at Majuba. The Gladstone government which came into office in 1880 had no inclination for further imperial adventures in southern Africa.

Gladstone's abhorrence of expansion was undoubtedly genuine, though his unctuous rectitude irritated those who considered him to be as amoral in politics as those whom he flayed. But politicians, particularly successful ones, cannot afford the luxury of devotion to abstract principles or to consistency. The world in which Gladstone lived and the British society that he governed imposed constraints upon his freedom of action. He could not ignore German or French ambitions; nor could he control the course of events in overseas areas, which often faced his cabinet with options all of which were distasteful. Out of power he could say that intervention in Egypt was madness;[75] in office he was required to demonstrate that it was not only sane but necessary. Likewise in South Africa, he could commit himself, particularly after Majuba, to nonintervention, but feel compelled by the threat of German expansion to authorize the

74. The circumstances of the deaths of the members of the party are uncertain. The Ndebele stated that they died from drinking poisoned water, but suspicion remained that they had been killed by some Ndebele. Rider Haggard thought Lobengula had ordered their deaths, but there was no evidence either to support or deny the king's complicity. See the chapter by H. Rider Haggard in W. A. Wills and L. T. Collingridge, *The Downfall of Lobengula*, 227–233.

75. Gladstone to Granville, November 17, 1876, PRO 20/29/29A, P.R.O., published in Ramm, *Political Correspondence*, 1:20.

extension of British influence into Bechuanaland and on the coast north of Natal. This response brought the British sphere to the borders of Matabeleland at the same time as the Transvaal was beginning to manifest interest in northward expansion and Portugal was reasserting ancient claims to the area. The preconquest era for Matabeleland had begun.

From the British perspective there were two threats to the status quo north of the Limpopo in the years between 1885 and 1890. Fear of German intentions had subsided, but the ambitions of the Transvaal and of Portugal caused increasing concern. The two problems were quite different. For the Boers, the land beyond the Limpopo was a natural extension of their pastoral frontier. To the Portuguese, Africa represented ancient glories and future hopes; its significance related more to self-esteem than to substance. For centuries Portugal had done little to develop its African possessions. The Portuguese presence was represented by little more than a few miserable settlements on the coast. But when other European states began to show an interest in Africa, Portugal revived long-dormant claims and asserted its rights to a swath of the continent from Angola to Mozambique. Old treaty rights were not enough to keep out other states; the Berlin Conference required "effective occupation" on the coast, and in the interior mouldering ruins, deserted since the seventeenth century, were evidence of the recession of Portugal rather than its rights.

Portuguese pretensions were vexatious to expansionist Britons. It was outrageous, they felt, that listless, decadent Portugal should hold on to possessions that it could not develop but would not relinquish to more progressive peoples. Delagoa Bay was a magnificent harbor, but would never realize its potentialities so long as the nearly bankrupt Portuguese government retained it. The MacMahon award had confirmed the Portuguese claim to all of the bay. But there was always a danger that some other European power might acquire it by purchase, despite Portugal's commitment to give Britain first refusal, or that the Boers of the Transvaal might break out to the sea at that point and thus become a menace to British paramountcy in southern Africa. Such views were current in Britain and Cape Colony. The much vaunted alliance counted for little against the frustrations of politicians, shipping interests, mining speculators, and others who desired what Portugal had but could find no way to take it. They were not deterred by sentiment or by principle. Most Britons looked upon the Portuguese with contempt. They considered them not quite Europeans—swarthy countenances and indolent habits betrayed an admixture of African blood. But Portugal was a European state; larceny against a member of the community was restricted by certain rules. Most important, Portugal was protected by the mutual jealousies of the great powers. Germany might have wished to have Delagoa Bay, but Britain would not allow it; Britain, Cape Colony, and later the British South Africa Company desired it, but Germany would not consent. Portuguese Africa survived, not so much from any Portuguese action but because other alternatives were deemed contrary to the interests of one or more of the great powers.

Portuguese claims to Mashonaland rested on the conquest of the Monomatapa empire which at its height had extended from the high veld between the Zambezi and the Limpopo to much of what became Mozambique. But in the 1870s there was little evidence of a Portuguese presence to support these claims. There were a few Portuguese settlements up the Zambezi, but all of them gave the impression of imminent demise. Sena, in the Manica district which was later to be an area of conflict with the British South Africa Company, had once been an important center. In 1874 there were only four civilian residents and one soldier. Tete, the capital of the Province of Zambezia, housed a battalion of almost 300 men, but none of the officers was white and most of the men were *degradados,* who had been exiled for crimes. The furthest settlement upstream was Zumbo where a nonwhite officer was stationed at the head of twenty-one soldiers. These forces were hardly sufficient to overawe Africans in the vicinity, or even to defend themselves.[76]

Symptomatic of the lack of vitality of Portuguese influence was the state of the *prazo* system. The *prazos da coroa* had developed as a response to a power vacuum resulting from the feebleness of Portuguese power and the inability of African states to establish hegemony over the lands on both banks of the

76. Eric Axelson, *Portugal and the Scramble for Africa,* pp. 3-4.

Zambezi from Tete to the Indian Ocean. This absence of established authority had enabled individual Portuguese, Goans, and
mestizos to establish control over large estates. These *prazeros*
owed nominal obligations to the Portuguese state, but in fact
they were virtually autonomous. For almost three centuries the
prazo system had dominated the political and economic life of
Portuguese Zambezia. The *prazeros'* power was sustained by
slave armies and they frequently exploited the people who lived
on their estates. But by the first half of the nineteenth century,
the *prazo* system was disintegrating. Its collapse had been accelerated by a great increase in the demand for slaves. Many *prazeros* had sought to profit from the vastly increased market in
Brazil by enslaving large numbers of the people who lived on
their estates, and thus produced a reaction against their authority, which had always lacked a traditional legitimacy recognized
by Africans and now was being exercised in a way destructive of
the welfare of the *prazo* community. Out of the wreckage of the
old *prazo* system there emerged new leaders, most formidable of
whom was Manoel António da Sousa, generally known as
Gouveia because of his Goan birth. Gouveia had arrived in
Mozambique in the 1850s to engage in the ivory trade but soon
took advantage of the disruption to gather around him an army
of ex-*prazo* soldiers and to establish himself in the Manica area
as an independent potentate who cooperated with the Portuguese officials only when it suited his convenience.[77]

Portuguese resources were poor indeed to counter an aggressive assertion of claims by subjects of another European state.
But energetic men in Portugal and Africa refused to resign
themselves to the end of empire. In the 1880s Foreign Minister
Barbosa du Bocage and his successor Henrique de Barros Tomes
fought for the recognition of Portugal's ancient rights, and in
southern Africa Colonel Paiva d'Andrada and Colonel A. A. de
R. Serpa Pinto, and others sought to give these claims substance
by establishing the Portuguese presence in the Zambezi watershed and beyond into the Nyasa region. All of these expeditions
reported that most of the natives they encountered welcomed
them. But, in the words of one expedition leader, Commander

77. The *prazo* system has recently been reassessed by Allen F. Isaacman, *Mozambique. The Africanization of a European Institution.*

Antonio Cardoso, they "complain a good deal of the English."[78] (Africans in the presence of English armed forces, of course, complained of the Portuguese, the French, or the Germans; prudence dictated such a response.)

The Portuguese also sought to strengthen their position by diplomatic activity. In 1886 and 1887 they negotiated treaties with Germany and with France by which these powers recognized Portugal's claims to the territories between Angola and Mozambique "without prejudice to the rights which other powers may have acquired there." The provision in effect meant that the Portuguese would have to argue their case with the British, and Lord Salisbury in 1887 refused to recognize claims in the interior unsupported by occupation.[79] In addition, Portugal from the mid-1880s on attempted to bolster its case by treaties with Africans and by showing the flag. Portuguese activity in southern Africa made it difficult for the British government to pursue the policy of *quieta non movere* which both Gladstone and Salisbury preferred. The resurgence of gold fever in Matabeleland and Mashonaland made it impossible.

After the disappointments of the 1870s the attraction of Matabeleland to miners and capitalists had declined, but it did not entirely subside. Lord Gifford in 1880 unsuccessfully offered Lobengula £100 for exclusive mining rights over the Mazoe River basin.[80] Gifford, then 31 years of age, had heard of the possible riches of Matabeleland and Mashonaland during his stay in Natal at the time of the Zulu War, in which he had participated.[81] His application was later to play a part in the background of the British South Africa Company. Another of the principal figures in the formation of the company appeared in 1885, when Lieutenant Edward A. Maund in company with another officer visited Lobengula on a goodwill embassy from Sir Charles Warren. Maund, like Warren, was an advocate of imperial expansion in Africa. Matabeleland impressed him as a prize worth acquiring, preferably by diplomacy, but, if neces-

78. Translation, *Diario de Noticias*, Lisbon, January 20, 1889, F.O. 179/269, P.R.O.
79. James Duffy, *Portuguese Africa*, p. 215.
80. A draft of this agreement, dated 1880, is in HO 1/3/4, N.A.R.
81. Gifford had previously served with Wolseley in his Ashanti campaign, and was awarded the Victoria Cross.

sary by force. British protection over Kgama presented a problem. Not only did the Ndebele look down upon the Ngwato as
inferiors but the two peoples disputed possession over the land
between the Shashi and Maklautsi rivers, within which were
some of the gold deposits that Europeans sought to exploit.

Maund thought that Lobengula could nevertheless be induced to accept British protection by exploiting his fear that
the Boers intended to invade his territory and seize his land. If
the object could not be achieved by peace, Maund thought the
Ndebele could be easily subdued, despite their vaunted military
reputation. He had arrived in Bulawayo just as a large impi was
returning from an expedition against the Tawana near Lake
Ngami in which they had been repelled with heavy losses, and
he derived the impression that the Ndebele were sick of war and
that the iron discipline that had made them so formidable was
rapidly eroding. A force of 1500 mounted men, Maund concluded, could easily drive out the Ndebele; and he reported that
he was certain that Lobengula and his senior indunas were
keenly cognizant of their inability by their own resources to
withstand a large encroachment of white men.[82] Maund's assessment of the decline of Ndebele discipline was overly affected by
his observation of a defeated impi; his impression of the outlook of their leadership was undoubtedly correct. Maund's report to Warren was not made public, but he also recorded his
impressions of the country in a memorandum that stimulated
the flood of white gold-seekers that Lobengula so much feared.
His report extolling the mineral wealth of Matabeleland was
made public in 1886, the same year that the gold rush began to
the Witwatersrand, where gold had been discovered in great
quantities after several false starts. Attention again focused on
Matabeleland; just as rich deposits had been found in the
Transvaal after disappointments, so might they exist in Matabeleland and Mashonaland; indeed, the ancient diggings were
impressive evidence that the gold must be there.

Among those who were attracted was Rhodes. Contrary to
most accounts, including his own, Rhodes's interest in Matabeleland came late. In July 1885 he described the area dominated

82. Notes on Matabeleland, n.d. [1885], Maund Papers, Rhodes
House.

by Lobengula as "fever-stricken" and unfit for settlement. Any colonization plan, he maintained, was "absurd" and the evidence of mineral wealth was not convincing. But in little over a year, reports from visitors to the area had drastically altered his opinion. He had come to realize that the land between the Limpopo and the Zambezi was indeed fit for European colonization and he had convinced himself that Matabeleland and Mashonaland might prove to be richer in mineral wealth than the Rand. Many others thought similarly, and Lobengula by 1887 was again confronted with a tide of gold seekers, some in their true guise, others masquerading as hunters. At the same time the threat to Matabeleland from the Transvaal became acute. Hemmed in by British on the east and west, the Transvaal's only direction of expansion was the north. The impulse to expansion which had driven the trekkers for generations was still there, indeed intensified by the gold rush. Burghers who had sold their farms to miners sought other lands. The territory beyond the Limpopo thus became an object of increasing attention, both from private individuals and from governmental representatives.[83]

In June 1887 Edward R. Renny-Tailyour, a young Englishman who had migrated to Natal, undertook what he described as a "hunting trip" to Lobengula's country. Renny-Tailyour was no ordinary hunter—the excitement of his life subsequently was associated with intrigue rather than the slaughter of animals—and his larger objectives were indicated by his prior consultation with Theophilus ("Offy") Shepstone, son of the renowned Sir Theophilus. "Offy" had become adviser to Mbanzeni, king of the Swazi, a position that was much more beneficial to "Offy" than to the Swazi king. Shepstone asked Renny-Tailyour to use the trip as an opportunity to promote good relations between Lobengula and the Swazi, and Renny-Tailyour took along an old Swazi induna to act as an adviser and interpreter. He arrived at Bulawayo in October 1887 and soon found that Lobengula and his indunas were preoccupied with how to deal with unauthorized gold seekers who entered his country and with the prospect of a Boer invasion. Lobengula asked about the implications of accepting British protection, but

83. Gann, Southern Rhodesia, pp. 71–72.

he made it clear that the question did not imply that he was considering making such a request.[84] Renny-Tailyour was not known for either modesty or integrity, but his report on Lobengula's agitation was undoubtedly correct. Three months before Renny-Tailyour arrived, Pieter D. C. J. Grobler reached Bulawayo as an emissary from the Transvaal to negotiate a treaty with Lobengula.[85] On July 30 Lobengula, after some hesitation, accepted an agreement which if it had been carried into effect, would have made his kingdom a dependent ally of the Transvaal. The treaty bound him to provide military assistance on request, to protect Transvaal citizens in his country who had a pass from the state president, and to accept a consul from the Transvaal who would have jurisdiction over all Transvaal subjects and over all civil cases between burghers and Ndebele.[86]

News of the treaty created a sensation among the expansionist minded of Cape Colony, who immediately branded it a fraud. Lobengula under pressure from the British side later denied that he had accepted the obligations written in the agreement. The king may have been literally truthful, for the treaty may have been interpreted to him as involving little more than a reaffirmation of the old Transvaal treaty of friendship with Mzilikazi.[87] But there seems little question that he agreed to an alliance with the Transvaal in an effort to prevent the feared Boer invasion of his territory which so dominated his conversations with Renny-Tailyour.

Lobengula could not cope with a rush of white men into his territories, whether they were Boer or British. They would not long accept his authority, and if they defied him, he would be unable to mete out punishment without bringing down upon himself the wrath of the entire white South African community. He sought to avoid or at least postpone this collision. In the

84. Memo, Renny-Tailyour, March 16, 1888, MISC/TA 5/2/1, N.A.R.
85. Renny-Tailyour stated that Grobler arrived while he was in Bulawayo. But Grobler's treaty with Lobengula was dated July 30, 1887, and Renny-Tailyour by his own testimony arrived on October 6.
86. Gann, *Southern Rhodesia*, p. 72.
87. The only whites who signed the document were Grobler and his brother. There were apparently no non-Transvaalers present to correct any misrepresentations.

Tati district early in 1887 he tried the expedient of appointing "Far Interior Sam" Edwards, an old and trusted friend, with full powers to make and enforce laws involving Europeans.[88] This establishment of a buffer between himself and the whites worked quite well at Tati.

The Tati Company, however, was not representative of the general problem with which he had to deal. Even before reports of Grobler's treaty reached Cape Colony, powerful men there were making plans which if successful would mean the end of Ndebele independence, but under British rather than Transvaal rule. Cecil Rhodes, now convinced that Matabeleland was a fair field for his ambitions, had resolved to seek a monopoly of mining rights. In 1887 he employed John Fry, who had been a shareholder in the Tati mines, to seek such a concession and promised Fry a fortune if he were successful.[89] Rhodes was indignant when he heard of the treaty and he acted with characteristic speed and force to prevent the Transvaal's stealing his north.

Prior to Rhodes's eruption, official British policy had been averse to further northward expansion. The Gladstone government had been ousted, but Salisbury's administration was no more inclined than had been its predecessor to incur further obligations in the South African interior. The high commissioner, Sir Hercules Robinson, though he privately favored extending the British sphere to the Zambezi, considered it hopeless to attempt to influence the British cabinet toward his views.[90]

Robinson's caution was highly vexing to his subordinates, in particular John S. Moffat and Sir Sidney Shippard. Moffat, son of the renowned Robert, had been one of the founders of the ineffectual Matabele mission of the London Missionary Society, but had tired of the frustrations of unheeded evangelism. He had left the land of the Ndebele in 1865 and subsequently in 1884 had joined the government service as assistant commissioner for Bechuanaland. Shippard had been appointed deputy commissioner for Bechuanaland and the Kalahari in 1885. Prior

88. Lobengula to Edwards, February 24, 1887, TA 1/2/1, N.A.R.
89. Reminiscences of Ivon Fry, September–October, 1938, FR 2/2/1, N.A.R. Fry's son later recalled that his father had a written contract by which he would receive £55,000 if the concession was granted through his work.
90. Shippard to Moffat, September 19, 1887, MO 1/1/4, N.A.R.

to his appointment he had been a lawyer in Griqualand West, where he and Rhodes became close friends, so intimate in fact that Rhodes in 1877 had named him and the British colonial secretary as executors of his will. This remarkable testament provided for the promotion of a secret society for the extension of British rule throughout the world and the colonization by British settlers of Africa, the Holy Land, the valley of the Euphrates, Cyprus and Candia, all of South America, islands of the Pacific, and the Malay Archipelago, as well as the ultimate reunion of the United States with the British Empire.[91] Shippard's imagination did not soar to such breathtaking heights, but he ardently advocated British expansion at least to the Zambezi. In May 1887 he wrote Robinson that the land between the Limpopo and the Zambezi "would form a most valuable addition to the British Empire and the necessary complement of a United South Africa under the British flag."[92] He argued: "The Power that can acquire that territory and also secure Delagoa Bay—the site of the future San Francisco of the Indian Ocean—will hold the key of the wealth and commerce of South and Central Africa."[93]

Shippard's assistant Moffat visited Lobengula during the last months of 1887, avowedly to discuss the boundary dispute between the Ndebele chief and Kgama but also to observe the state of affairs of Matabeleland. Shippard would have wished to go much further. He was constrained by the orders of Robinson to avoid commitments, but he did all that he could short of obvious insubordination to attach Lobengula to the British. When Lobengula in June 1887 complained about whites entering his country without permission, indicating that most if not all of these intruders were "Dutch," Shippard seized the opportunity. Britain, he reminded the king with more emphasis than accuracy, had always been friendly to the Ndebele during the half century since D'Urban had made his treaty with Mzilikazi. But other whites were treacherous and hostile, in particular the Boers, the Germans, and the Portuguese. He advised Lobengula

91. Will, September 19, 1877, RH 1/2/2, N.A.R.
92. J. L. Rademeyer, *Die Land Noord van die Limpopo in die Ekspansie Beleid van die Suid-Afrikaanse Republiek*, pp. 58–59.
93. *Ibid.*, p. 59.

to grant no concessions for prospecting, mining, grazing or any other purpose to these non-British whites without consulting Moffat.[94]

At the time that Shippard gave this counsel, he was unaware that during the time between the dispatch of Lobengula's letter and his reply, Grobler had secured his treaty. The first report of the treaty came to Shippard not from Lobengula but from Robinson. The high commissioner in December had heard from sources in the Transvaal that all of Matabeleland, including the Tati gold fields, had fallen under the control of the Transvaal, and that Lobengula had renounced the right of granting any concessions or making any agreements without the approval of the Transvaal. Shippard ordered Moffat to ascertain whether the rumors were true, and if they were not, to obtain an undertaking from Lobengula that he would not commit himself to any obligations with any government without the consent of Britain.[95]

This negative approach, denying rights to foreign powers rather than asserting British responsibility, was designed to avoid conflict with London. The initiative came from Robinson, pressed by Rhodes. Whether or not Rhodes's agents were the sources in the Transvaal which reported to Robinson, clearly the urgency with which Rhodes demanded action moved the high commissioner to respond. Rhodes did not transform Robinson into an advocate of positive action but he did convince him that he could no longer temporize. Rhodes saw Robinson on Christmas Day, 1887, and the two agreed on a course that involved legal formalization of the line that Shippard had taken. If Lobengula could be induced to accept a treaty binding him to make no agreements with any government without British consent, the immediate threat would be removed, and Britain would in effect have an option that could be exercised when the imperial government was willing to accept responsibility. One day later Robinson wired instructions to Shippard to act in this way. The result was the Moffat Treaty of February 1888.

94. Shippard to Lobengula, August 22, 1887, encl. in C.O. to F.O., December 3, 1887, F.O. 84/1875, P.R.O. In an amended version all reference to the Germans was stricken out.
95. Shippard to Moffat, December 26, 1887, MO 1/1/4, N.A.R.

From Moffat's testimony, Lobengula's consent was not obtained easily.[96] His reluctance may have related to his continuing resentment at British patronage of Kgama. More probably he was unwilling to commit himself witout ascertaining the consequences. What effect, for example, would a treaty with Britain have on his relations with the Boers? What assurance could he have that the British would protect him? Their record was not reassuring. Furthermore, written words were not always in accordance with oral interpretations. Moffat had explained to him that the Grobler treaty involved far more extensive concessions than Lobengula had thought. Might not the British treaty also ensnare him in involvements that he did not understand? Lobengula's testimony is not available. But in the end he accepted, convinced apparently that a relaxed British protection was preferable to domination by the Boers. There was no third choice of independence from both. What he could not yet foresee was that there was another alternative—domination by the chartered company of Cecil John Rhodes.[97]

At the time of the Moffat treaty Lobengula's significance for Rhodes was as a temporary occupier of territory pending ultimate absorption of the area into the British Empire. The ultimate fate of the Ndebele was of little consequence. Rhodes wrote his friend Shippard in April 1888 that it was not good policy at that time to move the Ndebele over the Zambezi, since the burghers of the Transvaal would rush in; consequently a policy that kept the Ndebele quiet under the protection of the Crown was the best expedient.[98]

The Moffat treaty also accorded nicely with the state of imperial policy. Robinson's letter communicating intelligence that the Transvaal had established a protectorate over Matabeleland including the Tati gold fields reached London at the end of February 1888. The report brought a mixed reaction. The Foreign Office's principal African expert, Sir Percy Anderson, considered it "very serious" if the news was correct. Salisbury, on the other hand, professed to be unworried. The London conven-

96. Moffat to Shippard, private, February 10, 1888, HC 1/1/16, N.A.R.
97. See Richard Brown, "Aspects of the Scramble for Matabeleland," in Stokes and Brown, *The Zambesian Past*, p. 75.
98. Rhodes to Shippard, April 14, 1888, RH 1/1/1, N.A.R.

tion, he maintained, proscribed any such protectorate. When Anderson pointed to the Colonial Office judgment that article 4 of the convention applied only to territories east and west of the Transvaal and that Derby had purposely excluded the north at the insistence of the Transvaal delegates, Salisbury remained unimpressed. He responded that the first part of that article prevented the Transvaal from making any treaty with any "state" or "nation," and that Matabeleland at least fitted into the latter category.[99]

The exchange between Salisbury and his adviser is significant on two bases. Salisbury was not prepared to approve of any action by Britain to assert imperial authority over Matabeleland. But neither was he prepared to allow the Transvaal or any European power to move into the vacuum. The Moffat Treaty fitted Salisbury's specifications of imperial influence without imperial responsibility.

No one involved in the formulation of Salisbury's South African policy was willing to concede Matabeleland to the Boers or to the Portuguese. On the character of positive action, there was division of opinion. Some members of the permanent staffs of the Colonial Office and the Foreign Office now favored the assertion of a British protectorate. But, as was the case in Lincoln's cabinet, one vote constituted a majority. Salisbury was content to maintain a vague aura of British influence south of the Zambezi. This policy of non-action applied only to the imperial government. Salisbury had no objection to the assertion of British authority by nongovernmental agencies, in particular chartered companies. He had not only endorsed Mackinnon's chartered company as the British presence in East Africa; he had welcomed it as a means of achieving imperial purposes. The Moffat Treaty opened the way for a chartered company in South Africa. It would be of a very different character than its counterparts in Borneo and in East and West Africa.

99. Notes on C.O. to F.O., March 6, 1888, F.O. 4/1917, P.R.O.

2

The Great Amalgamation

THE DISCOVERY IN 1886 OF THE GREAT MAIN REEF OF the Witwatersrand not only transformed the history of South Africa; the repercussions profoundly affected central Africa, in particular the lands of the Ndebele and the Shona. Though the full extent of the deposits was not known for several years, the reports of great riches attracted thousands of miners and assorted other fortune seekers. Cecil Rhodes wrote Charles Rudd in January 1887 that "opinion is steadily growing that the Randt [sic] is the biggest thing the world has seen."[1] Not all experts agreed with this impression—Rhodes himself subsequently became more cautious—but capital, much of it from the diamond fields of Kimberley, poured in to buy farms and to begin mining operations. Even before the development of deep-level mining, extraction of the gold of the Rand required great agglomerations of capital; competition for properties drove prices to levels that effectively excluded small speculators, and machinery was very expensive. The practices developed in the early years of the Rand for the generation of capital established a pattern that was followed north of the Limpopo. In 1888, for example, the cash investment in the mines was £1,200,000,[2] but the authorized capital of the companies was many times that amount, and the insiders who were able to sell shares at par were able to realize huge profits in the "Kaffir market" as the prices of their stocks were forced up to levels often unrelated to the

1. The Consolidated Gold Fields of South Africa, Limited, "The Gold Fields," 1887–1937, p. 6.
2. S. H. Frankel, Capital Investment in Africa, p. 95.

prospect of returns by exaggerated reports and gullible investors.

The boom in the Transvaal directly contributed to the rush
north of the Limpopo. The "land of Ophir" again became a
lure; the gold was there, as the ancient workings attested; it
seemed reasonable to expect that with modern techniques
wealth could be extracted from the old mines, and there was
always the prospect of great deposits as yet undiscovered. Men
who did not have the capital to compete on the Rand trekked
to Matabeleland in the hope that they would find their fortunes
there. And one great capitalist also directed his attention to the
north. Cecil Rhodes had early sought an amalgamation of interests on the Rand with J. B. Robinson and with Barney Barnato, and had failed. He was determined that he would not be
similarly frustrated in Matabeleland.

Most of the concession hunters who importuned Lobengula
for mining and land rights, however, were men with little capital at their disposal. One group, the Great Northern Gold
Fields Exploration Company, which has left fuller records than
most, later became involved with the plans of Rhodes. This
petty enterprise with the impressive title represented an association of Cape Town businessmen. The subscribers were a mixed
bag of businessmen and politicians. They included a wine mer-
chant, the ex-managing director of the Cape Commercial Bank,
the secretary of the Table Bay Harbor Board, and a cousin of
Alfred Beit, W. A. Lippert, of the prominent South African
firm of the same name. Among the politicians were two members of the Cape Assembly, the ex-mayor of Kimberley, and the
mayor of Cape Town. Probably none of them knew anything
about mining; they did know, however, that concessions could
be turned into gold. At the beginning of 1887 they dispatched to
Matabeleland a party led by Frank Johnson, a young man of
twenty-one who would later achieve fame as the leader of the
Pioneer Expedition into Mashonaland, and Maurice Heany, an
American who had fled the discipline of West Point for a life of
adventure and had later served with Johnson in the Bechuanaland Border Police.

The two young entrepreneurs reminded Lobengula that the

discoveries of gold in the Transvaal had intensified interest in
Matabeleland and Mashonaland and warned him that the tide
would soon pour into his country. Indeed, the first signs of the
gold rush were already evident. Shortly after Johnson and
Heany's arrival, a German party appeared headed by a man
named Schultz. A Grahamstown syndicate sent Joseph G. Wood,
William C. Francis, and Edward Chapman to seek a concession;
and already in evidence were several concession hunters with no
backing and no prospects but with hopes that somehow they
would be able to induce Lobengula to make them rich by awarding them rights to goldbearing land in exchange for a few
pounds.[3] Johnson and Heany pointed out to the king that the
best way to protect himself against this flood of unscrupulous
adventurers was to make an agreement with a responsible,
friendly group, the Great Northern Gold Fields Exploration
Company, which was prepared to pay a "certain sum" and, on
discoveries, annual payments, for the right to exploit the mineral resources of Mashonaland.[4] They presented a note from Sir
Sidney Shippard attesting to their good character and concluding that "you may safely grant them the concessions they seek in
return for which they are willing to pay you any reasonable sum
you may ask."[5] How much Shippard's endorsement was worth
must be a matter of speculation, but Lobengula did not immediately reject the proposition. Instead, he kept the party in sus-
pense for several months. He assured them that if he gave any
concession at all, it would be to them, but that he was not an
absolute monarch who could make decisions with such great
import without the approval of his people and that the Ndebele
were almost unanimously opposed to allowing white miners to
enter their country.[6]

Johnson and Heany's negotiations with Lobengula were strik-
ingly similar to those a year later between Rhodes's emissaries
and the Ndebele chief. In both instances the would-be concessionaires portrayed themselves and their backers as substantial

3. Johnson to Chairman and Members, Northern Gold Fields Exploration Syndicate, January 10, 1888, JO 3/1/1, N.A.R.
4. Johnson et al. to Lobengula, February 21, 1887, in ibid.
5. Shippard to Lobengula, March 19, 1887, in ibid.
6. Johnson to Chairman and Members, January 10, 1888, in ibid.

businessmen who could be relied upon not only to act responsi-
bly but to serve the interests of the Ndebele by keeping out adventurers who would swamp the kingdom. In both cases Sir
Sidney Shippard gave his benediction to the promoters. And in
both negotiations the fair professions of the concessionaires
covered a contempt for the people with whom they dealt. Johnson saw his trip as a means for spending the rest of his life in
ease and comfort, and Lobengula as a savage chief whose avarice
was the key to the realization of that object. In May, while he
was awaiting what he hoped would be a favorable decision,
Johnson wrote a friend, "I think I'll have the whip hand of the
old heathen in the coming talk, for I now know that he is the
most greedy old glutton under the sun for what he terms 'in-
simbi' (iron) by which he means money."[7] Johnson was more
forthright than most. Shortly after his visit with Lobengula he
concluded a letter to another African chief for whom he was
seeking a concession, "Now believe that as long as I can make
anything out of you I shall be your friend."[8] Presumably the
sentence lost something in translation to the chief.

Lobengula was not immune to the attraction of money. But
he was not so enamored of it as to lose sight of his position as
the head of the Ndebele, and Johnson's assumption that Lobengula would sell out his country's interests for the £100 which
was offered is probably more revealing of Johnson than of
Lobengula. The king was keenly aware of the menaces that surrounded him and his people. His regiments were eager to destroy the whites. His indunas were opposed to any concessions
that would allow whites to settle in their country, and his position was not so secure that he could defy them. On the other
hand he knew that the isolation of the Ndebele was nearly at an
end. The whites would soon swarm into his country, as they had
into that of his father. One possible course would be to follow
Mzilikazi's precedent and to trek north, in this case beyond the
Zambezi River. Such a necessity might eventually have to be
faced, but in the meantime he must temporize. His best hope was
for an accommodation with one section of the white population
which would then act as a barrier to other whites. A strong syn-

7. Scrap of letter, Johnson to Mrs. Saunders, May ――, 1887, in *ibid.*
8. Johnson to Ngomo, May 28, 1889, in *ibid.*

dicate backed by the British government could be such a barrier. Lobengula's dalliance with Johnson and Heany, consequently, may have related to such considerations rather than being mere dilatory tactics.

The area for which Johnson and Heany sought monopoly mining rights was the district east of the Hunyani River extending to the Mazoe and adjacent to that which Lobengula had granted verbally to Thomas Baines, a district in which alluvial gold deposits were known to exist. Lobengula finally, early in July 1887, referred the application to the council of indunas. After several meetings of the council, the king suggested that the syndicate accept instead a concession in the area between the Shashi and Maklautsi rivers, which was also claimed by Kgama. This diversion, which Johnson and Heany immediately refused, undoubtedly resulted from conflict between the indunas and Lobengula with regard to allowing mining operations in the Shona country. Lobengula did not immediately accept the opposition of his indunas as decisive; on July 20 he authorized the Johnson-Heany party to prospect in the country for which they sought a concession payment of £100 and, if they found payable gold, he would on their return to Bulawayo grant a concession on payment of £200 a year. But when the king's decision became known, the indunas manifested their hostility to the arrangement in such emphatic terms that he detained the party for ten days. Heany returned to the Ngwato country, where on the way to Matabeleland they had received permission to prospect for minerals. Heany's presence with Kgama was deemed essential to protect his and Johnson's rights. The remainder of the party under Johnson were finally allowed to proceed, but were accompanied by an Ndebele escort which manifestly was not sent to help them in their search. Despite the uncooperativeness of the Ndebele, the party found alluvial gold, but when they returned to claim their concession Johnson was instead summoned before the council of indunas to answer to the following charges: (1) Poisoning the head man of the escort, who had died of fever; (2) being a spy; (3) writing a letter saying Lobengula had two tongues; (4) kicking an Ndebele with his boot; (5) using a spade to look for gold.[9]

9. Johnson to Chairman and Members, January 10, 1888, in *ibid.*

After a trial lasting three days, the council fined Johnson £300, a wagon, oxen, and rifles, but Lobengula reduced the penalty to £100, ten blankets, and ten tins of gunpowder. Johnson interpreted the trial as a farce devised by the indunas to block the concession. This motive was undoubtedly central, but the action against him followed immediately after another party led by J. G. Wood had been discovered searching for gold when they had been given permission only to hunt, and experience with Wood undoubtedly heightened suspicion of others.[10]

Johnson had failed, but his reports of rich alluvial deposits in the Mazoe country stimulated interest in the area. Lord Gifford who had tried to acquire a concession in the area almost ten years before, decided to try again. Johnson's association with Gifford, however, came through Bechuanaland rather than Matabeleland. During his service with the Bechuanaland Border Police, Johnson had been impressed by the potentialities for gold mining in the Ngwato territory. At Shoshong, Kgama's capital, he had seen gold dust on vulture quills which had been brought in from the surrounding area,[11] and while he pressed Lobengula he kept in mind the alternative of a concession from the Ngwato. Where Johnson and Heany had failed with Lobengula they were successful with Kgama. He granted the syndicate the right to prospect, for a payment of five shillings a month, and to select up to 400 square miles for £1 per year per square mile and a royalty of two and a half percent.[12] Heany was left in charge of the concession, and Johnson proceeded on to Cape Town where he presented his sponsors with the prize, which they immediately turned into cash. They sold their concession to the Caisse des Mines of Paris, represented in London by Francis I. Ricarde-Seaver, whose agents in South Africa were on the alert for any opportunities to capitalize on the South African mining boom. Ricarde-Seaver in turn sold the rights to a new enterprise, the Bechuanaland Exploration Company, headed by Lord Gifford and George Cawston. Gifford had not recovered from the mining fever that had infected him during his stay in South Africa, and he seems to have convinced Cawston

10. *Ibid.*
11. Ian Colvin, *Life of Jameson*, 1:121.
12. Agreement, December 16, 1887, C.O. 879/32/392, P.R.O.

that there were good prospects for the discovery of rich gold deposits in the country beyond the Rand. Cawston had a remarkable combination of interests. He was a map maker and he was also a prominent stockbroker. The family firm was a member of the London stock exchange, and by the 1880s he had become the head of the firm that now bore his name. He brought Ricarde-Seaver and Gifford together, and the result was the Bechuanaland Exploration Company. The new company was registered in April 1888 with a nominal capital of £150,000, much of which was in paper to privileged insiders in the transaction with the Caisse des Mines. The Caisse agreed to contribute £10,000 in cash in exchange for 10,000 shares in the company and the right to offer an additional 50,000 shares for subscription on the condition that they not be transferred by the purchaser for one year or until dividends of at least 100 per cent had been paid on the paid-up capital, whichever was earlier. Other insiders received similar stock privileges. Among the first subscribers were Baron Henry de Rothschild and such city magnates as Henry Oppenheim and Messrs. Mosenthal and Sons.[13] The transaction was of the stock-jobbing sort which was increasingly characteristic of the practices of the "Kaffir circus."

While the Bechuanaland company was being organized, news reached London of the Moffat treaty with Lobengula, and Gifford and Cawston decided to revive Gifford's project of a mining concession in the Mazoe valley. Since the articles of association of the Bechuanaland Exploration Company did not provide for such extension, they formed the Exploring Company with a nominal capital of £12,000. The capital bore no relationship to the magnitude of the objective. Its founders gave it the mission not only of seeking gold in the land of the Ndebele and the Shona, but the construction of a railway from the Cape border through Bechuanaland.[14] In this latter venture they had assurance of the participation of prominent British capitalists, including Rothschild's.

Gifford and Cawston felt confident that with the backing they

13. Agreement, May 16, 1888, File 26499, Board of Trade, Register of Companies, London. A branch of the Mosenthal family was established in Port Elizabeth, Cape Colony, and was an agent for the Bechuanaland Exploration Company.

14. The Exploring Company, Ltd., B.T. 31/4176/26995, P.R.O.

could summon to their support they could establish an enterprise that could overpower the petty competitors with whom they would have to contend. In Bechuanaland their confidence was fully justified. The only serious problem they encountered was in the territory disputed by Kgama and Lobengula. Wood, Francis, and Chapman, who had roused the ire of Lobengula by seeking gold rather than game had been sufficiently restored to favor that they acquired a concession in the Shashi-Maklautsi disputed territory, which Lobengula had previously sought to give to Johnson and Heany. In their eagerness for gold, Wood, Francis, and Chapman grasped what Johnson and Heany had rejected. They sought to ensure their possession by acquiring a concession from Kgama to the same territory. Kgama told them that they could not properly ask him for a concession that they had already acquired from Lobengula and warned them that he would not allow them to work in land which was Ngwato territory. They responded by threatening him with war with Lobengula,[15] and reinforced their threat by an appeal to Lobengula to protect them against the Ngwato.[6] Lobengula declined; he had granted the concession as a means of reinforcing his claims, but he had no intention of sacrificing Ndebele lives for the protection of white mining speculators. The risks were theirs.

Wood, Francis, and Chapman were a particularly quarrelsome manifestation of the inconsequential whites whose pursuit of wealth irritated and sometimes disrupted African societies in the interior of Africa. But the great changes that were impending were not the work of men such as these. The land of the Ndebele and Shona was coveted by powerful capitalists, and the contest was between the Gifford-Cawston interests and Rhodes.

Each of the principal contenders had strong claims to the favor of an imperial government that desired the economic development of Matabeleland and Mashonaland but was not prepared to pay for it in either expense or responsibility. Each was vulnerable to the competition of the other. The power of Gif-

15. Hepburn to Moffat, December 15, 1887, MO/1/1/4, N.A.R.
bengula to protect them against the Ngwato.[16] Lobengula de-
16. Wood, Chapman, and Francis to Lobengula, December 15, 1887, LO 1/1, N.A.R.

ford and Cawston derived from the City of London, where they had the backing of influential financiers. They also had actual and potential allies in the concern of many British philanthropists and commercial men over the expressed desire of many Cape politicians, including Rhodes, to eliminate the "imperial factor" in South and central Africa and to make Cape Town the de facto capital of the British Empire in that region. The London group was powerful enough to impress the staff of the Foreign Office and the Colonial Office.[17]

Against such influential Englishmen, Rhodes could pit his own great fortune. But in 1888 he was still almost unknown outside the circles of the diamond merchants, and what was known to British politicians was not in his favor. His conflicts with Sir Charles Warren and the Reverend John Mackenzie had left a sour aftertaste, which flavored Salisbury's reference to him as "Rather a Pro-Boer M.P. in South Africa, I fancy?"[18] Rhodes's contribution in 1888 of £10,000 to Parnell's Irish Nationalists had reinforced the impression in London and Whitehall that he was a dangerous man. Furthermore, though he was an Oxonian, he was not a gentleman. His money could command power; it could not naturalize him into the elite of British society. Even after he had become "the Colossus" in the mid-1890s with the adulation of the multitude, including Queen Victoria herself, he was black-balled by an exclusive London club.[19] In 1895 an anonymous member of the Colonial Office staff tried to translate Rhodes into the establishment when he noted that "Rhodes is a gentleman to his finger tips. He is an Eton and Oxford man."[20] But Edward Fairfield who understood the qualities requisite of a gentleman, evaluated Rhodes in these terms:

> ... in some aspects of his character, Mr. Rhodes is apt not to be regarded as a serious person ... he is grotesque, impulsive, school-

17. Note by Herbert, June 1, 1888, on Cawston to C.O., May 30, 1888, C.O. 417/26, P.R.O.
18. H. H. Johnston, *The Story of My Life*, p. 221.
19. *Truth*, March 27, 1895. The club was the Travellers' Club. His sponsors, the Prince of Wales, the Duke of Fife, and Earl Grey, resigned.
20. Note on telegram, Robinson to C.G., received July 17, 1895, C.O. 417/141, P.R.O. Rhodes's brother Frank attended Eton and relived throughout his life his athletic achievements, in particular in the great Rugby match against Harrow.

boyish, humorous and almost clownish and . . . he has probably
been encouraged in the habit of uttering calculated indiscretions
by the fact that "nobody markes him" as Shakespeare says.[21]

Rhodes, then, had great disadvantages. But he also had great
assets even in 1888 when he was a relative unknown. Not only
was he a wealthy man but he was already a great force in Cape
politics, though he did not become prime minister until 1890.

The financial power of Rhodes was fed from two sources, the
celebrated De Beers trust deed which enabled him to use the sur-
plus funds of the company for imperial expansion, and the resources he derived from Gold Fields of South Africa. The Gold
Fields arrangement was no less remarkable than that with De
Beers, and no less significant for his ambitions. Gold Fields of
South Africa (later Consolidated Gold Fields) was the creation
of Rhodes and Charles D. Rudd, whose destiny it was to be remembered as the negotiator for Rhodes of the mining concession from Lobengula, even though he was a person of considerable weight in his own right.

Rudd's early life had remarkable similarities to that of
Rhodes. He was educated at Harrow and at Trinity College,
Cambridge, where he excelled as an athlete. But his health
failed, and on the advice of his physician he left Cambridge for
the sunshine of South Africa, where he spent several years with
the renowned hunter John Dunn. News of the diamond discoveries attracted him to Kimberley, where he was among the early
arrivals, and it was here that Rhodes and he began their partnership which lasted for most of the rest of their lives. They purchased a quarter share each in "Baxter's Gully," and through
their joint efforts began the acquisitions that would make
Rhodes famous and Rudd wealthy. The two complemented
each other; Rhodes had great plans and great energy, but little
background or interest in the details necessary to carry out his
ideas. Rudd supplied much of the business acumen that made
their partnership a success. The amalgamation with Barnato
which produced the great De Beers monopoly gave Rhodes the
scope and resources to pursue his passion for empire building
and the two partners in effect came to an understanding that

21. Note by Fairfield, February 22, 1895, on Kimberley to Malet, confidential, February 18, 1895, C.O. 537/129, P.R.O.

Rhodes would devote his attention to diamonds and northern expansion and Rudd to gold in the Transvaal. The Gold Fields of South Africa, which was the second pillar of Rhodes's financial power, was thus primarily the creation of Rudd, though Rhodes participated equally with Rudd in the rich profits that were derived from the conglomerates of mining properties that Rudd put together. The returns to shareholders were handsome—in the first five years after the company's registration in March 1887 shareholders received dividends totalling 97½ percent, in addition to great windfalls from allotments of shares at par.[22] In the fiscal year 1894–1895, the company paid a 125-percent dividend;[23] other years were comparable. But the two founders enjoyed far greater returns than these. By the terms of the company's incorporation they were entitled to three-fifteenths of the net profits and an additional fifteenth for their services as managing directors.[24] Predictably, shareholders protested against the huge profits paid the founders, and when the company reorganized in 1892 as Consolidated Gold Fields, the terms were changed to provide Rhodes and Rudd with 80,000 shares in the new company, the right to purchase an additional 25,000 at par, and two-fifteenths of the profits.[25] With these "reduced" profits Rhodes and Rudd still received as directors £232,532 in 1894–1895.[26] For these huge revenues Rhodes gave relatively little of his time and energy. From the founding of the company until his death he did not attend any annual meetings, and while he contributed advice on acquisitions, he left most of the responsibility to Rudd.[27]

Beyond the vast resources he was able to generate from his

22. *Financial News*, November 4, 1892.

23. *Ibid.*, October 26, 1895.

24. Charles Sydney Goldmann, *The Financial, Statistical, and General History of the Gold & Other Companies of Witwatersrand, South Africa*, p. 75.

25. Consolidated Gold Fields, *The Gold Fields*, pp. 34–36.

26. *Financial News*, October 26, 1895.

27. A. P. Cartwright, *Gold Paved the Way*, p. 51. In 1896 the agreement was further revised by giving Rhodes and Rudd 100,000 shares in exchange for their share of the profits. At that time, the market value of these shares was over £1 million. Consolidated Gold Fields, *The Gold Fields*, pp. 64–65.

access to the revenues of De Beers and Consolidated Gold Fields, Rhodes was able to use these companies themselves to bolster his extra-economic ambitions. Gold Fields had a half interest in the Rudd concession, and after the foundation of the British South Africa Company, both De Beers and Consolidated bought large numbers of shares, and their treasuries were tapped on several occasions to provide financial assistance in the form of loans when the chartered company's capital was nearly exhausted.

It is ironic that Rudd should be remembered in relation to the concession that led to the British South Africa Company. The company was the vehicle for the soaring ambition of Rhodes; Rudd had no interest in painting maps red; as time went on he betrayed more and more irritation with the megalomania of his partner; and the first fissures, which in 1896 became a complete break, appeared about the time of the concession that has linked his name to Rhodes. The two had needed each other as they worked to command the diamond fields; when that objective was achieved, Rhodes required not a partner but a supporter. He found that man in Alfred Beit, who was not only a financial genius but became a devoted follower. Beit was the same age as Rhodes. The two had become acquainted in the diamond fields and Rhodes had consulted closely with Beit when he effected the amalgamation of De Beers; he relied upon him heavily for financial advice thereafter. "Ask little Alfred" became the catch phrase of Rhodes and his associates whenever complex business issues had to be resolved,[28] and "little Alfred" was seldom wrong. Beit's great mistakes were those deriving from his loyalty to Rhodes, which caused him to reject judgment for sentiment. How much Rhodes reciprocated that sentiment can only be conjectured. He was generally contemptuous of Jewish financiers whom he described as "narrow-minded money grubbers,"[29] but he had no such feeling regarding Beit, in whom he reposed great confidence. Beit was caught up with Rhodes's

28. J. G. Lockhart and C. M. Woodhouse, *Cecil Rhodes*, pp. 100–101.
29. In a letter to Rhodes, n.d. [1896], Rudd refers to Rhodes's views in these terms. Notes by Basil Williams, Rhodes Papers, s134, Rhodes House.

zeal for expansion to the extent that he became a zealot himself.

Rhodes, Rudd, and Beit had relatively little influence with the imperial government in 1888, but with the high commissioner their position was quite different. Since their first association at the time of the Warren expedition, Rhodes and Robinson had become close friends and allies. Their kinship may well have been based on a common view of South African problems, but there is basis for suspicion that the common view in turn was related to Robinson's self-interest and Rhodes's ability to advance it. There is no direct evidence that in 1888 Robinson expected personal economic benefits from a pro-Rhodes course, but the characters of the two men suggest that such expectations were a factor. Robinson indeed was much closer to Rhodes's thinking than to that of Downing Street. In May 1889 he made a speech in Cape Town in which he stated that he opposed active involvement of the imperial factor in South African affairs, and in the furore that ensued he offered his resignation, which was accepted.[30] Such an ally was worth much gold.

When Cawston, at the beginning of May 1888, inquired of the colonial secretary, Lord Knutsford, whether the Colonial Office would endorse an expedition of his syndicate to Matabeleland, he received the reply that he must consult the high commissioner.[31] At the time the London syndicate was unaware of Robinson's partiality for Rhodes.

As their agent, Gifford and Cawston selected Edward A. Maund, whose experience in Matabeleland as one of Warren's emissaries seemed to give him special qualifications, particularly since Maund assured them that he had established an excellent relationship with Lobengula. Maund's career had been an exotic one and its hues were made more flamboyant by his artist's touch. After his Matabeleland journey he had been involved in bizarre events in Tunis, but at the time he was approached by Gifford and Cawston he was seeking employment which would be both adventurous and lucrative. Many years later he recalled

30. Noel Garson, *The Swaziland Question and the Road to the Sea, 1887–1895*, p. 306.

31. Cawston to Knutsford, May 4, 1888, MSS Afr. S. 78, Rhodes House, also in F.O. 84/1922, P.R.O.; Wingfield to Cawston, May 14, 1888, F.O. 84/1922, P.R.O.

that he had been about to leave for Australia to report on a coal mine and a railway.[32] But to Cawston he gave quite a different and much more alarming story. He stated that he had been offered the leadership of an expedition to take wagons from German South West Africa to the German sphere of influence in East Africa, thus establishing a claim to a band across the continent which would shut out Britain from the northern interior beyond Bechuanaland.[33] The two versions do not seem to be reconcilable, but Maund's later recollection has the ring of authenticity while his tale to Cawston seems to have been calculated to enhance his value to his prospective employers.

Rhodes visited London in the late spring of 1888, during which he received information on the London syndicate's negotiations with the imperial government and their decision to send Maund. This intelligence underscored the urgency of immediately selecting a successor to the ill-fated John Fry. Fry had been employed by Rhodes and Beit at the end of 1887 to seek a monopoly from Lobengula, but he was unsuccessful. Ill with cancer which soon killed him, he had returned to Kimberley without the concession—he died there in November 1888. Fry's tragedy evoked no sentimenal response from Rhodes; his epitaph for Fry was "never have anything to do with a failure."[34] Precious time had been lost; a new mission must immediately be dispatched to prevent the great prize falling into other hands; to head that mission, Rhodes and Beit turned to Rudd.

The decision to ask Rudd was based on the assumption that a successful negotiator with Lobengula required the same kind of attributes as those with a Boer whose farm might be a gold mine. There was a price for which a bargain could be made, and Rudd was the man to settle the price. Since Rudd knew nothing of African societies, Rhodes selected Francis R. "Matabele" Thompson to accompany him. Thompson had been in charge of the reserves in Griqualand West until 1886, when Rhodes asked him

32. Maund to Hole, September 24, 1926, Maund Papers, University of Witwatersrand.

33. Extract, Cawston's speech at Stafford, *Staffordshire Chronicle*, September 29, 1900. British South Africa Company Papers, Misc. V, Rhodes House.

34. Rhodes to Rudd, September 10, 1888, in notes by Basil Williams, Rhodes Papers, S. 134 Rhodes House.

to undertake the reorganization of the native compounds at De Beers in order to restrict illicit diamond buying.[35] From his acquaintance with Africans in the reserves and the compounds, he was assumed to be an expert on African societies. He also spoke Sechuana, which Lobengula understood. His experience with Africans, however, included the horror of witnessing his father's death at the hands of a rebel band by a ramrod shoved down his throat; he was understandably prone to nervousness in the midst of hostile people like the young members of Lobengula's regiments.

The third member of the party, James Rochfort Maguire, had a vague commission to be helpful in any way that his talents made appropriate.[36] Rudd was the businessman; Thompson the linguist. Maguire was a lawyer whose background might appear to qualify him for framing the precise terms of a legal document, but such an expensive attendant was not necessary to draft the kind of agreement sought from Lobengula. Maguire indeed was a most unlikely envoy to the Ndebele. In appearance he was a spoiled child of fortune, a caricature of the "effete snob" which was one of the less attractive products of a privileged aristocracy. It was not that Maguire was lacking in ability. He had been a brilliant undergraduate at Oxford, where he had become acquainted with Rhodes. He had won a "double first," had been elected a fellow of All Souls, and was subsequently called to the Bar. He fascinated Rhodes, as he attracted others, with his charm, wit, and well-documented intelligence, and he used his assets to advance himself on the social and economic scale. Like Rhodes, his father had been a clergyman; but Maguire's road to success was not through the camps of the miners but the salons of Britain. He knew the best people; he became a close friend of Baron Ferdinand de Rothschild, on whose yacht he was a frequent guest; a few years after his adventure, he married well.[37] Maguire enjoyed the good life. Not for him the dis-

35. Nancy Rouillard, ed., *Matabele Thompson, an Autobiography*, p. 81.
36. Unlike Rudd and Thompson, Maguire was not a shareholder in the syndicate.
37. In 1895 he married Beatrice Peel, daughter of a celebrated speaker of the House of Commons. The couple spent their honeymoon in a manor lent them by Rothschild.

comforts of the veld, the manured floors of African huts, or the uncivilized habits of savages who ate raw meat and drank foul-tasting beer. His imperfectly concealed revulsion against the habits of the Ndebele, and his lack of sensitivity to their customs jeopardized the success of the mission and the lives of its members.[38]

The London syndicate began with a head start over the Rudd party. Maund arrived in Cape Town at the end of June 1888 and had an interview with Robinson which he described as "very satisfactory,"[39] but which in fact revealed little of Robinson's position. The high commissioner told Maund that he was favorable to the development of Matabeleland by a company with impressive credentials like those of Maund's backers. But there were other contenders, principally Rhodes, and Robinson stated he was not willing to bless any project without a sign from Westminster clearer than he had thus far received.[40] The interview, however, underscored the urgency of reaching Lobengula before Rhodes's agents. Maund hurried off for the north, and arrived in Kimberley at the beginning of July, before Rudd and his party were ready to start.[41]

Sir Charles Metcalfe and other representatives of the London group's railway project arrived in July, and also had a conference with Robinson. The high commissioner was friendly, but beneath the pretense of impartiality, Metcalfe discerned a commitment to Rhodes. This was a shrewd and a correct perception. Between Maund's and Metcalfe's interviews, Rhodes had returned from London and had elicited Robinson's warm support for a Rhodes-dominated chartered company in central Africa with powers similar to those of the British North Borneo, Royal Niger, and Imperial British East Africa companies. Rhodes's company would acquire control over those parts of Matabeleland and Mashonaland "not in use"[42] by the African residents

38. For an account of Maguire's loathing of Ndebele practices, see E. T. Cook, *Edmund Garrett*, pp. 254–255.

39. Telegram, Maund to Exploring Company, June 29, 1888, BSAC Misc. I, Rhodes House.

40. Maund to Cawston, July 2, 1888, in *ibid.*

41. Maund to Cawston, July 8, 1888, in *ibid.*

42. The expression was Robinson's, but it may well have been used by Rhodes.

and provide protection for the Africans on lands reserved to them. The welfare of the Ndebele and the Shona would be safeguarded, and the interior of Africa would be developed at no expense to the British taxpayer. This proposal, said Robinson, merited acceptance by the imperial government. The extension of British influence into the interior by a chartered company based in South Africa would have a much more favorable reception from the Afrikaner community than the creation of another Crown colony.[43]

The sudden appearance of a chartered company as the instrument of Rhodes's ambitions is intriguing, for such an idea was not foreshadowed by any previous statements of his which have survived. There is, however, a striking similarity in the scheme to a plan that Cawston had laid out earlier in the year and which he was developing into a formal proposal at the time Rhodes met with Robinson. Maund may have described Cawston's plans during his discussion with Robinson, or Rhodes may have appropriated the idea some time during his visit to London. Whatever the antecedents, Rhodes anticipated his London rivals, who produced their draft charter for the "Imperial British Central South Africa Company" in September 1888.[44]

Rhodes had won an important advantage in Cape Town, and the focus of action now shifted to the interior—Maund left Kimberley early in July, several weeks ahead of his rivals, with the intention of reaching Lobengula no later than September 26.[45] But his penchant for dramatic involvement caused him to put aside his employers' urgent instructions to proceed to Matabeleland with the utmost possible speed. On the way to Mafeking he heard from Shippard that Kgama faced the threat of a Boer invasion as the result of the death of Grobler at the hands of some Ngwato. Maund, the ex-trooper, gallantly offered his

43. Robinson to Knutsford, July 21, 1888, quoted in "Minutes of Proceedings of the [Cave] Commission in continuation of Cmd. 1129," May 1921.

44. Draft Charter, September 1888, Maund Papers, Witwatersrand. The charter, like the title of the company, seems to be modeled on that of the Imperial British East Africa Company. Maund noted on the margin, "this proves the BSAC was not Rhodes' scheme but was formed under auspices of Exploring Co."

45. Maund to Cawston, July 8, 1888, BSAC Misc. I, Rhodes House.

services for the defense of this British-protected chief. He explained to Cawston that his defense of Kgama would give him the opportunity to get a concession for all of the disputed territory between the Shashi and Maklautsi rivers, and that he would then seek the same concession from Lobengula in order to eliminate the problem of rival claims.[46] Maund's essay into personal diplomacy evoked a peremptory order from Cawston to end his stay in Bechuanaland immediately and to proceed to Bulawayo with no further delay.[47] But a precious month had been lost, during which time Rhodes's agents arrived in Lobengula's kraal.

Maund, undaunted by the displeasure of his principals, proceeded to Bulawayo. His version of his journey was highly complimentary to himself. Other parties on the way to seek a concession were being turned back, but Maund said he had secured permission to enter by representing himself as an emissary of great people in England—Lobengula was allowed to assume that Maund represented the imperial government, and Maund's previous visit as the emissary of Warren lent color to the illusion.[48] Shippard's version of Maund's movements was less complimentary. From Baines's Drift on the borders of Lobengula's country, he reported that Maund had arrived from Shoshong in a famished state, representing himself to be a correspondent for the *Times*. Shippard knew him to be a concession hunter but allowed him to proceed on the assurance that he had permission from Lobengula to enter Matabeleland. In fact, Shippard said, he had had to order his self-invited guest to leave after Maund had imposed himself ten days.[49] The two versions are not mutually exclusive. In each case Maund was a liar, but by his ac-

46. Extract, Maund to Cawston, July 29, 1888, in *ibid*. Grobler had been attempting to return from Matabeleland through territory claimed by the Ngwato without their permission, and was killed in an altercation.
47. Telegrams, Cawston to Maund, September 19, 1888, September 28, 1888, in Cawston Papers, Rhodes House. The telegraph reached only to Mafeking and the messages had to be delivered by messenger on horseback.
48. Maund to Cawston, October 25, 1888, BSAC Misc. I, Rhodes House.
49. Shippard to Robinson, September 1, 1888, C.O. 879/30/369, P.R.O.

count a successful one. Duplicity was in fact the general practice. The Africans had christened Shippard "Amaranamaka"—the Father of Lies.[50]

By his own admission, however, Maund's adventure in personal diplomacy had cost him and his employers precious time. While he was in the Ngwato territory, he was passed by Rudd's party, which had arrived in Bulawayo on Sepember 21, 1888, almost three weeks ahead of him.[51] Also at the royal kraal at the time of Maund's arrival were a miscellaneous collection of traders and would-be concessionaires, several of whom were available to be co-opted by any capitalists who seemed to have greater chances of success than did they. Among them were representatives of syndicates from Kimberley, Port Elizabeth, and Johannesburg; Messrs. Renny-Tailyour, Boyle, and O'Reilly recently arrived from Swaziland representing Edouard Lippert, Beit's cousin; and Ivon Fry, now superseded by Rudd, but still hoping to get a concession. The suitors had presented the king with gifts ranging from Rudd's £100 to a horse and saddlery and champagne, but had received no sign of royal favor. Maund felt confident that in the guise of an imperial representative he would be able to capitalize on Lobengula's fears of the colonial whites, and interpreted the king's present of a sheep as an augury of success since none of the others had such a mark of favor.[52] Within three weeks Lobengula granted the concession to Rudd.

Maund had made one serious miscalculation. He had relied on his ability to delude Lobengula as to his sponsorship, and he had enlisted supporters from the local trading community who were known to be influential with the king. Among his adherents he counted his companion of the 1885 visit to Lobengula, Sam Edwards, "Far Interior Sam"; George A. "Elephant" Phillips;[53] and C. D. Tainton, another prominent trader, who served as interpreter. His performance as imperial representative prob-

50. William Plomer, *Cecil Rhodes* (Edinburgh, 1933), p. 58.
51. Maund arrived on October 10. See V. W. Hiller, "The Commission Journey of Charles Dunell Rudd, 1888," in Constance E. Fripp and V. W. Hiller, eds., *Gold and the Gospel in Mashonaland*, p. 181.
52. Maund to Gifford, October 10, 1888, BSAC Misc. I, Rhodes House.
53. Known to the Ndebele as "Elephant" because of his enormous size and great strength.

ably impressed Lobengula to some degree, but with all of the opposition eager to give the king the "facts," it is unlikely that the king was entirely taken in by Maund. Maund's failure came not from a misjudgment of his own strength, but from an underestimation of his opposition. Rudd had a trump card which won the game—the support of local imperial officials. With their backing he was able to neutralize Maund's claims to governmental favor. Robinson was committed to Rhodes, as were his subordinates, Shippard and Shippard's assistant, Francis J. Newton. So close indeed was their cooperation that bribery might be suspected. They undoubtedly were not "bribed" in the sense that they received money as an inducement. Such a direct bargain would have been both risky and unnecessary. They needed little encouragement because they shared Rhodes's enthusiasm for northward expansion and his aversion to Downing Street.[54] Also they supported Rhodes at least in part because he had power which could affect their futures, and all subsequently benefited. Robinson became a director of De Beers and a substantial shareholder in the Central Search Company and its successor, the United Concessions Company, which held the Rudd concession,[55] and Rhodes's support contributed to his return to South Africa in 1895 as high commissioner. Shippard looked to Rhodes for help in advancing his career in government.[56] In 1894 on his retirement from government service he was appointed legal adviser to Consolidated Gold Fields of South Africa, and in 1896 he was appointed a director of the British South Africa Company. Their advocacy of Rudd's suit was understandably enthusiastic; indeed they were accessories. Shippard advised Rudd on tactics,[57] and Newton pressed Moffat to do what he could to help Rhodes's interests: "I confess I

54. This is a view of Richard Brown, "Aspects of the Scramble for Matabeleland," in Eric Stokes and Richard Brown, eds., The Zambesian Past, pp. 78–79.
55. In October 1889 he held 250 shares in Central Search. In 1890 he was registered as holding 2500 in United Concessions and by January 1892 he owned 6250 shares. Daily Chronicle, November 1, 1895.
56. In 1891 he sought Rhodes's help with regard to a judgeship in Cape Colony. Rhodes to Shippard, January 11, 1891, RH 1/1/1, N.A.R. He decided eventually to stay in the imperial service where he remained until November 1895.
57. Shippard to Newton, September 1, 1888, NE 1/1/9, N.A.R.

should like to see a thorough Imperialist and good man of business at the same time, as he undoubtedly is, get a footing in that country."[58]

Shippard's mission to Lobengula just before the Rudd concession was granted was designed to advance the cause of his good friend Rhodes. In the commissioner's eyes the fate of the Ndebele was already settled. The "old savage" Lobengula could not prevent his country from being overrun by miners: "The accounts one hears of the wealth of Mashonaland if known and believed in England would bring such a rush to the country that its destiny would soon be settled whether the Matabele liked it or not."[59]

Beyond his general contempt for Africans, Shippard developed a special aversion for the Ndebele. His experiences at the king's kraal confirmed his judgment that the Ndebele were vermin whose extermination would benefit mankind. On the way back from his meeting with Lobengula, he unburdened himself to Newton. What was most needed for central Africa, he said, was not the railway but a "liberal supply of Gatling guns, magazine and Martini Henry rifles *with bayonets* and a good field battery with the proper men to handle the same effectively." He added:

> I do not think that I am naturally of a cruel or bloodthirsty disposition, but I must confess that it would offer me sincere and lasting satisfaction if I could see the Matebele Matjaha cut down by our rifles and machine guns like a cornfield by a reaping machine and I would not spare a single one if I could have my way. The cup of their iniquities must surely be full or nearly full now. Never till I saw these wretches did I understand the true mercy and love for humanity contained in the injunction to the Israelites to destroy the Canaanites. I understand it perfectly now.[60]

Shippard prided himself in his realism; he was contemptuous of the pious sentimentality of the negrophiles. Whatever pretenses might be necessary in negotiations with Lobengula, the question was not whether the country would remain under Ndebele control, but the character of the European influx which

58. Newton to Moffat, August 26, 1888, MO 1/1/4, in *ibid.*
59. Shippard to Newton, October 1, 1888, NE 1/1/9, in *ibid.*
60. Shippard to Newton, October 29, 1888, in *ibid.*

would dispossess the African inhabitants. There would either be a rush like that into other areas where gold had been found, with all of the attendant disorders, or the transition from African to European rule would be effected peacefully through a monopoly dominated, hopefully, by Rhodes. Lobengula, Shippard assumed, wanted imperial help to keep out Boers and miners; Shippard sought to capitalize on the Ndebele chief's fears by assuring him that the best way to do so was to grant a monopoly to Rhodes.

Shippard's "official visit" to Lobengula was, therefore, not that of a disinterested imperial official, and its timing could not have been more attuned to the Rudd mission's needs if there had been collusion, as there almost certainly was. Though Shippard for obvious reasons made no mention in his reports of any representations to Lobengula on behalf of Rhodes, the reports of the Rudd party indicated how valuable they regarded his intervention to be. Maguire wrote to Newton that "Sir Sydney's visit did a great deal of good removing much misunderstanding which was steadily growing worse," and that "Shippard and Moffat did all they could for us."[61] Rudd noted in his diary before Shippard's arrival that "the King talked to Moffat about so many white people coming into the country and as to how it could be avoided, and Moffat took the chance of putting in a good word for us."[62]

Moffat has been identified with the other local imperial officials as a protagonist of the Rudd party,[63] and there can be no question that he was helpful to them. But his motivations may have been somewhat different from those of his colleagues. Like them, he supported the grant of a concession to a "powerful company."[64] But that designation applied to Maund's backers as well as to Rhodes and Rudd. Moffat was irritated by Maund's efforts to suggest he had some official status derived from the imperial government, but did not object to Maund's telling Lobengula that he represented "Great Men" in England.[65]

61. Maguire to Newton, October 27, 1888, NE 1/1/10, in *ibid.*
62. Diary, September 29, 1888, in Hiller, *Commission Journey*, p. 187.
63. Brown, "Aspects of the Scramble," p. 186.
64. Moffat to Shippard, September 28, 1888, MO 1/1/5, N.A.R.
65. Maund to Gifford, October 10, 1888, BSAC Misc. I, Rhodes House.

Moffat may have used his position to favor Rhodes over the London rivals, but his indictment for complicity is unproved.

A similar accusation has been leveled aaginst Charles D. Helm, the missionary who interpreted the Rudd party's proposals to Lobengula. One biography of Rhodes goes so far as to suggest that Helm had "become one of Rhodes's men" who misled the chief as to the provisions of the proposed concession.[66] Another writer cites the biography as documentation that Helm was "a mere mercenary, a paid hack of Rhodes."[67]

The corrupt missionary is an appropriate performer with the bought government official as supporting actors in the amorality play of the Rudd concession. But there is no evidence that Rhodes "bought" Helm, only that he tried. There can be no doubt that Helm hoped the Rudd party would be successful, but his support came from other considerations than bribery. Like his associates in Matabeleland, Helm had been a missionary without converts, a pastor without a flock. Nor had he been able to modify the Ndebele way of life toward Victorian standards of behavior. The traders and concession hunters who infested Bulawayo he considered little better than the Ndebele, and he was convinced there would be chaos if the impending rush of concessionaires were not stopped. The Oxonians behind the Rudd concession were gentlemen of high principle as well as great wealth. A monopoly to a company controlled by them might result in a new era in which the Ndebele were gradually converted to civilized ways and where the missionaries might have opportunities both for conversion and for assistance to the new regime.[68] These views were like those of his fellow mission-

66. Lockhart and Woodhouse, *Rhodes*, p. 137.
67. Stanlake Samkange, *Origins of Rhodesia*, p. 67.
68. Helm's reactions to the prospect of the Rudd concessions are contained in a letter, Helm to Thompson (L.M.S.), October 11, 1888, LO 6/1/5, N.A.R. After the concession, "Matabele" Thompson offered Helm £200 a year to act on behalf of the concessionaires but Helm referred the proposal to the headquarters of the L.M.S. with the notation that he assumed the society would not approve. He was correct. Helm to Thompson (L.M.S.), December 22, 1888, and encl. "Matabele" Thompson to Helm, November 9, 1888, in Hiller, *Commission Journey*. The only Ndebele missionary recorded as acquiring shares in the British South Africa Company was W. A. Elliott who in 1893 had 100 shares. London to South Africa, BSAC, April 7, 1893, LO 3/1/13, N.A.R.

aries. W. A. Elliott wrote his superiors in London that "it is clear that Thompson and his party are gentlemen and equally clear the others are not.[69] David Carnegie was delighted to hear of the Rudd concession and disconsolate when he heard later that Lobengula had repudiated it. The way was now open, he feared, for the invasion of hundreds of filibusterers who would overrun the country.[70] Helm stated that he had received no personal inducement, and there seems no reason to disbelieve him, for his motivations to be of assistance were already compelling.

Allegations of bribery and corruption derive in large part from the assumption that Lobengula could not have agreed to concede a mining monopoly over his entire domain for the price offered. By the terms of the concession, Rudd and his associates agreed to pay £100 monthly and one thousand Martini Henry breech-loading rifles and one hundred thousand cartridges. He would also have the option of acquiring an armed steamboat, to be used on the Zambezi,[71] or an additional £500 in cash. For this Lobengula granted the concessionaires complete and exclusive charge over all metals and minerals "within his dominions, with the exception of the Tati concession, and full power to do all things that they may deem necessary to win and procure the same and to hold, collect and enjoy the profits and revenue if any." Furthermore, he authorized them to exclude other prospectors and concession hunters.[72]

In view of the experience of his relative by marriage, Mbanzeni of Swaziland, who had given away much of his country by concessions, Lobengula might have been expected to be particularly wary of any written documents he was asked to sign. But there were important reasons of state which predisposed him to

69. Elliott to Thompson (L.M.S.), March 27, 1889, LO 6/1/5, N.A.R.
70. Carnegie to Thompson, January 15, 1889, LO 6/1/5, N.A.R.
71. The suggestion of the steamboat came from Rhodes, who saw a parallel with Stanley's steamboat on the Upper Congo. The utility of such a vessel to the Ndebele was obviously not relevant to the proposal, though undoubtedly if they could have been able to operate and maintain it, they could have dominated the Zambezi and wiped out the "canoe power" of their rivals. Rhodes to Rudd, September 10, 1888, RU 2/1/1, N.A.R.
72. The text of the concession is in Hiller, *Commission Journey*, pp. 219–220.

make an agreement with one strong company. The arrival of more and more white men had inflamed his society. His young warriors needed only the word to kill all the whites; under his restraint they restricted themselves to threats and insults. The crisis was certain to become more and more grave. Not only did he have to contend with miners but there was the perennial threat of a Boer migration. The British government, as Shippard probably had made clear, was not prepared to defend his territory; a strong company in exchange for gold might do so.

Such considerations undoubtedly influenced the Ndebele leader but they do not explain his sanction of a mining monopoly for Rudd and his associates. When reports of the agreement became public, Lobengula insisted that the document was a fraud and repudiated it. But if Rudd's account of the final negotiations is to be believed, the proposals were not only understood but discussed in great detail by the indunas as well as by Lobengula. Lobengula, Rudd asserted, finally gave his consent after a brief conference with Thompson and Lotjie, a trusted induna who had favored the concession, at which no one else was present.[73]

The most likely explanation for Lobengula's insistence that he had been duped is not that the provisions of the concession document were mistranslated, but that oral assurances were given him which misrepresented its meaning. Helm later stated to his directors that the grantees had assured Lobengula that all that they wished was the right to dig for gold and to bring in the necessary machinery, that they would not bring in more than ten white men, and that they would abide by the laws of his country and "be his people." These promises were not put in the concession.[74] In November 1888 Lobengula did not yet know that the verbal promise of a maximum of ten white men would not be kept, but he had received disturbing reports that he had been tricked into "selling his country." One of the concession

73. *Ibid.*, p. 202. Lotjie was killed by order of Lobengula in September, 1889, allegedly for his support of the concession. Maund thought he had been killed because of his wealth.

74. Helm to L.M.S., March 29, 1889, in Hiller, *Commission Journey*, p. 227. Lobengula later referred to this promise when he protested to Rhodes against the entry of the pioneer column.

hunters, Edward R. Renny-Tailyour, who had allied himself with Maund, admitted that on instructions from Maund he had told Lobengula that the chief had given away his country,[75] but Renny-Tailyour was not alone in the attempt to upset the concession, and reports in South African papers which were communicated to Lobengula also indicated that he had in fact conferred rights far more extensive than he had been led to believe.

The subsequent execution of Lotjie followed by the flight of Thompson suggests an additional dimension in the duplicity of the Rudd concession. Lotjie and Thompson were the only people in attendance at the conference with Lobengula at which the fateful decision was made. Lobengula considered Thompson to be the principal to whom he had assigned the concession,[76] and the verbal stipulations made at that time were undoubtedly accepted as commitments. When Lobengula became aware of the full extent of the written document, his anger was naturally directed at Lotjie and Thompson. After Lotjie's execution, Thompson's panic was understandable; he expected that he would be next. Lotjie stood condemned for having deluded his king; what cannot be known is whether he himself was deluded. Thompson likewise seems to have been unaware of the intentions of Rhodes to use the Rudd concession as a vehicle for white settlement in Mashonaland and was apparently sincere in his assurances to Lobengula that only mining rights were desired by his syndicate.[77]

Whatever the translation may have been, Lobengula did not have the power, even if he had had the inclination, to alienate land. Also, leaving aside the issue of whether the Ndebele actually controlled the areas of Mashonaland where the gold deposits reputedly were, Lobengula could have granted the con-

75. Memo of conversation with Maund, January 24, 1889, by Graham Bower, imperial secretary, C. O. 879/30/369, P.R.O.
76. Rhodes after Thompson's flight urged him to return since "the King recognizes you as the concession and it will not be ratified unless you are present." Fragment, Rhodes to Thompson, September or October, 1889, RH 1/1/1, N.A.R. W. A. Elliott referred to "Thompson's concession." Elliott to Thompson, March 27, 1889, LO 6/1/5, N.A.R.
77. Rouillard, ed., *Thompson*, pp. 175–178.

cessionaires only the usufruct. The early history of the Rudd
concession, however, has little to do with legality. With the
Ndebele as with other African peoples, the language of the
European barrister provided a gloss of legitimacy to arbitrary
dispossession.

By the Rudd concession three white men acquired huge territories and reputed great riches for a few hundred pounds. None
of them had previously been to Bulawayo, much less to the
Zambezi; none had any knowledge of the interrelationships of
the peoples inhabiting the area over which they sought mastery.
Only one of them knew anything of African customs, and he
had had little experience with the Ndebele. These men in pursuit of their own ends credited Lobengula with an absolute
power over his own people which he did not possess and control
over other peoples which he did not exercise. "Matabeleland"
was aggrandized on the maps to include the Shona and the other
peoples, and this imagined empire was colored pink. The hue
was important—pink rather than red—because the object was
rule by a British company not by the imperial government. The
hope of the promoters, indeed, was that there would be no interference from Whitehall, which would confer full power and
exercise no controls.

The "rights" of the Ndebele over the territory of the Shona
were unquestioned on Downing Street because they were convenient. One member of the Colonial Office staff, Edward Fairfield, ventured to suggest that Lobengula's raids on the Shona
were more in the tradition of murderers, kidnappers, and thieves
than of "government." "At best," he noted, "I fear that our do-
ings as to Mashonaland are a transaction into which we have
been hustled by interested parties."[78] But Fairfield's declaration
of conscience was dismissed as exaggerated and irrelevant. As
his superior, Sir Robert Herbert declared, "Whatever may be
the actual truth about Lo Bengula—and I certainly doubt his
being anything like as bad as Mr. Fairfield makes out—it will

78. Note by Fairfield, December 29, 1888, on F.O. to C.O., December
28, 1888, C.O. 417/25, P.R.O. Fairfield's opinion remained unchanged.
In January 1890 he was still expressing doubt that an impartial tribunal would judge that Lobengula had the right to make any concessions in Mashonaland. Note by Fairfield, January 13, 1890, on
Bowler to Knutsford, December 20, 1889, C.O. 417/38, P.R.O.

never do for us to admit any doubt of his right over Mashona-land, or to open the door one inch to Portuguese claims."[79]

The Rudd concession immediately produced great disquiet among Lobengula's advisers and his position was seriously weakened. Moffat expressed concern as to whether the king could continue to hold his people in restraint,[80] and rumors circulated among the white community of an impending "private" filibustering attack from the Transvaal with the avowed object of supporting Gambo, one of the most powerful indunas, in a coup to depose and kill Lobengula.[81] Confronted with a threat to his leadership, Lobengula twisted and turned. On the one hand he continued to assure Maguire and Thompson, who had remained to protect their interests, that he had not repudiated the concession itself, merely the suggestion that he had given away his country. Maguire maintained that Lobengula in mid-January 1889 told him not to worry, that when the guns arrived all would be well and the concession would be honored. But at the end of November 1888 Lobengula had asked Maund to accompany two of his indunas to England with the official mission of presenting a letter to the queen protesting the encroachments of the Portuguese but also to seek advice on the crisis confronting him from the increasing pressure of Europeans on his country. The first object of the mission was public —his letter was witnessed by Helm, among other Europeans— the second was secret, though no one was deluded that he would at his own expense send a mission to England merely to deliver a letter regarding the Portuguese.[82]

Maund was jubilant. The chief's protest against the Portuguese involved encroachments in the Mazoe valley where Maund sought a concession for the Exploring Company, and his verbal message disavowing the Rudd concession would likely eliminate the threat of Rhodes's monopoly. Maund had not seen the Rudd

79. Note by Herbert, n.d., on F.O. to C.O., December 28, 1888, C.O. 417/25, P.R.O.
80. Moffat to Shippard, November 13, 1888, C. O. 837/30/369, P.R.O.
81. Shippard to Newton, November 17, 1888, NE 1/1/9, N.A.R.
82. Helm after hearing of the chief's intentions wrote Moffat that he hoped Lobengula would also inform Robinson. Helm to Moffat, November 22, 1888, MO 1/1/4, N.A.R. Rhodes and his associates were never under any doubt that the mission was directed against them.

concession. Rudd in his haste to depart had not left a copy—but Maund was assured by Lobengula and his indunas that the chief had conceded nothing. Maund concluded that even if there were a concession, the pressure of the Ndebele would compel Lobengula to repudiate it.[83] Maund maintained that he knew nothing of the concession to Rudd until after he left Matabeleland, which led Maguire to observe that it was difficult to understand how Maund could have advised Lobengula to disavow an arrangement of which he was unaware.[84] Also difficult to believe was Maund's later insistence that the initiative for the mission came from Lobengula and that Maund had reluctantly agreed to serve for fear of offending the chief. Maund also averred that the oral message which the chief entrusted to the indunas was entirely Lobengula's own.[85] This assertion was undoubtedly correct. Lobengula had great reasons of state for his initiative, and he must have been led to hope by Maund, still posing as the representative of "the great men in London," that the imperial government across the seas could be a source of succor against its South African representative. For his services to Lobengula, Maund extracted the promise that there be no more concessions or negotiations until the return of the indunas from England. The response to Maund's request for a concession in the Mazoe valley was less explicit. Lobengula replied, "Take my men to England for me; and when you return, then I will talk about that."[86] Lobengula's caution was understandable.

Whatever its antecedents, the mission to London provided a magnificent opportunity for the Exploring Company—as both its directors and Cecil Rhodes were keenly aware. The issue was not merely the Rudd concession. The document was vulnerable to challenge, and its worth might be eliminated if Lobengula were expressly to repudiate it. If the indunas were to convey

83. Maund to Gifford, December 5, 1888, BSAC Misc. I, Rhodes House.
84. Maguire to Moffat, January 4, 1889, MO 1/1/4, N.A.R.
85. Maund to Hole, October 7, 1926, Maund Papers, Witwatersrand.
86. Memo by Maund of meeting held at king's kraal, November 24, 1888, witnessed by Helm, Tainton, and J. W. Colenbrander, Maund Papers, Witwatersrand.

the message that Lobengula had been defrauded they would have support from British humanitarians as well as from the financiers who backed the Exploring Company. Rhodes's plan to use the concession as the basis for a charter might well be frustrated.

The news of the mission came as a shock to Rhodes. He had congratulated himself on the removal of what he thought to be the last obstacle to the concession—the prohibition on shipment of rifles. The compliant Robinson had accepted Shippard's argument that arming the Ndebele with firearms was in fact humanitarian because they would not know how to fire them and would become less formidable than if they used assegais. Bishop George W. H. Knight-Bruce, who sought to establish a mission in Mashonaland and who had denounced the "deviltry and brutality"[87] of providing the Ndebele with rifles to massacre the Shona, had been converted by Rhodes with unspecified arguments into a "cordial supporter." Rhodes had assured Rudd that "Matabeleland is all right for the future,"[88] but now he was confronted with a threat far greater than that from a mere bishop. His first response was to attempt to discredit the indunas as people of no standing, and to prevent their departure from South Africa.

Maund suspected that Rhodes would make such an effort. Before any orders for his detention could be received he traveled to Kgama's capital, where he arrived on December 22 and left the same afternoon. He told Moffat, who was now back in residency with Kgama, that Lobengula had "all but forced on him" the mission. Moffat was contemptuous of Maund, who was "phenomenally untruthful." He lamented to Shippard that he had no authority to put down "this kind of thing,"[89] but before any such authority could arrive, Maund had departed, proceeding through the Transvaal to avoid any complications from Shippard or his agents, reappearing in British territory at Kimberley in the freedom of Cape Colony where Shippard's writ did

87. Speech by Bishop Knight-Bruce, December 15, 1888, BR 8/1/1, N.A.R.
88. Rhodes to Rudd, December 6, 1888, RU 2/1/1, *ibid.*
89. Moffat to Shippard, December 24, 1888, C.O. 879/30/369, P.R.O.

not run. Rhodes, hearing of his arrival, sent Dr. Jameson to invite Maund to his cottage and Maund, though "scenting trouble," accepted.[90]

The interview was in the Rhodes style. Rhodes was first casually friendly and then turned to business—if Maund would "chuck" his London backers and join him, he would "make" him. When Maund refused to betray his employers, Rhodes stormed that he would see to it that the high commissioner stopped him and the indunas. Robinson did his best. He had previously tried unsuccessfully to discourage Maund from proceeding by warning him that the imperial government would not receive the deputation without the recommendation of the local authorities,[91] and when they arrived in Cape Town, he reiterated that they should not proceed on a hopeless mission. Robinson sought to ensure the futility of the mission by discrediting it in communications to the Colonial Office—Maund, he quoted Shippard as saying, was "a mendacious adventurer," "a dangerous man," the interpreter Colenbrander was "hopelessly unreliable," and the "natives" were not indunas or even head men.[92] Robinson's opposition might well have prevented the departure of the deputation. Cawston, after a fruitless plea to the Foreign Office, wired Maund that it was useless to proceed until the high commissioner's opposition had been removed.[93]

At this critical moment, Rhodes arrived in Cape Town. His mood was far different from that he had displayed in Kimberley. There was no bluster or attempted bribery. Instead, he asked to see the letter which Lobengula had addressed to the queen, and professed to see in the appeal and the mission an opportunity to strengthen the Rudd concession and his plans for northern expansion if the London group and he were to join hands in an amalgamated company, and he authorized

90. Maund apparently came to Kimberley not with the intention of meeting Rhodes but because it was on the railway to Cape Town.
91. Robinson to Administrator, Vryburg, January 15, 1889, C.O. 879/30/369, P.R.O.
92. Robinson to Knutsford, January 23, 1889, confidential, enclosing extract, Shippard to Robinson, January 17, 1889, C.O. 537/124B, P.R.O.
93. Telegram, Cawston to Maund, January 28, 1889, BSAC Misc. I, Rhodes House.

Maund to cable the Exploring Company to this effect.[94] Maund assumed that the threat posed by the mission, and his own persuasiveness had been responsible for Rhodes's change of front. But the initiative for amalgamation came from the Colonial Office. In December 1888 Knutsford advised Cawston and Gifford that their prospects of receiving a charter would be greatly enhanced if they worked together with Rhodes. Accordingly they cabled Rhodes, who was in fact responding to the London overture when he agreed to unite with the Exploring Company.[95]

With Rhodes's opposition removed, Robinson modified his position. He could not without loss of credibility shift to outright endorsement but he informed the Colonial Office that on further examination of the Ndebele whom Lobengula described as head men, he had concluded that they should be allowed to proceed. Their sole object was to see the queen to prove that she existed, and "in good hands the visit may be advantageous to British interests."[96]

Rhodes's decision to seek an amalgamation came as a great relief to Gifford and Cawston, for they and Rhodes were in stalemate. They believed that they had sufficient weight to frustrate his hopes for a charter. They had enlisted the support of prominent men in British commerce and politics who were concerned about the extension of the Cape Colony's interest into Bechuanaland and the north. The South African trade section of the London Chamber of Commerce had notified the government of its opposition to Bechuanaland Colony being transferred to the Cape and had sought support for the Bechuanaland Exploration Company's railway scheme.[97] Another influential committee, the South African Committee, was being formed to promote the same objects, including in its membership Earl Grey and his nephew Albert, Joseph Chamberlain, Sir Thomas Fowell Buxton, and other men of prominence.[98]

These were powerful allies, but the London group could not

94. Samkange, *Origins of Rhodesia*, p. 104.
95. Cawston to C. O., July 1, 1889, C.O. 879/30/372, P.R.O.
96. Telegram, Robinson to Knutsford, February 4, 1889, C.O. 879/30/369, P.R.O.
97. *South Africa*, January 11, 1889.
98. The committee is listed in C.5918, 1890.

hope to succeed without the cooperation of the Cape government and the high commissioner. In the last months of 1888 the
project for a railway through Bechuanaland had been stalled
by an impasse between Downing Street and Cape Town. The
Colonial Office would not negotiate an agreement for Bechuanaland without assurances from the government of Sir Gordon
Sprigg that it would build a railway to the Bechuanaland border, but the Sprigg government would take no action without
knowing the terms of the company's agreement with the imperial government, and the obduracy of the Cape was strengthened by opposition in Britain to the transfer of the Crown
Colony of Bechuanaland to the Cape.[99] Rhodes was a powerful
member of the Cape Assembly, made more formidable by his
alliance with the Afrikaner Bond, whose opposition to railway
extension into Bechuanaland had been a factor in the delay.
Rhodes could be the means to removing the block in Cape
Town. Most important, Rhodes would bring into the amalgamation the substantial resources he derived from De Beers and
Gold Fields, and the Rudd concession which would become
far more valuable if the London group's opposition to it were
to be withdrawn. Amalgamation with Rhodes had become essential to the Exploring Company, as cooperation with the Exploring Company had become essential to Rhodes.[100]

The union of interests took place as the Colonial Office was
considering an inquiry by Gifford as to whether the government
would be willing to grant a charter to a merger of the Bechuanaland Exploration and Exploring Companies. The subordinate
staff was cautious to hostile. Edward Fairfield was opposed in
principle to chartered companies,[101] and predictably condemned
the proposal:

99. Gifford to Herbert, December 3, 1888, and enclosures and minutes,
C.O. 417/26, P.R.O.
100. Metcalfe, who was a close friend of Rhodes though employed by
his rivals, later wrote, "There is no doubt that without the aid of the
Exploring Company, the Charter would not have been granted or
even thought of. The amalgamation made it possible." "My Story of
the Scheme," in Leo Weinthal, *The Story of the Cape to Cairo Railway
and River Route, 1887–1922*, 4 vols. (London [1923–1927]), 1:99.
101. It is ironic that several years later Fairfield should be saddled
with the indictment of having been an accessory to the Jameson Raid.

This is a mere piece of financing. Something is to be got which will look well enough to invite fools to subscribe to. Such a Chartered Company could never really pay. It would simply sow the seeds of a heap of political trouble and then the promoters would shuffle out of it, and leave us to take up the work of preserving the peace, and settling the difficulties. The existing system of chartering has not been such a success as to make us augur well for its extension to a poor inland country, the seat of political troubles. . . .[102]

Fairfield's colleague John Bramston agreed that there was danger in chartering a company in an area dominated by grave political questions. Their superiors acknowledged that there was a risk, as there were in any extensions of the British presence in Africa. But the issue was not whether Britain should refuse to be involved; the government had already involved itself by the Moffat Treaty. The questions for decision were whether the recognition of a chartered company would lighten or remove the burden on the exchequer for the support of the British presence in Bechuanaland and the interior and whether such a company could be regulated in such a way that it would not contribute to international complications or native disturbances. Lord Knutsford and his permanent undersecretary, Sir Robert Herbert, already impressed with the financial backing of Gifford and Cawston, were convinced that with the reported accession of Rhodes there was no problem of resources—there was now "a plethora" of funds available to the promoters.[103] The Colonial Office, therefore, replied that it would defer a decision until it had considered the effects of a charter on the financial and political condition of Bechuanaland, and had received a recommendation from the high commissioner.[104] The campaign for a charter was on the verge of success. Gifford wrote to Cawston in mid-March, "I am convinced that we are going to win, it is a grand game. I was dreaming of it last night, but my

102. Note by Fairfield, January 4, 1889, on Gifford to Knutsford, January 3, 1889, C. O. 417/38, P.R.O.
103. Notes by Herbert and Knutsford, on *ibid.* At the time Knutsford referred to Rhodes's joining forces with Cawston and Gifford, they were still in opposition. The origin of the premature report that they had combined is obscure and interesting.
104. C. O. to Gifford, January 10, 1889, F.O. 84/1995, P.R.O.

damned gun would not go off as the natives rushed to turn us out." [105]

Gifford's optimism may have been heightened by the arrival of Maund with the indunas. If Frederick Selous is to be believed, Maund also brought a document which purported to be a concession made out to Gifford in 1888 for all of Mashonaland including most of the Mazoe valley. Gifford showed this alleged concession to Selous who pronounced it as valid as any other concession given by Lobengula, being duly signed and witnessed. [106] But Maund later admitted he had nothing but a promise from Lobengula for consideration on the return of the mission. The mysterious document may have been Gifford's 1880 draft of a concession, but that referred only to the Mazoe valley, and was never executed. If Maund's concession ever existed, however, it disappeared. The attention of the would-be concessionaires focused on the mission of the indunas. With Robinson's opposition removed, the attitude of the Colonial Office had shifted from frigidity to welcome. A reception at Windsor was arranged, and when the indunas refused to go without Maund, Knutsford hastened to assure them that an exception would be made to the rule that British subjects could not attend such an audience since it would be "a matter of great regret to him both on account of the indunas themselves and of the relations between Lobengula and the British government if their proposed visit to the Queen were in any way to fall through." [107] The envoys delivered the letter protesting Portuguese encroachments, which was useful to the new combination, and Lobengula's oral message, which was not. The response of

105. Gifford to Cawston, March 13, 1889, BSAC Misc. I, Rhodes House.
106. Heany to Moffat, confidential, June 6, 1889, MO 1/1/4, N.A.R. Heany stated he was convinced Maund was guilty of fraud in inducing Lobengula to agree to a document under false pretenses and that neither Gifford nor Cawston had been parties to the deception.
107. Baillie Hamilton to Maund, March 1, 1889, Maund Papers, Witwatersrand. Maund gave the credit for the change of front to the influence of Lord Lothian, Secretary of State for Scotland, and Lady Frederick Cavendish, who were his shipboard acquaintances. "The Matabele Mission to Queen Victoria," n.d., Maund Papers, Witwatersrand. It is likely that Robinson's changed position and the agreement with Rhodes had made the Colonial Office more receptive.

Knutsford, speaking for the queen, was all that the Exploring Company could have desired in the circumstances of late 1888 but was directly contrary to its interests in 1889—"A King gives a stranger an ox, not his whole herd of cattle, otherwise what would other strangers arriving have to eat?"[108] This counsel, written in what Knutsford conceived to be the Ndebele style,[109] resulted from poor communication between the Colonial Office and the promoters. The Colonial Office had received protests against the Rudd concession not only from humanitarians but from influential London businessmen, and had concluded that it could not back an agreement which was at best dubious and which Lobengula now disavowed.[110] A letter from the Aborigines Protection Society to Lobengula reinforced the Colonial Office message in more explicit terms, that white men would make war for gold, just as Africans fought for cattle.[111]

These messages provoked dismay among the amalgamators. Rhodes, who had arrived in London to formalize the agreement just as the indunas were leaving, reacted characteristically by assuming that Maund was the culprit and denounced him as a traitor to his employers. Maund finally convinced him that he was not guilty. But the damage had to be undone, and Maund was given the task of betraying the confidence of the king. He was to pose as an adviser who had no thought of personal gain but to use every opportunity to strengthen the hands of the Rudd concession-holders. There was an additional complication which affected Maund's instructions. At the time of his departure there was considerable doubt that the imperial government would recognize the Rudd concession as valid. Consequently Maund was instructed to try to secure as many subconcessions as possible as an insurance against total loss if the Rudd

108. Message to Lobengula, March 26, 1889, in Knutsford to Robinson, March 27, 1889, C.O. 878/30/372, P.R.O.
109. Maund maintained that the parable of the ox was Knutsford's own idea, that Maund tried to get the sentence changed or eliminated but the message had already been approved by the queen. Maund to Hole, October 7, 1926, NO 1/2/1, N.A.R.
110. See note by Herbert, October 23, 1889, on F. O. to C.O. March 25, 1889, C.O. 417/36, P.R.O.
111. Buxton and Fox Bourne to Lobengula, March 19, 1889, MA 23/1/1, N.A.R.

concession was discarded. By June 1889, however, the amalgamation had had its effect, and the government was no longer disposed to raise embarrassing issues. Maund was now instructed to shift his ground again and to use his influence to induce the king to refuse any other concessions.[112] This feat of gymnastics Maund performed with great finesse. He advised Lobengula that the concession was undoubtedly legal and that the chief had no alternative but to accept it.[113]

While their agents in Matabeleland devoted themselves to salvaging the Rudd concession, Rhodes, Cawston, and Gifford proceeded with the organization of their monopoly and their campaign for a charter. At the end of May, Rhodes and Rudd on behalf of Gold Fields of South Africa, which had provided the funds for the Rudd mission, and the Exploring Company, negotiated an agreement with a new entity named the "Central Search Association, Limited," by which they sold to the new body all their claims to mineral rights in "the domains of Lobengula and adjacent territories."

The directors of the Central Search Association included Rhodes, Gifford, Cawston, Beit, John Oakley Maund, and C. D. Rudd and his brother Thomas. In essence, therefore, the creators were selling to themselves. The Central Search Association, the creation of the vendors with a nominal capital of £120,000, paid its creators £92,400 in shares, distributed as follows:[114]

Gold Fields of South Africa, Ltd.	25,500	Nathan Rothschild	3,000
Exploring Company, Ltd.	22,500	Rochfort Maguire	3,000
Cecil J. Rhodes	9,750	Rhodes, Rudd, and Beit	9,000
Charles D. Rudd	9,000	Austral Africa Exploration Company	2,400
Alfred Beit	8,250		

The Austral Africa Company, which claimed a prior concession from Lobengula, and other rivals were transformed into

112. Weatherley to Maund, June 14, 1889, Maund Papers, Witwatersrand.
113. Maund to Exploring Company, June 11, 1890, MA 23/1/1, N.A.R.
114. Memorandum of Agreement, May 30, 1889, B.T. 31/4451/28988, P.R.O.

supporters by being bought out. Recognizing the vulnerability of the Rudd concession, Rhodes had sought to absorb all potential rivals who had any shadow of mining rights which might be embarrassing. The Austral Africa Company had been founded in August 1888 with a nominal capital of £20,000,[115] with the usual complement of paper, to exploit an alleged verbal concession from Lobengula and the knowledge and influence of Alfred H. Haggard, brother of the celebrated Rider, and John Wallop, second son of Lord Portsmouth, with regard to Matabeleland and Mashonaland. They were not only unsuccessful in confirming their concession but were turned back at the border when they attempted to enter Ndebele territory after the Rudd concession.[116] Haggard returned to England vowing to expose the Rudd concession, and Wallop indicated that his own influential connections could be used to embarrass Rhodes.[117] Their blackmail value was enough for Rhodes to offer them participation in the Central Search Association, and the results for their company were impressive from its participation in the inflation of the Central Search shares.

Subsequently other useful individuals were admitted to participation in the spoils. Sir Hercules Robinson after his return from South Africa received 250 shares in Central Search. The capital was increased to £121,000 when Leander Starr Jameson received 1,000 shares for his services in Matabeleland in 1889,[118] and in 1890 an enormous inflation transformed Central Search into the United Concessions Company, with a nominal capital of £4,000,000. The largest shareholders in the new firm were as follows:[119]

Thomas Rudd	3,000	Cecil Rhodes	132,000
Thomas Rudd and		Nathan Rothschild	39,200
H. D. Boyle	336,200	Rochfort Maguire	49,000
Alfred Beit	112,400	Hercules Robinson	2,500

115. Austral Africa Exploration Company, B.T. 31/4208/2730, P.R.O.
116. Statement of Shares, Central Search Association, October 4, 1889, B.T. 31/4451/28988, P.R.O.
117. Rhodes to Rudd, January 10, 1888[9], RU 2/1/1, N.A.R.
118. Agreement between Central Search and Alfred Beit, June 27, 1890, in *ibid.*
119. Summary of Capital and Shares, November 21, 1890, B.T. 4815/31926, P.R.O.

C. D. Rudd	66,800	Exploration	
Francis R. Thompson	49,770	Company	80,000
Rhodes, C. D. Rudd,		Exploring Company	293,700
and Beit	90,000	L. S. Jameson	10,000
Austral Africa		Harry C. Moore[120]	10,000

Also in May 1889 the old Exploring Company was liquidated, and from its dead body emerged a new company of the same name, with a capital of £35,000, which included Rhodes as a director and Beit as one of its prominent shareholders. This pyramiding of paper capital which eventually would be converted into fortunes for the favored few took place unknown to the investing public and even to the government, which when it granted the charter to the British South Africa Company assumed that the chartered company owned the Rudd concession, where in fact it remained the property of the Central Search Association.

The shares of Central Search and its successor rested upon a concession that its possessors knew to be shaky at best. Those who might be embarrassing by contesting its validity had been bought off or absorbed, but the promoters required the imprimatur of government to legitimatize their monopoly and to advance their further ambitions in central Africa. As Rhodes admitted to "Matabele" Thompson, "The Concession was useless without the Charter—the Charter was useless without the Concession."[121] He and his allies now proceeded to insure the legitimacy of the concession by Royal Charter, confident that their joint power made their case irresistible.

120. Moore was an American who claimed to have an oral concession from Lobengula and was bought out despite doubts as to whether he had any rights because it was felt his abilities would be useful to the amalgamated enterprise and because of his possible blackmail potentiality if he remained an opponent.
121. Rouillard, ed., *Thompson*, p. 161.

3
The Grand Design

CECIL RHODES HAS CONVINCED HISTORIANS AND BIOGRA-
phers, as he convinced his contemporaries, that the dominating
purpose of his adult years was the expansion of the British
Empire not only in Africa but throughout the world. He was,
so orthodoxy runs, a man consumed by an ambition which far
transcended the material objectives of other millionaires. This
contrast assumes a distinction between "idealism" and "materialism" which is untenable. Most other millionaires did not
devote their energies to the appropriation of imperial estates,
but the nature of the ambition that leads a man to seek to dominate the gold mines or, for that matter, the clothing industry,
is not as far removed from that of Rhodes as the myth of Rhodes
suggests.

Rhodes has been cast in the heroic tradition. Heroes scorn
material rewards in their struggles for great ideals. The same
element in humanity which immortalizes a Gordon perpetuates
the myth of Rhodes. Neither was interested in wealth for the
sake of wealth, though Gordon was more unworldly than
Rhodes with regard to acquiring it. Both were men driven by
supramaterial ambitions. The identification would have been
even more impressive had Rhodes died romantically at the
hands of the Ndebele as did Gordon by the onslaught of the
dervishes.

The tale has been told and retold of the young man, so unlike
his fellows, who sat amid the Kimberley diamond fields dreaming great dreams while others grubbed for money, and who

made of his short life a dedication to the expansion of Anglo-Saxondom. His soaring nature reached for the stars, though he settled for Cape to Cairo, an ambition he went a long way toward realizing. But Rhodes was not the sole architect of the plans of the British South Africa Company. Its objectives were developed by several men, of whom Rhodes was one.

During the spring of 1889 Rhodes, Gifford, and Cawston agreed on the outline of a plan for the development of a chartered company empire in central Africa. Crudely stated in the terms used by F. Rutherfoord Harris who became secretary of the company in South Africa, the object was "to place our finger, waiting for the practical development which is sure to come" in any areas where treaties with African chiefs could have any show of validity. Such treaties cost little and the rewards could be prodigious.[1] The plans formulated in the spring embraced three major areas—Matabeleland and Mashonaland, the Lakes district, and the "Garaganze country" in the environs of the Congo Free State, where lay the rich copper deposits in what came to be known as the Katanga. Beyond these districts the promoters hoped to acquire territory claimed by the Portuguese both in Angola and in Mozambique, pushing into any areas where the Portuguese hold was weak. In the west the object was the port of Moçamedes; on the east, Beira and Delagoa Bay; and the means would be treaties with "independent chiefs." The Portuguese would be removed either by money or by force.[2] These great plans were made visual by Cawston who produced a map of Africa with these territories designated as belonging to the chartered company.[3] The map represented a composite of the ambitions of the founders, which were indeed tremendous. John Verschoyle, editor of the *Fortnightly Review*, was ecstatic at the prospects. He foresaw a "vast empire administered by as great or a greater company than the old East India Company."

1. Harris to Weatherley, Sec., BSAC, London, September 16, 1889, LO5/2/0, N.A.R.
2. Harris to Weatherley, November 11, 1889, in *ibid.*
3. Cawston to Rhodes, December 13, 1889, BSAC I. Misc. Rhodes House. Cawston refers to the "celebrated map" that he, Gifford, and Rhodes had developed in the spring of 1889. I have been unable to locate the map.

The thought "fills one's mind with an enthusiasm which one would scarcely be an Englishman if one did not feel."[4] The promoters also had no doubts that they served a great ideal for the advancement of which they expected to be richly rewarded in material as well as psychic terms.

In this grand scheme the primary focus of Rhodes's attention was the lands allegedly subject to Lobengula, which he hoped would prove to yield gold in quantities rivaling or surpassing the Witwatersrand. Harris in September 1889 described the Transvaal, Matabeleland, and Mashonaland as "one vast gold field."[5] This was typical Harris ebullience, but his confidence undoubtedly represented the optimism of his employer. The possession of this vast wealth would serve several purposes. It would give Rhodes the position as a gold magnate which had eluded him in the Witwatersrand, and it would thwart the Transvaal in its ambitions to expand to the north. Rhodes visualized himself as the instrument for the restoration of the Transvaal to the British Empire as part of a great union stretching from the Cape to the Zambezi. In 1889 he entertained no doubts that the eventual absorption of the Transvaal was inevitable; Kruger's burghers must give way before the mining age just as must the Ndebele. The Transvaal's ambition to annex Swaziland he professed to regard with indifference, particularly because the republic would still be landlocked. Indeed, he maintained, annexation would accelerate the return of the Transvaal to the British Empire, since most of the mining concessions were held by Englishmen, who would give additional force to their fellow Britons on the Rand.[6] But the northward extension of the Transvaal must be resisted. His energy was concentrated on establishing company authority so securely in Matabeleland and Mashonaland as to remove any temptation on the part of the Boers to trek north of the Limpopo. Mashonaland for Rhodes had become a symbol invested with mystical significance. In one of the flights of fancy which he directed to his admirer W. T. Stead, he described it as "the key to Central Africa," "worth

4. Verschoyle to Cawston [1899?], BSAC I Misc. Rhodes House.
5. Harris to Weatherley, September 16, 1889, LO5/2/0, N.A.R.
6. Harris to Weatherley, December 9, 1889, LO5/2/0, N.A.R.

more than all other African possessions." This was the land of
Ophir where the Phoenicians had extracted gold; Zimbabwe
was the work of their hands; Sofala in Portuguese Africa was
the port from which the gold had been shipped to Hiram. Sig-
nificantly, he followed his discussion of the riches of Mashonaland—"simply full of gold reefs"—with a discourse on his scheme
for a secret society modeled on the Jesuits which would be the
agency for the expansion of the British Empire. Gold reefs and
the secular religion of imperialism, the material and the meta-
physical, were blended in Rhodes's self-fulfilment. As he added
to Stead, "I find I am human and should like to be living after
my death."[7] His immortality would be Rhodesia.

Rhodes's objectives in Mashonaland involved the adjacent
Portuguese coastal possessions. Just as Kruger reached for the
sea to ensure Transvaal independence, so did Rhodes seek ocean
ports to realize the future he planned for Matabeleland and
Mashonaland. Beyond these centers of his attention, Rhodes
was less involved with the plans of the company. He participated
in plans for the acquisition of the areas, but the ideas were not
his and the execution was left to other men. In a rare moment,
Rhodes once admitted that his focus was south of the Zambezi.
This was the land he most coveted and about which he had
acquired the greatest amount of information.[8] Rhodes did not
often admit his limitations with such candor, but in the northern outreaches of the company's expansion he was dependent to
a large extent on the energy and thought of others.

The Lakes area came into the plans of the chartered company
promoters by several channels. The African Lakes Company
and the missionaries of the Lake Nyasa district had great political significance, particularly in Scotland, where any suggestion of a compromise on the Shiré highlands was certain to
produce a great outpouring of indignation from missionary
societies and civic groups. The assets of the Lakes Company
related to the region it occupied and the political power it could

7. Rhodes to Stead, August 19, 1891, strictly private, RH 1/1/1,
N.A.R. At the time of the letter the name of Rhodesia had come into
use.
8. Harris to Weatherley, June 2, 1890, LO5/2/1, N.A.R.

command. As a commercial venture it had been a failure—it paid its first dividend, 2½ percent, ten years after its founding.[9] In its philanthropic objectives, its performance was no more impressive. It had the power only to create disruption. Though its authorized capital was £100,000, its paid-up capital was only a little over £20,000,[10] and it could not dominate the Arab and African peoples with whom it frequently came into conflict. It also quarreled with its fellow evangelists of Christianity. But the realities of the company's impotence had little to do with its importance. It had immense symbolic significance as the inheritor of Livingstone's mission to bring light to Africa. Livingstone's son-in-law, Alexander L. Bruce, was a strong supporter and became one of its directors in 1889. Bruce's relative, Balfour of Burleigh, a political power in Scotland and Salisbury's secretary of state for Scotland, was also a strong supporter. Salisbury described the work of the company and the missionaries as "splendid monuments of British energy and enthusiasm."[11] But his professed admiration masked vexation. The missionary lobby and their numerous allies desired imperial protection for these "monuments," and Salisbury was not willing to provide it. There were no material interests in the area worth the expenditure of public money and the settlements were remote from the ocean and the Royal Navy. He would have preferred to allow the issue of sovereignty to remain moot, but the perverse Portuguese would not let him.[12] They insisted on their historic claims to the Shiré highlands and the area of Lake Nyasa itself, and they refused to accept Salisbury's contention that the Zambezi River, which with the Shiré was the route of access, was an international waterway. Salisbury wished to tidy up the map of Africa to remove points of irritation but the Scots and the Portuguese frustrated him in the Nyasa region. He was angry with Portugal, not angry enough for a direct confrontation with all

9. The *Times*, April 24, 1888.
10. Issue of additional capital, 1886, F.O. 84/1/1784, P.R.O.
11. H. L. Duff, *Nyasaland Under the Foreign Office*, p. 3.
12. In July 1888 Salisbury stated, "We must save (1) Matabeleland and Khama's country, (2) the waterways of the Zambezi, (3) neutrality of Nyassa." Note, n.d., on C.O. to F.O., July 19, 1888, F.O. 84/1924, P.R.O.

of its attendant diplomatic complications, but sufficiently to give his moral support to a private enterprise which was prepared to undertake the risks and expense.

Tension between Britain and Portugal had intensified during the course of 1888. In January the Portuguese attempted to prevent an African Lakes Company's steamer from using the Zambezi, and an attempt later in the year to resolve the dispute over the Nyasa territory was met with Portuguese refusal to abandon any claims in the area.[13] Petitions poured into the Foreign Office demanding that action be taken to prevent the "calamity" of Portuguese domination of the Shiré and Nyasa region and the closure of the Zambezi to international traffic.[14] The agitation centered in Scotland, but it spread widely throughout England as well. At the end of February 1889 a public meeting in Oxford attended by many heads of colleges and leading members of the university community passed resolutions deploring the Central African slave trade and urging the government either alone or in concert with other powers to take the lead in suppressing the evil.[15] Influential men added their weight to the pressure on the government. Sir John Kirk went to see Salisbury to ask him to be resolute; A. L. Bruce energetically took up the cause of his father-in-law. Livingstone's humanitarianism, Bruce maintained, was not only Christian but British. Had he not accepted an appointment as consul for inner Africa and carried the Union Jack in his last two expeditions? "The British public must understand that the supremacy of Britain in the Dark Continent is at stake at the present time though the Great opportunity [is] lost." The British government by its flabbiness had already lost much of Africa; unless dedicated imperialists immediately took a hand, it would surrender much of the rest, and it was imperative that "Britain must control the Dark Continent from Cairo to the Cape." Bruce appealed to his friend Albert Grey to enlist other leaders in the cause: "It is individuals and

13. R. J. Hammond, *Portugal and Africa*, pp. 111–114.
14. These petitions from various groups are in F.O. 84/1935, P.R.O. The word "calamity" was used in a letter from the African Lakes Company to Salisbury, December 26, 1888, but other appeals were in the same vein.
15. Hunter to F.O., March 1, 1889, F.O. 84/1990, P.R.O.

not the British Govt. who have built the British Empire. Individuals must move, the Govt. acts always too slowly. You must
join the Lakes Co. Board and put spurs in the Company to make
it move quickly...."[16]

Among the individuals whom Bruce hoped would involve
themselves was William Mackinnon, "an Imperialist strong for
a bold progressive forward African policy," whose Imperial
British East Africa Company might link up with the Lakes
Company to resist the Portuguese.[17] Mackinnon was not prepared to take an active part at that time, but he provided his
moral support, as did his friend the Reverend Horace Waller,
one of Livingstone's old associates and a prominent advocate of
British expansion in East Africa. Also enlisted in the cause was
Balfour of Burleigh. This combination of influence and numbers produced a political environment which restricted the government's freedom of action in negotiations with the Portuguese. In the spring of 1889 Salisbury commissioned Harry
Johnston, the newly appointed consul at Mozambique, to be
his emissary to Lisbon with the proposal that a compromise
boundary be arranged which would recognize the Shiré highlands as within the British sphere.[18]

The Portuguese foreign minister was willing to recommend
an agreement which would have recognized an uninterrupted
sphere of British influence north of the Zambezi to the western
shores of Lake Nyasa and conceded British rights over Matabeleland and Mashonaland, and access to the Zambezi. This was
a considerable withdrawal from the previous Portuguese position, but the arrangement would have recognized Portuguese
preeminence over the Shiré highlands.[19] The permanent staff
of the British Foreign Office thought the terms highly satisfactory, "far more favorable than we had any right to expect,"
stated Villiers Lister, usually a proponent of imperial advance.[20]

16. Bruce to Grey, January 1, 1889, 208/04, Grey Papers, University of
Durham.
17. *Ibid.*
18. Harry H. Johnston, *The Story of My Life*, pp. 214–217.
19. Telegram, Petre to Salisbury, April 6, 1889, F.O. 179/269, P.R.O.
20. Memo, "Proposed Agreement with Portugal in Africa," by T. V.
Lister, April 28, 1889, F.O. 84/1993, P.R.O.

But Salisbury rejected the proposal. What Portugal was willing to concede, he said, Britain could take for itself. Portugal could not prevent free passage on the Zambezi if Britain were inclined to make an issue of it, and the territorial concessions were a reflection of the weakness of the Portuguese case rather than of a generous spirit. The most important consideration dictating rejection was the strong opposition of the missionary societies and the African Lakes Company to the recognition of Portugal's rights to the Shiré highlands to the southern shores of Lake Nyasa.[21] The political implications of the issue were underscored by a petition signed by 10,494 ministers and elders of the three Presbyterian churches of Scotland,[22] and by a memorial from the Convention of Royal and Parliamentary Burghs meeting in Edinburgh.[23] Other calls for the defense of the missions poured in throughout the year. That they were not always entirely spontaneous is indicated by Bruce's comment that public meetings "might easily be got up say in London, Manchester, Newcastle, Edinburgh, and Glasgow to strengthen the hand of the Government and alarm the Portuguese."[24]

These pressures reinforced Salisbury's disinclination to be flexible with the Portuguese and in the spring of 1889, consequently, the governments of Britain and Portugal were at an impasse. Salisbury was annoyed with what he considered to be Portuguese attempts to use weakness as strength. The decision of the Portuguese government to cancel its concession to the Delagoa Bay Railway Company produced further tension. The railway project had had a tortured career.

Portugal had agreed to assist in the construction of a line to the Transvaal border by a treaty of 1875 with the republic which was finally ratified in 1882. The terms which Portugal was willing to offer were a subsidy of half the cost and various other privileges. At the end of 1883 a concession was awarded to Edward MacMurdo, an American citizen. MacMurdo declined

21. Memo, "Portugal," by Salisbury, April 26, 1889, F.O. 84/1993, P.R.O.
22. Marchbank to Balfour, April 30, 1989, F.O. 84/1994, P.R.O.
23. Agent, Convention of Royal and Parliamentary Burghs to F.O., May 7, 1889, in *ibid.*
24. Bruce to Grey, December 10, 1889, 208/4, Grey Papers, Durham.

the subvention but received substantial land grants, including a large block on Delagoa Bay, and his company had the right to fix its own rates. In exchange for these benefits, he agreed to complete the line to the border within three years.[25]

MacMurdo formed a Lisbon-based company to exploit the concession. During the next few years much more energy had been spent on questionable financial manipulations than on construction, and at the end of 1886 the Portuguese government had decided to construct the railway itself. The Lisbon board had agreed but MacMurdo, who was the principal shareholder and only bondholder, used his voting power to override the Portuguese directors and in effect transferred his rights to an English company—the Delagoa Bay and East Africa Railway, Ltd.—which was legally constituted as a subsidiary of the Portuguese company in order to avoid forfeiture of the concession.[26] Under the aegis of this new entity construction of the line moved forward vigorously, spurred by the hope of forestalling promulgation of the Portuguese decree. At the same time, influential shareholders, among them Lord Castletown, a prominent investor in African projects, protested that the impending Portuguese action was confiscatory and demanded governmental intervention to protect their interests. But the cabinet was not prepared to go beyond a "sharp warning" to Portugal that Britain would hold it accountable for any breach of obligations.[27] The Portuguese government withdrew its decision, but British high-handedness reinforced Portugal's determination not to give way before any further assaults.

Mounting animosity between the two governments made a collision more and more likely. One incident which might have produced a clash resulted from the refusal of Portuguese authorities to allow Bishop Smythies to land arms at Tunghi Bay which he intended to use for the defense of his party during their journey to the Lakes. Salisbury immediately ordered a warship to proceed to the area to back the bishop, but before

25. Confidential print, Colonial Office, February 1896, C.O. 537/129, P.R.O.
26. Hammond, *Portugal and Africa*, pp. 224–229.
27. Cabinet minute, June 29, 1889, CAB 41/41/29, P.R.O.

it arrived, the Portuguese had allowed him and his followers
to land with their arms.[28] The severity of Salisbury's response
surprised Gerald Portal, acting consul-general in Zanzibar, who
wrote that "if it was wished to raise the question of Portuguese
rights to Tunghi I would guarantee to find a better opportunity
in a month." [29] Salisbury noted, "Simply the key of the enigma
which puzzles Portal was that I wanted an opportunity of giving the Portuguese a hint—which I could defend in Parliament.
This was the first occasion on which they have put themselves
in the wrong." [30]

Salisbury, however, did not want war. His "hints" were intended to communicate to the Portuguese that the British government stood behind its citizens, but he had not modified his
position that imperial expansion must be by private initiative.
What the Lakes area required was a strong company which
could represent and defend the British presence as did Mackinnon's company in East Africa or the projected chartered company in Matabeleland and Mashonaland. His specifications
were met by the enlargement of the sphere of the proposed British South Africa Company. The development was not at his
behest, but neither was it without his knowledge and encouragement. During the months since the African Lakes Company
and the missionaries had begun their agitation for defense of
British interests in the Nyasa area, plans had developed to rein-
vigorate the Lakes Company. Bruce, Balfour of Burleigh, and
Grey had all been involved in the discussions that led to the
decision to seek a charter for this more vigorous enterprise. In
April 1889 the backers of the proposed charter informed Salisbury of their intentions, and received an encouraging response.[31]
Indeed, their objectives fitted so closely Salisbury's desires as to
suggest that the initiative was his and not theirs. Salisbury hoped
that a strong African Lakes Company under a charter would
provide the bulwark in the Lakes area against Portuguese am-

28. F.O. to Admiralty, May 20, 1889, F.O. 84/1995, P.R.O.
29. Portal to Barrington, May 17, 1889 A/79, Salisbury Papers, Christ
Church, Oxford.
30. Note by Salisbury, n.d., on *ibid.*
31. Ewing to Salisbury, May 3, 1889, F.O. 84/1994, P.R.O.

bitions. Like other professed servants of public opinion, Salisbury sought to manage it, and Balfour and Bruce were useful allies in stimulating indignation in Scotland which would impress the Portuguese.[32]

The developing plans for a South Africa Company provided an opportunity to supply new energy for the African Lakes Company. In mid-April, two weeks before the Lakes Company approached Salisbury, Cawston inquired of Ewing whether the application for "a Royal Central South Africa Charter" should include the area of operations of the Lakes Company to give that company "the advantage of Association with the Charter Company."[33] Discussions followed involving Rhodes, Cawston, Grey, Balfour, and directors of the Lakes Company, which culminated in a decision of the leadership of the two companies to fuse their enterprises rather than developing independently. Balfour accepted the chairmanship of a meeting in Glasgow at the beginning of May attended by directors of the Lakes Company and other influential men from the west of Scotland, at which the proposal to join hands with the Rhodes-London combination was presented. As a result of this meeting, negotiations began for an amalgamation of the two groups, with Balfour as the principal representative of the Lakes company. The advantages to the Lakes Company seemed great—large infusions of capital for commercial operations and guarantees of money for administration and for military forces. For Rhodes and his associates the union provided access to the Lakes area and a base for expansion north of the Zambezi.[34]

The two groups agreed that at least in the transitional period to complete fusion, Lakes Company interests would have special recognition through a "Northern Board" which would include prominent Scots in its membership—Lord Rosebery was among those suggested. In addition, the Lakes Company would have a representative on the London board of the chartered company.[35]

32. Roland Oliver, *Sir Harry Johnston and the Scramble for Africa*, p. 151.
33. Cawston to Ewing, April 18, 1889, BSAC I Misc. Rhodes House.
34. Rhodes and Cawston to Secretary, African Lakes Company, June 5, 1889, F.O. 84/2006, P.R.O.
35. "Memorandum of subjects talked on by the Hon. C. J. Rhodes

Amalgamation was strongly advocated by three men whose objectives were the advancement of the national interest—Balfour, Bruce, and Grey. All were much involved in the cause of British preeminence in the Lakes area. None was satisfied with the ramshackle management of the African Lakes Company. Balfour was also sufficiently interested in the South Africa Company to consider seriously becoming its president,[36] and Grey became one of that company's board of directors. In the early days of their planning they had looked to a linkage with energetic management of the South Africa Company and the munificence of Rhodes as the means to the realization of their objectives. Rhodes was highly susceptible to their appeal, and Harry Johnston, just back from Portugal and about to leave for Mozambique, added his persuasiveness. Salisbury's selection of Johnston as his emissary to Portugal was a sign of esteem which the chartered company promoters were quick to notice. Ricarde-Seaver after discussions with Rhodes, who was visiting in Paris, concluded that they should make contact with "a certain little explorer now in Portugal" to elicit his advice on strategy, and, hopefully, secure his good offices with Lord Salisbury. The intermediary was John Verschoyle, a frequent host to politicians and other prominent men at his flat on Fitzroy Square.[37] Verschoyle's contacts were useful, and he had been enlisted as a publicist for the charter project. On Johnston's return to England, Verschoyle brought him and Rhodes together, thus beginning a tempestuous association of two self-willed men which had great significance for central Africa.[38]

If Johnston's recollections are to be believed, he first met Rhodes at the end of April or the beginning of May at a dinner party at Verschoyle's and their conversation so exhilarated Rhodes that the two talked through the night about the great prospects for central Africa. The result, Johnston stated, was that Rhodes wrote him a check for £2000 to subsidize a treaty-

and J. W. Moir and approved by Mr. Rhodes," n.d. CT 1/16/1, N.A.R.
36. Balfour to Salisbury, May 24, 1889, File E, Salisbury Papers, Christ Church, Oxford.
37. Ricarde-Seaver to Cawston, April 21, 1889, BSAC Misc. I, Rhodes House.
38. Johnston, *Story of My Life*, p. 217.

making expedition north of the Zambezi.[39] Some such discussion no doubt occurred, and the enthusiasms of these two ardent spirits fed each other.

Johnston's version creates an oversimplified view of the course of events. But what cannot be gainsaid is that plans meant little without energy and commitment. Salisbury favored an active policy pursued by others, who would assume both the responsibilities and the risks. The Lakes Company directors lacked the drive or the resources to advance an ambitious project. Rhodes had both. He and Cawston with the backing of Balfour, Bruce, and Grey pressed forward with active negotiations. By the end of June they seemed to have resolved all major issues. They agreed that a company tentatively to be called the British South Africa and Lakes Company would be created with an authorized capital of £1 million in £1 shares. The Rhodes-London group would buy 200,000 shares. The Lakes Company would receive 30,000 shares credited as fully paid in consideration for its transferring all its assets. Its directors would also have the option of buying up to 20,000 additional shares at par for themselves or for their friends. The Rhodes-London interests would also contribute £20,000 toward a capital account and a subsidy of not more than £9,000 per year for administration of the territory in the neighborhood of Lakes Nyasa and Tanganyika. The Lakes Company would have a "fair representation" on the united board. The objectives of the chartered company in the Lakes area were stated in terms which were highly appealing to humanitarians. The promoters vowed to support the missionaries and to put a stop to the slave and liquor traffic.[40] The merger did not immediately take place; indeed it was bogged down for years by obstruction in which the Lakes Company representatives demonstrated that avowed humanitarianism was not incompatible with canniness. But the negotiations between the two groups had the full support of the government which considered that the union served an imperial interest.

The company's plan to extend its control over Barotseland and the territories between that country and Lake Nyasa also was conceived by more than one person. Johnston credited

39. *Ibid.*, p. 219. Ewing to Salisbury, July 1, 1889, F.O. 84/1998, P.R.O.
40. Same to same, August 14, 1890, and encls., F.O. 84/2079, P.R.O.

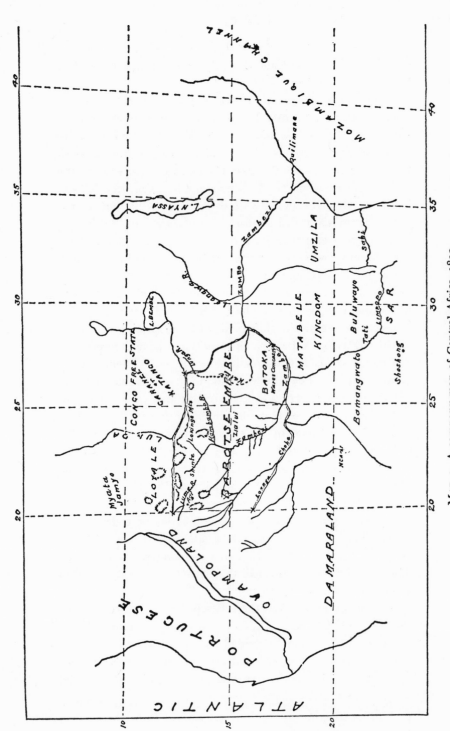

MAP 2. A company map of Central Africa, 1890

himself as the originator of the idea.[41] Again he ignored the contributions of other men, though his early advocacy of this objective is beyond dispute. Lewanika, the chief of the Lozi, had watched with alarm the advance of the concession hunters into the lands of the south; some had already appeared in his own country. Elephant hunters had destroyed so many elephants that there was an increasing shortage of ivory on which the Lozi depended in their barter trade.[42] Economic crisis weakened the already shaky power of the Lozi chief. For decades the Lozi kingdom had been wracked with power struggles. In 1884 Lewanika himself had been driven from power and he had reestablished himself at the end of 1885 after a bloody war. He had executed many of his enemies, but the instability of his regime made him fear that today's friends might be tomorrow's foes. The constant threat of Ndebele raids also hung over the kingdom. Beset by these dangers from within and without, Lewanika saw his possible salvation in the example of his friend Kgama, who had accepted British protection and had thus apparently ensured the security of his regime.[43] In September 1886 Lewanika sought the aid of the missionary François Coillard of the Paris Evangelical Missionary Society, who had established a mission to the Lozi, in drawing up a petition asking for British protection. Coillard was not eager to comply; he recognized that Lewanika's aim was the protection of his personal security, which was not necessarily the same as the interests of his people; and he advised the chief to wait until Kgama had had more experience with British protection.[44] Lewanika tried again in January 1887 and again Coillard temporized.[45] Then in October 1888 Lewanika called together a great meeting of his indunas and people and asked for their advice as to whether he should seek the protection of the great Queen Victoria. The response

41. Johnston to Rhodes, October 8, 1893, quoted in Oliver, *Johnston*, pp. 153–154.
42. Lewis H. Gann, *A History of Northern Rhodesia*, p. 46.
43. Gerald L. Caplan, "Barotseland's Scramble for Protection," *Journal of African History*, X, 2 (1969), 277–294; see also Mutumba M. Bull, "Lewanika's achievement," in *ibid.*, XII, 3 (1972), 463–472.
44. F. Coillard to C. Coillard, September 24, October 3–16, 1886, CO 5/1/1/1, N.A.R.
45. Notes by Coillard, January 23, 1887, MA 18/4/2/5, in *ibid.*

was not what he had hoped for. In the words of the missionary chronicler A. D. Jalla: "The answer was, If you want the English, let them come, but we shall no longer be there. We serve you because you are king, but if you become a slave we shall cease to serve you."[46]

Lewanika was not deterred and continued to press Coillard to act as his amanuensis. Finally the missionary gave way, and at the beginning of 1889 wrote a letter to Shippard, informing the commissioner of Lewanika's desire for imperial protection. But Coillard's description of Barotseland as excellent country for immigration and agriculture was almost certainly not at Lewanika's behest.[47]

Coillard's letter did not reach the Colonial Office until August 1889 and received the usual languid response to communications of no great moment.[48] But the prospect of exploiting the resources of Barotseland attracted much more interest from private citizens. Reports of Lewanika's desire for imperial protection had circulated widely in South Africa and England. Lord Gifford in September 1888 informed the Foreign Office that he had heard from the Bechuanaland Exploration Company's agents that Lewanika had made inquiries of Kgama about Kgama's experience with imperial protection and asking for advice as to how to obtain it for himself. Gifford thought Barotseland offered a promising field for investment and expressed willingness to raise capital for its development if the government were willing to extend its protection to the area.[49] When Gifford, Cawston, and Rhodes developed their "Grand Design" in the spring of 1889, Barotseland was colored pink.

The incorporation of the country between Barotseland and Lake Nyasa was a logical part of the plan, though Johnston claimed the suggestion as his own.[50] Lord Knutsford recommended to Salisbury on May 18, 1889, that the company be

46. Jalla to Harding, n.d., MA 18/4/1, in *ibid.*
47. Coillard to Shippard, January 2, 1889, encl. in C.O. to F.O., August 30, 1889, F.O. 84/2002, P.R.O. Coillard probably had in mind the Tonga dependencies along what is now the Zambian railway belt, rather than Barotseland proper.
48. Gervas Clay, *Your Friend Lewanika*, pp. 60–61.
49. *Ibid.*, p. 59.
50. Oliver, *Johnston*, p. 154.

"required" to include in its sphere "such portion of territory north of the Zambesi as it may be important to control with a view to security of communications with the Shiré and Lake Nyasa and the protection of British missionary settlements."[51] This idea almost certainly did not originate with Knutsford, but came from the promoters themselves, who must have seen it as a natural corollary to other elements of their scheme.

Beyond Barotseland lay the copper deposits of Katanga, an inevitable objective for the promoters of the "Grand Scheme." The existence of copper had been known to Europeans for some time. The people of the area had long used the metal for money, ornaments, arms, and a variety of other purposes. Livingstone in 1868 had encountered an Arab caravan on its way from Katanga with nearly five tons of copper, and Verney Lovett Cameron, who traveled across equatorial Africa in the 1870s, saw specimens of gold from Katanga, though he did not visit the copper deposits. The German explorer P. Reichard in 1884 saw two copper deposits, but had to leave abruptly because of the unfriendliness of the inhabitants of the area. Two Portuguese naval officers traversed Katanga on the way to Tete on the Zambezi in 1884 and 1885, and in 1886 the Scottish missionary F. S. Arnot saw a rich copper deposit.[52]

The existence of substantial mineral resources was certain to provide an irresistible attraction for European capitalists. The area was claimed by Leopold II's Congo Free State, but in 1889 Leopold's jurisdiction was not yet recognized by Great Britain, and the promoters of the British South Africa Company hoped to preempt him by making a treaty with Msiri (Msidi) the chief of the Garaganze, in whose territory the principal copper deposits were located. Msiri, a Nyamwezi trader, had gained control of the area by diplomacy and force, and had built up a commercial empire during the approximately three decades during which he had been the ruler. He now became important to Europeans in the same way as was Lobengula, and he suffered the same fate.

51. C.O. to F.O., May 16, 1889, F.O. 84/1995, P.R.O.
52. Joseph Rousseau, "The Story of the Union Minière du Haut Katanga," in Les Weinthal, The Story of the Cape to Cairo Railway & River Route, 1887–1922, 4 vols. (London [1923–1927]), 1:469.

The paternity of the company's plans to acquire Katanga is doubtful, though Johnston as usual claimed credit for directing the promoters' attention in that direction. Rich copper deposits in lands not clearly under any European power in any event were certain to stimulate the avarice of the founders, both the London group and Rhodes. The London directors and Rhodes all were eager to acquire the wealth of Katanga, though Rhodes was more reckless of political problems. Johnston, in terms of expression, was most reckless of all. He lectured to Salisbury on the importance of the company's acquiring Katanga "to complete the new province of British Central Africa," and asserted that Leopold had no rights to this area which was "the richest country in minerals (copper and gold) in all Central Africa."[53] Rhodes was also aggressive in words. Long after the campaign had been lost, he was still issuing peremptory orders. "You must go and get Katanga," he wrote Joseph Thomson in July 1891.[54] Two months before, the Foreign Office had made it clear to members of the London board that the imperial government considered the mining districts of Katanga as being under the sovereignty of the Congo Free State.[55] Rhodes's continued perseverance might be construed as merely another example of his defiance of any but the most explicit instructions from the imperial government. Salisbury complained to the queen that "the company as a whole are quite inclined to behave fairly; but Mr. Cecil Rhodes is rather difficult to keep in order."[56] But Rhodes's words were not matched by action. The company's probes toward Katanga were weak and ineffectual, in contrast to the power it manifested in the occupation of Mashonaland.

The company's defeat in Katanga may be attributed to the illness of Thomson, the energy of Leopold, or a variety of other causes. But throughout the whole of the campaign, Rhodes was on the periphery. He did not manifest the drive which characterized his actions in Mashonaland, and he became increasingly

53. Johnston to Salisbury, August 25, 1890, File E, Salisbury Papers, Christ Church, Oxford.
54. Rhodes to Thomson, July ——, 1891, quoted in J. B. Thomson, *Joseph Thomson*, p. 269.
55. Minute, "Katanga," Sir Percy Anderson, May 27, 1891, F.O. 84/2166, P.R.O.
56. Salisbury to the queen, April ——, 1891, CAB 41/22/5, P.R.O.

out of touch with the policies being pursued by the London board. While Rhodes was still fighting the battle of concessions, his board had already decided to make peace. George Cawston as the company's principal negotiator, was actively involved in negotiations by which the company would participate in the management of the Katanga Company which Leopold had licensed to exploit the Katanga mineral deposits.[57]

Though Rhodes professed to be as dedicated an expansionist north of the Zambezi as south of the river, his actions demonstrated that his focus was on Matabeleland and Mashonaland. In the territories beyond, his vision became somewhat blurred. He never identified himself with Nyasaland or with Katanga as he did with the land that became known as Rhodesia.

Analysis of origins of ideas frequently leads to the not surprising conclusion that they have more than one source. So it was with the "Grand Scheme" developed in the spring of 1889. But the power for their execution was supplied primarily by Rhodes. When he appropriated the ideas of others and made them his own, he gave these ideas a vitality which they would not otherwise have achieved. Cawston thought of a plan for a great chartered South African Company but such a company under Cawston would have borne little resemblance to that dominated by Rhodes. Harry Johnston had great energy and imagination, but he could not translate his ideas into reality. Rhodes did not create the British South Africa Company, but he molded it with his energy and his resources into a mechanism for the realization of his ambitions. His associates in the formation of the company, Gifford and Cawston, were businessmen with business ends. Rhode's objective far transcended theirs; how far, the world was made aware when Jameson invaded the Transvaal.

57. London to Cape office, BSAC, May 28, 1891, LO 3/1/3, N.A.R.

4
The Charter

AFTER THE UNION OF THE LONDON CAPITALISTS WITH
Rhodes, the positions of the parties involved in the future of
Matabeleland and Mashonaland underwent a considerable
change. The London interests adopted Rhodes's imperialism as
their own, abandoning their earlier, more modest ambitions.
Salisbury and the imperial cabinet blessed the undertaking,
with the reservation that it must not embarrass "high policy."
The colonial secretary who had expressed concern that Lobengula not give away his "whole herd" now favored a great chartered company which would promote civilization, inculcate
good work habits, and protect the Africans against Portuguese
aggression. No matter that Lobengula now apparently repudiated the Rudd concession. Lobengula's power to grant such
rights in any case had been doubtful; Edward Fairfield's assertions had gone uncontested that the Ndebele relationship to
the Shona was that of occasional raiders rather than that of
rulers, and that the concession would probably be invalidated
by any impartial tribunal.[1]

The company's promoters sought to prevent such a test by
buying up possible litigants and by pressing for speedy action
on a charter, and the government for its own purposes cooperated with them. An appeal by Lobengula to the imperial government that he had been defrauded now evoked no response.
His letter of April 25, 1889, was referred to Rhodes, who in turn
asked Maguire for comment. Maguire pronounced the docu-

---

1. Note by Fairfield, January 13, 1890, on Bowler to Knutsford, December 20, 1889, C.O. 417/40, P.R.O.

ment to be the work of conniving whites in Matabeleland. Lobengula must have been deluded by these malcontents, Maguire asserted, for he continued to accept the payment of £100 a month and had finally accepted the rifles as well.[2] This explanation, Rhodes suggested to the Colonial Office, should be conclusive, since Maguire had recently returned from Lobengula's kraal and his unimpeachable character was well known to the Colonial Office.[3] A reply to Lobengula was delayed until after the charter was granted, and he was then in essence advised to accept his fate.

The limits which the government sought to establish for the prospective chartered company had little to do with the rights of an African chief. The Lobengula who mattered was largely an artificial creation whose power was assumed to be unquestioned in the gold regions of the Mazoe Valley and other areas south of the Zambezi claimed by the Portuguese. This invention was essential to undergird the British claim to a sphere of influence as against Portugal, and the Rudd concession was the basis on which a great chartered company would develop this sphere at no expense to the British taxpayer. Lord Knutsford wrote the queen's secretary: "I am confident that a strongly constituted Company will give us the best chance of peaceably opening up and developing the resources of this country south of the Zambezi, and will be most beneficial to the native Chiefs and people. Such a Company has been formed, and all the capital subscribed without going to the public."[4]

In the eyes of Salisbury and the Foreign Office the plans of the promoters also offered a great opportunity to advance gov-

---

2. Maguire to Rhodes, June 21, 1889, encl. in Rhodes to Herbert, June 21, 1889, C.O. 417/38, P.R.O. Printed for Parliament, C. 5918, 1890. Maguire's statement that Lobengula had accepted the rifles was untrue. They were held under guard in various places, the king refusing to accept them, since "the guns do not belong to me." Finally in 1892 the king apparently accepted them. Colenbrander to Rhodes, December 11, 1891. Colenbrander to Harris, December 30, 1892. Both in CT 1/13/3; Diary of "Matabele" Wilson (typescript) WI 6/2/1, all in N.A.R.
3. Rhodes to Herbert, June 21, 1889, in ibid. As Oscar Wilde put it, "Untruthful! My nephew Algernon? Impossible! He is an Oxonian."
4. Knutsford to Ponsonby, July 11, 1889, in George E. Buckle, ed., The Letters of Queen Victoria, 1:512.

ernmental objectives. Salisbury prided himself on being a practical man; he was as much opposed as any Little Englander to
the addition of square miles to the British Empire merely for
the psychic pleasure it would bring to the imperially minded.
African land had no fascination for him; he was not captivated
by the sources of the Nile or by tales of legendary wealth. But
there were British interests in Africa he considered important
enough to justify governmental protection. The Zambezi and
its tributaries might become an important waterway of commerce if a way could be found through the bars which blocked
passage from the sea—the limitations of the river itself had not
yet been demonstrated—and he considered it essential that this
river system be recognized as an international waterway. Portuguese determination to thwart free passage was highly irritating
to him. Likewise, Portuguese claims to sovereignty over the
Shiré highlands presented him with a serious domestic problem.
Lake Nyasa and the Shiré area was the country of David Livingstone; the labors of British missionary societies were carrying
out Livingstone's injunction to spread Christianity and uproot
slavery. If Catholic Portugal, reputed to be benighted in its
attitudes toward slavery and the slave trade, were allowed to intrude into this British preserve there would be a storm of indignation, particularly in Scotland, which would threaten the
position of any government that was a party to an agreement on
these terms. Salisbury had no intention of making such a concession. In 1888 he was willing to settle for an understanding that
the Nyasa area would be neutralized, lying outside the British
or Portuguese sphere, but the probes of Portuguese expeditions
made him less inclined to be flexible. Salisbury also wished to
keep the Transvaal in a state of de facto dependency and supported the blocking of the republic in its ambitions to expand.
The plans of Rhodes and his colleagues served all these objects.
They would accept the expense and take the risks, and the imperial government need not be directly involved beyond providing its blessing to the company and recognition of its sphere of
operations.[5]

    Lord Salisbury's concern about the prospective charter did
not relate to Africans. The records of Foreign Office correspon-

5. See notes on C.O. to F.O., July 19, 1888, F.O. 84/1924, P.R.O.

dence with spokesmen for the company contain much with regard to the claims of Germany and Portugal but little with
regard to the rights of the inhabitants. Salisbury knew nothing
of the Yao or the Lozi, the Shona or the Ndebele; his preoccupation was with Germany, and with Portugal to the extent that it
related to Germany. In mid–1889 he saw a brief period of European calm coming to an end. The Near East was again sim-
mering, with disturbances in Crete and Serbia and the prospect
of a revolution in Rumania, and France was again being difficult
over Egypt. Under these conditions good relations with Germany were of paramount importance.[6] Accordingly, it was
essential that the proposed company's area of operations be
defined to avoid the prospect of a collision with German claims
in East and South West Africa. No such considerations of power
deterred him in responding to Portuguese pretensions. This
decadent, nearly bankrupt state seemed to have no energy for
any purpose beyond the assertion of vast claims based largely
on a vanished era. Salisbury had little doubt that this flimsy
empire was on the verge of collapse, and he viewed the prospect
with equanimity provided, again, that there were minimal repercussions in European diplomacy. He did not desire to push
over the tottering House of Braganza, but neither was he prepared to pay a high price to prop it up.[7]

Salisbury's position with regard to Portugal encouraged
Rhodes in his inclination to summary action, since the prime
minister's words were sometimes subject to the interpretation
that he would not restrain the company provided its actions
were not too glaringly aggressive. Salisbury was not in fact prepared to adopt such a laissez-faire line, but his subsequent restraints were to an extent made necessary by his own stimulus to
a man who needed little encouragement.

The Salisbury government sought to use the chartered company as an instrument of imperial policy. The proposal of the
chartered company backers in April 1889 to join forces with
the Lakes Company[8] was in part motivated by discussions with

6. Salisbury to Malet, private, June 12, 1889, F.O. 343/3, P.R.O.
7. See, for example, P. Currie to Grey, July 26, 1889, Grey Papers, File
184/6, Durham.
8. Cawston to Ewing, April 18, 1889, BSAC Misc. I, Rhodes House.

government officials on the ramifications of extension beyond
the Zambezi in terms of Anglo-Portuguese relations. The Lakes
Company was too weak to be effective. A powerful chartered
company could provide stability.

This consideration was emphatically in evidence in the Colonial Office's reaction to Gifford's application for a charter to
"develop the Bechuanaland Protectorate and the countries to
the north." The original application had been made in January,[9] before the decision to seek cooperation with Rhodes, and
an answer had been deferred pending an opinion from Robinson. The high commissioner predictably had been negative. The
Bechuanaland Exploration Company possessed only a mineral
concession from Kgama due to expire at the end of the year; the
Exploring Company had no grant at all from Lobengula and
only an as yet unapproved application for a railway concession
in Bechuanaland. Robinson was certain that both Kgama and
Lobengula were disinclined to part with any of their sovereign
rights and indicated that to grant a charter at this time would
be dangerous.[10] After Rhodes came to an understanding with
Gifford and Cawston, this concern about alienating Kgama and
Lobengula no longer seemed so compelling. Knutsford un-
reservedly endorsed the charter. In terms similar to those used
by this predecessors in approving charters for the North Borneo,
East Africa, and Niger Companies, he argued that such a course
would subject the company to much more effective control by
the government than if they were merely to incorporate themselves under the joint stock company acts in order to carry on
their commercial operations. More positively, the company
would assume responsibilities and expense currently shouldered
by the government. Every year Parliament was asked to vote
large sums for the administration of the Bechuanaland Protectorate, most of which were absorbed by the semi-military
force, the Bechuanaland Border Police. Each year demands
were made for police and for telegraph construction on the
justification that it was necessary to maintain the peace. For
all these expenditures there was little return. Bechuanaland was

9. Gifford to C.O., January 3, 1889, C.O. 879/30/372, P.R.O.
10. Robinson to Knutsford, confidential, February 6, 1889, in *ibid.*

a wasteland with no known resources to justify the expense, of significance not for itself but because it controlled the route to the north. The sooner the government could shift this burden to a private company the better. Furthermore, Knutsford suggested, it might be in the public interest to require the company to include in its sphere those territories north of the Zambezi which lay between that river and Lake Nyasa in order to secure communications to the missionary settlements and thus to protect them more effectively.[11]

These bright hopes were soon dimmed. Rhodes explained that the company would not immediately be prepared to assume responsibility for the Bechuanaland Protectorate. The justification for deferral was that an immediate transfer would bring down upon the company the wrath of John Mackenzie and his numerous and influential following who had been fighting for the retention of both British Bechuanaland and the protectorate under imperial control. They had opposed transfer to Cape Colony, and they would certainly resist shifting administration of the protectorate to a company whose most powerful director was Mackenzie's old antagonist, Cecil Rhodes.[12]

For this and other reasons, the language defining the company's field of operations had to be somewhat imprecise. Salisbury believed it impolitic in the first instance to specify that the company's field of operations extended north of the Zambezi, since such a public declaration would be interpreted by Portugal as an arbitrary act and might jeopardize a settlement with the Portuguese which he continued to hope might be effectuated. The extension northward could be granted at the appropriate time by a simple license.[13] This restriction the company's promoters sought to soften, and they were supported by Salisbury's principal adviser on African affairs, Sir Percy Anderson, who argued that in view of the continuing obduracy of Portugal, it might be desirable to define the area of operations as being

11. C.O. to F.O., May 16, 1889, F.O. 84/1995, P.R.O.
12. Note by Herbert, n.d., on F.O. to C.O., July 5, 1889, C.O. 417/36, P.R.O.
13. Note by Salisbury, on *ibid.*; F.O. to C.O., May 27, 1889, F.O. 84/1996, P.R.O.

east and west of the Portuguese possessions, east of German South West Africa, and south of the Congo Free State, thus leaving the company the opportunity to push its claims to the maximum degree.[14] Anderson's recommendation essentially was accepted. The language adopted in the charter provided that the company's "principal sphere of operations" was north of British Bechuanaland, north and west of the South African Republic, and to the west of the Portuguese possessions; no northern limits were assigned. The only specific restriction was the exclusion of the Tati district, where a mining company held a concession from Lobengula antedating that to Rudd.[15] Rhodes added to the government's satisfaction by offering to construct at his own expense a telegraph from the Cape through the Bechuanaland Protectorate. He also asked for the appointment of a British resident in Matabeleland, for which he would pay the full cost.[16] Sir Robert Herbert, the permanent undersecretary, whose opinions normally carried weight, commented that "those who pay the piper set the tune," and that the independence of the imperial representative might be compromised if his salary and expenses came from a company.[17] His objections were brushed aside. Also ignored was the fact that Lobengula had not asked for a resident. The idea of providing such an official had been put forward by Robinson in December 1888 when he inquired of Moffat whether he would accept such an appointment provided that Lobengula could be induced to give his consent.[18] Acting on Robinson's advice, the Colonial Office in March 1889 had suggested that a representative of the queen would be useful in protecting Lobengula's interests. A long silence had followed; at Rhodes's insistence the Colonial Office again pressed Lobengula for a reply. In August he sent his answer: "With regard to Her Majesty's offer to send me an envoy or resident, I

14. Note by Anderson, n.d., on C.O. to F.O., June 28, 1889, F.O. 84/1998, P.R.O.
15. L. H. Gann, *A History of Southern Rhodesia: Early Days to 1934*, p. 82.
16. Rhodes to Knutsford, June 1, 1889, F.O. 84/1996, P.R.O.
17. Note by Herbert, June 10, 1889, on F.O. to C.O., June 7, 1889, C.O. 417/36, P.R.O.
18. Shippard to Moffat, private, December 29, 1888, MO 1/1/4, N.A.R.

thank Her Majesty, but I do not need an officer to be sent. I will ask for one when I am pressed for one."[19]

Lobengula's attitudes, however, were not of great moment in Whitehall and Downing Street in the summer of 1889. The negotiations with regard to the future of his territory related to the affairs of white men, not black. One concern of the cabinet was the personnel of the board of the proposed company. In the original draft of the charter, provision had been made that two thirds of the directors must be British subjects. At the suggestion of Knutsford, this stipulation was changed to require that all directors must be British subjects except any person named in the charter as a director. In this way Alfred Beit, a German national, was able to take his seat.[20] But beyond nationality there was a question of "quality" in the managing board. The founders of the company were respectable. Rhodes had rehabilitated himself in the eyes of Salisbury. He was no longer a pro-Boer colonial, but a proven imperialist. At the Colonial Office Rhodes was in high favor. Even the cynical Edward Fairfield had become a convert, and now spoke of him as a "man of prudence"![21] Joseph Chamberlain who in March had been an opponent,[22] and had said that he knew only three things about Rhodes, all bad,[23] had been strangely silent in the ensuing months[24]—he would in time become a backer of the company. But Rhodes was not a pillar of British society. Gifford and Cawston were reputable men of business. What was lacking was participation on the board of men of character and social standing who would represent the public interest. As an intermediary in the search for distinguished names, the promoters utilized the services of Sir Charles Euan Smith, consul general of Zanzibar,

19. J. L. Rademeyer, *Die Land Noord van die Limpopo in die Ekspansie Beleid van die Suid-Afrikaanse Republiek*, p. 98.

20. C.O. to F.O., August 15, 1889, C.O. 417/38, P.R.O.

21. Note by Fairfield, August 23, 1889, on Sanderson to C.O., August 21, 1889, C.O. 417/36, P.R.O.

22. *Parliamentary Debates*, March 11, 1889, CCCXXXIII, 140.

23. "(1) he has made an enormous fortune very rapidly, (2) he is an Africander (i.e. not an Imperialist), (3) he gave £10,000 to Parnell," Basil Williams, *Cecil Rhodes*, p. 136.

24. The Fourth Earl Grey asserted that he had reassured Chamberlain that Rhodes was a "single-minded patriot." Interview, Basil Williams with Grey, July 7, 1914, Rhodes Papers s. 134, Rhodes House.

who had entree to court circles and social acquaintances with prominent people. At his behest they invited two well-known shipping magnates to join the board—Sir William Mackinnon and Sir Donald Currie.[25] Mackinnon's imperial mindedness had been amply demonstrated—he was founder-president of the Imperial British East Africa Company. Currie was well known as a gadfly for expansion in South Africa and he now advocated a great company on the model of the East India Company which would represent Britain in central Africa.[26] Both, however, declined. Lord Balfour of Burleigh was invited to be chairman of the board,[27] with the opportunity to select other board members.[28] Balfour was inclined to accept the appointment, but finally withdrew because of a possible conflict of interest with his position in the ministry.[29] The involvement of three such strong personalities with commitments in Africa might have made the London board an effective policy making body. But, on their refusal, the promoters at Euan Smith's suggestion invited the Duke of Abercorn and the Duke of Fife to be chairman and vice-chairman respectively. Their acceptance gave the chartered company the prestige of their names but little of their energy. Neither Abercorn nor Fife had any taste for the drudgery of reading reports and overseeing company administration. Fife had very little experience in business. Neither of them had previously displayed an interest in Africa. Before their appointment they probably knew as little of Matabeleland as did Euan Smith, who thought it fronted on the Indian Ocean.[30] After

25. Euan Smith to Salisbury, June 15, 1889, File A/79, Salisbury Papers, Christ Church, Oxford.
26. Currie to Salisbury, confidential, May 28, 1889, F.O. 84/1996, P.R.O.
27. The biographer of the Earl of Carnarvon asserts that Carnarvon was asked to be chairman of the board but declined. I have found no record of such an offer, which may have been before or after that to Balfour. Arthur Hardinge, *The Life of Henry Howard Molyneaux Herbert, Fourth Earl of Carnarvon, 1831–1890*, 3 vols. (London, 1925), 3:295.
28. Balfour to Salisbury, May 24, 1889, File E, Salisbury Papers, Christ Church, Oxford.
29. Euan Smith to Salisbury, June 15, 1889, File A/79, *ibid.*
30. Euan Smith to Salisbury, February 1, 1889, encl. in F.O. to C.O., February 27, 1889, C.O. 417/36, P.R.O. Fairfield commented that "Col. Euan Smith's ideas of the situation in Matabeleland are about

their appointment they knew little more. Abercorn spent much more of his time and thought on his estates in Ireland and Scotland than on the company's affairs. Fife had been selected in large part because he was the husband of the Prince of Wales's eldest daughter. Each, had he been so disposed, could have made contributions. Abercorn, fifty years of age at the time of his appointment, was a prominent member of the Conservative party and a close friend of Salisbury's. Fife, about the same age, was a wealthy man who had augmented his fortune as partner in the London banking firm of Sir Samuel Scott and Company, and was an influential member of the Liberal party.[31] By their failure to perform their functions as "public representatives," however, they became accessories to the subsequent actions of Rhodes.

During the six years he held office before the Jameson Raid, Abercorn showed no uneasiness about the activities of the Company's South African representatives. His only recorded outburst of annoyance was when Maguire, Rhodes's alternate on the board, became a Home Rule candidate in the duke's own county of Donegal. Abercorn was "greatly shaken" in his opinion of Rhodes for sanctioning such an affront.[32] Abercorn also mildly protested Rhodes's assumption of the Cape prime ministership in June 1890, though not to the extent of forcing him to make a choice between the two roles which the duke rightly considered incompatible.[33] If interest can be measured by the emphasis in communication, Abercorn's stake in the company was emphatically economic. The £1200 per year he received as chairman was not significant to a man of his wealth, but he also bought large quantities of shares at par which he was able to convert into substantial returns as the prices of shares rose. In 1895, for example, Cawston sold 4500 shares for Abercorn at over sixty shillings each, and he made numerous other transactions on Abercorn's behalf.[34] Abercorn was not alone; other

---

as accurate as Shakespeare's ideas about the Island of Bohemia." Note by Fairfield, February 28, 1889, on *ibid.*
31. *South Africa*, March 14, 1891.
32. Telegram, Cawston to Rhodes, June 16, 1890; Abercorn to Cawston, June 14, 1890, both in BSAC II Misc., Rhodes House.
33. Abercorn to Cawston, July 19, 1890, in *ibid.*
34. This correspondence is contained in BSAC Misc. V, Rhodes

members of the board were also deeply interested in the prices of shares and also avidly watched the stock exchange. But he and Fife can be specially indicted for somnolence in their functions as representatives of the public interest.

The third "public" member was Albert Grey, the future fourth Earl. Unlike the other two, Grey took his responsibilities seriously. He had long been interested in South Africa, in large part from his close association with the third Earl, who had been an outstanding colonial secretary and continued thereafter to think and write about colonial affairs. Albert was a member of the South African Committee and a supporter of John Mackenzie's advocacy of a more active imperial policy.[35] His inclusion on the board was consequently useful in reassuring the supporters of Mackenzie that the chartered company would not be controlled from the Cape. Grey was conscientious, and he was honest. Unfortunately he was also weak. Jameson described him as "a nice old lady, but not a genius, who does not like committing himself to any opinion."[36] The characterization was unduly harsh, but Grey was highly susceptible to the spell of Rhodes, and he became a votary. His well-known integrity thus became an immense asset to Rhodes without any corresponding obligation on Rhodes's part to adhere to Grey's standards.[37]

Of the three public members of the board, then, two devoted little time and effort to the affairs of the company and the third was converted to the religion of Rhodes. They consequently were worse than useless, for they gave a sheen of respectability to the operations of a company over which they exercised no control. Also named to the board in the original charter were Gifford, Rhodes, Beit, and Cawston. At the suggestion of Fife,

---

House. On March 28, 1895, Abercorn acknowledged Cawston's sale of 4,500 shares and authorized him to sell another 2,000 at 65 shillings. In November 1894 he had sold 150 shares at between 45 and 50 shillings.
35. W. D. Mackenzie, *John Mackenzie, South African Missionary and Statesman*, p. 435.
36. George H. Tanser, *A Scantling of Time*, p. 128.
37. J. G. Lockhart and C. M. Woodhouse, *Cecil Rhodes*, p. 165. See also Graham Sims, "Paladin of Empire, Earl Grey and Rhodesia," Local Series Pamphlet No. 26, Central Africa Historical Association (Salisbury; 1970).

the board subsequently added his banking partner, Horace P. Farquhar, a close friend of the Prince of Wales. Farquhar, "an aristocrat whom strong commercial abilities and a capacity to make money turned into a business man,"[38] added to the luster which gave the board respectability to match the company's financial power. His sense of responsibility to the chartered company was even less than that of his colleagues. Rothschild's offered him a directorship on their exploration company in the expectation that through him they would receive favorable treatment in mining claims in Matabeleland and Mashonaland. Cawston, who was also invited to accept a directorship, declined on the basis that he would be compromising himself, and Alfred Beit endorsed Cawston's position. But Farquhar unhesitatingly and apparently without embarrassment accepted.[39] Farquhar's business ethics belied his public reputation, and his presence on the board did not enhance its moral tone.[40]

With the formation of such a prestigious board there was only one remaining obstacle to the grant of a royal charter. The amalgamators had assumed that they had bought off all rivals who had even a shadow of a claim to gold-mining rights in Matabeleland and Mashonaland. Moore, the Austral Africa Company, Wood, Francis, and Chapman, and others had been satisfied by receiving shares, the right to peg claims, and other inducements. But in mid-summer four new claimants appeared. Sir John Swinburne, M.P., sought to postpone a decision until the next session of Parliament.[41] Swinburne had done nothing with the concession he had acquired almost twenty years before in the Tati district, but he now protested that the Rudd concession infringed on his rights. He indicated his opposition could be removed and his support assured for a payment of £20,000.

---

38. Paul H. Emden, *Money Powers of Europe in the Nineteenth and Twentieth Centuries*, p. 338.

39. Cawston to Rhodes, November 6, 1889, BSAC I Misc., Rhodes House.

40. Farquhar was later involved in a scandal with regard to misuse of Conservative party funds which were in his custody as treasurer. He died an undisclosed bankrupt. Lord Beaverbrook, *The Decline and Fall of Lloyd George* (London, 1963), pp. 203–204.

41. *Parliamentary Debates*, August 24, 1889, 3rd Series, CCCXL; 376.

Since delay was dangerous, Swinburne's opposition was serious. Alfred Beit settled with him for £10,000.[42] The second objector, the Tati Company, had been working its claims in the district between the Shashi and Ramaquabane rivers since 1880, and its rights were safeguarded by the specific exclusion of the Tati district from the jurisdiction of the British South Africa Company. The other two protestors sought to capitalize on the doubtful validity of the Rudd concession; their claims probably would not survive in a court of law, but in the process of exposing them, the Rudd concession itself might be called into question. They calculated that their potentiality for embarrassment was worth a considerable amount of money. One, the Matabeleland Company formed by the Ochs brothers, wealthy diamond merchants, had acquired the successorship to the verbal concession to Baines. They argued that their alleged rights were worth one-tenth interest in the chartered company, 25,000 shares. This was "madness,"[43] wrote the chartered company's solicitor. But the Matabeleland Company after much haggling and litigation, finally acquired shares worth over £30,000.[44] The Ochs brothers were unsuccessful, however, in their efforts to have one of their nominees appointed to the board. Rhodes indignantly declared, "Blackmail is quite bad enough without having some low cad or his acquaintances on the board. The whole crowd are low specimens of the Jewish race and the less we have to do with them the better."[45]

The other contest came from a syndicate that included several of the subscribers to the Northern Gold Fields Pioneer Syndicate which had sold its rights in Bechuanaland to the Bechuanaland Exploration Company. These speculators, headed by Edouard and William Lippert, developed a plan to capitalize on doubts about Lobengula's jurisdiction over the Shona. They sent an expedition under Frederick Selous to proceed from Quelimane in Portuguese East Africa up the Zambezi to Ma-

42. Cawston to Rhodes, September 18, 1889, BSAC I Misc., Rhodes House.
43. Hawksley to Cawston, September 13, 1889, in *ibid.*
44. *Financial News*, August 11, 1893.
45. Rhodes to Cawston, October 15, 1889, BSAC I Misc., Rhodes House.

shonaland.[46] Selous accomplished his mission, though in the process he demonstrated the impracticability of the Zambezi route.[47] He acquired a document which he asserted was a concession from an independent Shona chief. Edouard Lippert offered to sell this agreement to the British South Africa Company for an appropriate price. He also asked compensation in terms of an alleged agreement between the Rudd mission and his agent E. R. Renny-Tailyour by which Lippert would receive a share in the fruits if Renny-Tailyour cooperated with them. Renny-Tailyour had not been helpful. On the contrary he had done all he could to thwart Rudd and had cooperated with Maund in attempting to discredit the Rudd concession. But Lippert was not a man to discard a claim, however dubious. He calculated that the value of his assets to the British South Africa Company was 20,000 shares.[48]

The issue with Lippert had not been settled when the charter was granted in October 1889. But Selous's alleged Mazoe concession caused worry both to the company's board and to the imperial government, particularly because Lippert threatened to sell his rights in Germany if he did not get satisfaction. If the German government recognized the claim, warned Sir Robert Herbert, the British Foreign Office might not be able effectively to resist such a decision.[49] The chartered company decided to buy the concession, though a dispute over the terms continued to cause mutual ill will.

These problems with concession mongers reflected the weakness of the Rudd concession. The promoters could not afford to have it challenged, particularly before the grant of a royal charter. Consequently they bought off all contenders who might be obnoxious, however flimsy their claims. In the process they added to the already mountainous paper capital of the chartered company. The issuance of the charter gave the appearance of validity to the Rudd concession, particularly because the

46. Selous to Johnson, June 18, 1889, JO 3/1/1, N.A.R.
47. Selous to Johnson, July 18, 1889, in *ibid.*
48. *Cape Times*, September 2, 1890.
49. Herbert to Cawston, March 22, 1890, BSAC II Misc., Rhodes House.

promoters gave the government the impression that the British South Africa Company possessed the concession, when in fact it was owned by the Central Search Association which leased the rights to the chartered company in exchange for an equal division of the profits.

The imperial government and its South African officials had backed the promoters by rejecting Lobengula's protests. They had ignored his plea of April 23, 1889, that he had been defrauded. A subsequent letter from Lobengula dated August 10, was mysteriously delayed in transit and was not dispatched from Cape Town until October 25, too late to interfere with the issuance of the charter.[50] General H. A. Smyth, acting as high commissioner in the period between Robinson's departure and the arrival of his successor, recommended that Lobengula be informed that it was "prejudicial to the interests of the Natives and the prospects of peace" if the issue were to be reopened,[51] and Knutsford now informed Lobengula that it was in the interest of his people to concede a mining monopoly to a responsible body of white men, and that the queen approved of the Rudd concession. Further, Knutsford wrote, the queen understood Lobengula's aversion to deciding disputes among white men and recommended that he assign jurisdiction to the British South Africa Company. Finally, Knutsford announced that the imperial government would send John S. Moffat as a resident to watch over African interests. Moffat would from time to time "convey the Queen's words to the Chief and the Chief should always listen to and believe Moffat's words."[52] This dramatic shift in Knutsford's position may have been influenced by the advice of his permanent undersecretary, Sir Robert Herbert. In the months since the amalgamation of the major interests, Herbert had become an enthusiastic advocate of the charter. So helpful was Herbert indeed, that the promoters singled him out for special recognition in their appreciation for governmental cooperation in the swift approval of the charter. When a coat of arms was being devised for the company, they suggested

50. J. E. S. Green, *Rhodes Goes North*, p. 127.
51. Smyth to Knutsford, October 28, 1889, F.O. 84/2007, P.R.O.
52. Knutsford to Lobengula, November 15, 1889, in *ibid.*

that somewhere within the shield there be "some small emblem" representing Herbert's own crest or coat of arms.[53]

The "Queen's message" perfectly met the specifications of the chartered company. Its importance was dramatized by its mode of delivery. At Herbert's suggestion,[54] the letter was conveyed by a military mission of two imperial officers in full dress uniform complete with plumed helmets and glistening breastplates. They arrived at Bulawayo in a gaudily painted four-wheeled coach adorned with the royal monogram and drawn by eight mules—horses were not considered practical because of the horse sickness endemic to the region. The final touch was provided by Dr. Jameson, who pronounced the royal letter to be "unintelligible rubbish" and rewrote it; the Jameson version was interpreted to Lobengula with "excellent results."[55]

Lobengula was bewildered by the dramatic change in the queen's counsel. He later told Colenbrander that "the Queen speaks with two tongues."[56] But the impressive mission and the royal letter did not change his position that he had been deceived and that the Rudd concession was invalid. His appeals to the queen, however, were unavailing. Whitehall had decided to back the chartered company.

This decision in effect delivered the Ndebele and the Shona into the hands of the British South Africa Company. The actions of the government made it evident that the restrictive language of the company's charter had little force. The charter contained several clauses expressing benevolent intentions with regard to Africans. The company was enjoined to use its best efforts toward abolishing the slave trade and domestic servitude; it was required to regulate the liquor traffic; and all disputes between the company and any chief were subject, if the secretary of state should require, to final decision by his office.[57] During the critical early years the secretary of state did not so require.

Other provisions were much like those governing other char-

53. Cawston to Wyon, January 17, 1890, BSAC I Misc., Rhodes House.
54. Cawston to Rhodes, November 6, 1889, in *ibid.*
55. Green, *Rhodes Goes North*, p. 134.
56. Colenbrander's diary, December 10, 1890, CO 4/3/2, N.A.R.
57. The provisions of the charter are reproduced in John H. Harris, *The Chartered Millions*, pp. 301–312.

tered companies. The charter conferred no powers of government; such authority had to be derived from treaties with African chiefs, and the privileges granted to the company were subject to review after twenty-five years and every ten years thereafter.[58]

The language of the charter, in short, bore little relationship to the intentions of Rhodes and his associates, and its regulatory language counted for little without governmental commitment which was not in evidence before the Jameson Raid. The great significance of the charter was in its legitimization of the acts of a company which, so far as its relationships with African peoples were concerned, was virtually unrestrained.

The British South Africa Company had one distinctive attribute which set it apart from other chartered companies in Africa. It was not formed to engage in trade, mining, agriculture, or other productive occupations. What rights it possessed either directly or from United Concessions were intended to be the basis for concessions to others rather than for direct activity of its own. Its profits would derive from the work of subcontractors. The company, in short, was a giant concessionaire. But to make the country attractive to developers, it was necessary for substantial capital to be invested. By the amalgamation the participants agreed to provide £700,000 as initial capital of which £500,000 would be for railway construction and £200,000 for preliminary development of the country. In addition Rhodes agreed to provide from his own funds £30,000 for a telegraph and £4,000 for the salary and expenses of a British resident in Matabeleland. The money came from the following sources:[59]

	Railway	Development
Gold Fields of South Africa	£170,834	£68,334
Rhodes, Rudd, Beit, and various minor interests in South Africa	204,166	81,666
Exploring Company, Bechuanaland Exploration Company, Southern Land Company, and other smaller interests	125,000	50,000

58. *Ibid.*
59. Cawston to C.O., July 1, 1889, C.O. 879/30/372, P.R.O.

The bulk of the capital thus was provided by Rhodes and his associates, and with money went power. In addition to his membership with Beit on the London board, Rhodes was made chairman of the local board in South Africa and managing director with plenary powers. He interpreted his authority liberally and the complaisant London directors gave him full scope so long as he appeared to be successful.

The techniques employed by the company in protecting itself against attacks from Parliament and press bore the unmistakable stamp of Rhodes. No opportunity to secure influence was left untried. Through Euan Smith, Rhodes offered Salisbury's son Lord Robert Cecil the position of standing counsel for the company. Salisbury commented that "Rhodes' magnificence rather alarms me,"[60] but Cecil nevertheless accepted the position.[61] Such an approach was more delicate than that used with lesser men. As competitors had been silenced by golden arguments, so did Rhodes hope to quiet opposition from the press and from the Parliament. J. Scott Keltie, the well-known *Times* correspondent, was employed by the company to write articles favorable to the company in the guise of being an objective reporter.[62] John Verschoyle likewise continued to be a paid editorialist, though on occasion he complained that his remuneration was inadequate, and indicated that his "loyalty" had a price. He once threatened to expose the company if he did not receive £4000.[63] But he generally performed his function quietly and efficiently, even to the extent of editing out passages inconvenient to the company in an article submitted to the *Fortnightly Review* by Selous.[64] Flora Shaw, the colonial correspondent of the *Times*, was from the beginning an ardent advocate of the

60. Note by Salisbury, n.d., on McDonnell to Salisbury, July 10, 1889, Salisbury Papers, Christ Church, Oxford.
61. Cawston to Rhodes, November 6, 1889, BSAC I Misc., Rhodes House.
62. Keltie to [Cawston?], August 8, 1889, in *ibid.*
63. Verschoyle to Cawston, private, n.d. [December 1889?], in *ibid.* Verschoyle later withdrew his threat, which he said had been uttered in heat.
64. Verschoyle to Cawston [January 1890]; same to same, January 12, 1890, BSAC I Misc., Rhodes House.

company,[65] though her advocacy was probably idealistic rather than venal. Perhaps Rhodes himself had not yet captivated her to the degree she made manifest in later years,[66] but clearly she was already an unreserved supporter of his avowed objectives. The company early in 1890 acquired another powerful ally in Sir Charles Dilke, whose belief in the company as an agency of Greater Britain was reinforced by more material considerations. Rhodes, through Sir Charles Mills, the Cape's agent general, suggested that Dilke should apply for shares in the British South Africa Company, and Dilke after brief consideration bought at par 1,000 fully paid shares and 2,000 shares on which three shillings were paid.[67] His involvement was particularly useful to the company because he was a frequent correspondent on foreign and imperial affairs in the *Fortnightly Review*.[68]

Shares in the company were sold at par to many politicians and other influential leaders as a means of providing support for the company. Mills, the intermediary with Dilke, bought 200 for himself and smaller amounts for himself and relatives.[69] Precisely how many shares were distributed in these terms cannot be determined, but there is enough evidence to make it clear that the number was substantial. By April 1890 Rhodes had distributed most of the 34,000 shares allotted to him for influential people in Cape Colony[70] and he requested and received several thousand more during the course of the year. One special allotment was made to Barney Barnato who as a life governor of De Beers with substantial share holdings could be a factor in the diamond company's availability as a source of funds for the chartered company. Barnato insisted on being given a substantial block of chartered shares as the price of his support, and Rhodes gave him 10,000 shares, with the rights to purchase additional shares at par. He availed himself of the option by subscribing to 20,000 partly paid shares.[71]

65. Shaw to Cawston, January 30, 1890, BSAC II Misc., Rhodes House.
66. Margery Perham, *Lugard, The Years of Adventure, 1858–1898*, p. 570.
67. Dilke to Cawston, January 25, 1890, BSAC I Misc., Rhodes House.
68. Verschoyle to Cawston [December 27, 1889?], in *ibid.*
69. Mills to Cawston, private, January 22, 1890, in *ibid.*
70. Harris to London office, April 21, 1890, LO 5/2/0, N.A.R.
71. Rhodes to Abercorn, April 21, 1890, in *ibid.*

At the beginning of December 1890 the list of shareholders in South Africa indicated 59,916 allotted in fully paid shares and 69,434 with three shillings paid.[72] Not all of these were assigned to prominent capitalists and politicians. Many were purchased by employees of the company, but the intention was the same— to create a numerous and influential lobby. The number of shares thus distributed at par in Britain cannot be calculated,[73] but Alfred Beit gave some indication of the magnitude when he testified in a court case. Beit stated that he had distributed 6,000 shares in England at the same time as Rhodes had assigned his 34,000 in Cape Colony, to "people who wanted to enter the Company at par." On being asked who they were, he replied that they were people whom "it was considered in the interests of the Company should be interested in the undertaking."[74] Additional thousands were distributed by Beit on other occasions. Among the fortunate recipients were Leopold II and his adviser, Count John d'Oultremont, who in July 1890 took a total of 3,000 shares which were held in the names of others.[75] The total number of shares granted at par to influential people outside the company was certainly well in excess of 100,000. During the next few years shares fluctuated to as high as £5; and investors at par stood to gain handsomely. The prospect of three or four hundred percent profit was a powerful inducement to favor the company.[76] Financial involvement was frequently masked by the use of surrogates who concealed the identity of the real beneficiary.

For the promoters and the directors there were additional

72. Same to same, December 8, 1890, LO 5/2/5, in *ibid.* The first issue of company shares was £250,000 of £1 shares. These were taken in the main by the promoters and the bank. Soon after, an additional 500,000 shares were issued on which three shillings were paid.
73. Reportedly the London records were destroyed by bombing in World War II.
74. The case was Matabeleland Company v. The British South Africa Company. *Truth*, January 4, 1894.
75. d'Oultremont to Cawston (September, 1890), BSAC II Misc., Rhodes House. The intermediary was Sir William Mackinnon whose Imperial British East Africa Company was interested in cooperative arrangements with the Congo Free State. Mackinnon to Cawston, July 24, 1890, BSAC II Misc., Rhodes House.
76. Chartered shares rose to £8 in September 1895. *Economist*, October 19, 1895.

benefits. Each director was entitled to an allotment of 9,000 chartered shares at par. But in addition there were profits to be made in the shares of related companies. During the frantic speculation of the 1890s, Bechuanaland Exploration shares rose to 2⅝ in 1895, the Exploring Company to 6⅞.[77] Other companies spawned by the original amalgamators also participated in the boom. The Southern Land Company, formed to acquire land rights held by the Exploring Company,[78] paid 20,100 shares plus £3,000 in cash to the Exploring Company, in which Gifford, Cawston, and Maund were the most sizeable shareholders. The Southern Land Company did not fare as spectacularly as its parents—indeed its shares dropped below par—but the price of the stock represented a profit for Gifford, Cawston, and Maund on an insignificant original investment. Many other companies with impressive paper prospects came into existence in the early years of the chartered company. By 1896 the total nominal capital of these Rhodesian enterprises was £19,833,400.[79]

The Central Search Association and its successor the United Concessions Company provided an enormous amount of paper capital to the beneficiaries of the Rudd Concession. The shares of the United Concessions Company did not sell at par. In 1892 they were valued at as low as five shillings, and rose to ten shillings the next year.[80] But even at these low valuations they provided a market value of between £1,000,000 and £2,000,000 based on an investment of 1,000 rifles and £100 per month. When the United Concessions was bought up by the chartered company at the end of 1893 under pressure from the imperial government, the £4,000,000 in shares was translated into £1,000,000 in chartered shares. At the time, chartereds were selling at a little above par, and shortly thereafter rose sharply.

The focus of attention for the directors and other insiders was consequently on the stock exchange rather than upon the operation of the chartered company and on the development of the resources of the area within the company's zone of operations.

77. *Economist*, April 27, 1895.
78. The Southern Land Company was registered in February 13, 1889, with a capital of £100,000 shares of which 100,000 were ordinary and 100 were founders. B.T. 31/14966/28250, P.R.O.
79. *South African Telegraph*, May 11, 1896.
80. *Economist*, April 29, 1893.

This emphasis on speculation rather than production contributed to maladministration and near financial ruin for the company. It also was responsible for policies in Matabeleland and Mashonaland which from any standpoint, European or African, were profligate.

5

The Invasion of Mashonaland

WHITE MEN SEIZED MASHONALAND IN 1890 BY FORCE clothed in the mantle of civilization. The use of violence by one society to acquire the possessions of another is as old as humanity. The Ndebele had established themselves as masters south of the Zambezi by their superiority in war; they felt no need to rationalize their raids on the Shona—power was the ultimate morality. What distinguished the occupation of Mashonaland and the wars that followed it was not the dispossession of the inhabitants by a superior military force. The idealistic justification of seizure in terms of humanity, progress, and civilization was not unusual; indeed such arguments had become conventional in the expansion of Europe throughout the world. There was one element which was different. The domination of African societies in Central Africa was achieved by a private company operating within restrictions imposed by royal charter and subject to a government avowedly imbued with concern for the welfare of indigenous populations.

Sir Thomas Fowell Buxton, scion of a great line of humanitarians, represented thousands of his countrymen when he tried to protect African societies against the worst effects of European domination. The Aborigines Protection Society remained a significant force. Lobengula's indunas had carried home from London two letters, one from the queen and the other from the Aborigines Protection Society. Maund's involvement of the society represented his estimate of the power of humanitarian organizations in shaping British public opinion. After the company was chartered, the board of directors were concerned that opposition from humanitarian groups might wreck their plans, and took action to convince the humanitarians of the company's benevolent intentions. An opportunity was presented by the Anti-Slavery Conference which met in Brussels in 1889–1890. The company sent George Cawston to act as its representative with instructions to "cooperate cordially" with Leopold II and others in their efforts to secure international approval of measures to suppress the slave trade.[1] At the time, the company foresaw the likelihood of war with Lobengula, and the directors, in Cawston's words, were most anxious that the company should have a good "record" on which it could draw against unfavorable reactions from the British public. Cawston, therefore, was active in advocating action not only to suppress the slave trade but to curb the traffic in spirits and in arms.[2] This devotion to good causes involved no costs to the company, and if effective could produce considerable dividends. The control of liquor was essential to ensure a hardworking, reliable labor force; and, despite oft-repeated assertions about the ineffectuality of Africans with guns, the company had no desire to equip potential antagonists with such weapons. Efforts to secure a strong resolution against the liquor traffic were not entirely successful because of the opposition of Germany,[3] but Cawston and the board nevertheless congratulated themselves on having put the company publicly on record in support of a good cause.[4]

Potential opposition from humanitarian organizations was the more formidable because they had numerous allies who, for

1. For an account of this conference, see Suzanne Miers, "The Brussels Conference of 1889–1890: The Place of the Slave Trade in the Policies of Great Britain and Germany," in *Britain and Germany in Africa*, eds. Prosser Gifford and W. Roger Louis (New Haven, 1967), pp. 83–118.
2. Cawston to Rhodes, February 6, 1890, BSAC II Misc., Rhodes House. The company was required by its charter to use its best efforts to suppress the slave trade and the sale of intoxicating liquor to Africans. See charter in John H. Harris, *The Chartered Millions*, p. 305.
3. Miers, "Brussels Conference," pp. 112–113.
4. Abercorn to Cawston, February 14, 1890, BSAC II Misc., Rhodes House.

one reason or another, were opposed to chartered companies. Henry Labouchere had little interest in Africans but his political life was devoted to excoriating the misuse of power; many other Englishmen were opposed in principle to monopolies. An aggregation of such forces could be highly dangerous to the British South Africa Company. But the advocates of protection for non-European peoples fought like soldiers who expected eventually to lose. Buxton recognized that "the darkest day for many a heathen tribe was that which first saw the white man step upon its shores,"[5] but he had little hope that he and his supporters could effectively shield such peoples. The African traveler James Johnston remarked: "Dr. Guthrie[6] hit the mark when he said in reference to British colonization: 'Not more fatal to the Canaanites the irruption of the Hebrews than our arrival in almost every colony to its native population. We have seized their lands and, in a way less honorable and even merciful than the sword of Israel, have given them in return nothing but a grave.' "[7]

Most Britons who thought about Africa in the late nineteenth century had some stirrings of conscience about the prospective fate of indigenous peoples, but most also accepted the destiny of "lesser breeds" as being fore-ordained in the nature of life. Government officials, both politicians and permanent staff, Parliament, and the press were sensitive to humanitarian appeals; honor and fair play were no mere catch words in late Victorian society. But the government was not sufficiently concerned to oversee the actions of its authorized agents; perhaps it did not desire to see too much. Reports of atrocities would produce a strong response, but the less dramatic aspects of the subjection of Africans to Europeans did not attract the attention of imperial officials thousands of miles away. Many, indeed, considered it entirely appropriate that Europeans, particularly Britons,

5. James Johnston, *Reality versus Romance in South Central Africa*, p. 261.
6. Probably Dr. Thomas Guthrie (1803–1873) a Free Church minister involved in philanthropic causes.
7. Johnston, *Reality*, pp. 260–261. Guthrie was obviously engaging in hyperbole. The African population was not sent to the grave. They increased substantially under British rule, imposing ever-greater pressure on the lands left to them by the conquerors.

should develop the unused resources of Africa and inculcate in the Africans "desirable work habits." Local imperial officers were less restrained. They had lived among Africans, and felt that they had come to appreciate, as could no Englishman at home, the point of view of white South Africans. Shippard, Newton, and Moffat, whatever their differences on the character of Africans generally, agreed that the Ndebele were like beasts of prey, and that their extermination would benefit humanity. Moffat was not an uncritical supporter of the chartered company, yet with all of the sins of its leadership, he felt it served a higher purpose. "I do not like the ways of some of the more prominent men who figure in the Chartered Company," he stated after the occupation of Mashonaland, "but the issue seems to be of God all the same." [8] Sir Henry Loch, who became governor of the Cape and high commissioner for South Africa in December 1889, came to essentially the same conclusion. Loch is usually described as a "strong man," and if by that is meant that he was self-willed the designation is certainly justified. Unlike Sir Hercules Robinson, Loch was no enthusiast for the chartered company. Loch was determined to assert the imperial presence in the chartered company's territories as in other parts of South Africa, and Rhodes's disinclination to consult sometimes brought him into conflict with the high commissioner. But Loch as much as Rhodes was a believer in the natural inequality of the races. When he came to South Africa he was sixty-two years old. As a young man he had served in India, with the Bengal Light Cavalry and with Skinner's Horse. He had subsequently observed the "decadence" of China. The Ndebele he had not observed at first hand, but he had no doubt that the reports they were bloodthirsty wretches were correct and that their chief was a tyrant. Expediency might dictate for the time being some deference to Lobengula, but he was still a savage, and the title of "king" conventionally used in addressing him was a ludicrous exaltation of his status. When Lobengula expressed displeasure that Loch had not visited him in Bulawayo and Moffat reported that he had assured the chief that no disrespect was intended, Loch sharply rebuked him. He told Shippard that

8. Moffat to ————, September 28, 1890, quoted in Robert U. Moffat, *John Smith Moffat*, p. 234.

"Moffat should be informed this is not the proper tone to assume when speaking of the High Commissioner to a native chief. Language such as this tends to inflate the arrogance of the natives and to convey a false impression of the position and power of Her Majesty."[9]

Loch's differences with Rhodes had little to do with the Ndebele, much with the issue of authority. Loch was as dedicated as had been John Mackenzie in his advocacy of imperial paramountcy in southern Africa. Like Mackenzie he was resolutely opposed to the ambitions of those Cape politicians, Rhodes included, who sought to minimize the importance of the imperial factor in South Africa. Like Mackenzie, Loch confronted the fact that the imperial government was not prepared to accept the expense which responsibility involved. As one Colonial Office official complained, "Mr. Mackenzie always puts out of sight the British taxpayer and the Treasury. The money for his schemes is not forthcoming. . . ."[10] Loch's desire for effective supervision over the chartered company encountered the same response from his superiors. The impotency of imperial regulation of the company was manifest in the appointment of a resident for Matabeleland. The initiative for the official's appointment came not from the imperial government, but from Rhodes. In exchange for the payment of £1,500 per year for himself and staff, he would be expected "to advise Lobengula and give the Company moral support so far as can be done without entailing on Her Majesty's Government any responsibility or expense."[11] The proposal in short was to give to company policy the imprimatur of imperial sanction. Officially the resident would be independent of the company and subject to instructions from superior imperial officers. The selection for the position, John Smith Moffat, had the assets of his long experience with the Ndebele, and he supported the company as the best agency for the development of Matabeleland and Mashonaland. He had reacted like a company man to the letters brought back by the indunas; and he had done all in his power to convince

9. Loch to Shippard, December 26, 1890, MO 1/1/4, N.A.R.
10. Note by John Bramston, June 15, 1889, on Mackenzie to Knutsford, June 6, 1889, C.O. 417/38, P.R.O.
11. Rhodes to Knutsford, June 1, 1889, F.O. 84/1996, P.R.O.

Lobengula that he should put his trust in the company.[12] Moffat was thus a most valuable asset—an honest man whose convinced advocacy of the company made bribery unnecessary. To Moffat the opponents of the company were "obnoxious," "disreputable" disturbers of the peace and order of Matabeleland who should be expelled for the public welfare, and Rhodes was admirable in the "patient, waiting policy" he pursued.[13] The contribution of £1,500 was a small price to pay for such an ally. In the early months after the charter Moffat's concern for the welfare of the company was so extensive that Sir Henry Loch had to remind him that he should not involve himself in the company's commercial interests since such advocacy gave the appearance of excessive partiality.[14] His correspondence with Harris and Rhodes prior to that warning had displayed the attributes of a company agent rather than of an imperial representative, and his letters retained that flavor thereafter.[15]

The government controls which might have been exercised over the company were thus generally ineffective. The resident was a protagonist of company interests; the high commissioner at first had no objection to the company's policies provided that due deference was shown to him; and the Colonial Office was too far away to influence the course of events. Within the company no controls were imposed upon the acts of the South African representative. The London directors conceded plenary authority to Rhodes to act, and his power to act as he saw fit in the company's South African affairs was formalized by a power of attorney in May 1890.[16]

12. Rhodes to Cawston, October 4, 1889, BSAC Misc. I, Rhodes House. Rhodes in September 1889 had expressed the hope that Moffat would continue to represent the imperial government in Matabeleland because "no one else could carry on the post with the same credit as yourself." Rhodes to Moffat, September 26, 1889, MO/1/4, N.A.R.
13. Moffat to Shippard, November 18, 1889, HO 1/3/4, in *ibid.*, N.A.R.
14. Loch to Shippard, December 11, 1890, C.O. 879/33/403, P.R.O.
15. Moffat to Harris, April 14, 1891; Moffat to Rhodes, May 16, 1891, both in CTI/13/10, N.A.R.
16. Hawksley to Fairfield, May 12, 1896, C.O. 879/47/517, P.R.O. Rhodes was also "Managing Director," but no formal resolution was passed giving him that status.

Rhodes was thus free to use his own judgment as to the best means of achieving the company's objects, and he could proceed without undue worry about the reactions of company or imperial officials. The lack of interest of the government in the views of Lobengula was demonstrated by the fact that, though the appointment of the resident was cleared with the chartered company as well as with imperial officials, no one thought it necessary to ask the approval of the Ndebele chief. Lobengula had not requested a resident. On the contrary, he had indicated he did not need such help; and Moffat was not acceptable to him because he was identified in Lobengula's mind with the Rudd concession and with the British South Africa Company which he now saw as the great menace to the continued independence of the Ndebele.

By February 1890 Lobengula had lost his faith in the imperial government. His repudiation of the Rudd concession had been ignored; the advice brought home by his indunas had been followed by a message from the queen blessing the monopolists against whom she had previously warned him.[17] Two negotiators of the Rudd concession had decamped, and the third, Thompson, had fled, suggesting that he feared punishment for his acts. Now a new representative of the company had appeared, more beguiling than the rest. Dr. Leander Starr Jameson, accompanied by Major Thomas Maxwell, Denis Doyle, and Thompson, whom they had persuaded to return, arrived at Bulawayo in October 1889. Lobengula had met Jameson once before when he had paid a brief visit to Matabeleland in April when the first consignment of rifles had been sent up. On this visit Jameson's charge was to reassure the king that the company had no intention to seize his land and merely wished to dig for gold.[18]

While Jameson was in Bulawayo seeking to gain Lobengula's cooperation, Rhodes and the board of directors were debating strategy for the occupation of Mashonaland. Two routes had been considered, from the south via the Ngwato territory and from the east by the Zambezi river. The first preference of the

17. Lobengula to the queen, February 15, 1890, LO 5/2/0, N.A.R., also in C.O. 879/32/392, P.R.O.
18. Ian Colvin, *The Life of Jameson*, 1:116–118.

board was for the river route. An expedition by the Zambezi would accomplish several useful purposes. By its entry from the Indian Ocean it would challenge the claim of the Portuguese that they controlled the river system, and would do so with the assurance it would have the support of the imperial government. By approaching Mashonaland from the north, the expedition would minimize the risk of a clash with Lobengula, which most of the directors considered it desirable to avoid at least for the time being. And the river expedition could also be available for service in the Nyasa-Shiré area by the Shiré river route.

An expedition from the south at first seemed less desirable, though it was not ruled out as a possibility. Such a thrust would challenge Lobengula and the Ndebele, and they might respond by attack. This prospect was not necessarily cause to discard the plan. The power of the Ndebele might be awesome against other Africans, but the preponderance of opinion among "old Africa hands" was that they could not stand against white men, particularly mounted sharpshooters. Mzilikazi's impis could not master the Boers, and spirited young Britons in the view of Selous, Frank Johnson, and others were at least the equal of the Boers in military prowess. Rhodes was convinced that sooner or later war with the Ndebele was inevitable. Lobengula's temporizing frayed Rhodes's patience. He would not tolerate frustration of his plans by "a savage chief with about 8000 warriors." White settlers would soon occupy Matabeleland and Mashonaland, and the Ndebele could not resist them. Rhodes was determined that those whites would be under the flag of the company, and it was imperative that they move soon to prevent incursions by Boers or Portuguese.[19] Jameson's mission to Lobengula was thus of critical importance. If Lobengula refused to honor the Rudd concession, the company would seize the land it desired, with whatever justifications were necessary to placate humanitarian sentiment at home.

Even before the charter was approved, Rhodes and his associates in South Africa had begun to contemplate plans to occupy Mashonaland either by smashing the Ndebele if they should resist or by overawing them. In September 1889 he contemplated

19. Rhodes to Dilke, October 15, 1889, Dilke Papers, Addtl. MSS 43877, British Museum.

organizing a force of whites and Ngwato. Rhodes, like most
other white South Africans, had high esteem for Kgama, "the
most remarkable Kaffir that this or any century has seen."[20] The
Ngwato could put into the field 600 cavalry on "salted"[21] horses
and armed with Martini Henry rifles, in addition to several
thousand other warriors armed with rifles and spears. Many of
these guns had been shipped by the company which with the
assistance of the Sir Hercules Robinson had overcome initial
opposition from the Cape government with the justification
that these weapons were necessary to maintain the balance of
power between the Ngwato and the Ndebele.[22] With white commissioned and noncommissioned officers, the Ngwato cavalry
could become a formidable force, though they would require
"considerable stiffening" with a unit of white marksmen if they
were to face the feared Ndebele.[23]

Rhodes was convinced at the end of 1889 that peaceful occupation of Mashonaland was highly unlikely and that the
sooner war came the better for the company's interest. He was
supported in this belief by at least two of the missionaries in
Matabeleland, C. D. Helm and David Carnegie.[24] His feeling of
urgency was intensified by reports from the Transvaal of preparations for a Boer trek, perhaps 1,000 strong, into Mashonaland
at the beginning of winter, probably in May.[25] British negotiators had kept Kruger dangling on the issue of Swaziland, in
part as a means to deterring him from any adventures in the
north, but this diplomatic gambit might not succeed; and in any
event a trek might still take place without the approval of the

20. The phrase is Harris's but accurately reflected Rhodes's views.
Harris to Weatherley, September 16, 1889, LO 5/2/0, N.A.R.
21. "Salted" horses were those that had developed an immunity to
horse sickness.
22. Robinson to Cawston, private, October 7, 1889, BSAC, Misc. I,
Rhodes House. The line that rifles were less dangerous than assegais
did not seem to apply to the Ngwato.
23. Maguire to Grey, October 21, 1889, File 183/1, Grey Papers, Durham.
24. Jameson to Harris, November 1, 1889, CT 1/13/6, N.A.R.
25. Extract, anonymous ltr., September 19, 1889, in Herbert to Cawston, private, November 14, 1889, BSAC I Misc., Rhodes House. The
winter months in Mashonaland are from May to August.

Transvaal government. Thus Rhodes's desire for an early show-down with the Ndebele was reinforced. He developed a plan of action which was a modification of that previously mooted for a joint white-Ngwato force; the principal instruments for its execution were to be Frank Johnson and Maurice Heany. Johnson and Heany had not forgotten their treatment by the Ndebele two years before, but the reward they sought was much more substantial than vengeance. For a price they undertook to raise a force of 500 white men which with support from the Ngwato would carry out a sudden onslaught on Lobengula's kraal. Johnson had two alternative courses of action thereafter. The force might kill Lobengula, thus demoralizing the Ndebele by de-priving them of their leadership, and then "make a complete job of it" by smashing each of the Ndebele regiments. Or they might dig themselves in at Bulawayo holding Lobengula and his indunas as hostages and open negotiations with the Ndebele for the peaceful surrender of the Ndebele kingdom. Johnson somewhat favored the latter course. The excuse for the coup would be a manufactured "aggression" by the Ndebele in the disputed territory between the Shashi and the Maklautsi rivers.[26]

The plan was developed in considerable detail at a meeting between Rhodes and Johnson in Kimberley during the first week in December 1889. By the contract, dated December 7, Johnson and Heany were to receive £150,000 if they were suc-cessful as well as a grant of 50,000 morgen.[27] Johnson was to select the men and Rhodes undertook to have the necessary arms landed in Cape Town not later than the end of February. The consignment would include 1,800 Martini Henry rifles with short bayonets and 600,000 rounds of ammunition, 500 Webley revolvers with 50,000 rounds, and 500 "serviceable knives."[28]

The projected "Johnson coup" was remarkably like the plan

26. The existence of this agreement was first revealed by Johnson in an article in the *Cape Times* of September 12, 1930. Johnson remem-bered that he had discussed the plan early in 1889, but his memory was almost certainly in error. See Richard Brown, "Aspects of the Scramble for Matabeleland," in Eric Stokes and Richard Brown, eds., *The Zambesian Past*, pp. 88–90.
27. Typescript of Frank Johnson's *Great Days*, TO 3/6, N.A.R.
28. Harris to Johnson, Dec. 9, 1889, CT 2/11/1, N.A.R.

of the Jameson Raid of six years later by its reliance on the light-
ning strike delivered by an amateur commander. But in 1889
Jameson played a different role than he did in 1895. His efforts
were directed to making the raid unnecessary by inducing
Lobengula to give his consent to the peaceful occupation of
Mashonaland. Many years later Frank Johnson recalled that the
plan had been canceled because one of his associates, Heany, lost
his discretion under the influence of drink and told the missionary to Kgama's people, J. D. Hepburn, of the plan. Hepburn
felt obligated to report the immoral scheme to the high commissioner, who forced Rhodes to disavow the plan. This version
is an illustration of the unreliability of memory long after the
fact. Heany could hardly have revealed the plot to Hepburn because the missionary was himself involved in it. Hepburn was
the interpreter by which Kgama was informed of the plan and
who participated in the discussions between Heany and Kgama
about the coordination of the Ngwato and white forces.[29]

Rhodes testified to the administrator of British Bechuanaland
that after the death of Lotjie and the flight of Thompson,
Kgama had sent a message through Heany that there was no
longer any possibility of a peaceful settlement between the company and the Ndebele and that he would assist the company in
the war which now appeared inevitable. Rhodes asked Kgama to
confer with Heany about joint measures, but soon afterwards
the attitude of Lobengula changed, and action against him was
no longer necessary.[30]

Rhodes's version was true, though he did not mention his
agreement with Johnson and Heany. The plan was abandoned
because a report from Jameson seemed to make it unnecessary.
On December 21 Rhodes received word from Jameson that
Lobengula had abandoned his obstructionism and had agreed
to allow the company to begin prospecting north of the Ramaquabane River. Jameson added that Lobengula had been willing to authorize immediate entry into Mashonaland but his advisers had objected and had proposed the company first seek
gold in the south. But, said Jameson, Lobengula had promised

29. Typescript, Johnson's *Great Days*, TO 3/6, N.A.R.
30. Rhodes to Administrator British Bechuanaland [end of February
1890], C.O. 879/32/392, P.R.O.

to permit an expedition into Mashonaland if no gold was found in the Ramaquabane.

Lobengula's change of front was not caused by Jameson's morphia or the doctor's winning personality. The chief in his many years of dealing with whites had developed a more sophisticated appreciation of the problems of his kingdom than Europeans were willing to concede. Caught between the menace of the whites and the militancy of his young men, he sought an accommodation with the whites which would preserve his chieftainship and maintain the peace. In one meeting with his indunas he met an incipient revolt against his conciliatory policy by threatening to ally himself with the white men unless he was supported. His gamble succeeded; the indunas gave way and acquiesced in his agreement with Jameson.[31]

Lobengula's withdrawal of opposition caused Rhodes to reassess his plans. If Lobengula was sincere this expensive and risky foray was unnecessary.[32] Rhodes devised a second plan for the occupation of Mashonaland by a route that would bypass the Ndebele. On January 1, 1890, he and Johnson signed another agreement by which, instead of leading a war party into Matabeleland, he would be responsible for conducting an avowedly peaceful expedition into Mashonaland.[33]

This decision to carry out a flanking movement from the south followed on the conclusion of the company's directors that an expedition into Mashonaland by the Zambezi was unfeasible. Until December 1889 the Zambezi route had been favored by the London board, their support being reinforced by sibylline utterances from Lord Salisbury which seemed to suggest that he favored a test of strength with the Portuguese. Salisbury frequently was interpreted by his hearers to promise more than he later was willing to admit. The message which Grey and other company representatives derived from discussions with him and his parliamentary undersecretary, Sir Philip Currie, was that the company should act positively to back its claims for as much territory as possible, with the single restriction that it

31. Brown, "Aspects of the Struggle for Matabeleland," in Stokes and Brown, eds., *The Zambesian Past*, p. 87.
32. Harris to Hepburn, January 17, 1890, CT 2/11/1, N.A.R.
33. Memo of Agreement, January 1, 1890, CT 1/20/2, N.A.R.

should do nothing to antagonize Germany. Salisbury made it clear that he did not advocate a collision with the Portuguese and that the company must rely on its own resources in any actions it might take.[34] Information available to the company from military sources and from English travelers in Portuguese territory was that the Portuguese army in East Africa, manned largely by Africans, was derisory and would disintegrate with the first shots from any well-equipped British expedition. But wars even against contemptible opponents were costly, and at Alfred Beit's suggestion the company contemplated the less traumatic course of seeking a concession from Portugal to take over the Portuguese possessions on the coast north of Delagoa Bay for an amount to be negotiated.[35] Such a settlement would give the company peaceful access to the interior (possible African opposition was not considered). If the Portuguese were obdurate, however, the company was prepared to use force. The plan developed after consultation with the Foreign Office and with Lord Wolseley, the adjutant general, for an expedition of 300 men transported on armed steamers with a shallow draft. Wolseley believed that a picked contingent of that size would be sufficient to deal with any Portuguese resistance.[36]

By the end of 1889, however, serious doubts had developed as to the feasibility of the Zambezi plan. Most telling was the report of Frederick Selous. His journey to Mashonaland by the river route tended to confirm reports of Portuguese weakness. Tete, their "bastion" upstream, was a "damned hole," and ten miles beyond the river the Portuguese had "not a shadow of power."[37] But against this encouragement, there were overpowering deterrents. Most important, the river above its junction with the Shiré was not navigable throughout most of the year to vessels with over two feet of clearance. Further, the region between the river and the Mazoe valley was infested with

34. Note, Currie, July 19, 1889, F.O. 84/2000, P.R.O. Currie to Grey, July 26, 1889, Grey to Currie, July 31, 1889, both in File 184/6, Grey Papers, Durham; Cawston to Rhodes, November 6, 1889, BSAC I, Misc., Rhodes House.
35. Harris to Weatherley, November 11, 1889, LO 5/2/0, N.A.R.
36. Weatherley to Cawston, December 20, 1889; Gifford to Cawston, December 23, 1889, both in BSAC I Misc., Rhodes House.
37. Selous to Johnson, August 15, 1889, JO 3/1/1, N.A.R.

tsetse fly,[38] and the area from the sea upstream was fever country, and a white expedition might be incapacitated without firing a shot.[39] Selous presented his findings to Rhodes in Kimberley on or about December 7, 1889,[40] the day on which Rhodes signed the contract with Johnson and Heany for the invasion of Matabeleland.

The coincidence is intriguing. Selous was much less sanguine than was Rhodes about the chances of success of a 500-man invasion even if they were able to take the Ndebele by surprise. But the chances of failure were great. In Selous's view it was needlessly rash to risk all with a single throw when the game could be won by patience and more prudent measures. Over a year before he had suggested the occupation of Mashonaland by a route skirting Matabeleland. He had not altered his opinion that this course was the best one.[41]

The combination of Selous's advice and Jameson's reports of Lobengula's pliability decided the issue. The Zambezi route to Mashonaland was rejected, though talk continued about a possible expedition into the Nyasa region by the Zambezi and the Shiré river. Selous's proposed route into Mashonaland was adopted, and the outlines of the new plan were presented to Sir Henry Loch on January 10, 1890.

The involvement of Selous with the proposed expedition in a central role took away some of the authority of Johnson who by the agreement of January 1, 1890, had been assigned plenary power to recruit the expedition, to lead it, and to determine its route. Johnson's responsibility was further restricted by the decision to provide the expedition with an escort of an armed force which would be under the command of a military officer.[42]

When Rhodes presented his plan to Loch, he indicated that

38. Harris to Weatherley, December 9, 1889, LO 5/2/210, in *ibid.*, N.A.R.
39. Harris to Weatherley, December 23, 1889, in *ibid.*
40. Note, December 24, 1889, reporting communication from Mrs. Slous (Selous), F.O. 84/2009, P.R.O. Beit to Cawston, December 7, 1889, BSAC I Misc., Rhodes House. Beit reported receiving a cable that day from Rhodes reporting his conversation with Selous.
41. J. E. S. Green, *Rhodes Goes North*, pp. 174–177.
42. Minutes Meeting, Govt. H., January 10, 1890, C.O. 879/32/392, P.R.O., S1428/17/10, N.A.R.

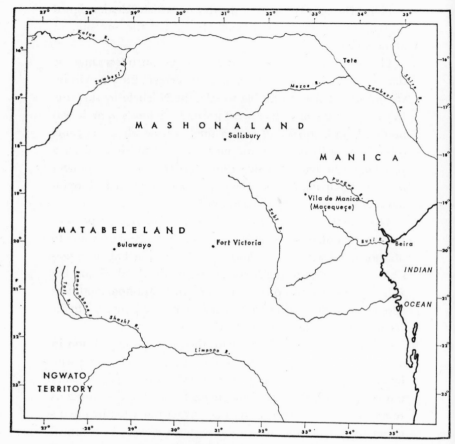

MAP 3. Matabeleland and Mashonaland

he expected the expedition would consist of 125 miners with a military escort of 250 men. The strength of the armed force had been raised from the 100 authorized by the Colonial Office for the British South African Police in November 1889. But Rhodes and Loch soon concluded that the number was still too small to guarantee safety, and the force was further increased to 480 men.[43]

Where were the dangers that justified such military strength? Lobengula, by Rhodes's own testimony, had acquiesced in the company's entry in Mashonaland. John Moffat could not understand why such a large contingent was required. It appeared to him that the company was challenging the Ndebele by a display of military might at a time when Lobengula was resisting the importunities of his young men to fight. The chief had not only agreed to the entry into Mashonaland but he had promised to provide some of his own people to assist in the road building. In response the company treated him as a potential enemy and the expedition as planned would subject him to humiliation by flaunting an armed force before him and his people.[44] The response of Rhodes was that prudence dictated adequate protection of the pioneers against all hazards. The Ndebele were "restless and suspicious," and the company was in fact supporting Lobengula's position by letting his people know that any attack would be repelled.[45] But on another occasion Rhodes explained that the size of the force was necessary because, though Lobengula had given his permission, "with a treacherous savage as he is, we must take every precaution."[46] Abercorn found this argument convincing—Lobengula would have to be carefully watched, as he "seems to be full of suspicion, like most sav-

43. BSAC Minute Book, LO 8/1/1, N.A.R.
44. Moffat to Shippard, February 23, 1890, S1428/17/10, N.A.R.
45. Harris to Bowen, March 18, 1890, in *ibid.*
46. Rhodes to Abercorn, March 31, 1890, C.O. 879/32/392, P.R.O. Many years later Frank Johnson in his autobiography recalled that the military force had been required by Sir Henry Loch who would not authorize the expedition without a "force of at least 400 mounted men to hold the base and, if necessary, go to his [Johnson's] assistance." Frank Johnson, *Great Days*, p. 112. Loch may well have insisted on the force being larger than the 250 to which it had been in-

ages."[47] Gifford, the veteran of African wars, also advocated a force strong enough to eliminate any risk of disaster.[48]

This formidable force bore little relationship to the mining party for which Jameson had sought "the road" from Lobengula. Jameson stated that he proposed to tell the king that the force was necessary to protect the miners and settlers against the Portuguese and the Shona,[49] but Lobengula later insisted that he had been asked for permission only for a few miners and that, without his authorization or prior knowledge, the company had invaded his territories with an armed force. Lobengula blamed Denis Doyle, who had acted as Jameson's interpreter, for falsely translating their exchanges.[50] As with the Rudd concession, Lobengula made the interpreter the scapegoat. In so doing, he may have sought to convince his advisers that he had been deluded without his directly clashing with the South Africa Company. Whatever Lobengula's motive, Rhodes's decision to send an armed force was a provocation which placed the Ndebele chief in a difficult position. He was under great pressure to order his regiments to destroy the invaders; if he failed to do so, he might be overthrown. Rhodes recognized that Lobengula might give way to pressure from his people, and his plans provided for that contingency. If Lobengula did nothing when the column entered his territory, Mashonaland would be occupied with adequate force to repel any subsequent Ndebele attack. If Lobengula ordered an immediate attack, his forces would have to fight not only with a formidable European military force but Kgama's cavalry as well, for the Ngwato chief had agreed to provide support. Rhodes believed that he had provided for all eventualities, and that Lobengula could not frustrate his plans. In the words of Rutherfoord Harris: ". . . If he attacks us, he is

creased, but Rhodes in his communication to the directors did not indicate that Loch had been the source of the decision. Johnson was certainly in error in ascribing the genesis of the British South Africa Police to Loch's ultimatum.

47. Abercorn to Cawston, March 29, 1890, BSAC II, Misc., Rhodes House.
48. Robert Cary, *Charter Royal*, p. 80.
49. Jameson to Harris, January 8, 1890, CT 1/13/6, N.A.R.
50. Doyle to Harris, July 7, 1890, CT 1/13/4, N.A.R.

doomed, if he does not, his fangs will be drawn and the pressure of civilisation on all his borders will press more and more heavily upon him, and the desired result, the disappearance of the Matabele as a power, if delayed is yet the more certain."[51]

The armed force also provided security against possible attack from Boers of the Transvaal, though that threat had been largely eliminated by diplomacy. For months before the organization of the British South Africa Police rumors had been circulating that a trek might take place into Mashonaland, and Sir Henry Loch used this danger as justification for sanctioning an increase in the company's police.[52] But Rhodes was not unduly worried about Boers as he planned the pioneer expedition. The imperial government had a check on President Kruger by withholding an agreement on Swaziland until it was satisfied that he would not encourage his burghers to trek north. Rhodes and Loch met with the president in March 1890. The conference was not conclusive. Neither Kruger nor Loch made any commitments, but Rhodes left the meeting convinced that Kruger could be trusted to keep his burghers out of Mashonaland.[53]

Rhodes and Loch also cited the possibility of a Portuguese attack as justification for a sizeable military force, but privately they had no fear that the Portuguese would initiate hostilities in Mashonaland. The only serious threat was that from the Ndebele and the provocation of the entry of an armed force made that danger greater. If the company had sent a small mining party into Mashonaland the risks of Ndebele attack would have been small. The company had not felt it necessary to provide military protection for the miners who had been sent to the Ramaquabane River, much closer to the Ndebele. One of the missionaries, Carnegie, protested that a crisis had been created by the company's decision to seize Mashonaland with a military force rather than to work in an accommodating fashion with Lobengula.[54] Moffat also advised the company that the Ndebele

51. Harris to Hepburn, January 17, 1890, CT 2/11/1, N.A.R.
52. Loch to Knutsford, February 20, 1890, C.O. 879/32/392, P.R.O.
53. Harris to Weatherley, March 17, 1890, LO 5/2/0, N.A.R.
54. Carnegie to Doyle, May 5, 1890, MA 1/1/1, N.A.R. Carnegie told Doyle that the "dangerous situation" of the missionaries "was brought about by your policy."

would almost certainly not attack unless the company challenged them with an armed force. Frank Johnson had opposed the military escort from the beginning, arguing that the police force would be an incitement to the Ndebele, and that war was probable if Rhodes insisted on sending the police. He insisted that the company guarantee to make good all financial losses he suffered as a result.[55] All these warnings were brushed aside. The police were a necessary part of Rhodes's plan, for the expedition had much larger objects than prospecting for minerals. It was conceived from the beginning as an occupation that would effectively wrest the area from the Ndebele and from the Shona themselves. Rhodes and the London directors envisioned Mashonaland not only as another Rand but as a colony where white families would settle and raise the herds and crops necessary to sustain the new economy. Africans would provide labor for the mines and for the farms, but this would be white man's country, an extension of the Cape. Such a plan obviously involved risks of war with the Ndebele, who could hardly be relied upon to accept quietly the forfeiture of their claims to the area (the Shona were not considered at all). The large force also had significance with regard to the Portuguese, not so much for defense against Portuguese attack as to provide the power to drive Portugal from East Africa if it should refuse to part with its possessions peacefully.

The purpose of the Mashonaland expedition, then, was to establish a settlement which would be the nucleus of the company's empire in central Africa. The pioneers were not recruited on the basis of any expertise in mining, and few of them were interested in the hard work of discovery and development of gold mines. The recruits were brought together by the lures of adventure and avarice; they had little else in common.

One of the police officers described the police and the pioneer corps in these terms:

> . . . Such a mixed lot I never saw in my life, all sorts and conditions, from the aristocrat down to the street Arab—peers and waifs of humanity mingling together like the ingredients of a hotch-potch. Prospectors predominate, but nearly every trade and profession under the sun is represented. Clerks and business

55. Johnson to Rhodes, May 6, 1890, CT 1/20/2, N.A.R.

men of all kinds jostle one another, and one troop is called the gentlemanly troop because the majority in it are brokers. . . .[56]

Most of the pioneers considered themselves South Africans, and many were Afrikaners. Included among them were members of leading families of Cape Colony. Frank Johnson later recalled that he had recruited these young men at the instance of Rhodes, who thought that if the expedition was in danger their influential fathers would put pressure on the imperial government to save their sons.[57] The volunteers were each promised 15 mining claims and 1500 morgen (about 3000 acres) of land. The contract they accepted as a commitment, not a contingency awaiting the approval of an African chief. They had heard that Mashonaland contained gold deposits far richer than the Rand, and that the wealth lay at the surface easily accessible to inexperienced men with no capital, unlike the low-grade ore of the Transvaal. The gold fields were dotted amidst pastures which were the lushest in South Africa and the soil and climate were admirably adapted for agriculture. Those who had been disillusioned in the Rand now looked to Mashonaland as the land of their destiny.[58] Some of the officers invested their money in chartered shares, which they were allowed to buy at par, in the expectation that there would be a rapid rise as Mashonaland was developed.[59]

Johnson, as the leader of the corps, had much more substantial inducements than the rank and file. He was authorized to spend £88,340 for all purposes.[60] He would pay for supplies and weapons, which included four Maxims and two seven-pounder guns. In addition to any monetary profits he was promised 40,000 morgen as soon as the company was able to grant him valid title.[61]

The contingency in Johnson's contract reflected the fact that the company had no land to give. The Rudd Concession, as ex-

56. A. G. Leonard, *How We Made Rhodesia*, p. 26.
57. Johnson, *Great Days*, p. 109.
58. See, for example, A. Tulloch, "The Rhodesian Dawn," TU 1/1/1, N.A.R. Tulloch was one of the pioneers.
59. Twenty-five applications are on record, for a total of 6200 srares. LO 5/2/3, N.A.R.
60. Harris to Weatherley, April 28, 1890, LA 5/2/1, N.A.R.
61. Johnson, *Great Days*, pp. 326–332.

pansive as it was, conferred no title to land, and no spokesman of the company contended that Lobengula had subsequently conceded such rights. Archibald R. Colquhoun, who was selected to be civil administrator of Mashonaland, was instructed that there could be no legal land title until Lobengula gave his consent. But Colquhoun was further advised that if the pioneers pressed him for farms, he should allow them to "ride off" the boundaries in accordance with the Boer custom and grant them provisional titles. He was also instructed to select one or more town sites of at least 25,000 morgen each.[62]

The recruits expected to get titles to land, and Rhodes intended to provide them with land, whether or not Lobengula assented. In the last resort, the Shona could be "liberated" from the Ndebele, since as Selous and others maintained they were not subject to the Ndebele and they could be expected to accept company rule in exchange for protection.[63]

The ambitions of the company to become masters of Mashonaland had the unqualified support of Sir Henry Loch, though Loch distrusted rule by a private company. And he particularly distrusted Rhodes, whose ambitions he saw as subversive of the authority of the queen and of himself as her representative. Rhodes as prime minister was abrasive to Loch as high commissioner. Rhodes's impatience with moral considerations when great objects were to be won was met with Loch's insistence that action be in accordance with the "rules of game." When rumors reached Loch of Rhodes's agreement with Johnson and Heany to manufacture an incident to justify the invasion of Matabeleland, the high commissioner required Rhodes to disavow such intentions, so contrary to the British ethic.

Loch, however, was in agreement with Rhodes on the one principle that was essential. He, fully as much as Rhodes, believed that it was the destiny of the British people to occupy the high plateau north of the Limpopo. He, like Rhodes, believed that the Ndebele military system must sooner or later be swept away. And he, like Rhodes, favored sooner rather than later. Loch consequently pressed the Colonial Office to authorize the

62. BSAC, Kimberley, to BSAC, London, May 19, 1890, C.O. 879/32/392, P.R.O.
63. Selous to his mother, April 30, 1890, SE 1/1/1, N.A.R.

expansion of the British South Africa Company's police to 500. His justification was the threat of a Boer trek; his safeguard, his control over their use.[64]

From the perspective of Downing Street the urgency communicated by the company and by Loch seemed to be unjustified by any documented emergency. The Colonial Office saw no evidence of an aggressive intention on the part of Lobengula. On the contrary, the danger of war seemed to come from the company which proposed to invade Mashonaland with a military force. When and how, asked Knutsford, the colonial secretary, did Lobengula sanction this occupation of Mashonaland with a police force?[65] The imperial government had asserted his sovereignty over the Shona as against the Portuguese; how now could it authorize the entry of an armed force without his express consent?[66]

The fastidiousness of the Colonial Office with regard to Lobengula's rights seemed unrealistic to Salisbury and the Foreign Office. Much weightier considerations were involved than the wishes of an African chief. While Downing Street was dotting i's and crossing t's, Boer trekkers might make such concerns of no consequence. Far better to leave discretion in the hands of the high commissioner, who was much closer to the scene and much better able to judge the best course of action.[67] The Colonial Office grudgingly capitulated. Loch was given discretionary authority. Knutsford suggested that it would be desirable to secure support from Lobengula against any invasion by trekkers from the Transvaal.[68]

The injunction was hopelessly unrealistic, and it is difficult to believe that the staff of the Colonial Office were so naive and uninformed as to accept the company's line that the occupation of Mashonaland was for the protection of the Shona and the Ndebele. In 1890 the great menace to the Ndebele was not the Boers but the company. Lobengula was in no position to pro-

64. Telegram, Loch to Knutsford, February 20, 1890, C.O. 879/32/392, P.R.O.
65. Telegram, Knutsford to Loch, February 22, 1890, in ibid.
66. C.O. to F.O., confidential, February 26, 1890, F.O. 84/2075, P.R.O.
67. F.O. to C.O., March 7, 1890, F.O. 84/2076, P.R.O.
68. Telegram, Knutsford to Loch, March 10, 1890, C.O. 879/32/392, P.R.O.

vide assistance to anyone; he desperately needed protection, and he had no advocates. He mistrusted the missionaries—had not one of them been an accessory to the Rudd party? The imperial resident, Moffat, he considered a lackey of the company. Had Moffat not advised approval of the Rudd concession? The high commissioner far away in Cape Town had no interest in justice for the Ndebele. Had he not refused to visit Bulawayo when he was on tour nearby? And the queen's government at home on which he thought he could rely had now repudiated its earlier good advice and advised him to submit quietly to the company which he was certain intended to steal his land. He had no resources that could be effective against such odds. At best, he would buy time in the hope that by such temporizing some development might yet occur which would salvage his position. He fenced with Jameson, at times appearing to give his consent to the expedition into Mashonaland, and then beclouding his permission. He appealed to the queen to intercede.[69] He called upon Rhodes to visit Bulawayo to arrange an agreement with regard to Mashonaland.[70] Finally, when the invading column was already on the move, he made one last desperate effort to deflect destiny. He sent Mtshete, one of the indunas who had journeyed to London, to see the high commissioner and inform him of the Ndebele opposition to the company's entry into Mashonaland. Mtshete was accompanied by Frank Boyle, Renny-Tailyour, and the Reverend C. D. Helm. Boyle and Renny-Tailyour had been among the whites in Bulawayo who had tried to undermine the Rudd concession, and Helm accompanied the party as an interpreter, his role in the Rudd concession notwithstanding. Rhodes was present at Loch's invitation, as were the imperial secretary, Graham Bower, and Major General Paul Methuen, commander of British forces at the Cape.[71]

The mission was hopeless; while it was en route, the letter

69. Lobengula to the queen, February 15, 1890, in *ibid*.
70. Selous to his mother, March 26, 1890, SE 1/1/1, N.A.R.
71. "Shorthand Report of Interview between Loch and Umshete," July 29, 1890, C.O. 879/32/392, P.R.O. Renny-Tailyour visited Shepstone in Natal before proceeding to Cape Town to join Mtshete.

from Loch was on its way to Lobengula informing the chief that he had authorized the company's expedition to enter Mashonaland "to guard your country against enroachments" and that they came as friends "who desire only your good."[72] The bristling military force which the Ndebele saw poised at the Maklautsi River seemed to Lobengula neither peaceful nor friendly. He sent the commander a message dripping with irony: "Why were so many warriors at Macloutsie? Had the King committed any fault, or had any white man been killed, or had the white men lost anything that they were looking for?" Jameson as Rhodes's representative replied that the soldiers were not directed against Lobengula but were merely an escort for protection on the way to Mashonaland by the road the king had approved.[73]

The meeting in Cape Town was thus in the nature of a meaningless ritual. Mtshete spoke in a hopeless cause, but he had no choice but to carry out this commission. He repeated that the Rudd concession was not valid, since Lobengula had not accepted the guns which were part of the agreement and that the chief had followed the advice of the queen not to give all his cattle to one man. Rhodes's men were not content to dig a hole at the place assigned them; they wanted to "eat up" the Ndebele; Moffat was their accessory and should be replaced. Thus went the litany of grievances; the supplication was unavailing.

Loch waved aside Lobengula's repudiation of the Rudd concession; the issue, he said, could not be reopened since the queen had approved the charter and with it the concession. Moffat would continue to be the queen's resident. The expedition proceeding into Mashonaland was in search of gold, not land, and Lobengula should cooperate with Rhodes rather than listening to the evil counsel of ill-disposed whites. Loch concluded by warning Renny-Tailyour and Boyle that he would have them banished if they or their agents continued to sow mistrust in Lobengula's mind toward the chartered company.[74] Loch's per-

72. Loch to Lobengula, June 12, 1890, C.O. 879/32/392, P.R.O.
73. Secretary, BSAC, Kimberley, to Imperial Secretary, July 14. 1890, in ibid.
74. Shorthand reports, July 29, 30, 31, 1890, August 5, 1890, in ibid.

formance was all that the most ardent company man could have desired. Lobengula's complaints had been flatly repudiated, and the Mashonaland column had been invested with the sanction and approval of the principal imperial officer in South Africa.

The entry of the pioneers into Mashonaland was delayed, not by Lobengula's protests, but by internal problems of organization. The police and Johnson's pioneers had to be organized into a harmonious relationship, and this was not easy. There were difficulties involving divided authority and rival egos, most of them centering on Johnson who rankled over Rhodes's actions to circumscribe his authority. He continued to complain that the decision to impose the police on his pioneers was a great blunder which might prove tragic. Not only did this endanger the lives of the pioneers by making a war likely, but the police were an encumbrance, producing dangerous delay in preparations for the journey. The combined force was under the command of an imperial officer, Lieutenant Colonel Edward G. Pennefather, who had been seconded for this assignment. Johnson suggested that Pennefather was not well qualified for the responsibility. "Left to our own devices," he complained to Rhodes, "we will do the work with little or no loss of life and quickly but I fear the tactics which the Police are going in for." The police, he said, were being trained as mounted infantry, who would form a square to meet the Ndebele rush. This was lunacy. "When I receive such an order I shall refuse to obey it and would sooner be tried by a dozen courts martial than *murder* the splendid lot of men I have here." Johnson also had an abrasive relationship with Selous, who "is more bother to me than all the Matabele."[75]

Finally, in July 1890 a mixed force of about 100 pioneers and about the same number of police crossed the Shashi River. In the first stages of the journey they were accompanied by 200 Ngwato under the command of Kgama's brother Radikladi, a demonstration of Kgama's enthusiastic cooperation in the discomfiture of Lobengula and the Ndebele. The Ngwato were helpful in opening up the road, but inevitably irritations developed between them and the whites who were not accustomed to treating Africans as equals—the Ngwato smelled bad, they

75. Johnson to Rhodes, private, May 29, 1890, CT 1/20/2, N.A.R.

said—and by mutual consent the Ngwato went home to do their ploughing.[76]

The expedition proceeded without incident, except for a brief alarm occasioned by a message from Lobengula repeating his opposition to the movement into Mashonaland, and they arrived in September at the site of what would become Salisbury, jubilant at their success and optimistic as to their future. They had enrolled in part for adventure, but the ruling passion was gold.[77] As soon as they were disbanded many rushed to stake claims which they hoped would make them rich; others sold their rights to speculators. The occupation of Mashonaland had been accomplished bloodlessly it seemed. But the blood price had yet to be paid.

Lobengula had kept his restive people in check and allowed the column to pass without challenge. He had dexterously parried his young men and some of his indunas in their demands for action and thus had avoided a war. The price for peace was unconditional surrender. In 1890 the company wanted only Mashonaland. But Lobengula had won only a brief respite; his demise would come in 1893 rather than three years earlier. Whatever course he adopted there was no escape from his fate. One observer commented, "Never, surely, did a shepherd open the door of his fold to the wolf more foolishly than did Lobengula when granting the Chartered Company's concession."[78] Lobengula was not foolish; perhaps he was not brilliant; but the qualities of his mind had no relationship to the fate of his people. The Ndebele possessed what Europeans coveted; and they were dispossessed. They could succumb "peacefully" or they could fight; the result would be the same.

---

76. Green, *Rhodes Goes North*, p. 219.
77. Leonard, *How We Made Rhodesia*, p. 171.
78. Ralph Williams, *How I Became a Governor* (London, 1913), p. 187.

6

The Company and
Portuguese East Africa

AFTER THE JAMESON RAID OF DECEMBER 1895, AN-
alysts sought to relate the fiasco to changes in the character of
Cecil Rhodes which could have led him to stake his fortunes on
a gambler's throw with prohibitively long odds. Some suggested
that he had suffered a mental aberration which had disturbed
his normally clear perception.[1] Others speculated that he might
have been impelled by his belief that he had not long to live.

Such interpretations ignored the fact that the characteristics
which brought Rhodes's downfall were essentially the same he
had displayed in his rise to power. In 1889 he had contemplated
a sudden descent on the Ndebele; in 1890 he planned a light-
ning stroke against the Portuguese.

Unquestionably what had been tendencies in his earlier life
became hardened characteristics in his later years. Years of success, years of adulation had made him imperious. The bully who
is unchecked becomes even more the bully. While most humans
must modify their conduct to the requirements of society,
Rhodes was able to impose on society acquiescence in his aber-
rant conduct. Indeed, once he became the "Colossus," otherwise
fastidious English society found his rough ways endearing—he
was not to be judged by ordinary standards. The explorer
Joseph Thomson explained Rhodes's manners thus: ". . . His

1. Among those who had this view was Harry Johnston. In *The Story
of My Life*, pp. 281–283, Johnston states that Rhodes in 1893 was very
different from the man he had met in 1889.

THE COMPANY AND EAST AFRICA

education is that of the mining camp grafted on a University training and he consequently often expresses himself and acts in a manner calculated to shock people at home accustomed to the refined statesman full of suave language."[2]

As Rhodes's power increased, so did his arrogance. Any checks on his designs enraged him, whether the person responsible was humble or great. When the driver of his cart was not available when Rhodes was ready to leave he exploded, denouncing all Africans as shiftless and irresponsible, deserving to be flogged.[3] When a secretary of state for the colonies mildly inquired about the truth of allegations made in a British paper, Rhodes responded that he was sick of the Colonial Office pandering to blackmail and declined to reply.[4] His language concerning British politicians when he toured the hustings in South Africa frequently exceeded the usual limits of political rhetoric; when Sir Henry Loch protested at one of his outbursts the reply was that he should not be answerable for what he said in public speeches, which were not to be taken seriously.[5] Even Salisbury was the target of Rhodes's vituperation. When the Foreign Office thwarted Rhodes in his plan to deal summarily with the Portuguese, he was enraged—he accused the British prime minister of cravenness and held him responsible if the settlers of Mashonaland died for lack of supplies because Rhodes had been unable to open the route from the sea.[6] The language was stronger than that usually used by the representatives of an unfriendly state. As T. Villiers Lister of the Colonial Office stated on another occasion, Rhodes's expressions of his demands were always "absolute alcohol," with no bland language to reduce the bite.[7]

Rhodes in his ascent to power had judged men by their usefulness for his ends. As time went on, his judgment took on more

2. James B. Thomson, *Joseph Thomson*, pp. 296–297.
3. A. G. Leonard, *How We Made Rhodesia*, p. 104.
4. Rhodes to Ripon, June 25, 1894, Ripon Papers, Addtl. MSS 43637, British Museum.
5. Loch to Ripon, private, January 9, 1894, Ripon Papers, Addtl. MSS 43562, British Museum.
6. Rhodes to Salisbury, September 12, 1891, F.O. 84/2174, P.R.O.
7. Note by Lister, September 20, 1890, on Herbert to Lister, same date, F.O. 84/2091. P.R.O.

and more of a moral tone. Those who opposed his will were not
only wrong-headed but benighted and, if they were his servants
—traitorous. He expected loyalty from those whom he paid, not
independent judgments. Harry Johnston, whose administration
in Nyasaland was subsidized by a grant from the company, was
accused of disloyalty because Rhodes assumed he had been involved in the terms of a treaty with Portugal which Rhodes
could not accept. He accused Johnston of "desertion."[8]

Related to these manifestations was an increasing tendency to
personalize achievements with which he was identified. The
company became his creation; its life was the extension of his.
His speeches more and more referred to his accomplishments.

These attributes did not appear suddenly. Edward Maund
found the Rhodes of 1895 "very different" from ten years earlier
—"more dictatorial, not to say autocratic."[9] But the transformation was accelerated by events in 1890 which brought Rhodes's
career into a new phase. In May the company assigned him "absolute discretion" as its managing director.[10] This authorization
was merely formal recognition of the plenary powers he already
enjoyed, but the act was still significant. Then in July he became prime minister of Cape Colony, the head of a coalition including the Afrikaner Bond. The combination of these two
offices gave him enormous power, and the checks on his use of it
were generally ineffective. The London board of the company
would not or could not control him. Among the directors were
men who were more knowledgeable than he on various aspects
of its operations. Cawston had become in effect the company's
chief representative in great international commercial negotiations involving Katanga and Mozambique. Grey was much
better informed on Anglo-German relations affecting the company's interests. Particularly on issues north of the Zambezi,
Rhodes was often unacquainted with the facts. But the strength
of Rhodes was unrelated to mastery of detail. He had sought to
build an empire which would stretch from the Congo Free State

8. Rhodes to Johnston, September 22, 1890, quoted in Johnston Papers, Royal Commonwealth Society; Roland Oliver, *Sir Harry Johnston and the Scramble for Africa*, pp. 176–177.

9. Maund's recollections, March 22, 1925, Afr. s 229 (4), Maund
Papers, Rhodes House.

10. Power of Attorney, May 14, 1890, C. 8117, 1896.

to the Indian Ocean, and he would not be deterred by mere arguments or remonstrances from his board or from the imperial government. If the board demurred, his threat of resignation was enough to end all resistance. He was the man whose energy, power, and wealth would make the fortunes of others. The Duke of Abercorn acknowledged him to be the "mainstay of the Chartered Company." The duke explained to Salisbury that the board depended on Rhodes because he was "on the spot" and had an "intimate knowledge of the locality."[11] But Rhodes before 1891 had not visited any of the territories within the chartered sphere. He was "on the spot" in the sense that he was in South Africa, but his vista from Cape Town or even from Kimberley was hardly close enough to provide an "intimate knowledge of the locality." Abercorn and other directors did not depend upon Rhodes for his expertise, but by the summer of 1890 they acknowledged him to be the vital force of the company.

Within Cape Colony the limitations on Rhodes's political power were generally unrelated to his expansionist ambitions. The Afrikaner Bond applauded his assertion of Cape imperialism, as did most of his supporters of British stock. With predominant support from both white elements, he had political weight to match his economic power. No other South African had ever enjoyed such influence with the imperial government. Even with lesser prime ministers, Downing Street had displayed great deference. Several years earlier Bismarck had been incensed when in response to his inquiry about the status of South West Africa, the British had consulted with the Cape government, occasioning a delay of several months. He was convinced that this reference to Cape Town was a device, a mere pretense to cover a desire to avoid the issue.[12] He did not understand the significance of colonial autonomy to British policy. The imperial government sought to maintain the loyalty of its self-governing colonies not only by respecting their control over their internal affairs but by consulting them on questions affecting their security. This relaxed relationship provided an opportu-

11. Abercorn to Salisbury, September 22, 1890, File E, Salisbury Papers, Christ Church, Oxford.
12. William O. Aydelotte, *Bismarck and British Colonial Policy. The Problem of South West Africa*, pp. 3–4.

nity which Rhodes exploited. Colonial secretaries, both Conservative and Liberal, sought to avoid confrontation with Rhodes which meant, in effect, that they avoided interference except when they had no alternative. Sidney Olivier who as a youthful member of the Colonial Office staff observed the reactions of his superiors to Rhodes, later commented: "That Office [the Colonial Office], indeed, had no more control over the Chartered Company than the League of Nations has now over a mandated Power (the relations are closely parallel), and had far too much delicacy to act in any manner that might have been rebuffed as 'inquisitorial.' Short of revoking the Charter, it could do nothing."[13]

One of the most vehement critics of imperial expansion in general and chartered companies in particular, Henry Labouchere's *Truth* put the indictment more strongly: "The Colonial Office dreaded Mr. Rhodes. It did not dare oppose him and his schemes for fear of his putting himself at the head of a government to establish a South Africa Republic, as he more than once threatened. They, therefore, winked at his misdeeds and permitted the British flag to be disgraced by him."[14]

Between 1890 and 1896 the energy and ambition of Rhodes was under no effective control, except when his activity became involved in considerations of high policy and Salisbury asserted his authority. Salisbury in many respects was the antithesis of Rhodes. He was cautious and calculating; Rhodes was impetuous. Rhodes's imperialism was simple; the strong had the right to dominate the weak; the progressive and industrious, to rule the lazy and the shiftless. The imperial government whenever it had intervened had done so for the worse; the destiny of South and Central Africa should be determined by its white inhabitants—the adjective excluded Portuguese but included Afrikaners. Salisbury's world was complicated. The security of Britain depended not only on her naval and military power but on the astuteness of her diplomacy. Until 1890 he had to contend with Bismarck; and the two old masters made their moves with great mutual respect and the conviction that none of their subordinates understood the complexities of the game. On great issues

13. Lord Olivier, *The Anatomy of African Misery*, p. 51.
14. *Truth*, November 29, 1894.

he did not even confide in the staff of his own Foreign Office, who were consequently often uninformed. Salisbury supported British commercial interests overseas within the framework of the national interest; he did not identify the two as being the same or necessarily harmonious. He considered chartered companies as a means of preserving potentially valuable assets for Britain, but he expected their leaders to adapt their policies to his. Sir William Mackinnon of the Imperial British East Africa Company incurred his wrath when he did not so conform.[15] But Mackinnon was a minor problem compared to Rhodes. The attributes of Rhodes which fascinated Salisbury also alarmed him. Rhodes was building a great African empire, but Salisbury was not sure for whom. His earliest impression had been that Rhodes was pro-Boer, but he had been reassured by the South African's manifest zeal for the imperial cause. But by 1890 it had become evident that Rhodes's imperialism was not entirely compatible with Salisbury's. In the negotiations with the Portuguese, the threat to unleash Rhodes might be useful in promoting a settlement. The problem was to put on the leash and to keep hold of it. Rhodes's manifest intention to oust the Portuguese from Mozambique threatened international complications far beyond little Portugal—perhaps even a rift with Germany. As the crisis intensified, complicated by Rhodes's actions and words, Salisbury became increasingly irritated with Rhodes.[16] But as Cape prime minister, supported by both Afrikaners and English South Africans, Rhodes was a formidable problem. Perhaps if provoked too far he might carry out the threat suggested in his speeches and lead South Africa out of the British Empire. Remarks by Rhodes in Kimberley in September 1891 as misreported in the *Times*[17] seemed to document Rhodes's readiness to lead a movement to oust the imperial factor from South Africa if he did not have his way. Despite Rhodes's subsequent disclaimers and professions of devotion to the Union Jack,

15. John S. Galbraith, *Mackinnon and East Africa, 1878–95*, pp. 132–134, 181.
16. On September 28, 1890, before the worst of the crisis, Abercorn wrote to Cawston that Salisbury "apparently has had enough of Rhodes." BSAC II Misc., Rhodes House. It was not the only time that such a sentiment was attributed to the British prime minister.
17. The *Times* (London), September 6, 1890.

Salisbury remained concerned that he might indeed try to establish an Anglo-Dutch republic.[18] Such an eventuality must be avoided; consequently Rhodes could not be treated too summarily.

Rhodes's voracity for Portuguese territory developed at a time when that territory had taken on great psychological significance. Africa had become a national symbol to the Portuguese people. After centuries of torpor, Portugal had awakened to reassert her ancient claims. Expeditions across Central Africa led by Serpa Pinto and Ivens and Capelo were manifestations of this new energy; the retention by Portugal of her ancient territories became a national cause.

The focus of Portuguese attention was at first on the possession of the two great waterways of Central Africa, the Congo and the Zambezi. The Berlin Conference stripped Portugal of control over the Congo and the bitterness of the blow was intensified by what the Portuguese considered British desertion at the critical stage. The loss of the Congo intensified Portuguese determination to retain the Zambezi and to join Mozambique and Angola; bitterness at British perfidy was reflected in the German-Portuguese convention of 1886 by which Germany recognized Portuguese claims to a transcontinental swath of Africa. The provisions of the convention did not become fully known to Britain for several months, when they were published in a Portuguese White Book.[19]

Mutual irritations involving Africa had produced a testy relationship between the two governments when Salisbury returned to office in 1886. Such statesmen as Henrique de Barros Gomes, who became foreign minister in 1886, fanned the national fervor of the Portuguese, but in turn were compelled to follow the popular will they had helped to create, even when cold reason indicated that they risked grave consequences for the nation in doing so. The Portuguese, particularly their "men on the spot" in Africa, defended their national honor in ways

18. Cawston to Rhodes, October 29, 1890, BSAC II Misc., Rhodes House.
19. An excellent presentation of the issues as seen by a British statesman is in a memo by Sir Percy Anderson, January 6, 1890, CAB 27/26/2, P.R.O.

that Salisbury considered impudent and presuming on their weakness as a defense against a great power.

Portuguese claims to vast territory seemed to Salisbury to rest on the flimsiest of elements—ancient treaties with rulers of vanished peoples, mouldering forts, a few wild orange trees presumably descended from some Portuguese plantations—but little evidence of occupation beyond the coast, and little development of the coastal zone. The general opinion among financial experts was that Portugal was on the verge of bankruptcy— the issue was not whether but when she would collapse. At the end of October the *Financial News* reported that the economic ruin of Portugal was imminent. Its bonds had been steadily dropping far below par value, and commerce was languishing.[20] Yet the Portuguese government persisted in asserting its rights over territories it could not possibly develop; the farce could not long continue. Already what economic activity there was in the Portuguese colonies was generated by foreign capitalists. The façade of Portuguese control would soon collapse—either Portugal would finally face realities and sell its holdings or it would lose them by force, by the direct action of some other state or by filibusterers who would seize control. Albert Grey stated the view of the chartered company board that most if not all of the Portuguese territory south of the Zambezi was "bound by the eternal laws of gravitation to tumble into our lap,"[21] and the board and Rhodes were eager to assist the process. The restraints imposed by the British government on the company's forces seemed to Rhodes both incomprehensible and intolerable. The Portuguese had no more rights than did the Africans. "They are a bad race," said Rhodes, "and have had 300 years on the coast and all they have done is to be a curse to any place they have occupied."[22]

Salisbury's search for an agreement had no relationship to sentiment—the prime minister was not a sentimental man. The "ancient alliance" related to past myth, not present reality. Re-

20. *Financial News*, October 29, 1890.
21. Grey to Harris, private, January 1, 1891, File 183/4, Grey Papers, Durham,
22. Extract, Rhodes to ———, June 15, 1890, encl. in Abercorn to Currie, July 16, 1890, F.O. 84/2086, P.R.O.

peated warnings that the monarchy might fall if the government capitulated to British pressure did not impress him. A monarchy so decrepit that it would fall over such an issue, he maintained, was not worth propping up, for it would collapse in the next crisis. He hoped, however, that its fall would be as untraumatic as possible. Like the chartered company board, he saw the Portuguese as fighting the inevitable. If they could not colonize and develop their dependencies, others would certainly do so:

> These Portuguese are the most unsatisfactory people to negotiate with I have ever had any experience of. . . . The difficult point to bring home to them is that it is of no use for them to claim rule over African territory unless they can colonise it. If they cannot provide settlers of their own blood, we can of ours; and we shall do so, whether we—that is Great Britain—desire it or not, and a country once inhabited by men of English or Dutch race, the Portuguese had better allow us to govern it; for it is quite certain that *they* will not be able to do so.[23]

Salisbury, however, did not believe it to be the function of government to accelerate the workings of "natural law." He sought an agreement which would recognize British claims in the Nyasa-Shiré area and in Mashonaland, and the rights of all nations to travel on the Zambezi as an international waterway. Beyond these conditions, he was prepared to negotiate, but he would react emphatically to any Portuguese attacks on what he considered to be British rights. Thus when a Portuguese expedition under Serpa Pinto penetrated into the Shiré area and collided with the Kololo, who had been declared under British protection, Salisbury responded to public outcry by issuing an ultimatum in January 1890 to Portugal to withdraw. The British cabinet prepared plans to seize part of the Portuguese dominions if Portugal was defiant. They considered occupying Goa with Indian forces as a cheap and easy means of making war but shelved this plan when the Indian government protested that such seizure would cause alarm among the Indian princes who might see their own future foreshadowed by this

23. Salisbury to Morier, February 11, 1891, quoted in Ronald Robinson and John Gallagher, *Africa and the Victorians*, pp. 247–248.

action.[24] Instead the government dispatched a squadron to Gibraltar and another to the Canary Islands,[25] and made plans also for the occupation of the island of Mozambique if the Portuguese did not give way. Such a show of force, the cabinet thought, might in fact be secretly welcomed by the Portuguese government which did not dare to confront popular feeling without the excuse that it was conceding to overwhelming physical power.[26]

Salisbury's emphatic action evoked cheers in Britain, not all spontaneous. Propagandists for the chartered company and the African Lakes Company were active in expressing public opinion. Verschoyle at the *Fortnightly Review* wrote a militant article on "Portugal's Aggression and England's Duty" in which he urged the government to seize Delagoa Bay; the harsh tone, he averred, was adopted at the instance of the government.[27] In Scotland the Lakes Company directors likewise took steps to manifest public support for a "no compromise" position.[28]

Jingoism in Britain was matched by indignation in Portugal, but the Portuguese government surrendered to the ultimatum. There was no rational alternative. Without the help of a great power, it would be madness to go to war, and no state was prepared to offer Portugal anything more than sympathy. Italy, Austria, and Germany all expressed concern for the survival of the Portuguese dynasty, the fall of which might also topple the Spanish monarchy and produce reverberations which would disturb the tranquillity of Europe. But their appeals to Britain for forbearance were couched in language devoid of threats.[29] A

24. As early as November 30, 1889, the British cabinet agreed that if the Portuguese proved obdurate, Britain should occupy Goa to bring them to reason. CAB 41/21/33, P.R.O. Salisbury referred to the opposition of the government of India in a letter to Portal, March 8, 1892, File A/80, Salisbury Papers, Christ Church, Oxford.
25. Eric Axelson, *Portugal and the Scramble for Africa, 1875–1891*, p. 229.
26. Cabinet meeting, December 23, 1889, CAB 41/21/34, P.R.O.
27. Verschoyle to Cawston, December [24?], 1889, BSAC I Misc., Rhodes House.
28. Bruce to Grey, December 29, 1889, File 208/4, Grey Papers, Durham.
29. Salisbury to Paget, January 13, 1890, F.O. 179/276, P.R.O.

Portuguese attempt in the spring of 1890 to gain the support of the Vatican was likewise unsuccessful. An application to the pope for spiritual jurisdiction across Africa north of the Zambezi from the Atlantic to the Indian Ocean was rejected in part at least through Cawston's connections in Rome.[30] After the signature of the Anglo-German agreement on Africa in June 1890 Portugal lost all hope of German intervention. It stood alone, virtually defenceless. Salisbury felt free to deal with the Portuguese, subject only to the constraint that any breach of the peace between the two countries must appear to be by Portuguese action rather than British aggression. He was not insensitive to the dangers of republicanism, though he considered republicanism a symptom rather than a cause of Portuguese political instability. He had no desire to humiliate the Portuguese, but neither was he willing to make concessions which would be interpreted at home as a surrender of British interests. Thus, the retention by Britain of Nyasa and the Shiré highlands and the recognition of the Zambezi as an international waterway were not negotiable. On the basis of both exploration and occupation, the Nyasa-Shiré area he considered to be rightfully British, and his conviction was reinforced by the strength of Scottish opinion. But possession of this interior area was of little value without access, and the only practicable route was that by the Zambezi and Shiré. The recent discovery by Daniel Rankin of the Chinde mouth offered the prospect of access to the Zambezi without land transit, and surveys by naval vessels ordered to the Chinde seemed to confirm the practicability of using that entrance.[31] Mashonaland, the eastern boundary of which was not defined, must also be British. Salisbury had no desire to wrest the coast from the Portuguese. Their right to Delagoa Bay, the most valuable harbor, had been confirmed by the MacMahon award of 1875, and their possession of the coast north to the boundaries of the German sphere he did not dispute.

---

30. Cawston to Herbert, private, April 3, 1890; Errington to Cawston, private, April 4, 1890; Errington to Cawston, private, April 18, 1890, all in BSAC II Misc., Rhodes House.

31. Macgregor to F.O., May 5, 1890, immediate; F.O. to Admiralty, confidential, pressing, May 7, 1890, both in F.O. 84/2081, P.R.O.; Cmdr. in Chief, East India Station, to Admiralty, July 25, 1890, confidential, F.O. 84/2087, P.R.O.

Later, Salisbury observed that his terms had been to assign to Britain the highlands where white men could work and thrive, while leaving to the Portuguese the disease-ridden, sweltering lowlands of the coast.[32] This was afterthought, for the bases for his decision had no such cynical symmetry.

In the formulation of the British positions, the Foreign Office consulted with the British South Africa Company, but the spokesmen of the company were the London board, in particular Cawston, rather than the irascible Cecil Rhodes. The government assumed that the board of directors spoke also for Rhodes. The assumption was not entirely justified. Liaison between the board and Rhodes was often defective, and policies agreed to when Rhodes was in London did not necessarily represent his views after he returned to the heady environment of South Africa. From Cape Town Rhodes came to the conclusion that no agreement was desirable, since the Portuguese would thus be confirmed in the possession of territory which they did not have the power to hold or the energy to develop. Particularly after the Anglo-German boundary agreement of June 1890 which he felt removed any threat of German intervention, he believed that the issue of the Portuguese boundary should be left to the free play of forces in Africa rather than being determined by diplomacy. If left alone, the British South Africa Company would occupy the territory south of the Zambezi all the way to the coastal belt and, if the Portuguese chose to fight, the result of the collision would surely be their rout and the company could then seize the coast itself from Delagoa Bay to the border of the German sphere.[33] Provided the imperial government did not intervene, the Portuguese thus would have the choice of peacefully accepting company control of most of the territory in dispute, or resisting and losing all their East African possessions.

Rhodes maintained that the fate of Africa should be decided by those who lived there, not by imperial officials who drew lines in accordance with the dictates of diplomacy in Europe, advised by dreary legalists pondering archaic treaties and ancient claims. The London board was more cautious. Perhaps the

32. J. E. S. Green, *Rhodes Goes North*, p. 233.
33. Extract, Rhodes to ———, June 15, 1890, encl. in Abercorn to Currie, July 1, 1890, F.O. 84/2086, P.R.O.

company's forces were superior to the African levies of the Portuguese, but they preferred not to put the issue to a test. Wars were costly, and the company's resources were limited. And, if hostilities broke out, it was imperative that the Portuguese seem to be the aggressors. If the company appeared to be engaged in aggression, the imperial government would certainly take action, even possibly revoking the company's charter.

The board of directors thus sought to curb Rhodes's impetuosity. But they and he were in agreement as to the basic strategy the company should employ. Between Mashonaland and the coast there were two regions reputed to be rich in gold—Manica and Gazaland. The principal chief in Manica was Mutasa (Umtasa), who lived in a mountainous area which offered protection against attack. Mutasa was an important element in the company's plans, for if they could demonstrate to the satisfaction of the British government that he was an independent chief while making him their client, they would gain control of the region which was both rich and strategic, for it was adjacent to that area of the coast closest to Mashonaland. The company hoped to establish a transport route from Pungwe Bay, on which Beira is situated, up the Pungwe River through the tsetse fly country, thus providing much easier and cheaper access than was possible from the south. If Mutasa could be inflated into a chief whose territories extended all the way to the coast, so much the better; at the very least, his recognition as an independent chief would give the company control of the gold region. Mutasa at various times had declared his vassalage either to the Portuguese or to the Shangaan chief of Gazaland to protect himself against the other. The company's object in 1890 was to discount these actions as of no validity (later, when its interests changed, it would discover that Mutasa was indeed a tributary to Gungunyana, chief of Gazaland).[34]

The Gazas (also known as Shangaans, Vatuas, or Landeens) were a Zulu-speaking people who had migrated to the area south

---

34. The company's concession from Gungunyana included rights to land, whereas that from Mutasa involved only mineral rights. Consequently it became convenient to treat Mutasa's territory as being under Gungunyana, which the company did in 1892. Memo, Fairfield to Ripon, December 2, 1892, C.O. 417/87, P.R.O.

of Lourenço Marques in the 1820s after they had suffered defeat at the hands of Shaka. Under the chief who had led them on this trek, Soshangane Manikusa, they had expanded their territory to include the territory between the Zambezi and the Limpopo and from the Sabi River in Shona territory to the sea. They occupied Lourenço Marques itself for a time, and the Portuguese for half a century paid tribute to the Gazas.[35]

After Shoshangane's death there was a struggle for the succession. The eldest son, Mzila, finally ousted his half-brother, with some assistance from the Portuguese who furnished him with arms and African levies. Thereafter, Portugal treated him as a "Portuguese-protected person."[36] Mzila denied any dependency on Portugal. In the 1870s he sent missions to Natal seeking to promote trade, but the Natal government was wary of any arrangements which would challenge Portuguese claims. Under Mzila's successor, Gungunyana, the power of the Gazas declined. They were still able to dominate their African neighbors, but they were hard pressed by the Portuguese. The Goan Manoel António da Sousa (Gouveia) forced the Gazas from the territory between the Zambezi and the Busi-Revue rivers, and the Gazas lost all control of the coast. Gungunyana accepted a Portuguese resident at his headquarters, and two Gazas claiming to represent him were taken to Lisbon where they accepted a treaty recognizing Portuguese overlordship. Gungunyana disowned these alleged agents, and in 1887 sought assistance from Natal, but the Natal government again declined to contest Portuguese claims to protection over Gazaland.[37]

This was the state of affairs when the company appeared as a factor. For the company's plans, recognition of Gungunyana's independence was of great importance. Like Mutasa, he occupied a territory which was reportedly gold-bearing; like Mutasa, he might be the vehicle for the company's march to the sea. The Limpopo River which coursed through Gazaland was said by travelers to be navigable most of the way to the Transvaal border and might offer a route into Mashonaland and Matabele-

35. P. R. Warhurst, "The Scramble and Politics in Gazaland," in Eric Stokes and Richard Brown, eds., *The Zambesian Past*, pp. 47–48.
36. *Ibid.*, p. 49.
37. *Ibid.*, pp. 51–52.

land. Consequently, Gungunyana in the eyes of the company
became a great African chief, unfettered by any dependence on
Portugal. The essence of the company's case as developed by
Rhodes was presented by Cawston to the imperial government
at the beginning of 1890. Citing the authority of Frederick Selous and a trader named Reuben Benningfield, Rhodes maintained that Gungunyana was a "much more powerful chief than
Lobengula," with a great standing army, and that he desired to
be the friend of Britain. With the friendship of Mutasa and
Gungunyana the company would be able to build a railway to
the coast and the Portuguese would be foiled in their hopes of
strangling the development of the interior, provided the British
government refused to recognize paper claims not supported
by actual occupation.[38]

"Occupation" was a word of uncertain meaning, and the
company used it as convenience dictated. But essential to the
company's case was the recognition of Mutasa and Gungunyana
as independent chiefs in alliance with Britain. This campaign
to protect the "independence" of the two chiefs, of course, was
a façade; the objective was to make them mere puppets of the
company. Neither, in the opinion of the company's officers, was
competent to govern.

Beyond the intellectual limitations assumed to be common
to most Africans, Mutasa and Gungunyana were particular objects of contempt. Mutasa's pretensions to be a great king were
considered to be ludicrous, for he was craven, "ready to grovel
by daylight before anyone who made a show of strength."[39]
His word was worthless, he was "greedy, venal, double dealing
and untruthful."[40] After he was safely under company control
he was treated with rudeness and, sometimes, brutality by company officials.[41] Gungunyana also allegedly had neither intelligence nor strength of character; he was described as an alcoholic
besotted by Portuguese rum and wine, who was rarely sober

38. Harris to London board, December 23, 1889, encl. in Cawston to
Currie, February 3, 1890, F.O. 84/2074, P.R.O.
39. Hugh Marshall Hole, *The Making of Rhodesia*, p. 161.
40. Fort to Scott, August 22. 1894, S 1428/15, N.A.R.
41. C.O. to F.O., July 30, 1892, F.O. 84/2255; F.O. to C.O., August 6,
1892, C.O. 417/87, both in P.R.O.

enough to make a rational decision.[42] These were the judgments by company representatives of the men whom they publicly portrayed as able leaders fighting to retain their people's independence against the treacherous Portuguese. Grey put the company's policy honestly and cynically: ". . . Let Gungunyana and Umtassa be the declared sovereigns. We can pull the wires from behind the curtain. They pose before the civilized world as independent chiefs and nobody can complain if they choose to use their independence in a way that is pleasing to us."[43]

The strategy was to negotiate an agreement with the two chiefs before the Portuguese came to terms and to press the imperial government to adjust its position accordingly. Consequently, Archibald R. Colquhoun, the prospective administrator of Mashonaland, was ordered to detach himself from the pioneer column as soon as it was safe to do so and make his way to Manica to negotiate a concession from Mutasa which, if possible, should extend all the way to the sea.[44] Also, Dr. Aurel Schulz, a Natalian whom Rhodes had known for several years, was instructed at the end of May to proceed to Gazaland on a similar mission. In addition to seeking a concession, Schulz was to attempt to induce Gungunyana to accept British protection.[45] For his services, Schulz was to receive £2,000 in cash, and he was promised an additional £8,000 in chartered shares if the company acquired Gazaland.[46]

Colquhoun and Jameson, guided by Selous. left the pioneer Column at Fort Charter at the beginning of September. Jameson had to turn back because of injuries caused by a fall from a horse, but Colquhoun and Selous arrived at Mutasa's kraal with no further mishaps. Negotiations with Mutasa involved no difficulties. He professed to look upon the company as his deliverers from the Portuguese menace, and on September 14 he approved a treaty by which he conferred extensive powers on the company

42. Hole, *Making of Rhodesia*, p. 191.
43. Grey to Harris, private, January 1, 1891, File 183/4, Grey Papers, Durham.
44. C.O. to BSAC, confidential, January 24, 1890, F.O. 84/2085, P.R.O.
45. Harris to Schulz, May 29, 1890, CT 1/7/9, N.A.R.
46. Currie to Harris, May 16, 1891, A1/2/1, N.A.R.

for an annual subsidy of £100 per year. In addition to exclusive mineral rights the company was granted monopolies of public works, including railways, banking, coining money, and the manufacture and importation of arms and ammunition.[47]

Colquhoun had been instructed to define Mutasa's domain in the most expansive terms which could be credible, if possible to the Indian Ocean. But it was soon evident that such claims could not be sustained. Not only was Mutasa a mere petty chief, but in much of the highlands area prospectors were at work under license from the Mozambique Company. The most that Colquhoun could claim for Mutasa was a strip of Manica extending to 34°E and 20°S, and even this claim was clouded by the fact that officials of the Mozambique Company were in residence at Maçequeçe, almost 60 miles to the west of Colquhoun's "boundaries."[48] Mutasa had accepted an alliance with the company as a means of self-preservation. But perhaps the company was not in fact stronger than the Portuguese and could not defend him. To protect himself against this contingency, he sent messengers to the Portuguese at Maçequeçe informing that he had signed the agreement only under duress.[49]

Schulz's mission to Gungunyana was complicated by the fact that though the Gaza chief claimed mastery over hundreds of miles of coastline, including the Limpopo mouth, the Portuguese were on the alert and might intercept an expedition to Gazaland. Consequently, Schulz made his way to the chief's kraal at Manhlagazi, about a hundred miles inland, and on October 4 secured Gungunyana's promise of a concession granting land and mineral rights, contingent on his receiving a thousand rifles, twenty thousand rounds of ammunition, and a payment of £500 per year. Schulz's party returned to Durban shortly thereafter to wrestle with the problem of how to deliver arms and ammunition without being apprehended by the Portuguese.[50]

The environment surrounding Gungunyana was similar to

47. The text of the concession is given in Green, *Rhodes Goes North*, pp. 365–367.
48. Summary, Manica Concessions, S 428/17/2, N.A.R.; Hole, *Making of Rhodesia*, p. 163.
49. Axelson, *Portugal and the Scramble for Africa*, p. 264.
50. Philip R. Warhurst, *Anglo-Portuguese Relations in South-Central Africa*, pp. 83–84.

that confronted by Lobengula at the time of the Rudd concession. Like the Ndebele chief, Gungunyana was besieged by concession hunters; like him also, he was aware that his independence was in mortal danger. The old Portuguese enemy he
knew; his new friends might be even more dangerous. Contrary
to the impressions of Schulz and others, Gungunyana was not a
muddle-headed weakling; on the contrary, he was an able negotiator who sought by diplomacy to play off his antagonists
against each other. He consequently declined Schulz's offer of
British protection, and cautiously avoided formally committing
himself to the concession until the weapons he needed were delivered. His subsequent failure was a further commentary on
the hopelessness of statecraft without supporting power.[51]

For the company directors as for Rhodes, Mutasa and Gungunyana were of significant only as counters in the diplomatic
contest. The company sought to establish control over as much
gold-bearing territory as possible in any arrangement reached
between Britain and Portugal and to secure at least transit rights
from the sea to Mashonaland. They attempted to convince the
imperial government of the worthlessness of Portuguese claims
and the validity of their own. The Colquhoun and Schulz missions thus represented deliberate company policy, not merely
that of Rhodes. But policy as developed in London and as interpreted and executed in South Africa were quite different. The
directors recognized constraints on company action which
Rhodes was not willing to accept. They acknowledged the necessity of submission to imperial authority; Rhodes railed
against the timidity of Whitehall and sought to create conditions which would force the imperial government to follow the
aggressive line he wished to pursue. Rhodes had an ally in Sir
Henry Loch, who was as ardent as the Cape prime minister in
advocating terms which would satisfy Rhodes's ambitions. If the
Portuguese were unwilling to cede their rights over Gazaland
and Manica, Loch suggested, their opposition might be removed
by an appropriate money payment.[52] But Loch was not kept in-

51. *Ibid.*, p. 82; Douglas L. Wheeler, "Gungunyana the Negotiator: a
Study in African Diplomacy," *Journal of African History*, IX, 4
(1968): 585–602.
52. Telegram, secret, Loch to Knutsford, July 21, 1890; same to same,

formed of the details of the negotiations until the convention had been essentially settled, and his suggestions carried little weight with the Foreign Office.

The Foreign Office in its negotiations with Portugal maintained close communication with the company, but the company with which it dealt was in London, not in Cape Town; the negotiator was Cawston, not Rhodes. The consequences were further alienation between Rhodes and the imperial government. Like his fellow directors, Cawston was a reasonable man. His discussions with Sir Philip Currie, the permanent undersecretary for foreign affairs, convinced him that the imperial government would not modify its position that Gazaland and most of Manica were within the Portuguese sphere, and he and the London board at the beginning of July agreed to a settlement with Portugal embodying these elements,[53] which were incorporated in the treaty concluded between Salisbury and the Portuguese negotiator in August 1890. The limits of British Nyasaland were all that the missionaries and their allies could have desired, but south of the Zambezi, Portuguese hegemony was recognized over Gazaland and the bulk of Manicaland. In the west Salisbury accepted a line between Angola and Barotseland which assigned to Angola approximately half of the territory claimed for the Lozi chief Lewanika by the company. Portugal agreed not to cede any territory south of the Zambezi to a third power without the consent of Britain; the Zambezi was to be internationalized and several acres of land at the Chinde mouth was to be leased to Britain. Portugal committed itself either to build or to allow others to build a railway from the Pungwe mouth to the British South Africa Company's borders.[54]

The terms produced an angry response from the zealots on both sides. Portuguese patriots denounced the requirement of British consent to alienation of territory as an affront to national dignity which reduced a proud European people to the

July 31, 1890, both in C.O. 537/126, P.R.O. The suggestion of a money payment almost certainly came from Rhodes.

53. "Terms agreed at meeting with Meade and Cawston," July 10, 1890, F.O. 84/2087, P.R.O.

54. Axelson, *Portugal and the Scramble for Africa*, p. 252; R.J. Hammond, *Portugal and Africa*, pp. 136–137.

level of African savages.[55] Rhodes was furious. He had insisted that the ownership of Manica and Gazaland should be determined by occupation which he confidently expected would be by the company, and his demands had been overridden.[56] Rhodes's backers on the board—Grey and Beit—and Rhodes's alternate, Maguire, went to the Foreign Office in a last minute effort to secure modifications of the convention in accordance with Rhodes's views,[57] but without success. Their extreme position was annoying to Salisbury—"they are quite hopeless," he noted.[58] The Foreign Office did not authorize notification of Rhodes himself until two weeks after Cawston had accepted the terms.[59] Loch likewise was given the opportunity to comment only after the provisions of the convention had been essentially determined by the Foreign Office.

The Foreign Office hoped that Rhodes would not "make difficulties"; they sought to moderate his opposition by asking Cawston to indicate support of the agreement; Beit likewise was induced to acquiesce.[60] But they did not really expect to convert Rhodes, and they were correct in their assumption. Rhodes emphatically protested that the imperial government had sacrificed the company's interests to Portugal, but his opposition had no effect. It was now "too late to draw back," said Currie, and in any event, Rhodes's position was far too militant for the imperial government to accept. Currie wrote Cawston:

> I am quite unable to understand Rhodes's policy, unless he proposes to make war on Portugal, seize her territories, and occupy her ports. The arrangement we have proposed is a vast improvement on the present state of things, and the utmost possible without the use of force. It is not probable HMG would sanction the Company engaging in hostilities with a European

55. Hammond, *Portugal and Africa*, p. 137.
56. Cawston to Currie, private, July 11, 1890, BSAC II Misc., Rhodes House. Currie asked Cawston not to telegraph Rhodes as to the terms of the convention, and Cawston agreed not to do so.
57. Cawston to Fife, July 18, 1890, BSAC II Misc., Rhodes House.
58. Note by Salisbury, n.d., on Abercorn to Currie, F.O. 84/2086, P.R.O.
59. Villiers to Meade, July 24, 1890, C.O. 537/126, P.R.O.; telegram, Currie to Cawston, July 24, 1890, BSAC II Misc., Rhodes House.
60. Currie to Cawston, July 28, 1890, BSAC II Misc.

Power and they are likely to have their hands full dealing with Lobengula and other colored potentates.[61]

Currie's description of Rhodes's desires was much closer to the truth than he probably realized. Rhodes was quite prepared to use force against the Portuguese, confident that the "black mercenaries" of the Portuguese would flee rather than fight in any encounter with the company. Responsibility for any collision would be Portuguese, for the company would be defending its rights against aggression. The treaty frustrated this policy, and Rhodes in his dual capacity as managing director and prime minister strongly pressed Salisbury to alter the convention to concede to Portugal only a narrow strip of the East African coast. In this campaign he had unexpected assistance from the Portuguese Cortes which balked at certain provisions of the treaty—particularly those which proscribed Portugal from ceding territory without the consent of Britain.[62] Salisbury warned Portugal that he would withdraw his restraints on Rhodes and the Cape government unless the treaty was ratified soon,[63] but the Portuguese ministry faced with public indignation avoided the issue by allowing the Cortes to adjourn without taking any action.[64] Efforts by Portugal to induce Salisbury to modify the treaty were largely unavailing, though he finally agreed to modify the obnoxious "consent" provision to a British first option to purchase.[65] The ministry resigned, leaving the whole issue moot.

Portuguese pride and politicians' cravenness had given Rhodes an opportunity which the British prime minister had attempted to deny him. "I am sorry to say," Salisbury noted, "that Portugal is playing Rhodes' game."[66] Rhodes had demanded that the map of South East Africa should be drawn by the men on the spot; those who had the power should have the

61. Currie to Cawston, private, August 14, 1890, BSAC II Misc., Rhodes House.
62. Axelson, *Portugal and the Scramble for Africa*, p. 259.
63. Telegram, Salisbury to Petre, September 21, 1890, F.O. 179/279, P.R.O.
64. Axelson, *Portugal and the Scramble for Africa*, p. 270.
65. Hammond, *Portugal and Africa*, p. 140.
66. Note by Salisbury, n.d., on Herbert to Lister, September 20, 1890, F.O. 84/2091, P.R.O.

prizes. Rhodes's determination to take all the land that power could seize was too blatant even for his own directors to accept; and the majority of the board had acquiesced in Salisbury's decision. They thus displayed more courage than was their wont in the face of Rhodes's insistence on having his way, but their resistance crumbled when Portugal failed to ratify the treaty. They capitulated in mid-September when they asked the Foreign Office to abandon the agreement.[67] Having reduced his board to submission, Rhodes shifted his assault to the imperial government. His major weapon was the threat of resignation both as managing director and as prime minister. He was confident that Britain would defer to him rather than face the wrath of Cape Colony, where he believed he had support from all parties in his campaign to drive the Portuguese into the sea;[68] and he knew that the company's directors would use all their influence on his behalf rather than risk losing him. His communiques from Cape Town took on an imperious tone, and the board showed appropriate deference to his desires. In private, Abercorn grumbled that Rhodes was "a little bit of an autocrat,"[69] but he nevertheless obeyed Rhodes's dictates and appealed to Salisbury to heed the demands of a man who had "great influence, power, and knowledge."[70] Rhodes's dispatches from Cape Town took on a hectoring tone. Toward Harry Johnston, whom he held accountable for the treaty, he was rude and bullying. "The least I can ask you to do," he wrote Johnston, "is to repair the mischief you have done by getting the Portuguese treaty dropped."[71] Toward the Foreign Office he was importunate. He did not deign to use the polite language of the statesman, and he communicated directly rather than following the established channels of correspondence.[72]

The bluster which was so effective in cowing company directors did not intimidate Salisbury. This great imperial statesman

67. Hawksley to F.O., September 13, 1890, F.O. 84/2090, P.R.O.
68. Weatherly to Currie, September 19, 1890, F.O. 84/2091, P.R.O.
69. Fragment, Abercorn to Cawston, [September 1890?], BSAC II Misc., Rhodes House.
70. Abercorn to Cawston, September 21, 1890, in *ibid.*
71. Rhodes to Johnston, September 22, 1890, quoted in Oliver, *Johnston,* p. 177.
72. Rhodes to Currie, September 21, 1890, F.O. 84/2091, P.R.O.

who prided himself on his ability to defend his country's interests would not be blackmailed by threats by a Cape prime minister who lacked both manners and political sophistication. The
bogey of a movement for Cape secession if Rhodes resigned as
prime minister did not dismay him. It was unlikely that Rhodes
would give up office, and even more unlikely that his departure
would produce the traumatic effect which the company's directors feared. Salisbury, in a letter to Abercorn which was as chilly
as Rhodes's were hot, let the company know that he had "had
enough of Rhodes."[73]

Salisbury instead of giving Rhodes his head chose to accept
the plea of the new Portuguese government that it had not repudiated the convention. When reports came of an impending
move by the company into territories assigned to Portugal by
the treaty, he informed Sir Henry Loch that the imperial government would not recognize any such acquisitions.[74] In November 1890 he formalized this position by accepting a *modus
vivendi* which essentially recognized as the status quo the provisions of the August treaty.[75]

While Salisbury negotiated with Portugal Rhodes was planning his campaign to oust the Portuguese, confident in his assumption that the August convention would be buried. This
expectation was reinforced by reports from the board that Portuguese antagonism to Britain was so strong that no agreement
could be reached.[76]

During the hiatus between the impasse on the treaty and the
modus vivendi, Rhodes took vigorous action to assert the company's authority in territories Salisbury had conceded to the
Portuguese. If a new treaty was negotiated, he hoped that these
acquisitions would be recognized; if no agreement was reached
with Portugal, they would belong to the company by right of
occupation. The strategy continued to be to establish the independence of Mutasa, Gungunyana, and other Gaza chiefs and

73. Abercorn to Cawston, September 28, 1890, BSAC II Misc., Rhodes
House. Abercorn did not enclose Salisbury's letter, probably because
the language in it was such that he felt it dangerous to circulate it.
74. Note by Salisbury, n.d., on C.O. to F.O., immediate, October 20,
1890, F.O. 84/2093, P.R.O.
75. Axelson, *Portugal and the Scramble for Africa*, p. 273.
76. London office to Kimberley, October 16, 1890, LO 3/1/1, N.A.R.

their right to the possession not only of the plateau but of the coast as well. The company as the protector of its African allies would send its forces to defend the coast against Portuguese attack. Thus the problem of communication with Mashonaland would be solved, for the company would acquire Beira and the control of a short route rather than the long and expensive route from the railhead at Mafeking. Harris, who by now spoke almost as the voice of Rhodes, expressed the hope that Downing Street would not obstruct "the rightful development of the English race in South Zambesia, out of respect to such a slave-raiding gin-drinking set of scoundrels as the Portuguese."[77] Harris, for Rhodes, notified Colonel Pennefather that he had a free hand to send forces through Manica as far as the sea and instructed him to do so without delay. "Now or never," he wired Jameson.[78] Pennefather was on leave at the time, but Colquhoun sent a small force of a sergeant-major and ten men into Manica, and ordered Captain H. M. Heyman, in charge of the police at Fort Charter, to send reinforcements as soon as possible. At the end of October Colquhoun appointed Captain P. W. Forbes in charge of Manica. Forbes's orders were explicit—to "occupy as much as Manica as possible" under Colquhoun's treaty of September and to negotiate further treaties with chiefs in the Busi River area. Colquhoun empowered Forbes to use whatever measures he deemed necessary if the Portuguese threatened Mutasa.[79] Given the character of Forbes, these orders made a collision with the Portuguese almost inevitable. He was a man of action, not a diplomat, and his orders encouraged him to act.[80]

Rhodes developed a further plan in accordance with his assumption that the Foreign Office would wink at aggressive actions provided they were adequately disguised. Colquhoun was advised to send company employees into the area between the Sabi River and the thirty-third meridian. They would pose as independent prospectors having no connection with the company, and the company would then send in its forces to establish order,

77. Harris to Grey, October 20, 1890, File 183/4, Grey Papers, Durham.
78. Telegram, Harris to Jameson, October 18, 1890, A 1/3/5, N.A.R.
79. Axelson, *Portugal and the Scramble for Africa*, p. 273.
80. He demonstrated these qualities in the Matabele War of 1893.

thus pointing up the fact that the Portuguese exercised no authority in the area. Rhodes stressed to Colquhoun the importance of maintaining the scenario that the company was responding to an initiative of prospectors of which it had no advance knowledge.[81]

The campaign in Manica represented Rhodes unrestrained. The controls in Britain were not operative, and Salisbury was to a considerable extent responsible. Cawston and Beit in their consultation with the Foreign Office had made no effort to dissemble about Rhodes's intentions. An explicit statement from Salisbury might have stopped the campaign in Manica, but it was not forthcoming. Instead, he advised the board that "what HMG will do depends on what takes place."[82] Such a remark could only be interpreted by Rhodes as an encouragement to proceed without asking questions of the imperial government.

The plan to send in "independent" miners was superseded when the company was presented with an opportunity for direct action when Forbes's forces collided with the Portuguese at Maçequeçe (Vila del Manica). Colonel Paiva d'Andrada, administrator of the Mozambique Company, and António da Sousa (Gouveia) had arrived at Maçequeçe on the Manica plateau to extract from Mutasa an affirmation of his submission to Portugal; and he complied, providing Sousa with an elephant tusk filled with earth as a symbol of his friendship and participating in the ceremony of raising the Portuguese flag. Forbes, acting on his orders, issued an ultimatum to the Portuguese to withdraw, and when they did not do so, attacked and took Andrada and Sousa prisoner, sending them off under guard to Fort Salisbury.[83]

Maçequeçe was on the Portuguese side of the boundary as described in the convention of August 1890 but the company's version of the affair was that an armed force of 300 men had attacked Mutasa and, in spite of his repeated protests, torn down the British flag and hoisted that of Portugal. Forbes had then

---

81. Harris to Colquhoun, Confidential Strictly, November 21, 1890, A 1/2/5, N.A.R.
82. Note by Salisbury, n.d., on Anderson to Hopwood, October 21, 1890, F.O. 84/2093, P.R.O.
83. Warhurst, *Anglo-Portuguese Relations*, pp. 27–30.

come to Mutasa's defense, disarmed the Portuguese force and taken their leaders prisoner.[84] The facts seem to have been different. Mutasa was attached to whatever European force was in his vicinity, and his alleged fervor for the Union Jack represented Forbes rather than himself. Andrada and Sousa undoubtedly put pressure on Mutasa by their presence, but their "army," as Forbes described it appears to have been largely a collection of bearers and other untrained men who were unprepared for attack by a disciplined force.[85] Andrada was probably correct in his assertions that he had been taken by surprise and that Mutasa had connived with the company's police to deliver his party into their hands.[86]

The altercation at Maçequeçe occurred on November 15, the day after Salisbury and the Portuguese negotiator had signed the *modus vivendi* accepting a temporary status quo. The agreement had no immediate effect on the Company's campaign in Manica; Forbes, after his "victory" at Maçequeçe, proceeded with his detachment of police toward the sea. But one week after the *modus vivendi*, the company's board advised Rhodes that there should be a change in tactics. The company should avoid any appearance of aggressive action. The company's employees in Manica should no longer be referred to as police but as miners, prospectors, and pioneers engaged in peaceful pursuits under licenses from the chiefs of the area. So long as the company did not actually assume administration east of the boundary of the *modus vivendi*, the imperial government was not likely to object.[87]

The company's directors interpreted Salisbury's views as filtered through his staff to be that he preferred not to be informed on what was taking place in Manica,[88] and that when a new treaty was negotiated, the company would reap at least some of the fruits of its clandestine activities. Their assumption was that

84. Kimberley office to London office, BSAC, December 4, 1890, F.O. 84/2096, P.R.O.
85. Axelson, *Portugal and the Scramble for Africa*, p. 267.
86. See J. C. Paiva d'Andrada, *Report and Protest of the Affairs Occurred at Manica*.
87. London office to Kimberley office, BSAC, November 21, 1890, LO 3/1/1, N.A.R.
88. Same to same, November 28, 1890, in *ibid*.

the *modus vivendi* would end in another stalemate, and that the imperial government would soon consider the agreement abandoned. The Duke of Fife, after reading reports in the newspapers at the beginning of November to this effect, wrote in congratulatory terms to Salisbury. "The baneful tendency of Portuguese rule in Africa" he asserted, had lasted far too long. The vigorous British South African colonies looked to the adjacent territories as their inheritance. No treaties could keep out the inevitable occupation of these undeveloped lands by English-speaking whites. Manica was already occupied by the company's pioneers; soon Gazaland would follow, including the coastal zone; company agents had acquired interests in Barotse country assigned by the 1890 convention to the Portuguese. Salisbury's enlightened decision to abandon the convention would expedite a process which in any case was irreversible.[89]

This interpretation of British policy was not what the Foreign Office had in mind. There was no immediate intention to cancel the convention, and the forays of company employees in the guise of miners were not what the government considered to be bona fide occupation. Salisbury branded Fife's letter "insolent."[90] But the company directors were almost certainly following what they considered to be broad hints from the Foreign Office in the line they were advising Rhodes to follow in Mozambique.

Confusion was compounded by first reports, from company officials, of the Maçequeçe incident which indicated that the Portuguese had been the aggressors and that the encounter had occurred on the British side of the treaty line. This version was initially accepted by the Foreign Office,[91] and by Sir Henry Loch who urgently called for the dispatch of a man-of-war to Delagoa Bay and to the Pungwe River mouth to demonstrate to the Portuguese that further aggression would not be tolerated.[92]

While these misapprehensions beclouded perception in London, Rhodes resumed his campaign to reach the sea. After the

89. Fife to Salisbury, November 7, 1890, F.O. 84/2094, P.R.O.
90. Note, Salisbury, n.d., on *ibid.*
91. Notes on C.O. to F.O., December 5, 1890, F.O. 84/2096, P.R.O.
92. Notes on F.O. to C.O., December 6, 1890, C.O. 417/50, P.R.O.

Maçequeçe incident Forbes and his little troop had continued east with the intention of reaching Pungwe Bay, and had arrived at a point not far from Beira when they were overtaken by a messenger from Colquhoun ordering them to withdraw.[93] Accordingly they broke off the expedition and instead concentrated, with the assistance of Doyle and Selous, in securing mining concessions from chiefs between Manica and the sea. In each of these concessions, the chief granted a right of way for the railroad.[94]

The withdrawal of Forbes's force was a setback to Rhodes's plans. He had a further setback when he was informed of the *modus vivendi*.[95] But Rhodes did not remain passive long. He resolved to try again to take Beira. The action would be justified by the Portuguese "aggression" on Mutasa at Maçequeçe and by alleged Portuguese responsibility for the raising of the Portuguese flag by chief Lomagundi, whose headquarters were about eighty miles southwest of Salisbury. The chief must have been intimidated, Rhodes maintained,[96] though he had refused to lower the flag when called upon to do so by company officers.[97] On these justifications Rhodes on December 4, 1890, ordered the police under Forbes, augmented by additional men sent from Fort Victoria, to occupy Beira and the lines of communication between that port and Mashonaland.[98] At the same time Rhodes considered a scheme by which the company would send 100 "picked young men" who would be transported to the Manica plateau, supplied by De Beers with wagons, food, tools, and dynamite to settle the future of Manica and preclude the return of the territory to Portugal.[99]

93. Warhurst, *Anglo-Portuguese Relations*, p. 50.
94. Harris to Bower, January 8, 1891, CT 2/4/2, N.A.R.
95. On November 24, 1890, the Kimberley office notified London that Rhodes had instructed Colquhoun not to proceed with "prospectors" beyond 33° E latitude in accordance with the *modus vivendi*, LO 5/2/5, N.A.R.
96. Rhodes to Colquhoun, December 1, 1890, A 1/2/5, N.A.R.
97. Telegram, Colquhoun to Sec., BSAC, Kimberley [Nov.] 23, 1890, CT 1/12/8, N.A.R.
98. Telegram, Rhodes to [Colquhoun?], December 4, 1890, LO 5/2/7, N.A.R. The telegram was received in Salisbury on December 14.
99. Harris to London office, December 14, 1890, LO 5/2/5, N.A.R.

A combination of circumstances frustrated the execution of these plans. Forbes was courageous but he was not a fool; he had been through the land between Maçequeçe and the coast and knew the dangers, natural and human, he would encounter. His troop must first pass through tsetse fly country, necessitating African bearers because of the mortality to animals. The rainy season had set in, making roads swampy or impassable. He was ill with malaria and already most of his men were unfit to march the 150 miles from their base on the plateau to Beira, and their equipment was sadly deficient—many did not even have serviceable boots. Those who would get through would have to confront a substantial body of black troops who had been brought in from other parts of Mozambique, and a Portuguese man-of-war stationed in the harbor. Such odds, Forbes considered, made an attempt on Beira lunatic. If he had been ordered to take the port in November, during the dry season and before the arrival of reinforcements, he considered that he could have done so. Now the operation would involve the senseless loss of his force for a prize not worth the battle. He had already secured rights to both sides of the Pungwe except for the site of Beira itself, by treaties with chiefs in the area. It would be better to occupy the high ground which commanded the Pungwe route and leave the issue of Beira for the future.[100]

Before Rhodes received this intelligence, he had been explicitly ordered by the imperial government to end aggressive action. Loch, acting on instructions from the Colonial Office, directed Rhodes on December 18 to withdraw the company's forces from Maçequeçe, which the Foreign Office now conceded was Portuguese by right of occupation as a station of the Mozambique Company, and to retire in other parts of Manica beyond the thirty-third meridian.[101] At the same time the London board requested Rhodes to pull back the police to the west of the water parting between the Pungwe and Sabri rivers, which would have involved a withdrawal even further to the west, but he declined to do so on the basis that the effect would have been "disastrous

100. Administrator, Fort Salisbury, to Sec. BSAC. December 17, [1890]; Forbes to Administrator, Mashonaland, December 20, 1890, both in LO 5/2/7, N.A.R.
101. Loch to Knutsford, December 23, 1890, F.O. 84/2098, P.R.O.

to our prestige" with the Africans whom the company had promised to protect from the Portuguese.[102]

Harris attributed the abortion of the Beira raid to Rhodes's adherence to the *modus vivendi* and his instructions to Colquhoun to resrtict himself to the protection of Mutasa and the company's Manica concession.[103] This version bore little relationship to reality. Rhodes expected his agents to interpret his intentions rather than to be guided by his words. It was one of the causes of Rhodes's discontent with Colquhoun that the administrator lacked this imagination. Jameson, on the other hand, was a man who could be relied upon to act as Rhodes wished without the necessity of explicit instructions. Consequently, Jameson was put in charge of Mashonaland and Manica as managing director in December 1890, though Colquhoun was allowed to save some face by retaining the title of administrator but with his functions strictly limited to administration under Jameson's control. All "political" matters, including relations with the Portuguese, were assigned to Jameson. Jameson arrived in Salisbury on Christmas Day, 1890.[104] It is interesting to speculate what the result would have been had he, rather than Colquhoun, been the recipient of Rhodes's instructions to seize Beira, which arrived only eleven days before.

What Rhodes had hoped to take by force Salisbury sought to win for the company by diplomacy. At the same time as he was imposing restraints on company action he was insisting to the Portuguese that there would be no settlement unless the Portuguese agreed to a "substantial rectification" of the frontier in Manica and conceded unrestrained access from the sea into Mashonaland by a railroad, which must be built within a fixed time.[105]

The negotiations were complicated by the fact that Portugal had granted a charter to the Mozambique Company to control the territory between 22° south latitude and the Zambezi—the

102. Harris to London office, December 22, 1890, LO 5/2/5, N.A.R.
103. *Ibid.*
104. Ian Colvin, *The Life of Jameson*, 1:171–172.
105. Telegram, Salisbury to Petre, December 23, 1890; telegram, Petre to Salisbury, December 24, 1890; telegram, Salisbury to Petre, December 26, 1890, all in F.O. 84/2154, P.R.O.

districts of Manica and Sofala. The Mozambique Company was
the latest in a series of ventures by which Paiva d'Andrada had
attempted to develop Portuguese African territory to the mutual benefit of himself and the state. In 1879 while he was a military attaché in Paris, he had formed a company called La So-
ciété des Fondateurs de la Compagnie Générale du Zambèse to
exploit a concession granted by the Portuguese government.
The company was a failure, and in 1883 he organized two other
companies. One, the East Africa Company, was still-born, and
the other, the Companhia Africana, died of malnutrition
shortly after birth. Then in 1884 he created the Ophir Company
with a nominal capital of £20,000 of which approximately
£6,600 was actually subscribed.[106] The concession of this company was embraced by the Mozambique Company which was
chartered in the spring of 1888, with a capital of £40,000,
which in the latter part of 1889 was increased to £80,000.[107]

The problems of the Mozambique Company and its predecessors reflected the plight of Portugal, with a near-bankrupt government and a colonial estate which required large capital resources to become profitable. These resources could not be
found in Portugal itself. Consequently, Paiva d'Andrada and
other company promoters had to seek investors in other countries, principally France and England. But financial circles in
Paris and London were wary, as the fate of his early ventures
demonstrated. Rothschild's, which had excellent intelligence on
financial transactions, reported in 1881 that French capitalists
would not invest because they had no faith in the capacity of
any Portuguese company to compete successfully with English
capital and enterprise in South East Africa.[108]

This reluctance was to an extent overcome by the inclusion of
French and British capitalists in the board of directors of the
Mozambique Company. Though the headquarters was required
to be in Lisbon, almost half of the directors were from London

106. Petre to Salisbury, August 1, 1889, F.O. 179/269, P.R.O.
107. I.D. 1889, *A Manual of Portuguese East Africa*. Compiled by the
Geographic Section of the Naval Intelligence Division, Naval Staff,
Admiralty, p. 154.
108. Lytton to Salisbury, December 31, 1881, C.O. 417/50, P.R.O.

and Paris. The vice-president, Edmond Bartissol, a member of the French Chamber of Deputies, was a powerful force, as was Charles A. Moreing of the London firm of Bewick and Moreing, who had particular expertise on the financing of railway construction. The international character of the Mozambique Company was further reflected in its subconcessions which were assigned principally to British investors. By 1890 the company had granted eight major subconcessions, all to Britons or Americans.[109] The prize of the Manica gold fields thus was contested by British capitalists on both sides; with the rights of the Mozambique Company being advocated by British members of its board of directors and of the subcompanies under its franchise. Among the prominent Englishmen who opposed the "aggression" of the British South Africa Company were the Duke of Marlborough and Lord Castletown.[110] Marlborough had recruited his fortune by marriage to a wealthy American, and had invested in the Mozambique Company,[111] and Castletown was a large investor in African companies, including the Delagoa Bay Railway. Among the other protestors were spokesmen for the Ophir Concessions, Zambesi (Gaza) Concessions, Zambesi (Sofala) Concessions, African Prospecting Syndicate, East Africa Exploring Syndicate, and Massi Kessi Gold Mines, who claimed

109. "List obtained by Mr. Kergarion of Concession holders under leases and licenses from Companhia de Mozambique," n. d. [1890], F.O. 84/2154, P.R.O. The list is the same as that in a letter from Colquhoun to BSAC, September 21, 1890, LO 5/2/4, N.A.R. The concessions were:
1. Gaza, Sofala, and Zambesi concession, represented by Messrs. Crampton and Harrison.
2. Ophir Concession, represented by E. de Kergarion and his assistants Moodie and Crampton.
3. Austen Concession, represented by Messrs. Holliday, Taylor, and Bailey.
4. Manica Syndicate Transvaal Concession, represented by Jeffreys, Harrington, and Harris.
5. Kergarion Concession, represented by himself.
6. Maritz Concession.
7. Leuter Concession.
8. Ochs Brothers London Concession, not being worked.
110. Castletown to Salisbury, December 10, 1890, F.O. 84/2096, P.R.O.
111. Weatherley to Hill, September 18, 1891, F.O. 84/2175, P.R.O.

to represent a collective capital of £1 million.[112] "These Companies wd. lead us to believe that there is prodigious mining activity in Manica," Anderson remarked.[113] In fact there was little mining but much activity in establishing claims which could buoy the price of shares in the London stock market regardless of the amount of gold that might be extracted. But these claims were now threatened by the advance of the chartered monopoly. In Parliament, and in his newspaper *Truth*, Labouchere could be relied on to attack the "filibustering activities" of the chartered company.[114]

The collective weight of these protestors did not match that of the British South Africa Company, But Salisbury's position was not determined by the resultant of these commercial forces. He sought an agreement that would fall between what he considered to be the excessive pretensions of Rhodes and the excessive claims of Portugal. To that end he suspended diplomatic action while the London directors of the South Africa Company negotiated with their counterparts in the Mozambique Company for a settlement which would have included a substantial South Africa Company voice in the management of the Mozambique Company.

Mutual overtures between the two companies began soon after the South Africa Company was chartered. In the autumn of 1889 Cawston heard that the Mozambique Company had obtained a concession from the Portuguese government to build a railway from the coast to Maçequeçe and that the Mozambique Company was negotiating with a banking group in Paris for the capital necessary for construction. Toward the end of 1889 Lord Nathan Rothschild invited Cawston to meet the Portuguese chargé d'affaires, L. P. de Soveral, who told Cawston that his government was anxious to reach a settlement with Britain and was willing even to give up mining rights but that it could not

112. Memorial to Lord Salisbury, January 30, 1891, F.O. 84/2155, P.R.O. Other protests are in F.O. 84/2096 and F.O. 84/2098, P.R.O.
113. Note, Anderson, December 13, 1890, F.O. 84/2096, P.R.O.
114. *Truth*, January 8, 1891. Question in Parliament, January 29, 1891, February 9, 1891, February 23, 1891 in F.O. 84/2155, F.O. 84/2156, F.O. 84/2157 respectively, P.R.O.

ratify a convention that would outrage Portuguese public opinion.[115]

Negotiations proceeded fitfully thereafter, as economic issues were affected by British-Portuguese tensions and the aggressive actions of the chartered company in Africa. The Mozambique Company, however, had great difficulty in raising capital. The Paris bankers whom they had engaged as their representatives found that potential investors were not eager to risk their funds, particularly in view of the tension between Britain and Portugal. Efforts to find the necessary money in the City of London were also unsuccessful. When Portugal failed to ratify the August convention which required the construction of a railway from Beira, Cawston approached Bartissol with the suggestion that the Mozambique Company authorize the South Africa Company to build the railway and also sell the chartered company its mining rights. Thus the two major economic issues would be eliminated. Bartissol was receptive, and by the end of 1890 negotiations between Cawston and Bartissol had brought the two companies close to an arrangement.[116]

Bartissol proposed that the British South Africa Company buy controlling interest in a reorganized Mozambique Company. Portuguese sensitivities would be soothed by the façade of the company's being legally Portuguese and its head office would be in Paris, not London. When public opinion in Portugal quieted down, the headquarters could be moved, but in the meantime the management would be securely in the hands of the British South Africa Company through its nominees on the board of directors.[117] Bartissol was authorized by the board of the Mozambique Company to offer the South Africa Company seventy percent interest if the British company would spend £200,000 in development, including the construction of a railway.[118]

Bartissol's proposal was acceptable to the South Africa Com-

115. "Report by Cawston of his negotiations having Reference to the Mozambique Co.," n. d. [1890], LO 8/3/1, N.A.R.
116. Cawston to Currie, March 13, 1891, F.O. 84/2159, P.R.O.
117. Memo by Bartissol, encl. in *ibid.*
118. Cable, London board to Kimberley office, December 16, 1890, LO 5/2/5, N.A.R.

pany's board, but two factors appeared which frustrated the settlement. The Portuguese government made it clear that it would approve no takeover until the August convention had been modified to meet its objections,[119] and the unavailability of Rhodes delayed final approval by the two companies. Rhodes had not been involved in the details of Cawston's negotiations. While Cawston had been promoting a commercial union, Rhodes's energies had been directed to seizing by force what Cawston would have acquired by money. The activities of the company's troopers further inflamed Portuguese animosity and made the commercial settlement more difficult. But Rhodes was nevertheless now the dominant force in the company; the directors would not take final action without his approval. Salisbury, though he was annoyed by Rhodes's perversity, nevertheless respected his power. Both the company's Board and the imperial government pressed Rhodes to hurry to England to discuss the major unresolved issues. The imperial government also called Loch home for consultation on South African questions, and Rhodes agreed to accompany Loch on the voyage.[120] Consequently Rhodes's departure was delayed several weeks. Instead of arriving in England in December, he did not land until the third week in January. Thus when Bartissol insisted on a final answer by the South Africa Company before the end of December, he was informed that no further discussions could take place until January when Rhodes was present.[121]

The tardiness of Rhodes's arrival was probably not decisive in the breakdown of negotiations. By December 1890 Portuguese anger at the activities of the company's agents had developed to such an intensity that the government was no longer willing to approve the kind of contract that Bartissol had proposed earlier in the year. When Cawston visited Bartissol at the end of January, he was informed that the Portuguese minister of marine had given orders that no further negotiations with the South Africa Company should be carried on without reference to Lisbon.[122] After Bartissol visited Portugal, the atmosphere turned frigid. Instead of seventy percent, the South Africa Company's participation in the new company was reduced to forty percent. Then even this option was removed, and the new Mozambique Company was prohibited from making any arrangement.[123] The charter of the new Mozambique Company provided that the majority of the directors must be Portuguese citizens living in Portugal and that the headquarters must be in Lisbon.[124]

Frustrated in their attmept to purchase and control Portuguese East Africa, Rhodes and his fellow directors resumed their efforts to take what they wanted by force and by diplomacy. Salisbury encouraged them by his acceptance of the company's position that any new agreement must guarantee communication with the sea, and his support of alteration of the frontier line in the company's favor.[125]

The impasse between the two governments provided the company with the opportunity to put into operation the plan that Rhodes and the London directors had discussed before they had been ordered to withdraw their forces. Gungunyana and Mutasa would be supported as independent chiefs; the Portuguese would menace them or attack them, the chiefs would call on the company for help, and it would respond by repelling Portuguese "aggression." If the Portuguese were not cooperative in playing the role assigned to them, an incident could easily be manufactured. Arrangements for assistance to Mutasa and Gungunyana would be made while Rhodes was absent on his trip to England, and would be without his "official knowledge," thus giving him the option of disclaiming the actions of his agents if it became necessary to do so.[126] At Dr. Schulz's suggestion[127]

122. Cawston to Currie, confidential, January 28, 1891, LO 8/3/1, N.A.R.
123. Cawston to Currie, March 13, 1891, BSAC III Misc., Rhodes House.
124. I.D. 1889, *Manual of Portuguese East Africa*, p. 155.
125. Telegram, Salisbury to Petre, December 23, 1890, F.O. 84/2154, P.R.O.
126. Cable received through Grey and Beit, January 13, 1891, LO 5/2/6, N.A.R.
127. On January 20, 1891, the Kimberley office reported that Schulz's position was "impregnable" with Gungunyana. Cable, Kimberley office to London, January 21, 1891, F.O. 84/2155, P.R.O.

Gungunyana announced his determination to defend his territory against the Portuguese and expressed the desire to send two
of his principal indunas to Britain to ask for the protection of
the imperial government.[128] The first response of the government was that the mission should be discouraged,[129] but, as had
been the case with Lobengula's envoys, his sponsors were persis-
tent, and the government indicated it might be willing to receive the envoys at an appropriate time.[130] Meanwhile the company's officers on the spot were active. Forbes reported that
Andrada had publicly expressed the intention of driving the
company's police out of Manica and that soldiers had hoisted
the Portuguese flag in two places in Mashonaland, one eighty
miles west of Fort Salisbury and the other a few miles west of
Fort Charter.[131] At the same time, Forbes reported that chiefs
from Manica to the coast with whom he had negotiated mineral
and railway concessions were fearful of Portuguese attack, and
he asked permission to assist them by opening the route from
the sea.[132]

Portuguese counter-measures gave additional urgency to
Forbes's request. At the end of December a mission arrived at
Gungunyana's kraal to seek reaffirmation of his vassalage to
Portugal. In the presence of Schulz, Gungunyana protested his
loyalty to the Portuguese and insisted that he had made no
commitments to the South Africa Company. He further asserted
that Mutasa was his tributary and thus likewise under Portuguese protection.[133] The company denied that Gungunyana had
made any such professions,[134] but the incident made it imperative to move quickly to secure the concession he had granted to
Schulz on the condition that he received arms and ammunition.

128. Cable, Kimberley office to London, January 21, 1891, encl. in
Weatherley to Currie, January 22, 1891, F.O. 84/2155, P.R.O.
129. Note on *ibid.*
130. Cable, London office to Kimberley, February 8, 1891, LO 5/2/7,
N.A.R.
131. Kimberley office to London, encl. in Weatherley to Currie, January 30, 1891, F.O. 84/2155, P.R.O.
132. Cable, Kimberley office to London, encl. in Weatherley to Currie, January 31, 1891, F.O. 84/2155, P.R.O.
133. Axelson, *Portugal and the Scramble for Africa*, p. 278.
134. Rhodes to Currie, March 5, 1891, F.O. 84/2158, P.R.O.

On February 17, 1891, a decrepit little steamer of about 100 tons bearing the proud name of the *Countess of Carnarvon* entered the Limpopo River. The ship had been purchased by the South Africa Company for £2,000 to transport 1,000 rifles to Gungunyana in fulfillment of the condition of his concession.[135] The captain of the ship had been recruited on the basis of the promise that if he did his job well he could expect a permanent position in the company's service.[136] The company's contention was that the Portuguese had no right to block passage on the Limpopo, and that the vessel was being sent in accordance with Gungunyana's desire that it make use of "his waterway," the Limpopo.[137] The Portuguese had no customs house on the river, the company maintained. The Limpopo should be opened to international commerce in accordance with Gungunyana's desires, and it was navigable for a considerable distance inland, probably as far as the Transvaal.[138] This report of the value of the Limpopo was greatly exaggerated, as was the description of Gungunyana's power. The actual events bore little relationships to the reports emanating from the Kimberley office of the company. The incident had the attributes of broad farce. The ship ran by a Portuguese customs post, ignoring the command to stop, and dropped anchor at a village named Chai Chai, about forty-five miles from Gungunyana's kraal, where the rifles were unloaded, and a messenger was sent to Gungunyana to send carriers to pick up the consignment. The next day an officer from the customs post arrived but, instead of protesting the violation of Portuguese territory, left without comment to report to a senior official whose station was forty-five miles away. The trip took him three days. Meanwhile the superintendent-in-chief of Gazaland had heard about the arrival of the steamer

135. Harris to London office, March 2, 1891, LO 5/2/7, N.A.R. The company bought the steamer rather than hiring it for £450. The cost of hire was high because no insurance company including Lloyd's would insure the voyage, considering the gun-running venture too risky.

136. Harris to Chaddock, confidential, January 15, 1891, CT 2/11/2, N.A.R.

137. Harris to Imperial Secretary, confidential, February 25, 1891, F.O. 84/2160, P.R.O.

138. Weatherley to Currie, March 4, 1891, F.O. 84/2158, P.R.O.

from Gungunyana and from Schulz, who stated the rifles were a gift from the British government. He sent a detachment to arrest the crew and seize the vessel and the cargo. The commander of the detachment arrived late in the day and decided to defer boarding the ship until the next morning, but when dawn broke the *Countess of Carnarvon* was gone. Members of the crew had cut the cable, and she floated quietly down the stream. There were eight men left on shore, but instead of arresting them and impounding the rifles, the Portuguese officer accepted a personal bond from a company official of £2,000 as security for payment of customs dues and released the weapons, which were promptly delivered to Gungunyana.[139]

The *Countess of Carnarvon* mission was ordered by Jameson, who took seriously the injunction that Rhodes should not be officially cognizant of such actions. He was not entirely responsible for the fiasco that followed—no man, however imaginative, could have written such a scenario of ineptitude—but the operation was reckless of odds. It relied on the gambler's throw, much as did his more famous escapade five years later.

When the guns were delivered to Gungunyana, Jameson was in Umtali, where he was receiving disturbing reports of Mutasa's dissatisfaction with his company alliance. There was a possibility that Mutasa might declare his concession to the company invalid on the basis that he was a dependent of Gungunyana and if Gungunyana were to be recognized as under Portuguese protection, the foundation of the company's strategy would collapse. Accordingly, though the rainy season was at its height Jameson, Denis Doyle, and Dunbar Moodie, a mining prospector, made a journey to Gungunyana to bolster his attachment to the company. In the presence of Jameson, Gungunyana confirmed in writing his verbal concession.[140] Precisely what Gungunyana had promised subsequently became a matter of dispute. The document to which he affixed his mark provided that he accepted an alliance with "Her Britannic Majesty Queen Victoria." But the Portuguese superintendent-in-chief of Gaza-

139. Warhurst, *Anglo-Portuguese Relations*, pp. 87–88; Axelson, *Portugal and the Scramble for Africa*, pp. 279–281.
140. Green, *Rhodes Goes North*, pp. 256–257.

land, who was also present, reported that Gungunyana had repeated in front of Jameson his allegiance to Portugal and that Gungunyana had been deluded as to the contents of the document he had approved.[141] Gungunyana's position was indeed a difficult one.

While Jameson was at Manhlagazi, the *Countess of Carnarvon* reentered the Limpopo, after refueling in Durban, and Jameson resolved to join the ship. But when he arrived he found the *Countess* in the custody of the Portuguese, and guarded by a gunboat. Jameson and his party were taken prisoner, with the exception of one man whom Jameson had prudently entrusted with the concession with instructions to proceed overland to Delagoa Bay.[142]

The seizure of the *Countess of Carnarvon* was precisely the kind of incident for which the company's directors had been hoping. The first report from the London board to the imperial government indicated that the ship had made a voyage up the Limpopo at the request of Gungunyana and had delivered cargo, including arms and ammunition without interference from Portuguese officials.[143] Gungunyana as an independent chief who controlled the coast had the right to issue his invitation; there was no Portuguese customs house or any other visible evidence of Portuguese authority.[144] On the second voyage—when the ship had been sent to pick up Jameson and other company officials who were on their way from Mashonaland to report to Rhodes on his return to Cape Town but was seized by a Portuguese man-of-war—one version indicated the warship had fired on the *Countess*, thus menacing the lives of its crew. This action by Portugal, the company maintained, was a clear case of aggression calling for intervention by the imperial government. Salisbury's reaction was cautious. He would not be rushed into precipitous action, but he rejected Portugal's protest of the violation of its territory—the fact that a ship could enter the

141. Axelson, *Portugal and the Scramble for Africa*, p. 280.
142. Warhurst, *Anglo-Portuguese Relations*, pp. 88–89; Green, *Rhodes Goes North*, p. 258.
143. Weatherley to Herbert, March 18, 1891, F.O. 84/2159, P.R.O.
144. Kimberley office to London, March 21, 1891, F.O. 84/2160, P.R.O.

Limpopo without being stopped, as had the *Countess of Carnarvon*, indicated that the Portuguese did not have effective authority in the area.[145]

In South Africa, Sir Henry Loch's response to reports of the ship's seizure was much more militant. Whatever his differences with Rhodes, Loch shared his prime minister's contempt for the Portuguese, and this outrage on British subjects he believed called for immediate and decisive action. As soon as he heard about the seizure of the vessel, he telegraphed the Colonial Office urging that warships be sent simultaneously to the Limpopo, Beira, and Delagoa Bay, and that the one directed to the Limpopo should carry a message to Gungunyana recognizing his independence of Portugal.[146]

Portuguese authorities were equally ardent in their response. The governor of the Mozambique Company, Colonel J. J. Machado, was outraged at what he considered acts of war by company officers and insults to Portuguese pride. After the arrest of Andrada and Sousa at Maçequeçe the home government had sent an expeditionary force of over 900 men to assert Portuguese authority in Mozambique, and they arrived in February and March. Machado now had the military power to back his indignation. In mid-March he proclaimed martial law in Sofala and Manica and closed both Beira and the Pungwe River to the British South Africa Company.[147]

These warlike preparations of the Portuguese were used by Rhodes to incite Loch to action. The high commissioner telegraphed to London that unless he was countermanded he would immediately send a man-of-war to protect British interests, but Salisbury still refused to sanction military action. Rhodes decided to take action himself. He would use the Portuguese closing of Beira and the Pungwe River as justification for the dispatch of a force to occupy the port and open the river. The Portuguese, he maintained, were in violation of the *modus vivendi*; they threatened the lives of the settlers in Mashonaland and the south. Rhodes on April 6, 1891, announced

145. Axelson, *Portugal and the Scramble for Africa*, p. 281.
146. C.O. to F.O., immediate, March 26, 1891, F.O. 84/2160, P.R.O.
147. Axelson, *Portugal and the Scramble for Africa*, p. 283; Green, *Rhodes Goes North*, p. 259.

that 250 men with supplies were en route to Beira; their mission was peaceful, to carry food to Mashonaland as permitted in the *modus vivendi*. Portugal should be warned not to interfere, for the men would defend themselves.[148]

The Foreign Office correctly interpreted this announcement as an attempt by Rhodes to force the hand of the imperial government, and Loch was ordered to stop the expedition, but it was too late.[149] On April 13 the company's men appeared off Beira, escorted by a Portuguese gunboat. Their object was certainly not a pitched battle with the Portuguese. The entire party consisted of thirteen white men and ninety-two Africans who were to be employed in road building.[150] They were transported on one small ship and two tugs, none of which had any armament. The purpose was to force the Portuguese to take an action that would cause a crisis. The commander of the expedition was perfectly in character for the part he had to play. Sir John Willoughby was a certified gentleman—Eton and Cambridge—with a record of bravery in battle, but his credentials did not include good judgment. Willoughby had not been sent to fight or to negotiate; he was to insist on his right of passage and thus produce an incident that would excite indignation in England. He well understood what he was supposed to accomplish. As he wrote to Harris: "Now I think I see very well what you all want, cause a disturbance and for me to take the blame if it does not turn out well. All right, I don't mind so long as Rhodes does not blame me privately...."[151]

He performed his assigned part perfectly. When the Portuguese refused to let him proceed, he started upstream and did not stop until a Portuguese warship had fired a warning shot. The round was blank. Willoughby became a hero without risk or penalty and Rhodes had his cause célèbre. Newspapers friendly to the company in Britain and South Africa fanned public indignation with demands for war, and Abercorn on behalf of the company called upon Salisbury to demonstrate that Great

148. Telegram, Loch to Knutsford, April 1, 1891, F.O. 84/2161, P.R.O.
149. Telegram, Currie to Salisbury, April 6, 1891, in *ibid.*
150. Green, *Rhodes Goes North*, p. 264.
151. Willoughby to Harris, confidential, April 14, 1891, CT 1/12/9, N.A.R.

Britain was still a great power, prepared to fight against mal-
treatment of its citizens, by at least sending one or two gunboats
to the area. If the government remained passive in the face of
Portuguese provocations, not only would Portugal be encouraged to commit further acts of aggression, but British prestige
with the natives of South Africa would be destroyed, with consequences that were horrible to contemplate.[152]

Salisbury responded to the company demands. He extracted
from Portugal the commitment to reopen the River Pungwe to
the transport of passengers and goods to Mashonaland and dispatched two gunboats and a cruiser to Beira. The commander
of the cruiser was instructed to remain until he was satisfied that
local officials were following the instructions of their government,[153] and the channel fleet was ordered to remain for the
present in one of the Spanish Atlantic ports as a reminder to
Portugal that the imperial government would protect Englishmen against mob violence.[154] But Salisbury resisted demands for
more stringent measures.

As the "Beira incident" illustrated, Salisbury was not easily
moved by the demands of "public opinion" as manifested by the
press. When he found it convenient, he would use public opinion as justification for his policy, but he was cynical about press
campaigns, which on occasion he himself had helped to manufacture. The company's version of the affair he had ascertained
was false; he assumed that any Portuguese rebuttal would likewise be false.[155] Scare stories from any source evoked a skeptical
reaction at the Foreign Office. When the governor of Natal reported "from two independent sources" that the Portuguese government had offered 2,000 Boers large acreages in Manica and
Mashonaland if they would help to repel the British, the Foreign Office labeled the story "unlikely," another of the many
rumors started in South Africa with the object of influencing
British policy. That policy continued to be for a peaceful
settlement.

152. Abercorn to Salisbury, April 20, 1891, File E, Salisbury Papers,
Christ Church, Oxford.
153. F.O. to Admiralty, April 22, 1891, F.O. 84/2163, P.R.O.
154. Notes of cabinet meeting, April, 1891, CAB 41/2215, P.R.O.
155. Note by Currie on telegram, Willoughby to Harris, April 22,
1891, F.O. 84/2165, P.R.O.

By the beginning of April 1891 Salisbury and the Portuguese government had reached a tentative agreement, and Cawston had expressed himself as satisfied.[156] The new convention was much more favorable to the South Africa Company than the treaty of August 1890. The boundary was moved from the Sabi River to 33° east longitude, thus giving the company the whole Manica plateau and northern Gazaland, which also was on the healthier upland. Free passage on the rivers of Portuguese East Africa was guaranteed, and duties on imports and exports were limited to three percent, whether goods were carried by road, river, or railway. Further, Portugal agreed to the speedy construction of a railway from Beira to Umtali in the company's territory. The terms gave the company most of what it had demanded; the only major loss was that most of Gungunyana's territory was assigned to the Portuguese sphere.[157] Even Rhodes expressed mild pleasure that terms were better than he had thought they would be, though he continued to insist that it was essential that Gungunyana's independence be recognized—abandonment by Britain was a "shameful proceeding."[158] Gungunyana's indunas who had arrived in Cape Town on their way to seek an audience with the queen were hurried on to London in the company of Denis Doyle, in the hope that the mission would be as successful as that of Maund two years earlier.[159] This decision was entirely Rhodes's own; he had not previously informed his own directors and he acted in the face of warnings from the Foreign Office and the Colonial Office that the mission was undesirable at that time.[160]

The prospective arrival in London of envoys from Gungunyana was one small aspect of a large problem, that the governments in Europe had only partial control over the "wild men" in southern Africa. As the fate of the August 1890 convention demonstrated, the quiet negotiations of the diplomats could be undermined by outbursts of national fervor, and another col-

156. Currie to Herbert, April 3, 1891, C.O. 537/127, P.R.O.
157. Warhurst, *Anglo-Portuguese Relations*, p. 99; Green, *Rhodes Goes North*, pp. 269–270.
158. Rhodes to London office, April 12, 1891, LO 3/1/2; Harris to London office, LO 5/2/8, both in N.A.R.
159. Harris to London office, May 6, 1891, LO 5/2/8, N.A.R.
160. London office to South Africa, May 8, 1891, LO 3/1/2, N.A.R.

lision between British and Portuguese forces could make it po-
litically impossible for Portugal, and perhaps for Britain, to
ratify the treaty. On the Portuguese side, rancor was still high at
the various insults committed by South Africa Company officials. Sousa still burned at the memory of his humiliation by
Forbes at Maçequeçe and was eager for revenge, and officials on
the company's side were equally eager to teach the Portuguese
another lesson on the superiority of the British race. In Whitehall reports of an impending collision caused considerable
alarm. Despite the confidence of the company's troopers, it did
not seem likely that they would be able to repel a Portuguese
assault. The troops from Portugal had substantially increased
Portuguese power, and they had been supplemented by African
contingents from Angola and Mozambique. The Foreign Office
also expected that Sousa would be able to organize an African
force and feared that Lobengula might use a clash as an opportunity to attack the pioneers in Manica.[161]

The menace of Sousa had been temporarily removed by a revolt among the peoples over whom he held sway,[162] but this fact
had not yet been communicated to Whitehall. There was deep
concern that the company's police might be overwhelmed and
that Britain might be required to use force on behalf of its subjects, and the months of delicate negotiations would be negated.
In that eventuality, Salisbury was prepared to punish Portugal;
". . . I do not regard the refusal of the Portuguese to disband
their force with any apprehension. If they commit one good
open flagrant outrage on our international rights, we shall shake
free of much criticism in this country, and some pressure from
friendly courts. Once armed with a solid grievance, we can recognise Gungunhana and hand over Sofala and Gaza to the
South African Company."[163]

Salisbury did not want a war; he would not be an accessory in
the use of any "trumped-up incidents"; but a clear-cut Portuguese aggression into territory claimed by Britain he was ready
to punish emphatically. The clash that occurred, however, was

161. Note by Anderson, May 7, 1891, F.O. 84/2164, P.R.O.
162. Axelson, *Portugal and the Scramble for Africa*, p. 283.
163. Note by Salisbury, n.d., on note by Anderson, May 7, 1891, F.O.
84/2164, P.R.O.

in territory assigned by the treaty to Portugal, and resulted in another humiliating defeat for the Portuguese. At the beginning of May 1891 a contingent of about 100 Portuguese volunteers and 120 Africans from Angola and Mozambique arrived in Maçequeçe after an arduous journey from the coast during which many had become ill with malaria. This occupation was in accord with the terms of the *modus vivendi*. But the further objectives of this force were not clear. By the company's version, the governor of Manica, Major J. J. Ferreira, told Captain H. M. Heyman, commander of the company's police in the area, that the *modus vivendi* was about to expire and that unless the police withdrew west of the Sabi he would drive them out.[164] But as the Portuguese were advancing toward Maçequeçe, Heyman had asked for instructions and had received orders from Rhodes to "turn them out of Massi-Kessi."[165] In the clash that followed, a Portuguese attack was repelled by thirty-five company police, and the Portuguese retreated from Maçequeçe, leaving supplies and belongings.[166]

Again Rhodes was unable to capitalize on a collision. His plea to be allowed to seize a strip of land from Mashonaland to Beira was rejected, and even his erstwhile ally Sir Henry Loch deserted him. Instead of supporting Rhodes, he sent an imperial officer to Mozambique to ensure that the company's forces withdrew from Maçequeçe and respected a neutral zone imposed to prevent a further collision. Loch believed that by his enforcement of the neutral zone, he was in fact saving Rhodes from his own rashness. The high commissioner believed that there could be considerable loss of life if the company's forces attacked Beira. They would have to fight a numerically stronger force far from their base and without horses, since they must pass through the tsetse country. The company's men might be victorious, but the price would be high.[167]

Loch considered this contretemps with Rhodes further evidence of the hazards of loose control and the need for a strong

164. Axelson, *Portugal and the Scramble for Africa*, p. 286.
165. This was the finding of Commander Winslow, R.N., who was appointed by the British government to investigate the clash. Warhurst, *Anglo-Portuguese Relations*, p. 74.
166. Axelson, *Portugal and the Scramble for Africa*, pp. 287–288.
167. Loch to Sapte, May 31, 1891, SA 10/1/1, N.A.R.

administrative authority directly responsible to the high commissioner to govern the chartered company's territories. Assignment of plenary authority to company officials, Loch said, was
an invitation to further turmoil in southern Africa, and the imperial government would be embroiled in the consequences of
actions for which its agents had no responsibility. Comparisons
between the advance of the company in Africa and expansion
of the East India Company created a false analogy. There was no
wealth in Africa to be compared with that which the East India
Company had extracted. Indian expansion had been paid for by
Indians; poverty-stricken Africa could not sustain European
armies. But in any event, the East India Company had been subject to far greater control—a board of control had regulated political affairs, and the governor general had been appointed
both by the British government and the company.[168] Loch desired to rein in Rhodes and the South Africa Company in similar fashion. So far as the immediate issue of the Maçequeçe
affair was concerned, he asked for and received the right to impose a neutral zone five miles to the west of the village.[169]

The Maçequeçe incident took place too late to affect an
Anglo-Portuguese settlement. Even if negotiations had not been
far advanced, Rhodes probably could not have used the clash to
his advantage. Experience with the fire-brand of the Cape had
convinced British officials in London that he was reckless, irresponsible, and untrustworthy, a man who would not hesitate to
sacrifice imperial interests to his own personal ambitions. It
was far preferable to accept a continuing Portuguese presence
in South East Africa than to continue to confront interminable
crises stimulated or manufactured by the Cape prime minister.
Consequently the last-minute efforts of the company to prevent
or delay the treaty were unavailing. Gungunyana's indunas accompanied by Doyle arrived at the end of May and were lavish-
ly entertained by company directors at Ascot, Aldershot, Wool-
wich Arsenal, and the zoo,[170] but they were not received by the

168. Loch to Knutsford, confidential, May 25, 1891, S 1428/17/7,
N.A.R.
169. C.O. to F.O., May 29, 1891, immediate, F.O. 84/2166, P.R.O.
170. London office to Cape, May 28, 1891; same to same, June 12, 1891,
both in LO 3/1/3, N.A.R.

queen until after the treaty was ratified and all possibility of misunderstanding with Portugal had been removed. Grey appealed to Salisbury "at the eleventh hour" to suspend negotiations, arguing that the certain result of the treaty would be the creation of a white, English-speaking republic between the chartered territories and the sea. The occupation of Gazaland by uncontrolled white adventurers, Dutch as well as English-speaking, would create an additional problem for Britain in South Africa, and Britain could not prevent the inevitable unless it went to war with its own colonists, which public opinion would not allow.[171] Grey's plea did not deter Salisbury. The prime minister agreed that the Portuguese would be "very bad owners" of African territory. They would not develop their lands and they would probably maltreat the Africans. Perhaps their weakness would attract turbulent white men who would give trouble both to Mozambique and its neighbors. But these filibusterers could not succeed in establishing a republic. Portugal could not alienate any part of its territory without British permission, and Britain would intervene if necessary to prevent the success of any coup. The possession of Mozambique by Britain would undoubtedly benefit Britain, South Africa, and the human race generally. But the territory had been recognized as Portuguese by treaties as far back as 1817, and in determining the limits of Portuguese authority inland he had been guided by the principle of international law that in ordinary cases possession of the coast implied possession of the interior to the nearest watershed.[172] Grey, as he usually did in cases of great importance, consulted his aged uncle, the third Earl, who assured him that Salisbury's "accepted principles" of international law were quite exotic—the rulers of Egypt had never contended that their possession of the coast gave them the right to govern Ethiopia.[173] But the issue was not really one of international law—Salisbury was adept at adducing whatever arguments were convenient to his case. He had decided that the imperial interest was best served by leaving Portugal in the pos-

171. Grey to Salisbury, May 30, 1891, File 231/3, Grey Papers, Durham.
172. Salisbury to Grey, June 3, 1891, in *ibid.*
173. Earl Grey to Albert Grey, File 183/2, Grey Papers, Durham.

session of the coast while recognizing the company's rights over much of the high country and guaranteeing it access from the sea. This the treaty provided, and thus he signed it.

Again at the last moment reports that the Cortes might refuse to cooperate in the ratification gave the company a momentary surge of hope. Jameson gleefully wrote his brother that the news from Portugal was good, though it might be necessary for the company to promote another "rumpus" to help its cause.[174] But his joy was short lived.

The Portuguese government preferred to face the indignant nationalists at home rather than risk the consequences of non-ratification. Ritual speeches were made in deference to national pride, but both chambers voted overwhelmingly for ratification, and the treaty was signed by the king on June 11, 1891.[175]

The treaty of 1891 did not satisfy Rhodes; no agreement would have done so. But in Britain the reaction was generally favorable. Even the company's board of directors conceded that the terms were much better than those of the treaty of 1890, provided, of course, that the Portuguese could be held to their promise to build a railroad expeditiously. Relations between the South Africa Company and Portuguese East Africa entered a new phase in which the issue of communication from the sea to Mashonaland was paramount. Rhodes did not easily give up his hope of a forcible solution to the "Portuguese problem." As late as March 1894 he tried to seize upon an incident involving an attack on a telegraph crew near Tete as an excuse for a raid on Beira.[176] The time had passed for such actions. Now the issues with Portugal would be resolved, not by force—Salisbury had decided that—but by negotiation. But the aftermath of the events of 1890 and 1891 would continue to poison relationships between the chartered company and Portugal.

174. Axelson, *Portugal and the Scramble*, pp. 296–297.
175. Jameson to S. Jameson, June 8, 1891, JA 1/1/1, N.A.R.
176. Note, confidential, Rhodes to [Duncan], (March 5, 1894); Duncan to [Rhodes], March 9, 1894, both in CT 1/16/412, N.A.R. He contemplated sending a force of fifty men from Umtali to Beira under the command of Captain J. Spreckley. The telegraph incident however was peacefully resolved. Spreckley was later privy to the Jameson Raid and as senior officer of the Rhodesian Horse had been asked by Jameson to be ready to come to his assistance.

7

North of the Zambezi

"CAPE TO CAIRO" WAS A DREAM WITH LITTLE RELA-
tionship to reality. The British South Africa Company did not
invest in dreams. Whatever higher purposes its founders envisaged, they expected substantial financial returns for their investments. Rhodes, it is true, promoted independently of the
chartered company the construction of a telegraph which
reached as far north as Ujiji on Lake Tanganyika before lack of
funds and small revenues caused the suspension of the project.[1]
But the development of territories from South to North Africa
was far beyond the resources of any private corporation even if
international diplomacy had not destroyed any possibility of an
"all-red" swath. If these vast areas had been rich in natural resources the capital required to exploit and to administer them
would still have been immense. Much of Central and East Africa, however, had little to offer in the way of returns to investors. Mackinnon's East Africa Company had gone bankrupt
within a few years and Leopold's Congo Free State nearly suffered the same fate. The Grand Scheme developed by the promoters of the British South Africa Company involved an empire
embracing Matabeleland, Mashonaland, Barotseland, Nyasaland, and Katanga, but the first focus of attention was on the
gold fields of Mashonaland which, it was hoped, would provide
the wealth necessary to generate development in other areas.
When this expectation proved illusory and the costs for construction of railways and other facilities strained the capital and

1. Leo Weinthal, *The Story of the Cape to Cairo Railway and River
Route, 1887–1922*, 4 vols. (London [1923–1927]), 1:211–217.

credit of the company, little money was available for projects north of the Zambezi.

Heavy expenditures in Mashonaland made it impossible for the company to spend much money north of the Zambezi. The company's promoters regarded the trans-Zambezi lands as territory to be held for future speculation rather than immediate development. This was evident in the response to the request of Lewanika, chief of the Lozi, for British protection. The offer must be accepted, Rhodes insisted in August 1889, and the company should offer to relieve the home government of all costs. He envisaged no other expenditure than "perhaps £100 a year" to be paid to Lewanika for a monopoly of all mineral rights in his kingdom. Barotseland, with the greatest possible area assigned to it, was to be held for future exploitation. As Rhodes asserted to Grey, "My plan is to secure all territory before it is gone." "But," he added, "I shall not rush you into needless expenditure."[2]

Possession of Barotseland was important also as a means of access to Katanga. The company hoped to establish claims to control over the deposits in that area before Leopold could incorporate Katanga in the Congo Free State. Neither Leopold nor the British South Africa Company had the capital to develop Katanga themselves. They expected to derive income by concessions to others, as Leopold intended to do in other parts of the long basin and as the South Africa Company was doing in Mashonaland.

The company's interest in the Lakes area had little to do with immediate economic development. Nyasaland had significance for any plans for northern extension but the mineral resources of the territory were unknown and there was nothing in the record of the African Lakes Company to suggest that the chartered company could soon make it profitable. The initiative which led to the South African Company's involvement was at least as much from government as from the company.

The African Lakes Company and the missionaries of several British societies lived a precarious existence. With small resources at their disposal, they threatened the economic and political interests of peoples who were too powerful for them to

2. Rhodes to Grey, August 30, 1889, BSAC Misc. I, Rhodes House.

dominate. Their opposition to the slave trade and slavery embroiled them in wars which they could not win, and their trials were compounded by the threat of Portuguese expansion from the south. They expected succor from the imperial government —at the minimum, diplomatic support against Portugal.

These hopes and expectations did not accord with the desires of the Foreign Office. Beyond the general principle that the imperial government should avoid the responsibility and expense of taking a territory, the Nyasa area had special liabilities. It was far from the sea and the reach of the Royal Navy, and there were no evident economic advantages in its acquisition. Wistfully, some members of the Foreign Office staff expressed regret that an arrangement with Portugal could not be worked out guaranteeing the right of the Lakes Company and the missionary societies within a Portuguese sphere. But no government, Liberal or Conservative, would risk its political life by negotiating an agreement which would assign the Shiré-Nyasa area to Portugal. The ground was hallowed by the spirit of Livingstone. His successors, humanitarians in England and Scotland knew, were actively engaged in evangelizing Africans and in uprooting the slave trade. Portugal stood for the evils against which these devoted Christians strove—papism, an abomination to "true" Christianity, and the slave trade, in which Portuguese officials reputedly connived. That these assumptions involved both ignorance and prejudice was of no consequence. Politicians were convinced that the voters would turn on any government that recognized Portuguese sovereignty over the area. But at the same time British rule seemed to be out of the question. Portugal controlled access to Nyasa. Any force sent to assist the British residents would have to be granted passage by Portugal. Any merchants using the Zambezi would be subject to Portuguese customs dues.[3] Gladstone's foreign secretary, Lord Derby, observed that there was "obvious objection in declaring a protectorate over territory which we cannot reach except by passing through the territories of the nation which is most likely to feel aggrieved by our claim."[4] Salisbury also wanted to avoid the

3. Minutes, "British Protectorate in the Nyassa District," [March, 1885], F.O. 84/1735, P.R.O.
4. Note by Derby, March 13, 1885, in *ibid.*

government's being embroiled in the convulsions that wracked the Nyasa area: "It is not our duty to do it. We should be risking tremendous sacrifices for a very doubtful gain. . . . We must leave the dispersal of this terrible army of wickedness to the gradual advancement of civilization and Christianity."[5] But mere negativism, Salisbury recognized, did not solve the problem. Unless an effective government was established in the area, Britain might be drawn in to protect the lives of its subjects.

One possible way out of the dilemma was the creation of a chartered company with sufficient capital to undertake the governance of the area. Sir Percy Anderson in 1885 had suggested that the African Lakes Company with augmented resources might receive a charter which would impose responsibility for police and other governmental functions.[6] This idea had already occurred to the directors of the Lakes Company, who saw the prospect of a charter as the means of converting failure into success.

In May 1885 John Moir, manager of the Lakes Company, secured signatures from various chiefs to documents ceding their territories to the company.[7] On the strength of these agreements the company formally applied to the government for a charter. When news of the company's intentions reached the missionary societies, however, it created a furor. Spokesmen for the societies made it clear that the missionaries did not wish to be governed by the company, and the chiefs who had allegedly ceded their sovereignty and land rights repudiated the treaties.[8]

These manifestations of opposition might have been a serious deterrent to a charter if the issue had reached the stage where the government had to make a decision. But the strongest argument against a charter was the Lakes Company itself. If the company had been an active one, with adequate capital to finance its operations, the Foreign Office would probably have given its claims serious consideration. Anderson in January 1886 noted

5. *Hansard,* 3rd series, CCCXXVIII, col. 550, quoted in Ronald Robinson and John Gallagher, *Africa and the Victorians,* p. 224.
6. Minute, Anderson [March, 1885], F.O. 84/1735, P.R.O.
7. A. J. Hanna, *The Beginnings of Nyasaland and North-Eastern Rhodesia,* pp. 84–85.
8. Memo, "African Lakes Company," February 27, 1886, F.O. 84/1781, P.R.O.

that the Lakes Company was "another prospect for a charter," but its lack of energy concerned him. Later in the year he expressed regret that the directors of the company "do not seem to be very active" and added that "if they are to occupy such a position as the Royal Niger Co. they should bestir themselves."[9]

The Foreign Office concluded that the Lakes Company could not be an effective instrument for administration in the Nyasa area, but the problem of the alternative remained. The coalition of Rhodes and London capitalists provided an opportunity for a solution. With the encouragement of the Foreign Office, Rhodes and Cawston in the spring of 1889 proposed that the African Lakes Company associate itself with the new chartered company. Part of the arrangement would be a subsidy from the British South Africa Company for the administration of Nyasaland. The original intention was that the Lakes Company as a subsidiary of the chartered company would accept the responsibility for governing the territory, but at the insistence of the Foreign Office this idea was dropped. The primary consideration in the Foreign Office's intervention was not the opposition of the missionary societies, but concern about Portuguese and, particularly, German reactions.

In the spring of 1889, while promoters of the chartered company were pressing their case, diplomatic negotiations were in progress with Portugal to delimit British and Portuguese spheres in Central Africa. A premature extension of the company's chartered powers to the lands north of the Zambezi could frustrate a settlement. The reaction of Portugal, however, was far less important than the attitude of Germany. The boundaries between the British and German spheres in both South West and East Africa remained unsettled. In the west Germany hoped to extend its jurisdiction to the Lake Ngami district and the Zambezi River.[10] In the east the "hinterland" which Germany sought to establish for its sphere reached the shores of Lake Nyasa. When Bismarck expressed disquiet at reported intentions of the South Africa Company's promoters, Salisbury

9. Hugh W. Macmillan, "The Origins and Development of the African Lakes Company, 1878–1908," pp. 235–236.
10. Salisbury to Hatzfeldt, September 2, 1889, encl. in F.O. to Malet, February 17, 1890, F.O. 244/470, P.R.O.

assured him that the charter would not be extended to Nyasa-land at least until the Anglo-German boundary was settled.[11]

A combination of economic and political considerations consequently prevented the company's devoting great energy and resources to the territories north of the Zambezi. They "pegged out claims for posterity," with the object of acquiring land and mineral rights which in time could be developed by other capitalists who would reward the company for its foresight. Such arrangements, of course, were the pattern in Mashonaland, but there the company expended great amounts of capital to open up the country for exploitation. North of the Zambezi the capital employed was comparatively insignificant. The contrast in the intensity of company actions had great implications for the African peoples involved. Lewanika, chief of the Lozi, frequently complained that the company had not kept its promise to open up his country. But the price for such development was high, as the Ndebele and the Shona could attest. There was no Barotse War, and Lewanika died of old age.

Barotseland

The country known to Europeans as Barotseland was of indefinite extent and with undetermined resources. In the 1880s the trans-Zambezi country was in a similar stage of European contact to that of the Ndebele twenty years before. A few traders had visited the territory, and one, George Westbeech, who visited the Lozi in 1871 or 1872,[12] had stayed on. In time he became the principal trader on whom the Lozi depended for firearms and other requirements, and he also became an influential adviser to the Lozi on matters relating to their relations with the Europeans. His station at Panda-ma-Tenka consequently was frequented by whites desirous of doing business with the Lozi. But in the mid–1880s Westbeech had fallen out of favor with Lewanika, and his place as confidant to the chief was taken

11. Notes, Anderson, Salisbury, n.d., on Ewing to Salisbury, July 1, 1889, F.O. 84/1998, P.R.O.
12. Gervas Clay, *Your Friend Lewanika*, p. 16, states that Westbeech arrived "about 1871," and Gerald Caplan, *The Elites of Barotseland, 1878–1969* p. 14, citing Gann, says the date was 1871.

by François Coillard, of the Paris Evangelical Missionary Society. Coillard had first arrived in Lozi country in 1878 when it was convulsed by a civil war in which Lewanika for a time was ousted, but during the period Lewanika held control of his capital he had given permission to Coillard to establish a missionary station. In 1884, after a fund-raising campaign in Europe, Coillard returned to take up permanent residence.

Coillard had a low opinion of the people over whose spiritual welfare he sought to preside. They were backward, he felt, not only by European standards but by those of the Sotho, among whom he had previously served. "These poor Barotse," he wrote shortly after his arrival, "How difficult to love them! The best do not amount to much."[13] His Scottish-born wife was even less enamored of the humanity among whom they labored. She confided to her niece that "if only you knew how hard-hearted, and cruel and ignorant are the poor Zambesians, you would pity them."[14] Lewanika, to Coillard, was a source of constant vexation—petulant, capricious, and weak[15]—and their relationship fluctuated. Like his fellow missionaries in Matabeleland Coillard was depressed at his inability to reach the chief and his people with the message of the Gospel and unhappily conscious of the fact that his significance to the Lozi related to the temporal rather than to the eternal. Lewanika accepted him, he knew, because the king believed he could be useful as an intermediary with Europeans, in particular with the British government.

Coillard and his fellow missionaries knew that the issue of their readmission to Lozi country had caused a deep division between Lewanika and many of his advisers. Many of the council opposed the entry of missionaries whose doctrines were subversive of Lozi beliefs and who could be the advance guard of European penetration into their country, but they were overridden.

Lewanika accepted the missionaries as a means to bolster his position against the external threats to his kingdom. He, no

13. Note by Coillard, October 27, 1884, MA 18/4/2/5, N.A.R.
14. Mrs. Coillard to her niece, December 13, 1885, in ibid.
15. See, for example, Coillard to Mackintosh, October 29, 1890, CO 5/1/1/1, N.A.R.

more than his conservative advisers, desired the missionaries to interfere in the domestic affairs of his society. He was conscious of the instability of his tenure and recognized that the presence of the missionaries could further weaken his position. Consequently the missionary role was restricted to the teaching of women and children and missionaries were forbidden to involve themselves in the "business of men."[16] But Lewanika saw a prospect of safeguarding himself from both internal and external threats by following the course of his friend Kgama and accepting a British protectorate, and Coillard could be useful in negotiations with imperial officials.

The greatest immediate external threat to Lewanika on his return to power continued to be the Ndebele, whose periodic raids terrorized the peoples north of the Zambezi. By the testimony of the missionary Frederick Arnot, who lived among the Lozi between 1882 and 1884, some time during his residence emissaries from Lobengula appeared to offer Lewanika an alliance to stand together against the encroachments of white men. Arnot maintained that he had convinced Lewanika that Kgama, Lobengula's bitter rival, was a better ally.[17] The incident almost certainly occurred, though Arnot may have exaggerated his own influence in Lewanika's decision. An alliance with the old enemy, the Ndebele, had short-term advantages for the Lozi in protecting themselves against an Ndebele onslaught, but Kgama offered the prospect of far greater advantages. Kgama had a degree of security against the Ndebele from British protection, and the power and prosperity of his people were augmented by the guns and other goods provided by white traders.

Observing the apparent advantages to Kgama of friendship with the British, Lewanika decided to seek the same protection. In this decision he met with opposition from some of his councillors. In part this negativism may have been based on the fear of some dissidents among the Lozi aristocracy that British intervention would make it impossible to overthrow Lewanika, but probably the primary source of concern was that such a step

16. Caplan, *Elites of Barotseland*, p. 43.
17. Ernest Baker, *The Life and Explorations of Frederick Stanley Arnot*, p. 97.

could mean the end of the independence of the Lozi people and perhaps the loss of their land.[18]

Coillard at first resisted writing on Lewanika's behalf because he was convinced that the motives were entirely selfish—protection against internal revolt—and he insisted that any overtures to the British government should be made only after consultation with the council.[19] Lewanika became increasingly importunate, but Coillard continued to refuse. Finally in late 1888 the chief gathered his council together and informed them of his desire to ask for British protection as a means of shielding his kingdom both against internal and external enemies. Kgama, he said, was happy and secure, because he had British soldiers to back him; Lewanika intended to follow his friend's example. Lewanika's insistence on seeking the aid of foreign troops met with considerable opposition. The council at first refused to accept the loss of Lozi independence which they believed a protectorate would involve,[20] and it was only after considerable pressure and intimidation that Lewanika was able to have his way. At the beginning of January 1889 Coillard wrote Sir Sidney Shippard that Lewanika was anxious for British protection. The Lozi country, the missionary asserted, was not densely populated, and the land offered excellent prospects for agricultural development by Europeans in addition to the ivory trade which at the moment was the principal attraction.[21] Coillard's letter is a curious document. His description of the Lozi territory as a fair field for agriculture bore little relationship to reality. The Lozi lived on the flood plain of the upper Zambezi which was inundated each year, requiring the people to move to higher ground, and this annual migration could hardly have been considered a desirable way of life by Europeans. But the advertisement of Barotseland's attraction for permanent European settlement was almost certainly Coillard's own. It is inconceivable that Lewanika could have suggested or endorsed a course of action

18. Caplan, *Elites of Barotseland*, pp. 44–45.
19. Journal, January 23, 1887, MA 18/4/2/5, N.A.R.
20. François Coillard, *On the Threshold of Central Africa*, pp. 329–332; copy ltr., A. Jalla to Col. Colin Harding, n.d., MA 18/4/1, N.A.R.
21. Coillard to Shippard, January 2, 1889, encl. in C.O. to F.O., August 30, 1889, F.O. 84/2002, P.R.O.

that would mean the death of his kingdom. Coillard's letter made no reference to minerals which were becoming the principal source of attraction drawing Europeans north into Lewanika's country.

Coillard was not the only source of information either on Lewanika's intentions or on the resources of the Lozi country. Lewanika had sent emissaries to Kgama asking how British protection could be obtained, and this intelligence was communicated to the Bechuanaland Exploration Company. Lord Gifford in September 1888 informed the Foreign Office of Lewanika's receptivity and indicated that the Exploration Company was prepared to invest capital in Barotseland if the imperial government blessed the undertaking.[22] The attraction was minerals. But at this time the focus of attention for Gifford and his friends, as for Rhodes, was south of the Zambezi, and the imperial government was not interested in extending its sphere of influence further into Central Africa. Consequently Lewanika's appeal went unanswered for some time.

Barotseland, however, was included in the "Grand Scheme" developed by Gifford, Rhodes, and Cawston in the spring of 1889. Shortly thereafter a trader named Henry Ware applied for a mineral concession in the region north of Victoria Falls between the Machili and Kafue rivers, inhabited by the Toka, a people tributary to the Lozi. The Toka had been falling increasingly under Ndebele influence, and Lewanika and his councillors probably thought that acceptance of Ware's offer involved selling an asset which was more and more doubtfully theirs. Accordingly, Lewanika in June 1889 granted Ware a concession of Toka territory for £200 a year and a four percent royalty on all minerals extracted. Ware also promised not to exploit any land under cultivation. Coillard witnessed the document, and it was probably at his instance that two other stipulations were included—a prohibition on the importation of liquor and a requirement that only men of "good character" would be brought in by the concessionaires.[23] Ware had no capital at his disposal. He was a concession monger and he sold his rights to a Kimber-

22. Clay, *Your Friend Lewanika*, p. 59.
23. Copy of Ware Concession, June 27, 1889, MA 18/4/1, N.A.R.

ley syndicate which in turn made public its willingness to transfer the concession for an appropriate compensation.

The British government heard about the concession in the
summer of 1889 at about the same time as it received Lewanika's
petition. There was nothing in the credentials of the concessionaires to excite a positive response and there was no disposition to undertake the expense of still another protectorate. Consequently, the Colonial and Foreign offices agreed that the response to Lewanika should be noncommitally friendly. The
British government should promise to use what influence it had
with Lobengula to deter him from sending his impis north of
the Zambezi.[24]

At this point the chartered company made an offer that
changed the character of the response. Rhodes proposed that
the company underwrite the expense of the protectorate, which
he estimated might be £100 a year.[25] And Rhodes's friend Sir
Sidney Shippard sent a message to Lewanika which, deliberately
or not, implied that the company was an agency of the imperial
government. He told Lewanika that the imperial government
was considering his request for protection but meanwhile the
South Africa Company would "be able to afford to Lewanika
and his people the fullest protection" and that Rhodes was
sending a mission to the Lozi.[26]

Shippard's message deceived both Lewanika and Coillard,
and the company's agent in his negotiations with Lewanika
took full advantage of this misapprehension. In September
1889 Rhodes appointed Frank Lochner, a former British official,
to proceed to the north with the object of acquiring a mineral
monopoly from Lewanika and then proceeding to the Garaganze country to seek a similar concession from Msiri.[27] Lochner was equipped with a letter of introduction to Coillard from
J. D. Hepburn, a missionary at Kgama's capital of Shoshong,
which reinforced the misconception that the company represented the imperial government. Hepburn told Coillard that

24. C.O. to F.O., August 30, 1889, F.O. 84/2002, P.R.O.
25. Rhodes to Grey. August 30, 1889. BSAC Misc. I., Rhodes House.
26. Caplan, *The Elites of Barotseland*, p. 49.
27. Kimberley to London office, BSAC, HO 1/3/4, N.A.R.

Lochner had "full power to offer Lewanika protection against
the Matabele I am told and that will be a great blessing in itself." Acceptance of the company's offer would mean that Lewanika would be as safe from the Ndebele as was Kgama, Hepburn assured Coillard.[28] Both Hepburn and Kgama warned the
Lozi against Ware. Hepburn called him "self-serving" and told
Coillard to put Lewanika on his guard.[29] Kgama labeled him a
"self-seeker" and advised Lewanika to listen to Lochner, who
had the means to make the Lozi as prosperous as the Bechuanaland Exploration Company had made the Ngwato.[30] This line
reflected Rhodes's conclusion that the price demanded by the
purchasers of Ware's concession was too high and that attacks
on the concession at the best might invalidate it and at the worst
would lower the price. The warnings did not have quite the
effect that was intended, for by casting doubt on Ware the chartered company added to the weight of another rival whose object was to discredit both Ware and the company.

While Lochner was en route, George Middleton was advising
the Lozi to have nothing to do with either Ware or the company. Middleton, who had been a lay member of Coillard's mission until 1887, had returned to seek more material rewards.
Ware had defrauded the Lozi, Middleton asserted, and Coillard
and his fellow missionaries had been accessories. Lochner was
an even worse menace. If Lewanika made an agreement with
him, "your country will be sold, you will not have enough
ground to sit upon."[31]

When Lochner finally arrived among the Lozi at the end of
March 1890, Middleton's efforts had succeeded in producing
considerable uneasiness among Lewanika and his councillors.
Coillard, on the other hand, at first had no apprehensions. The
advent of the chartered company meant to the missionary the
arrival of postal service, telegraph, and railways, the opening
up of a backwater area to the vitalizing influence of civilization.
Lochner's exuberant descriptions of the new era which the
company would bring at first captivated Coillard. "What a

28. Hepburn to Coillard, November 23, 1889, MA 18/4/1, in *ibid.*
29. *Ibid.*
30. Lochner to Harris, November 27 [1889], LO 5/2/0, in *ibid.*
31. Caplan, *Elites of Barotseland*, p. 50.

wonderful thing money is," he wrote his friend John Smith, "It never struck me as it has lately. It is not only the 'sinews of war'—it is the sinews of our civilisation."[32]

Coillard's reaction was similar to that of his counterparts in Matabeleland and elsewhere. Like them he had no doubt that successful conversion could not be effected without the transformation of African cultures into societies in conformity with the Victorian ethic, and they assumed that economic development was a powerful agency for Christianity and civilization. That these changes were inevitable made them no less desirable.

Coillard was almost as much an innocent as Lewanika in dealing with Rhodes and his agent. The missionary was flattered to receive from Lochner a letter from Rhodes himself asking him to accept the position of resident in the new regime which the company intended to establish. Like Helm in Matabeleland he had regretfully to decline. He assured Rhodes, however, that without any official title he would do all that he could to be of assistance to the company and to counteract those mischievous influences that were attempting to frustrate Lochner's mission.[33] In this first phase of uncritical acceptance, Coillard believed Lochner's assurances that the company as the instrument of the imperial government would soon establish an effective administration, that it would begin a regular postal service within a few months, and that soon after the railway would follow. The country, he thought, would then enter a new era under the auspices of a company that combined commerce and philanthropy.

Shortly before Lochner's arrival at Lewanika's capital, Rhodes decided that the company's interest would be served by buying the Ware concession rather than trying to undermine it. Ware was converted into an active advocate of the chartered company. He now devoted his efforts to convincing Lewanika that the chief's best interests would be served by putting his trust in the company.[34]

Acquisition of the Ware concession served the dual purpose of eliminating a potentially troublesome opponent and estab-

32. Coillard to Smith, April 19, 1890, CO 5/1/1/1, N.A.R.
33. Coillard to Rhodes [April 8, 1890], LO 5/2/1, in *ibid.*
34. Ware to Coillard, November 23, 1889, CT 2/11/1, in *ibid.*

lishing the company interests north of the Zambezi, thus coun-
tering the Portuguese plan to extend across Africa from east to
west. The price paid for this concession was £9,000 and 10,000
shares in the chartered company, a substantial reward for the
small sum Ware had paid Lewanika. For Rhodes's purposes,
however, the price was not excessive. The Ware concession, previously described as fraudulent, now was put forward as a valid
grant of a mineral monopoly to all of Lewanika's domain, and
Lochner's mission became one of reconfirmation rather than of
invalidation.[35] Rhodes ignored the patent fact that at best the
Ware concession applied only to an outlying district, and he was
apparently unaware of the requirement that sale of a concession
to a second party required confirmation by the Colonial Office.
"He is very unmethodical in his conduct of business details,"
commented Edward Fairfield.[36]

Rhodes could be careless of technicalities because no one in
authority was disposed to press them. In the spring of 1890 the
imperial government sought to establish the British presence
north of the Zambezi as against the Portuguese. If the Portuguese were successful in establishing their claims to territory between the lower Zambezi and Lake Nyasa, Barotseland could
provide an alternative route north to the Lakes. The Colonial
Office, responding to Loch's importunities, was particularly
eager to claim the territory. The Foreign Office, perhaps because
it had no intention of allowing the Portuguese to block the
Zambezi-Shiré route, was less anxious. But both departments
were predisposed to accept any agreements with African chiefs
north of the Zambezi which had the look of legitimacy.[37]

Lochner consequently was closer to truth than he himself believed when he allowed the Lozi and Coillard to believe his
mission was under the auspices of the imperial government.
Even with this deception, however, he had difficulty in accom-
plishing his object. Middleton's intrigues had revitalized the

35. Rhodes to Abercorn, March 31, 1890, private and confidential,
C.O. 879/32/392, P.R.O.
36. Note, Fairfield, March ——, 1890, on F.O. to C.O., March 11,
1890, C.O. 537/126, P.R.O.
37. C.O. to F.O., April 12, 1890, and F.O. notes thereto, F.O. 84/2079,
P.R.O., Currie to Cawston, June 28 [1890], private, BSAC II, Misc.,
Rhodes House.

opposition to white penetration. This hostility was particularly strong among the Sesheki chiefs in the territory around the confluence of the Zambezi and the Chobe who had only recently been incorporated in the Lozi kingdom and whose allegiance to Lewanika was by no means reliable.[38] This formidable opposition caused Lewanika to hesitate. Lochner's requests for an interview were turned aside with the explanation that "all the headmen have gone to war," and that Lochner should wait quietly until the chief was ready to receive him.[39]

During his wait Lochner lost time and had to delay the mission to Msiri which he had been instructed to undertake after a settlement with Lewanika. Then he fell victim to illness which eventually made it impossible for him to continue his journey. But he pressed on with his suit of the Lozi. He had a staunch ally in Coillard who continued under the illusion that the company represented the imperial government. With this misapprehension, Coillard had no doubts that he was serving the higher interests of the Lozi against "the old heathen conservative party" which was opposed to opening up the country to civilization.[40] Even with these convictions, however, he believed that the proposed annual subsidy of £500 was inadequate and advised Lewanika to insist on payment of at least £2,000 per year in addition to retaining the four percent royalty promised in the Ware concession. Lochner interpreted Coillard's argument for better terms as an attempt on the missionary's part to regain favor with Lewanika and his councillors.[41] This interpretation may have reflected more of Lochner than of Coillard; but whatever his motive Coillard succeeded in gaining the terms he recommended. The opposition among the Lozi collapsed and at a public meeting on June 27, 1890, Lewanika gave his consent to an exclusive mineral concession over all Barotseland.[42]

This agreement later gave rise to much controversy, with Lewanika maintaining that he had been defrauded. One of the causes of dispute was the translation of terms which were un-

---

38. Coillard to Mrs. Malan, May 29, 1890, C.O. 5/1/1/1, N.A.R.
39. Lewanika to Lochner, May, 1890, LO 5/2/3, in *ibid.*
40. Coillard to Mrs. Hart. May 28, 1890, CO 5/1/1/, in *ibid.*
41. Lochner to Harris, April 23, [1890], LO 5/2/2, in *ibid.*
42. Caplan, Elites of Barotseland, p. 54.

translatable into meanings which were unacceptable to one or
the other of the parties. Coillard translated "chartered company" to the Lozi as *lekhotla* (king's council) and "grant" in
the English version became "borrow" in the Lozi translation.[43]
Linguistic misunderstandings, however, were not the primary
cause for subsequent controversy. Lochner used whatever arguments and made whatever promises he felt necessary to win a
concession. Coillard hoped for strong effective British administration and the opening of Barotseland to development by the
advent of the railway. Lochner assured him that these would be
among the fruits of the concession agreement, and Rhodes contributed to the missionary's delusion with his descriptions of the
rapid progress of the railway and telegraph to the north.[44] Coillard was convinced that a great new era was at hand. He wrote:

> A break in the darkness of our horizon seems to be the estab-
> lishment of the Chartered South African Company, should the
> pending transactions come to a good issue. We should at least
> have the advantage of regular Postal communication & our trans-
> port would also become easier if not cheaper. Here they expect
> to push the railway through to Cairo![45]

Lewanika, on the other hand, was assured that the advent of
the company would mean security for himself and great prosperity for his kingdom. Before the full national council Lochner
had declared that by accepting the concession the Lozi would
"grow rich, make progress, graze your flocks and cultivate your
land with full security." An emissary for Kgama appeared at a
critical stage in the negotiations to warn any dissidents who
might be plotting against their chief that Kgama would use his
power to protect his friend. Coupled with this warning was the
assurance that the "Queen's men" of the company would bring
to Barotseland the blessings of British protection which the
Ngwato already enjoyed.[46]

The disillusion that inevitably followed was a consequence
both of the duplicity of Lochner and the naiveté of Coillard.

43. *Ibid.*, p. 52.
44. Harris to Lochner, July 5, 1890, MA 18/4/1, N.A.R.
45. Coillard to Mrs. Hart, May 28, 1890. CO 5/1/1/1, in *ibid.*
46. Caplan, *Elites of Barotseland*, p. 53.

The missionary had pushed the price of the concession to £2,000 per year, yet he seemingly expected that the company would recompense itself primarily in psychic satisfaction. When he cried out that he had been duped into becoming an unwitting accomplice in a "gigantic mining and land-securing scheme,"[47] he was confessing an almost incredible lack of comprehension of the provisions of the concession and of the objectives of those who sought it.

Perhaps in part Coillard's protestations of violated innocence were caused by the anger of Lewanika when he discovered that he had been misled. The agent of this revelation was George Middleton, who returned to Barotseland in September 1890. Middleton convinced the king that Lochner had deceived him and that he had sold the mining rights to his country without acquiring the imperial protection that he had sought.[48] Middleton's testimony naturally cast suspicion on the missionary interpreters, a suspicion that he no doubt was happy to encourage. At Lewanika's direction Middleton wrote Salisbury in October 1890 that the king repudiated the Lochner concession, that he had not understood its meaning and had thought that he was granting a concession merely for twenty years rather than in perpetuity.[49] Little was done to conciliate Lewanika. Loch in September 1890 had sent him a soothing message assuring the chief quite inaccurately that he was "under the protection of Her Majesty the Queen" and promising him that an agent of the queen, Harry Johnston, would soon arrive to "explain Her Majesty's wishes and feelings in regard to your country."[50] The letter arrived at the end of the year. But Middleton's communication experienced considerable delays en route to London, as did other messages embarrassing to the company, and it did not arrive at the Foreign Office until October 1891![51]

The British South Africa Company in 1890 had no immediate

47. Coillard to Harris, June 5, 1891, quoted in James Johnston, *Reality versus Romance in South Central Africa*, p. 147.
48. Caplan, *Elites of Barotseland*, p. 55.
49. Middleton to Salisbury, October 27, 1890, F.O. 84/2177, P.R.O.
50. Loch to Lewanika, September 19, 1890, CT 1/4/4, N.A.R.
51. Note on Middleton to Salisbury, October 27, 1890, F.O. 84/2177, P.R.O.

intention of exercising its rights under the Lochner concession
either directly or through subconcessionaires. Its purpose was to
hold claims to as wide an area as possible as against other European powers, in particular Portugal. The boundaries of Barotseland thus became an important issue in Anglo-Portuguese
negotiations. On June 28, 1890, the day after the Lochner concession was signed, the Foreign Office inquired of Cawston as to
what steps the company had taken to secure the country west of
the upper Zambezi.[52] Pending news of Lochner's fortunes,
Cawston could reply only in vague terms, but in September,
Rhodes wired that the Lozi nation had accepted British protection and that the western boundary of the kingdom was 20° east
longitude.[53] This absurdity of defining the boundaries of an
African people by a meridian derived loosely from the expansive claims made by the Lozi themselves to domination over
other peoples.[54] But any claims, however flimsy, had to be
pressed into service, for during the time between the signature
of the Lochner concession and its receipt in Cape Town, the
Anglo-Portuguese convention of August 20 had been signed,
which placed the boundary between Angola and Barotseland
considerably further to the east. Rhodes and Loch in South
Africa and the board in London protested this surrender of
territory which was "clearly" under Barotse influence and thus
within the British sphere by an agreement that antedated the
convention.[55] The Foreign Office was not prepared to reopen
the boundary issue at a time when the convention was being
submitted to the Portuguese Cortes, but assured the company
that if it could be established that the Lozi had rights west of the
convention boundary the imperial government would seek an
adjustment with Portugal involving, perhaps, a mutual exchange of territory.[56] This assurance was not acceptable to
Rhodes, who with the support of the directors tried to induce

52. Currie to Cawston, private, June 28 [1890], BSAC II Misc., Rhodes
House.
53. Harris to London office, September 8, 1890, LO 5/2/3, N.A.R.
54. Caplan, *Elites of Barotseland*, p. 54.
55. Harris to London office, September 8, 1890, 5/2/3, N.A.R.; Loch
to Knutsford, September 8, 1890; Abercorn to Currie, September 9,
1890, both in F.O. 84/2090, P.R.O.
56. Currie to Abercorn, September 11, 1890, F.O. 84/2090, P.R.O.

the imperial government to abandon the agreement.[57] These importunities were received differently in Downing Street than in Whitehall. Knutsford, the colonial secretary, urged Salisbury to seek an extension of the British sphere to encompass the territory claimed for the Barotse by the British South Africa Company or, alternatively, to ask Portugal to allow the company to exercise sovereign rights in that portion of the Barotse country in the Portuguese sphere.[58] These proposals evoked a cool reception from the Foreign Office. "The Company seem to have very loose ideas about agreements and signatures," noted T. Villiers Lister.[59] "The letter of the Colonial Office is really not creditable to them," wrote Salisbury.[60] Both statements were correct, but the Portuguese Cortes made the issue moot by declining to approve the convention, and the company again considered itself free to compete with the Portuguese in acquiring treaties with African chiefs. The company, however, could generate little momentum north of the Zambezi to advance its objects. Lochner, shattered in health, had to return to Palapye, and was unavailable to pursue either his original mission to Msiri or to lead an expedition to the west. His companions Fraser and Bagley were instructed to proceed westward as far as the Cunene River to acquire mineral concessions,[61] but they were unable to accomplish this objective. Their failure was caused not by the Portuguese but by the Lozi. Lewanika, angered by the company's misrepresentation and constantly goaded by Middleton, refused permission to Fraser and Bagley to cross the Zambezi into Barotseland.[62] Consequently the company had little more documentation for expansive claims in 1891 than it had advanced through the Lochner concession. The treaty of 1891 assigned Barotseland to the British sphere but left the western boundary undefined. Eventually, in 1905,

57. Nawksley to F.O., September 13, 1890, F.O. 84/2090, P.A.O.

58. C.O. to F.O., confidential, September 16, 1890, F.O. 84/2090, P.R.O.

59. Note by Lister, n.d., on Hawksley to F.O., September 13, 1890, F.O. 84/2090, P.R.O.

60. Note by Salisbury, n.d., on C.O. to F.O., September 16, 1890, F.O. 84/2090, P.R.O.

61. Harris to London office, October 6, 1890, LO 5/2/3, N.A.R.

62. Extract, Coillard's journal, January 29, 1891, CO 5/1/1/1, in *ibid.*

the issue was resolved by the mediation of the King of Italy who establish a boundary which was a compromise between British and Portuguese claims.[63]

The company displayed more energy in claiming territory north of the Zambezi than it did in developing it. Coillard waited in vain for the great new era which Lochner had led him to believe would soon come to pass. Almost four years after Lochner's arrival in Barotseland, Coillard was still complaining, with complete justification, that the company had not even fulfilled its promise to establish regular postal service much less railway communication. A letter addressed to him from South Africa in May 1892, arrived in April 1894![64] Loch in 1891 had promised that her majesty's commissioner Harry Johnston would pay Lewanika a visit as a manifestation of British interest. Johnston, however, was preoccupied with affairs in Nyasaland, and did not make the journey. When Lewanika in late 1894 protested to Sir Henry Loch that he had not sent the representative promised three years before, and that he saw no evidence that the queen had any interest in his people, Loch could only reply weakly that he regretted the delay and that he hoped Lewanika would not listen to mischief-makers who cast doubt on the friendship of her majesty's government for the Lozi people.[65] Not until June 1895 did the company send an administrator to Barotseland. Major Patrick W. Forbes, who had fallen into disfavor with Rhodes, was sent to this post, an act which he correctly interpreted as a form of exile, for he had practically no resources at his disposal and little to do beyond overseeing the progress of the telegraph line and taking an occasional tour around the country over which he had a title but little else.[66]

The Lakes Company

Negotiations between Rhodes and Cawston and the African Lakes Company in the spring of 1889 were significant for what

63. Caplan, *Elites of Barotseland*, p. 88.
64. Coillard to Mrs. Malan, April 7, 1894, CO 5/1/1/1, N.A.R.
65. Lewanika to Loch, August (?) 1894; same to same, October 30, 1894; Loch to Lewanika, January 2, 1895, LO 5/2/42, N.A.R.
66. Lewis H. Gann, *A History of Northern Rhodesia*, p. 75.

was not discussed as well as for the issues considered. The participants were concerned with creating an enterprise that would be a business success. In their calculations they dealt with such factors as markets, resources, and trade routes, but they devoted no thought to the indigenous population except in terms of its potentialities for disruption. This omission, of course, was characteristic of European attitudes toward Africans. The missionary did not consider the destructive consequences of his teachings on the cohesion of African societies. The commercial man did not consider the effect of his activity on indigenous traders. In Nyasaland both the missionaries and the Lakes Company had disrupted social and economic patterns throughout the area, but the consequent convulsions they interpreted in terms unrelated to understanding. The slave trade must be opposed because it was evil, and the "Arabs" who engaged in it were evil men. The wars which inevitably occurred were clearly over moral principles. Likewise those African chiefs who attacked the missionaries and the Lakes Company were tyrants fighting the new light. Whatever reassurance such convictions produced, they reflected no comprehension of the complex social and economic patterns of the area.

No one people dominated the region. Yao peoples who had been driven from their country east of Nyasa had resettled on the west side of the lake, where they had established a commercial relationship with Arab-Swahili traders in slaves and other commodities. The Yao lacked centralized leadership. There were four main groups, within each of which local chiefs exercised a considerable measure of autonomy. Also west of Nyasa were elements of the Ngoni, whose Zulu forebears had moved north in the upheavals of the 1820s, and who were dreaded for their military power which they employed to raid other peoples for cattle, crops, and slaves to be used by themselves. To the south on the lower Shiré the Kololo, once associated with Livingstone, had established their hegemony. Besides these peoples there were dozens of other groups who lived in varying degrees of subordination to their more powerful neighbors.[67]

Consequently there was no one African authority in the

67. Ake Holmberg, *African Tribes and European Agencies*, pp. 225–228.

Nyasa area who could be represented by Europeans as paramount, with power to sign treaties and make concessions for the entire region. Furthermore, the cross-currents among the various peoples complicated the problems of establishing effective European administration, as Harry Johnston discovered. But these considerations were absent from the thinking of the negotiators who in the spring of 1889 were planning the amalgamation of the South Africa and Lakes companies. Like other Europeans, they considered European interests to be paramount. Their point of view was candidly expressed by a chief secretary for Nyasaland a few years later:

> I do not pretend, of course, that we took charge of Nyasaland solely or even primarily for the benefit of the natives. Our first and most natural care was to protect the interests of the British settlers there . . . the natives of the country thus taken over are to enjoy the benefits of a strong and humane government, and are to participate in all such advantages of modern civilization as, from time to time, may be safely extended to them.[68]

The negotiators of the two companies were little more concerned with the advancement of European civilization than they were with the elevation of Africans. Rhodes's interest in Nyasaland was to some extent motivated by its strategic importance for communication to the entire Lakes area, but he was also intent on securing options for the South Africa Company to exploit any mineral wealth which might be found in the area. He expected substantial returns for his investments. In Sir John Kirk's words, he always received good value for what he paid.[69] When he contributed £2,000 to Harry Johnston in the spring of 1889 to assist in a treaty making expedition to the Nyasa area,[70] it was on the understanding that Johnston would serve the company as well as the imperial interest. Johnston for this money was supposed not only to secure British supremacy but to acquire "other claims to the British South Africa Company between Lake Nyasa and the Barotse country."[71] Other payments

68. H. L. Duff, *Nyasaland under the Foreign Office*, p. 198.
69. Kirk to Cawston, November 13, 1894, private, BSAC V Misc., Rhodes House.
70. Harry H. Johnston, *The Story of My Life*, p. 219.
71. Johnston to Rhodes, October 8, 1893, F.O. 2/55, P.R.O.

to Johnston as imperial commissioner likewise were made with the same expectation, and when Johnston did not act as a servant of the company Rhodes's rage was incandescent at Johnston's "disloyalty." Salisbury recognized that "free gifts" were not free when he told Johnston that the Foreign Office should pay his traveling and treaty making expenses, since "we do not want to commit ourselves to handing over that region to a Chartered Company." But he did not object to Rhodes's £2,000 being used for other purposes.[72]

Salisbury correctly assumed that the chartered company had ambitions to extend its administration over Nyasaland. Control of the Lakes Company was a means toward that end, but the Lakes Company had other assets. Among them were the treaties negotiated in 1885 by John Moir with the chiefs west of Lake Nyasa and in the Shiré highlands. There were twenty-four of these agreements, which purported to grant the Lakes Company sovereignty.[73] Only one of the agreements, that with the Nkonde people in the Karonga area at the end of the lake, gave the Lakes Company trading, mineral, or land rights, but the Lakes board maintained that such rights were implicit in all of them.

Harry Johnston described these treaties as worthless, but in fact they were much like the treaties he himself had distributed and which he pronounced valid. Most of the treaties had been made with weak peoples who hoped for protection. The only powerful chiefs who agreed to the treaties, the Kololo, were concerned over the threat of Portugal.[74] Later most of the chiefs repudiated the agreements when questioned by a British consul.[75] But evidence that an African chief understood the signifi-

72. Johnston, *Story of My Life*, p. 222.
73. "Treaties Negotiated between the African Lakes Company, Limited, and Nyasaland Chiefs," printed, CT 1/16/1, N.A.R. Typical of the agreements was that in which Ramakuhan, chief of the Kololo, agreed to "give over" his country and promised to send people to work for the Lakes Company. For this Moir gave one percussion gun, one piece (8 fathoms) of cloth, one long knife, and one clasp knife. Also he promised to give two pieces of cloth each month if the chief fulfilled his obligations.
74. Macmillan, "The Origins and Development of the African Lakes Company, 1878–1908," pp. 240–243.
75. Note, Clement Hill, n.d., on Weatherley to Currie, August 13, 1891, F.O. 84/2173, P.R.O.

cance of a treaty had never been a requirement for imperial approval; such a condition would have invalidated many, if not
most, such agreements. Nor was mere repudiation by a chief
sufficient in itself to annul a concession, as Lobengula and
others could attest, and the treaty rights were consequently potentially valuable. Beyond these rights, there was always the
possibility that the infusion of new money and energy might
make the Lakes Company a profitable trading enterprise,
though this was not paramount in the minds of the South Africa
Company's negotiators. Many years later Dr. Jameson compared
the South Africa Company with other imperial-tinged African
ventures in terms highly unfavorable to the latter. The Lakes
Company was "a philanthropy plus five per cent show," and
Rhodes's aims, unlike those of Goldie or Mackinnon, were to
develop white settlements, not merely to "rule niggers."[76] Whatever validity this observation may have had for the lands south
of the Zambezi, it did not apply to Nyasaland. So far as Rhodes's
own intentions were concerned, the important object was to acquire land and mineral rights to as much of Nyasaland as possible, with an emphasis on minerals that could produce quick returns.[77] Some of the board, Gifford and Cawston in particular,
saw opportunities for trade. But neither the board nor Rhodes
was prepared to invest large sums in development and indeed
were unable to do so as expenses mounted south of the Zambezi.

The Lakes Company's interest in amalgamation was manifestly to rescue a foundering enterprise, but the Scottish directors were intent on driving as hard a bargain as possible, and
their actions were scarcely on a more elevated level than those
of the South Africa Company's negotiators. The terms of the
arrangement hammered out between Rhodes and Cawston and
the Lakes Company in the summer of 1889 were straightforward
enough. They agreed that the South Africa Company would
immediately subscribe for 100 shares of £50 each as part of a

76. Interview, Basil Williams with Jameson, April 1, 1914, s. 134,
Rhodes Papers, Rhodes House.
77. Bruce to Grey, August 13, 1891, File 20814, Grey Papers, Durham.
Bruce wrote, "I know that Mr. Rhodes looks to minerals solely, as
agricultural development is too slow, but the permanent prosperity
of the country must depend upon the latter."

capital outlay of £20,000 for the Lakes Company and in addition would contribute maximum of £9,000 per year for administration of the country north of the Zambezi (this despite the fact that the Lakes Company had no administrative authority). The Lakes Company in turn would have the opportunity to acquire South Africa Company shares at par. For the time being each company would remain distinct pending the resolution of all issues involving exchanges of shares and other problems.[78] After several months of negotiations a draft understanding was reached in April 1890 by which the chartered company agreed to take over at par up to 639 £50 shares of Lakes Company stock, and Lakes Company stockholders would receive an equivalent amount of South Africa Company shares at par value. In addition Lakes Company shareholders would have the opportunity to purchase up to 8,050 of a first issue of 270,000 in new chartered company £1 shares. The Lakes Company would have one representative on the South Africa Company board, and the expenditure of the South Africa Company subsidy would be administered by a joint committee of five, three from the Lakes Company and two from the South Africa Company.[79] The exchange of shares was carried out, but the rest of the agreement was suspended amidst mutual charges of bad faith. The Lakes Company complained that the capital funds promised by the chartered company had not been delivered beyond the £5,000 paid for shares,[80] and the chartered company board charged that the canny Scots were stalling in the execution of the agreement in the hope of securing better terms. In fact, the chartered company itself was not anxious to press ahead in fulfillment of the terms of the April 1890 understanding. The territory north of the Zambezi was peripheral; Mashonaland was the central focus. The Lakes Company's appeals to proceed with the formation of the northern board and the definition of its powers received benign responses but produced no action.

78. Rhodes and Cawston to Ewing, August 8, 1889, F.O. 84/2006, P.R.O.
79. Memorandum of Agreement between the British South Africa Company and the African Lakes Lompany, n.d., in Ewing to Salisbury, April 14, 1890, F.O. 84/2079, P.R.O.
80. Stevenson to Bruce, May 12, 1892. F.O. 84/2250, P.R.O.

The acquisition of the ramshackle Lakes Company enterprise no longer appeared to be a great prize.

While both sides were expressing outraged virtue, the Foreign Office received private information from Albert Grey that the Lakes Company had been guilty of duplicity bordering on fraud. He alleged that in July 1889 just before it concluded its first tentative understanding with Rhodes and Cawston, the Lakes Company had granted a monopoly of its mineral rights in Nyasaland to "a Mr. Antoneki, a Pole naturalized as a German." "Antoneki" had formed the Scottish Exploration Company with capital of £2,000. The obvious intent of the transaction was to hold these rights for sale to the highest bidder, and the shareholders of the Scottish Exploration Company—Antoneki and four directors of the Lakes Company—would enjoy a further windfall. The existence of this company, Grey indicated, had come to light over a year after its formation. This was an ugly indictment, and Sir Percy Anderson of the Foreign Office commented on the hypocrisy of the avowed Christians on the Lakes Company board.[81]

The facts were far different than Grey had alleged. Charles E. A. Antonieski had acquired a mineral concession in the Nyasaland area which he sold to a group composed predominantly of directors of the African Lakes Company, who in July 1889 formed the Scottish Exploration Company. The company's objectives as set out in its articles of incorporation were extensive—involving not only prospecting and mining, but the cultivation of agricultural products, and the operation of transport services in support of these activities. The nominal capital to carry out these great ends was ludicrously small—£3,000, of which only £2,000 was actually called up.[82] There was obviously no intention of immediately engaging in mining and agriculture. But the creation of the Exploration Company was not the deliberate fraud on the chartered company which Grey thought it to be. And at least one prominent member of the South Africa Com-

81. A brief account of this episode is given in a note by Sir Percy Anderson, November 1, 1890, F.O. 84/2094, P.R.O.
82. Scottish Exploration Company, Ltd., Articles of Incorporation, July 2, 1889, BT 2/1874, West Register House, Edinburgh.

pany's board of directors was well aware of the Exploration Company's existence—Cecil Rhodes became a shareholder some time between July and November 1889.[83]

Grey's integrity was beyond reproach, and the obvious explanation for his misinformation was that Rhodes had not informed the members of the London board. The board, however, even though it mistakenly believed the Lakes Company to be guilty of a breach of ethics, had to restrain itself from a public charge of fraud. The alleged arrangement was embarrassingly similar to that between the chartered company and the United Concessions Company by which the public and the government had been led to believe that the chartered company held mineral rights when in fact it was merely the lessee.[84] Precisely when Rhodes informed the directors of his involvement in the Scottish Exploration Company is not clear, but the London board decided that this independent entity must be liquidated, and in February 1891 Rhodes and the Lakes Company directors agreed to the liquidation of the Scottish Exploration Company as part of a broader settlement. The chartered company gave 2,000 shares of stock for the "assets" of the Exploration Company, and the Lakes Company released the South Africa Company from its obligation to pay £9,000 a year for "administration" of Nyasaland. The Lakes Company as a partial set-off was granted £2,500 per year as a subsidy for maintaining steamers on Lake Nyasa.[85]

The withdrawal of the £9,000 per year subsidy was justified by the chartered company on the ground that a subsidy for administration was unwarranted when there was no administration. The logic of this position was impeccable, but there was another factor in the decision. The South Africa Company had grown increasingly impatient with the fractiousness of the Lakes Com-

83. List of Shareholders, November 13, 1889, in *ibid.* The incident is briefly described in Macmillan, "The Origins and Development of the African Lakes Company, 1878–1908," p. 335.

84. A. L. Bruce pointed out this parallel to Grey in a letter of August 21, 1891, Grey Papers, File 208/4, Durham. The reminder was probably unnecessary as the South Africa Company was already aware of the similarity in the two arrangements.

85. Minutes, BSAC Special Meeting, February 27, 1891, Grey Papers, File 208/4, Durham.

pany and its lack of energy in serving the chartered company.

The evidence poured in that the Lakes Company was coma-
tose except in defense of its vested interests. Rival concession
hunters had appeared in the Nyasa country but despite the pleas
of the South Africa Company to move quickly to anticipate
them, the Lakes representatives were inactive, even though they
were assured that all expenses for buying up rights would be
borne by the chartered company.[86] Joseph Thomson, who arrived in the area in August 1890, had reported woeful mismanagement, "store houses absolutely empty or filled with an incredible amount of absolute rubbish," an unbusinesslike business "on its last legs."[87] Testimony such as this convinced the
chartered board that "Scotch jealousies and cussedness"[88] could
no longer be tolerated. During the months since the first agreement more and more Lakes Company shareholders had taken
advantage of the profitable option of exchanging their stock for
that of the South Africa Company. Indeed, 599 out of the total
639 shares in the Lakes Company were so transferred, the remaining 40 being left unexchanged in order to enable Lakes
Company directors to hold meetings and pass valid resolutions.[89]

The time seemed at hand when amalgamation should be
completed and new arrangements made for the administration
of the territory north of the Zambezi. In November 1890 an approach had been made to the government to ascertain whether
it would accept direct administration if the company transferred its subsidy to an imperial commissioner, and the response
had been favorable.[90] Consequently the chartered company pursued negotiations with the Foreign Office which culminated in
the establishment of the Nyasaland Protectorate in May 1891,
with Harry Johnston as administrator.

With the chartered company in control of 97½ per cent of
the Lakes Company stock and the subsidy withdrawn it might

86. Hanna, *Beginnings of Nyasaland*, p. 175.

87. Thomson to Cawston, August 11, 1890, encl. in Weatherley to
Anderson, December 20, 1890, F.O. 84/2097, P.R.O.

88. Grey to Cawston, November 30, 1890, BSAC II Misc., Rhodes
House.

89. Weatherley to F.O., July 30, 1892, F.O. 84/2255, P.R.O.

90. Note, Anderson, November 1, 1890, F.O. 84/2094, P.R.O.

have been assumed that the Lakes directors would have quietly
accepted their fate and voted themselves into extinction. But
with great tenacity they fought a delaying action which frustrated the chartered company's intentions for two years. In June
1892 they secured in the courts a writ interdicting the South
Africa Company from carrying out the liquidation.[91] When that
recourse was exhausted they appealed to the Foreign Office under a provision of the agreement, alleging that the chartered
company had not fulfilled its financial obligations.[92] Finally, all
appeals having been unavailing, the Lakes Company passed out
of existence, and to carry on the trade and transport functions
the chartered company created a new entity, "The African
Lakes Trading Corporation," which formally came into existence in August 1893.[93]

With the shift of the subsidy from the Lakes Company to
Harry Johnston as the imperial commissioner the stage was set
for the inevitable collision between Johnston and Rhodes.
Johnston saw his function as the representative of imperial interests. Rhodes saw Johnston's role as a servant of the company.
Johnston favored the company's interests so far as he could do
so consistently with his obligations as the imperial representative. Rhodes demanded more—any deviation by Johnston from
the company line he treated as a dereliction.[94] Johnston's posi-
ton was an unenviable one. In the Nyasaland Protectorate he
was the imperial agent; in the other territories north of the Zambezi over which the charter was extended he was the company's
man. For both these functions, the company paid him £10,000
per year. Rhodes expected Johnston not only to act in the company's interest in Nyasaland but aggressively to direct treaty

91. Notice of Suspension and Interdict for the African Lakes Company Ltd. against the British South Africa Company, June 21, 1892,
F.O. 84/2253, P.R.O.; "Inventory of Process in Suspension and Interdict," CS 275/54/14, West Register House, Edinburgh.
92. Memorial, African Lakes Company to Secretary of State, Foreign
Affairs, August 1892, F.O. 84/2256, P.R.O.
93. Annual Report, BSAC, March 31, 1893, C.O. 417/110, P.R.O.;
Hanna, *Beginnings of Nyasaland*, p. 177. The name was later short-
ened to "African Lakes Corporation."
94. Roland Oliver, *Sir Harry Johnston and the Scramble for Africa*,
p. 175.

making expeditions in the territories to the west and especially to Katanga.[95]

Johnston on accepting administrative responsibility for Nyasaland had assumed that he and Rhodes were both zealous for the extension of the British Empire north of the Zambezi and that Rhodes and the South Africa Company were eager to back ideas with substance by energetic economic development. Neither assumption was correct. Rhodes may have evinced such desires when he and Johnston had their all-night orgy of imperialist ecstasy in the spring of 1889,[96] but the cold grey realities in Mashonaland had chilled Rhodes's ardor. Johnston's pleas to the company for additional action to "open up" Nyasaland consequently either went unanswered or provoked a hostile response. After several months of unsuccessful effort to stimulate action, Johnston concluded that the chartered company was "a little weary of British Central Africa and somehow inclined to drop it."[97] He was, he said, "metaphorically hoarse from pleading with the company to act aggressively to capture the trade of the Lakes."[98] Johnston continued to be a gadfly with his appeals for the active prosecution of commercial development in Central Africa, but his stings produced only irritation rather than substantive action.

The company, however, was much concerned to secure the recognition of all the land rights to which it could possibly lay claim, and it expected Johnston to support it by affirming the validity of the Lakes Company's treaties of 1885.[99] Indeed, in compensation for the annual subsidy Rhodes demanded preferential rights to all lands and minerals in Nyasaland.[100] As much as he was disposed to favor the company, Johnston could not give his full endorsement to the company's claims. The 1885 treaties, he insisted, were "downright frauds," and to recognize

95. London office BSAC to Cape office, July 3. 1891, LO 3/1/3, N.A.R. This letter quotes a private telegram from Rhodes, "Re Katanga, leave it to Consul Johnston."
96. Johnston, Story of My Life, p. 219.
97. Johnston to Weatherley, October 22, 1891, LO 5/1/12, N.A.R.
98. Johnston to Weatherley, private, December 16, 1891, CT 1/16/4/1, N.A.R.
99. Weatherley to Currie, August 13, 1891, F.O. 84/2173, P.R.O.
100. Harris to London office, March 15, 1893, LO 5/2/25, N.A.R.

them as valid would be not only dishonest but stupid. The Lakes Company treaties collided with many other land claims which he considered legitimate, and beyond that the Foreign Office would repudiate him if he made a judgment affirming the validity of the 1885 agreements.[101]

Such considerations were dismissed by Rhodes. To him the issue was simple—the company expected a return on its investment, and Johnston must act loyally to the company or lose its support. After months of mounting vexation he put the issue to Johnston bluntly and crudely. The company, he said, was prepared to relieve Johnston's financial difficulties by raising its expenditure north of the Zambezi to £17,500 yearly for at least five years and it would also construct the telegraph into Nyasaland. The condition was that the imperial government must recognize the company's preferential rights to land and minerals in the British sphere north of the Zambezi. If this condition was not accepted, the company would devote its subsidy of £10,000 entirely to development in the territory outside of Nyasaland.[102] These were the terms Rhodes presented to Johnston when the two met in Cape Town in May 1893. Johnston felt himself in a poor position to bargain. His military operations in Nyasaland had produced a sizeable deficit, and he saw little prospect for relief either from revenue raised locally or by subsidy from the imperial exchequer. Without development and communication, land was worth little and he saw no alternative but to accept in substance Rhodes's offer.[103] The long-term welfare of the territory was thereby sacrificed to immediate necessities. At the time of Rhodes's proposal the company as heir to the Lakes Company claimed one-fifth of Nyasaland, another fifth belonged to the Crown, about two-fifths was recognized as being in African hands, and another fifth had been alienated to other Europeans. What Rhodes demanded was that the Crown land be transferred outright to the company and that it be given the right of preemption to the two-fifths in African hands, with the imperial commissioner using his best efforts to induce the Africans to alienate their lands to the company.

101. Johnston to Weatherley, March 22, 1893, LO 3/1/14, N.A.R.
102. Rhodes to Johnston, April 30, 1893, F.O. 2/54, P.R.O.
103. Oliver, *Johnston*, p. 228.

Johnston agreed to support these terms with the proviso that the company must pay a "fair price" for land purchased from Africans and that the Crown have the right to retain sites necessary for buildings or for other governmental purposes.[104]

Rhodes had expected that the threat to withdraw financial support would make the government amenable to his terms since it was heavily dependent on the subsidy for administration of Nyasaland, and the treasury and Parliament were not prepared to assume the obligation. He was correct in this assessment. Both the Foreign Office and the Colonial Office were disposed to accept Rhodes's terms in principle. The Foreign Office was not concerned about the alienation of land as a price for financial relief. Percy Anderson commented that the best coffee land had already been appropriated and the remaining land was not likely to be in demand for some time unless there were such a dramatic development as a great gold strike.[105] The Colonial Office was concerned that the price might not be high enough if the subsidy were for only five years, but was prepared to support the transaction if the contract were extended to ten years.[106]

These terms were embodied in a draft agreement. The company was to pay £17,500 a year for ten years and to purchase a steamboat for Lake Tanganyika and another for Lake Nyasa. It would extend the telegraph to Nyasaland. In exchange the imperial government would transfer all Crown land in the protectorate and use its "best endeavors" to induce the Africans to grant concessions to the company for land and mineral rights.[107]

The agreement was not consummated, but the reasons had little to do with concern as to the effect of the contract on the welfare of Africans. One consideration which caused hesitation was the fear that if the company paid for the administration, it might expect the administrator to act as its agent, and the imperial government might as a result be embarrassed by commitments made by its representative which it did not wish to

104. Johnston to Rhodes, May 3, 1893, in *ibid.*
105. Memo., Anderson, May 27, 1893, F.O. 83/1240, P.R.O.
106. C.O. to F.O., June 24, 1893, F.O. 83/1240, P.R.O.
107. Draft Agreement, encl. in note, Anderson, July 12, 1893, F.O. 83/1241, P.R.O.

assume.[108] Negotiations, however, were terminated not by the initiative of the government but by Rhodes. The Foreign Office revised the draft agreement further to provide that all of the subsidy must be expended in Nyasaland rather than to be used anywhere north of the Zambezi, and it imposed a requirement that the company be liable for taxation[109] despite a protest from the Colonial Office that it seemed unfair to ask the company to pay taxes in addition to its subsidy.[110]

These modifications substantially altered the terms of Rhode's offer and provoked his celebrated denunciation of Johnston which permanently estranged the two men. Rhodes assumed that he had made a binding contract with Johnston in Cape Town, and that Johnston had modified it after his departure. Just as he had assumed in 1890 that Johnston had been the culprit in an Anglo-Portuguese agreement adverse to Rhodes's ambitions he now concluded that Johnston had betrayed him. The language used by Rhodes—"disloyalty," "desertion," "treachery"—reflected his simplistic view of imperial policy. Johnston as the "man on the spot" he considered to be the key figure; if the imperial government did not follow Johnston's recommendations it must be because Johnston in private had for his own reasons repudiated his commitments. He had expected Johnston as the recipient of the company's bounty to be loyal to his benefactor; he was outraged at what he considered to be Johnston's faithlessness to his trust. Rhodes had expected him to serve the company and he now sought to demonstrate his independence by advocating a line contrary to the company's interests. The "impudent" proposal to tax the company that subsidized the Nyasaland administration Rhodes assumed was inspired by Johnston.[111]

The harshness of Rhodes's attack evoked indignation at the Foreign Office. Villiers Lister called the denunciation of Johnston "a most undeserved slur" and Percy Anderson said that he

108. Buxton to Ripon, August 12, 1893, Ripon Papers, Addtl. MSS. 43553, British Museum.
109. Holmberg, *African Tribes*, p. 300.
110. C.O. to F.O., August 14, 1893, F.O. 83/1242, P.R.O.
111. Telegram, Rhodes to Harris, October 13, 1893, CT 1/16/4/2, N.A.R.

had "treated Johnston brutally."[112] But the fault was not entirely Rhodes's; by acceding to an agreement which made the company the principal financial support of administration, the imperial government had invited great expectations from a man who was accustomed to be well paid for his "benefactions"; and Johnston had been placed in the impossible position of serving two masters.

Rhodes eventually offered Johnston what for him was a form of apology, and invited him to visit in Cape Town on his way to England.[113] The company in London also indicated its willingness to negotiate an agreement based on the Rhodes-Johnston understanding of May 1893, and continued its payments at the rate of £17,500 a year pending a settlement.[114] But the government's receptivity had faded away in the wake of Rhodes's outburst, and the Foreign Office began to consider alternative arrangements. This shift was accelerated by a further demand from Rhodes. At the end of 1893 Johnston undertook an expensive amphibious campaign against the powerful Yao chief Makanjira, and he drew on Rhodes for £10,000 to pay for the operation. Through his secretary Rutherfoord Harris, Rhodes made it clear that he expected in compensation recognition of the company's claims to land and mineral rights.[115] Johnston was inclined to meet this demand by assigning Makanjira's country to the company as a reward for its philanthropic contribution, but he referred the matter to the Foreign Office. The response was emphatically negative. Percy Anderson noted: "There is nothing philanthropic about it; if there were, philanthropy should not be mercenary. It does not justify compensation in concessions or land grants. We allow no such compensation for 'philanthropic expenditures' in return for the far larger outlay of the East Africa Company. . . ."[116]

The company nevertheless received handsome dividends for its philanthropy. In November 1894 the Foreign Office and

112. Notes on Johnston to Rhodes, October 8, 1893, F.O. 2/55, P.R.O.
113. Rhodes to Johnston, February 6, 1894, Johnston Papers, Royal Commonwealth Society; JO 1/1/1, N.A.R.
114. Canning to F.O., March 9, 1894, F.O. 83/1310, P.R.O.
115. Harris to Johnston, confidential, March 10, 1894, LO 5/2/33, N.A.R.
116. Memo, Anderson, February 20, 1894, F.O. 83/1309, P.R.O.

Rhodes made a settlement embracing the whole range of disputes in the territory north of the Zambezi. The company obligated itself to assume direct administration of the territory north of the Zambezi outside of Nyasaland not later than June 30, 1895. In Nyasaland it agreed to continue the annual payment of £10,000 to January 1, 1896, in addition to £10,000 in liquidation of its obligation to provide the imperial commissioner with the free use of steamers on Lake Nyasa. In compensation for all the company's outlays, the government recognized the validity of mining claims by the company in the Protectorate in the districts of Marimba and Central Angoniland.[117] These in addition to the rights acquired by the company as heir to the Lakes Company, gave the chartered company vast land and mineral rights in Nyasaland.[118]

These holdings were supplemented by acquisitions of other claims, most important of which was the so-called "Wiese concession." The passage of the rights from the original African owners to the South Africa Company presents a fascinating view of concession-mongers and of company formation in Africa. Carl Wiese was a German-born trader who had been active south of Lake Nyasa since about 1885 and had acquired considerable influence with several African chiefs, most powerful of whom was the Ngoni chief Mpezeni. Wiese was courted by both British and Portuguese agents who sought to use his influence to sway Mpezeni to their sides. Wiese supported the Portuguese, and consequently Mpezeni rejected the overtures of Alfred Sharpe and Joseph Thompson to accept British protection.[119] Harry Johnston repeatedly attempted to woo Wiese to change his allegiance but was unsuccessful[120] and his subsequent vilification of Wiese as a slave trader and an "utterly unscrupulous" man[121] may have been related to this failure.

117. Memorandum of Agreement with South Africa Company respecting British Central Africa, November 24, 1894, F.O. 83/1318, P.R.O.
118. For a discussion of land alienation, see Hanna, *Beginnings of Nyasaland*, pp. 177–178, 190–194, 229–238.
119. J. K. Rennie, "The Ngoni States and European Intrusion," in Eric Stokes and Richard Brown, eds., *The Zambesian Past*, pp. 324–325.
120. Great Britain. Colonial Office, *North Charterland Concession Inquiry. Colonial No. 73*, p. 5.
121. Hanna, *Beginnings of Nyasaland*, pp. 237–238.

Wiese claimed to have received verbal concessions from Mpezeni and from other chiefs embracing approximately twenty-five thousand square miles. These claims were on both sides of the Anglo-Portuguese boundary established by the convention of 1891. Wiese reinforced his verbal concessions with written documents purporting to be signed by Mpezeni and other chiefs. These concessions were highly questionable. That alleged to come from Mpezeni had no mark of either the chief or any of his councillors; Mpezeni's "signature" had been affixed by the Portuguese associate of Wiese.[122] Even if they were genuine their validity was questioned by the Colonial Office because they granted monopolies not only of minerals but of trade, industry, and communication, contrary to British policy.[123] Johnston pronounced them worthless.[124] But Wiese proceeded to seek buyers for his rights. He sold the Portuguese portion to the Zambesia Company,[125] and found a buyer in the British sphere who hoped to resell the rights at a substantial profit. His rights in Nyasaland were bought by the Mozambique Gold, Land, and Concession Company, which had been registered in 1893 with a nominal capital of £1,000, only eleven pounds, three shillings of which was actually paid up. This company was a corporate front for two mining engineers, C. A. Moreing, one of the principal shareholders in the Mozambique Company, and B. T. Burrell, and their intentions were to use their expertise to sell their acquisition rather than to develop it themselves.[126] They in turn sold their "rights" to the Oceana Company, which specialized in the acquisition of mining properties throughout South and Central Africa, most of which it gained control over by allocation of shares rather than payments of money,[127] and the fluctuations of its shares and that of its subsidiaries were the objects of considerable attention of speculators in the London stock market. Its £1 shares at one time reached £25, driven up

122. *Ibid.*, p. 237.
123. C.O. to F.O., August 3, 1894, F.O. 83/1314, P.R.O.
124. Johnston to Anderson, October 17, 1894, F.O. 83/1316, P.R.O.
125. Canning to Maguire, May 3, 1895, LO 3/1/28, N.A.R.
126. C.O. to F.O., immediate, September 15, 1894, F.O. 83/1315, P.R.O.
127. The records of this company are in B.T. 31/3763/23462, P.R.O.

by hopes and expectations which were largely unrealized.[128] Johnston not inaccurately described the promoters of the Oceana Company as "a collection of Stock Jobbers and Speculators" who had no intention of spending large sums of money in the development of their estates. The South Africa Company desired to acquire the Wiese concessions, and Johnston stimulated the Oceana Company's willingness to negotiate by threatening to reopen the issue of the validity of the concessions unless the company came to terms.[129] To avoid investigation, the two companies agreed to form a new company of £1,000,000 capitalization in which the South Africa Company would be assigned thirty percent of the shares, and which would be subject to chartered company mineral and land rules which entitled the company to fifty percent of the profits.[130] The Oceana promoters individually and the Oceana Company itself had substantial holdings in this new company, the North Charterland Exploration Company.[131] This company was assigned a vast estate of 10,000 square miles; its assertion of these rights produced an Ngoni revolt in 1897, quickly put down by an imperial government which had earlier expressed grave doubts as to whether the concession was genuine and whether, even if it were, it could legally be transferred from one party to another. Percy Anderson in assessing the issue had commented that one of the worst practices in Africa was that of hawking concessions. Such a system, he maintained, was not admissible in any administration whose duty it was to protect Africans against the theft of their lands by unscrupulous speculators.[132] But Anderson's observations were not translated into policy.

Johnston had complained that the chartered company had been interested in acquiring land rights rather than in develop-

128. F.O. to C.O., August 11, 1894, C.O. 417/133, P.R.O. The shares slumped to under 1 1/2 after revelations that the company's properties were not producing. *Financial News*, September 1, 1894.
129. Johnston to Anderson, October 17, 1894, F.O. 83/1316, P.R.O.
130. London office, BSAC to Rhodes, March 13, 1895, LO 5/2/41, N.A.R.
131. Summary of Capital and Shares, August 13, 1895, B.T. 31/15483/44129, P.R.O.
132. Memo, Anderson, July 3, 1894, F.O. 83/1312, P.R.O.

ment of trade and agriculture. His complaint was largely justified, but members of the chartered company board did involve
themselves in the promotion of a great trading venture which, if
it had been successful, would have given its principals a monopoly of the trade and transport of Central Africa. One element of this monopoly was to be a new company with a capital
of £1,000,000 which would succeed the African Lakes Company,[133] and the plan envisaged cooperation with Belgian, Portuguese, and perhaps German interests. The principal backers
of the scheme on the South Africa Company board were Gifford
and Cawston, and Messrs. Mosenthal and Company of London
and South Africa were to be the concessionaires for that part
of the operation which was within the chartered company's
sphere.[134] Cawston envisaged the establishment of steamer and
railway services from Lake Tanganyika to the sea and he elicited favorable responses to the idea from Leopold and from
Albert Thys, the principal figure in the development of communications in the Congo Free State, and from directors of the
Mozambique Company,[135] but negotiations were suspended during the protracted stalemate with the Lakes Company, and the
great project faded away.

Katanga

The company also failed to wrest the riches of Katanga from
Leopold's Congo Free State. There was neither force nor direction in the Katanga campaign. Some called it a "race" with
Leopold. Bourchier Hawksley, the company's solicitor, more
accurately referred to the Katanga project as a "Will of the
Wisp." Hawksley years later recalled that Rhodes and Beit,
especially the latter, had "always wanted Katanga."[136] They

133. Bruce to Grey, January 20, 1892, File 189/9, Grey Papers, Durham.
134. Gifford to BSAC, February 22, 1893, and other correspondence,
LO 5/2/13, N.A.R.
135. Grey to Cawston, September 20, 1893; Cawston to Tiano, September 30, 1893; Cawston to ————, October 31, 1893, d'Oultremont
to Cawston, July 29, 1893, all in BSAC IV Misc., Rhodes House.
136. Hawksley to Cawston, June 22, 1911, BSAC IV Misc., Rhodes
House.

competed, however, with a wily adversary, and they did not want Katanga sufficiently to give its acquisition a high priority. The first concern of Rhodes and the South Africa Company was the occupation of Mashonaland and, if possible, access to the gold fields from the Indian Ocean. In 1890 when the possibility still glimmered that the company might win the race against Leopold, the race was not run.

Even if the company had devoted considerable resources to an energetic campaign, it probably would have lost the contest. Leopold, hard pressed as he was financially by the demands of the Congo on his personal fortune, nevertheless had formidable assets in defending his claim. With consummate artistry he had utilized the tension and jealousies of the great powers to carve out the Congo Free State; his weakness had been his strength. At the Berlin Conference he had secured recognition for his International Association against the strenuous opposition of the Portuguese. Subsequently he had secured French recognition of his claims to most of Katanga for the price of the French right of preemption if he should decide to withdraw from Africa. French recognition did not commit other powers but neither Britain nor Germany had protested when the association had announced its boundaries as including the Katanga area.[137]

In diplomacy as in seduction, though silence does not necessarily mean consent it can easily be so construed, and in the 1880s both the Gladstone and Salisbury governments had regarded Leopold's Congo venture benignly. When the South Africa Company challenged Leopold's right to Katanga, several years had passed during which no opposition to the southern Congo Free State boundary had been expressed by the imperial government. In the late 1880s the British position was influenced by the negotiations with Germany for territorial delimitation in Africa, for Germany's claims extended to the borders of the Congo Free State, the eastern boundaries of which Germany had not recognized. Germany might conceivably contest Leopold's claims on the basis of Paul Reichard's explorations in the Copper Belt and the absence of any Free State authority in the

137. A Berriedale Keith, *The Belgian Congo and the Berlin Act* (Oxford, 1919), 64n.

Katanga area.[138] The British government might have entered a claim to Katanga based on the explorations of Verney Lovett Cameron and others, but there was no disposition to do so without more positive evidence of British activity in the area. Prior to the advent of the British South Africa Company there was no such evidence, and the Foreign Office had no inclination to support the extension of a British protectorate over Katanga on behalf of the commercial interests of the company. The company, if it acquired a concession from Msiri, could enjoy the fruits of its good fortune even if political control were assigned to Leopold. When Cawston visited the Foreign Office in February 1890, consequently, he was informed that the government accepted Leopold's claim that Katanga was part of the Congo Free State.[139] This intelligence was conclusive for Cawston; it was not so regarded by Rhodes, to whom nothing less than an explicit official announcement by the imperial government was considered to be a deterrent.

The contrasting responses of Cawston and Rhodes reflected a difference in viewpoint which was always present between the London board and Rhodes but which was thrown into high relief on the Katanga issue. Where Rhodes's energy and money were committed, the board deferred to his judgment so long as he was successful. But Rhodes's concentration in 1890 was on Mashonaland. He had little time and no capital to devote to Katanga, and his attention was diverted in that direction only fitfully. Cawston, on the other hand, viewed the prospects as a businessman. The issue of sovereignty was of little consequence to Cawston, as compared to the opportunity for profit. He later became chairman of the South West Africa Company, a predominantly British corporation organized to acquire mineral concessions under the German flag,[140] and expressed interest in participation in joining a similar enterprise in German East Africa.[141] He supported an international transport company in

138. Kirk to Salisbury, June 22, 1890, File E, Salisbury Papers, Christ Church, Oxford.
139. Cawston to Rhodes, February 6, 1890, BSAC II Misc., Rhodes House.
140. The company still exists. Its reports are filed in the Companies Registration Office, London, File 37031.
141. Fairfield to Sanderson, July 2, 1894, C.O. 537/128, P.R.O.

central Africa. He later became chairman of a large mining company in China. He was, in short, interested in profits wherever they could be made, and he saw greater prospects in Katanga by cooperating with Leopold than by competing with him, particularly in view of the Foreign Office's attitude.

The company was first brought into communication with Leopold through the Brussels Anti-Slavery Conference of 1889–1890, called avowedly in response to Cardinal Lavigerie's call to Christian nations to join in a crusade against the slave trade. The conference had little to do with slavery, much with the ambitions of the powers in attendance. Leopold sought international recognition for the boundaries of the Congo Free State extending from Bahr-al-Ghazal on the Nile to Katanga.[142] The British South Africa Company which was invited to send an observer saw an opportunity to win favor with British humanitarians which might be useful in case of collision between the company and the Ndebele during the march of the pioneer column. Thus Cawston was sent to Brussels with instructions to take an enlightened position on all issues relating to slavery, strong drink, and the arms trade.[143] While Cawston was in Brussels a further development drew him into close contact with Leopold. Britain was engaged in negotiations with Germany on boundary issues in Africa, and Lord Salisbury's well-known deference to Germany caused members of the board to fear that he would make large concessions for the sake of amity with Germany. These sacrifices would likely come at the expense of the British East Africa and South Africa Companies. Germany desired a boundary between Lake Nyasa and Tanganyika which would have eliminated any British line of communication between the two lakes. The possibility that Salisbury might agree led Cawston to be receptive to a proposal from Leopold offered in the guise of his deep friendship and concern for Britain and Britons. Leopold offered to grant to the company a five-mile strip through the Congo Free State which would provide an al-

142. Suzanne Miers, "The Brussels Conference of 1889—1890," in Prosser Gifford and W. Roger Louis, eds., *Britain and Germany in Africa* (New Haven, 1967), p. 107.
143. Cawston to Rhodes, February 6, 1890, BSAC II Misc., Rhodes House.

ternative route of communication in case the "Stevenson road" between Lake Nyasa and Lake Tanganyika were lost to the Germans. But Leopold's gifts were never cheap. In return he suggested that he would like to have the following: a port on Lake Nyasa, to be reached through a corridor five miles wide from the Congo Free State, the right of engaging up to 800 Africans annually from the company's territories for service in the Free State police, and acceptance by the company of a northern limit of 14° south latitude in order to leave to the Free State some high lands suitable for European settlement.[144] This limitation would have assigned much of what is northern Zambia to the Congo Free State, including part of the copper-producing region. Leopold's reputation as a hard bargainer was well deserved. The company considered his terms either exorbitant or impossible. Cooperation with Leopold in the supply of manpower would expose the company to charges of trafficking in slaves; his demand for a port on Lake Nyasa and access thereto was rejected out of hand, as was his proposal for acceptance by the company of the 14° northern limit. Not only was this last suggestion unacceptable to the company but it was not within the company's power to concede, since any agreement on boundaries involved the imperial government. For all of this Leopold offered only a lease, since Leopold had conceded to France the right of preemption. Any inclination by the company to bargain for better terms disappeared when Germany conceded the Stevenson road to Britain, and the draft treaty became only an eloquent testimony to the remarkable effrontery of Leopold II.

While negotiations with Leopold were still in progress, the company considered its strategy with regard to Katanga. Cawston and other members of the London board accepted the Foreign Office's advice that Katanga was within the Congo Free State but believed that they could still outmaneuver Leopold by grasping the prize that made Katanga important, its mineral deposits. If the company won mineral concessions from Msiri and other chiefs, it expected that Leopold would have to recog-

144. Report by Cawston on interviews with Leopold on April 24, 1890, for submission to board meeting on April 30, 1890, F.O. 84/2081, P.R.O.; Cawston to Rhodes, June 20, 1890, BSAC II, Misc., Rhodes House.

nize them. The king's resources were strained already in the Congo basin, and he could not move swiftly to occupy Katanga; a rapid movement by the company could anticipate him. To accomplish this important mission, Cawston proposed Joseph Thomson who, though only 32 years old, had already established himself as one of the great African explorers, with a reputation for speed and endurance which seemed to make him an ideal selection for the task at hand. This was not the first time that the representatives of the company had approached Thomson. In the summer of 1889, when euphoria for the Grand Design was at its rosiest, a spokesman of the company, probably Cawston, had inquired if Thomson would be available to lead an expedition into the region around Lake Nyasa. He had indicated that he was interested, but had heard no more of the prospect.[145] On this occasion, however, the board, on the recommendation of A. L. Bruce, made Thomson a firm offer, in which Rhodes concurred. Thomson was employed at £100 a month to lead the expedition to Katanga.[146]

Thomson's subsequent failure was almost foreordained by the conditions surrounding his mission. Though Cawston and Rhodes had agreed on his appointment, they had not agreed on precisely what his objectives were to be or even the route he was to take. There was no unified plan of campaign. The contradictions between Cawston's and Rhodes's expectations became painfully apparent in May 1890. Thomson discovered on arrival in Kimberley that he was one of several with whom Rhodes wanted to discuss northward extension. Also in Kimberley were James A. Grant, son of the famous explorer, and Harry Johnston. Thomson was dispatched with Grant to trans-Zambezia via Quelimane and the Zambezi-Ruo Rivers. He understood that he was to lead an expedition to Msiri's but on the way was to make treaties with chiefs and to make contact with Lochner, who was to be placed under his orders. In selecting the river route, Thomson successfully resisted the suggestion of Johnston that he proceed overland from Bechuanaland. Johnston wrote to Cawston, "Thomson is a terribly obstinate man as I dare say

145. Thomson to Bolton, November 7 [1889], HO 1/3/3, N.A.R.
146. Robert I. Rotberg, *Joseph Thomson and the Exploration of Africa*, p. 267.

you know. He would not take any advice as to the route he should follow nor would he listen any more to Rhodes. . . ."[147] Thomson's version of his experience was quite different. He had arrived at Kimberley with the expectation of carrying out a mission outlined by Cawston of a rapid expedition to Katanga, and he had now received instructions from Rhodes to enlarge his mission to include treaty making activity in the intervening country. He complained to his friend John Bolton, the geographer, "I must confess I am rather at a loss between Rhodes and Cawston."[148]

An additional complication was provided by the involvement of Harry Johnston. The "Grand Design" of the spring of 1889 Johnston considered as much his creation as anyone's, and from his base in Nyasaland he was prepared to do all he could to make the plan a reality. Johnston needed no explicit instructions to act; he assumed great latitude in his campaign to win central Africa for Britain. While Cawston was negotiating with Thomson, Johnston had commissioned his vice-consul Alfred Sharpe to proceed on a treaty making expedition westward toward Katanga. Johnston had not been consulted by the London board about the appointment of Thomson, and he was much annoyed at the decision to send what he considered to be a competing expedition.[149]

Rhodes may or may not have been aware of Johnston's assignment to Sharpe; probably he was; but there was no coordination between the plans for Sharpe's expedition and those of Cawston for Thomson. Sharpe and Thomson first discovered each other's missions when they met in Nyasaland, which Thomson reached in July 1890, after a harrowing encounter with Portuguese soldiers who sought to stop his passage down the Ruo River.[150] Sharpe had recently returned from a treaty making expedition into the Luangwa valley and had now been instructed by Johnston to make a second journey into the valley, and then to proceed to Katanga. The two explorers could see no reason for the

147. Johnston to Cawston, June 16, 1890, quoted in *ibid.*, p. 271.
148. Thomson to Bolton, May 28 [1890], HO 1/3/3, N.A.R.
149. Macmillan, "The Origins and Development of the African Lakes Company, 1878–1908," p. 326.
150. Rotberg, *Thomson*, p. 276.

dispatch of two uncoordinated expeditions and therefore decided that Thomson would traverse country to the west of
Nkhoto Kota on the south end of Lake Nyasa and Sharpe would
take the northerly route from Karonga at the north end of the
lake, each making treaties with chiefs en route. Neither expedition achieved its ultimate objectives and Thomson's was an
almost total failure, partly because of his own attributes, but
principally from a natural disaster. Thomson's expedition was
struck by a smallpox epidemic which not only killed his porters
but caused the peoples on their route to shun contact with them.
Before the disease wiped out his chances, Thomson had man-
aged to secure a few agreements with Africans whom he described as chiefs but the documents were highly suspect. In his
haste to move on he had not taken the time to ascertain the credentials of the leaders with whom he negotiated and he had not
engaged in the extended palavers which would have been necessary by African custom. With the courage that had characterized
his African exploration throughout Thomson pushed on at the
head of a rapidly dwindling and increasingly debilitated expedition, but he failed to reach Msiri. Seriously ill with cystitis
and deserted by most of the remaining able-bodied porters, he
turned back, negotiating on the way more agreements with the
same defects as his earlier treaties.[151]

Sharpe reached Katanga, but failed to win the prized concession from Msiri. His expedition had also been attacked by
smallpox and he had allowed himself to be convinced by Kazembe, an enemy of Msiri, that he should leave his white associates and most of his caravan behind in Kazembe's country for
fear he would be attacked and robbed. Consequently he did not
impress Msiri with either his power or his opulence when he
arrived at Bunkeya, the capital of Garenganze.[152]

The prospects of Sharpe's success had been poor in any event.
Msiri had been described in various uncomplimentary terms by
European visitors and missionaries—cruel, capricious, blood-

151. *Ibid.*, p. 284. The Foreign Office considered the treaties probably
invalid, but nevertheless they were later officially certified by Johnston
and became, with Sharpe's agreements the basis for much of the company's claims to Northern Rhodesia.
152. René J. Cornet, *Katanga*, p. 65; G. E. Tilsley, *Dan Crawford,
Missionary and Pioneer in Central Africa*, p. 146.

thirsty were favorite adjectives. But no one had referred to him as credulous or stupid. He had risen to power through shrewd perception of the contending forces in the area. He had used the proceeds of his trade to acquire guns. By a combination of force and diplomacy, he had expanded his empire. But he was aware that his power rested on an unstable basis. As he had risen so might he fall, and he was vigilant to repel any threats to his position. By the time of Sharpe's arrival Msiri had become aware of the greatest menace of all, the intrusion of Europeans seeking the mineral wealth of his kingdom. The story has been told that he was superstitious and had believed the prophecy of Swahili traders that he must beware of white people from the east who would seek to "eat" his gold, and that Sharpe was rejected because he arrived from the east.[153] But Msiri's fear of Europeans went beyond superstition. Whether they came from the south, the north, or the west they wanted what he could provide only by the loss of his power and, if he resisted, his life. He was aware of the advent of the Belgians in the Congo and the British in Mashonaland, and he needed no soothsayers to stimulate him to be on his guard.

Sharpe had hoped to find Frederick Arnot, a missionary of the Plymouth Brethren, at Bunkeya, but Arnot was no longer there. Consequently Sharpe tried to enlist the services of another missionary, Charles Swan, to act as an interpreter and to advise Msiri to sign a concession. But Swan told Sharpe that the agreement as written would not be acceptable to Msiri and refused to perjure himself by telling the chief that a document transferring his mineral rights was merely a declaration of friendship with the British people. Msiri refused to sign the agreement and Sharpe departed without the prize he had been sent to win.[154]

Neither Cawston's nor Rhodes's object had been served, and the ineffectuality of their agents was in large part attributable to their failure to plan a campaign with the resources necessary for success or even to agree as to what precisely they sought to achieve. Critical decisions were made by each without consultation with the other. In July 1890, at about the time when

153. Tilsley, *Crawford*, p. 139.
154. Charles A. Swan, "Difficulties and Dangers in Early Days," *A Central African Jubilee* (London [1932?]), pp. 107–108.

Thomson was arriving in Nyasaland, Cawston on behalf of the board invited Lieutenant William Stairs to lead an expedition to the country between the Congo and the Zambezi.[155] Stairs, after some consideration, declined the offer,[156] and later accepted service under Leopold and led the force that ended Msiri's rule and his life. The precise relationship between his mission and that of Thomson and Sharpe was not made clear. The company seemed to be committed to a series of probing operations throughout Central Africa designed to acquire whatever rights were available, but there was no unified leadership. Communications were slow and what efforts were made to achieve unity were consequently useless. In December 1890, after Thomson and Sharpe had already failed in Katanga, the London board asked that Sharpe be notified that Thomson was working for the company and that Thomson be similarly informed with regard to Sharpe.[157] The message was a measure of the gaucherie of the trans-Zambezian campaign.

Remarkably, in view of the paucity of planning, Rhodes and the board expected their efforts to be successful. Cawston, confident that Thomson would not only reach Msiri but charm the chief into making the concession, began to lay plans for a friendly accommodation with Leopold by which the company and the Belgian king would jointly exploit the mines under the sovereignty of the Free State.[158] But as the silence from the interior continued, this optimism began to evaporate. Anxious telegrams went from London to Kimberley inquiring about the results of Thomson's and Sharpe's missions.[159] It was not until the end of May 1891 that the board learned definitely from Rhodes that neither Thomson nor Sharpe had made any treaties in Katanga. Their hopes had been raised briefly by receipt of a treaty Thomson had made with a chief, probably an Nkana of

155. Cawston to Stairs, confidential, July 18, 1890, BSAC II Misc., Rhodes House.
156. Stairs to Cawston, July 26, 1890, *ibid.*
157. London office to Kimberley, December 4, 1890, LO 3/1/1, N.A.R.
158. Cawston to Kirk, December 22, 1890, BSAC II Misc., Rhodes House.
159. Telegrams, London to Kimberley, February 2, 1891, February 8, 1891, both in LO 5/2/7; London to Kimberley, February 5, 1891, LO 3/1/2, all in N.A.R.

the Lamba tribe, who was called Mshiri.[160] Could this, the board
asked, be a misspelling for Msiri?[161] A negative response forced
the company to change its strategy.[162]

The urgency of the board's communications to Rhodes was
not entirely related to the mineral concession itself. Despite the
Foreign Office's insistence that it would not contest Leopold's
political rights in Katanga, the more aggressive members of the
board were encouraged to hope that Salisbury would support
boundary adjustments which would give the company at least
part of Katanga if only they could produce a treaty from Msiri
which could support a British claim. Salisbury's position on
Katanga was highly equivocal. While he did not contest Leopold's claims under the circular of 1885 and his German and
French treaties, he was not willing to admit that these documents interdicted the company from seeking treaties in the
mineral districts of Katanga. When Leopold appealed to him to
order the company to stay away from Katanga, Salisbury replied
that the southeast boundary of the Congo Free State by the
treaties was 6° south latitude, far north of Msiri's kingdom and
thus that Leopold had no basis for protest against the chartered
company's activities.[163] In August 1890 he had expressed annoyance at Johnston's presumptuousness in lecturing to him about
the importance of Britain's laying claim to Msiri's kingdom.[164]
In March 1891 he assured his parliamentary undersecretary, Sir
Philip Currie, that he had explicitly instructed Johnston not to
interfere in any way with the territories of the Congo Free State
as defined in the circular of 1885.[165] Yet, two weeks before, he
had advised Johnston that it "would be a very good thing" to
send "anybody you can trust" to determine whether Britain
should contest the boundary.[166] Salisbury thus showed one face

160. Rotberg, *Thomson*, p. 279.
161. Telegram, London to Kimberley, May 28, 1891, LO 3/1/3,
N.A.R.
162. Lister to BSAC, May 29, 1891, F.O. 84/2166, P.R.O.
163. Salisbury to Vivian, May 10, 1891, File A/49, Salisbury Papers,
Christ Church, Oxford.
164. Johnston to Salisbury, August 25, 1890, File E. *ibid.*
165. Salisbury's note, n.d., on note by Currie, March 19, 1891, F.O.
84/2159, P.R.O.
166. Salisbury to Johnston, March 4, 1891, Johnston Papers, Royal
Commonwealth Society.

to his staff and another to activists like Johnston. He was technically consistent, since he maintained that the circular did not extend to Katanga, but he was in effect applying the bellows to a fire his Foreign Office staff was trying to put out. While Salisbury was encouraging Johnston to send a reconnoitering party, Sir Percy Anderson was telling Albert Grey and Rochfort Maguire that the circular of 1885 unquestionably included the mining districts and that Britain accepted Leopold's rights under that document.[167] Salisbury's personal diplomacy thus contributed to the difficulties of the Foreign Office. Grey and Maguire who represented the Rhodes faction on the board had hoped to send out Thomson again to Msiri's country to try for a treaty by which the chief would accept British protection. They had heard that a Belgian expedition under Stairs was being sent to Katanga from the east coast and they sought to block it by denying him the use of African Lakes Company vessels and obstructing him in every way possible.[168] Anderson's emphatic response ended any further discussion in the board of this plan.[169] Rhodes continued for a time to act independently of the realities as seen from London. In July he told Thomson, "I want you to get M'siri's, I mean Katanga."[170] Thompson, despite his infirm health, responded enthusiastically to this call for action, but he was in no condition to withstand the rigors of such a journey. The decision to stop him, however, was not made out of consideration for his health. Before Thomson could start for Katanga Rhodes finally gave way to Foreign Office pressure, and countermanded the instructions.[171] Leopold consequently had to contend with no British rival when he dispatched Stairs's expedition to Katanga. In December 1891 Stairs raised the Free State flag over Msiri's territory and declared Msiri's rule at an end, and Msiri was killed by one of Stairs's officers.[172]

The Foreign Office's intervention thus thwarted the Rhodes-Johnston desire to compete with Leopold, but their hopes had

167. Minute, Anderson, May 27, 1891, F.O. 84/2166, P.R.O.
168. *Ibid.*
169. London office, BSAC, to Cape, June 5, 1891, LO 3/1/3, N.A.R.
170. James B. Thomson, *Joseph Thomson*, p. 269.
171. Rotberg, *Thomson*, p. 289.
172. Tilsley, *Crawford*, pp. 199–200; Edgar Verdick, *Les premiers jours au Katanga (1890–1903)*, pp. 56–57.

already been confounded. They might blame the ill luck of the smallpox epidemic among Thomson's porters, but Rhodes had not been sufficiently involved with Katanga to mount an expedition with the power to force Msiri to accept British protection, and the chief would not have given up his independence voluntarily, as Sharpe and the expeditions that preceded Stairs discovered. The failure of the Rhodes line of direct action shifted the emphasis to Cawston's policy of seeking an accommodation with Leopold. Cawston had been annoyed with Rhodes's and Johnston's aggressiveness. The issue of political control he thought insignificant; what was important was the economic prize, and Rhodes and Johnston he considered were compromising his negotiations. Johnston had never been a man to let public policy stand in the way of his enthusiasms, and the cautionary advice of the Foreign Office had not prevented his forays in personal diplomacy, not only in private communications but in appeals to the patriotic British public. In June 1890 he had distributed a map showing Msiri's kingdom as British territory. This map, or one like it, was published in the *Graphic*, and produced a heated protest from Leopold to Salisbury in which the king in effect suggested that this wayward official should be removed.[173] Johnston's map-making caused Cawston great concern, and he asked Sir John Kirk to reassure Leopold that the chartered company was not a party to this provocation.[174] This declaration of innocence Leopold did not accept, particularly since Rhodes fully supported Johnston's course of action.[175]

The company was in fact divided on the best course to pursue with regard to Katanga, and the confusion of its representatives on the spot was a manifestation of uncertainty at the top. The advocates of aggressive action to claim political control were

173. Rotberg, *Thomson*, p. 271; Oliver, *Johnston*, p. 194.
174. Cawston to Kirk, December 22, 1890, BSAC II Misc., Rhodes House.
175. Leopold protested to the queen against Rhodes's efforts to seize political control over Katanga. Salisbury responded to Victoria that the boundary was not as clear as the king maintained, but he assured her that the company would not be allowed to act in opposition to the laws of the Congo on "territory which really belongs to the latter." He added that "the Company as a whole are quite inclined to behave fairly, but Mr. Cecil Rhodes is rather difficult to keep in order." Salisbury to the queen, April 1891, CAB 41/22/5, P.R.O.

not equally committed to immediate economic development of the area. Indeed, the reverse was the case. Expenditures in Mashonaland continued to draw away the company's liquid resources and in the view of most of the directors it was in no position to make financial commitments in new areas. Grey and Maguire, consequently, who supported Rhodes in his desire to take Katanga, were wary of any involvement that required capital. Shortly after he had accepted the Foreign Office interdict as final, Grey expressed to Rhodes his concern that Leopold not ensnare the company in his financial ventures. The king, he asserted, looked upon the company as "une vache a train," and it would be unwise for the company to become involved in any Katanga company until it became a paying concern. For the present the best course was one of "masterly inactivity."[176]

Cawston in his negotiations with Leopold consequently was representing a wary board. But he was also representing himself. If the company were not interested in any arrangement he considered advantageous, he was prepared to seek associates outside the company in the City of London. When the Katanga Company was organized in 1891, however, neither the British South Africa Company nor Cawston was included among its subscribers. Leopold was willing to allow the South Africa Company to participate, but only on conditions which the company found unacceptable. He proposed that the chartered company contribute two-thirds of the working capital but receive only one-third of the fully paid shares.[177] Leopold again demonstrated that he was a hard bargainer. On the rejection of his terms by the chartered company, Leopold turned to other sources. The Katanga Company's capital and direction was largely Belgian, and the English contributors included Verney Lovett Cameron and the London financier, Albert L. Ochs, neither of whom was an ally of the South Africa Company, and its only British director was Sir John Kirk.[178] Leopold had not

176. Scrap of ltr., Grey to Rhodes, June 5, 1891, File 189/9, Grey Papers, Durham.
177. London office, BSAC, to Cape office, May 28, 1891, LO 3/1/3, N.A.R.
178. Compagnie du Katanga, Statuts, 1891, F.O. 84/2244, P.R.O. *Financial News*, March 24, 1891. Sir William Mackinnon also was a subscriber.

only won the battle for Katanga but had succeeded in assuring that its exploitation would be under Belgian control. Rhodes's force north of the Zambezi had been more than matched by Leopold's tenaciousness. Rhodes had the Katanga episode in mind when he later told Sir Robert Williams, "I thought I was clever, Williams, but I was no match for King Leopold."[179]

179. Weinthal, *Cape to Cairo*, 1:114.

8

Years of Disillusionment
1890-1893

THE CHARACTER OF THE OCCUPATION OF MASHONA-
land was foreshadowed in the pioneer column. The young men
who enrolled were a variegated lot. Some were English, most
were South African, including a large number of Afrikaners.
Some were gentlemen, others were tradesmen. But they were all
akin in one respect—their common excitement at the prospects
for adventure and riches, to them an irresistible combination.
A brush with the Ndebele would be exhilarating, but even
more stimulating was the thought that they would literally find
gold at the end of their trek. The company had contracted to
pay them in gold claims and in farms. The farms might be sold
—most of the pioneers did not intend to become settlers—but
gold was the focus of their concentration. The gold, they were
confident, was there in abundance and easily accessible. Had
not eye-witnesses such as Mauch and Hartley told of vast gold
fields like none else in the world, with rich surface deposits that
could be extracted with no more effort than the use of a pick
and shovel? Baines's *Gold Fields* had not only confirmed these
reports, but had given specific instructions as to where the richest fields were to be found.[1] These stories, told and retold, made
recruitment easy and the company was relieved of the burden of
monetary payments for the pioneers' services.

The success of the company depended upon the continuing

1. Hugh Marshall Hole, *The Making of Rhodesia*, p. 175.

credibility of the myth of Ophir. Contrary to the original assumptions of the Colonial Office,[2] the promoters had never contemplated the employment of the company's capital in mining
operations. Rather, they hoped that individuals and syndicates
would be sufficiently impressed with the opportunity for profit
to invest money and that the company would share in the returns of these lessee enterprises. This line of policy was dictated
both by preference and by necessity. The creation of syndicates,
it was anticipated, would enlist new sources of capital, and the
risks would be borne by these investors. In any event there was
no choice for the company, for the capital available to it was far
too small to finance development of the chartered territories.
The million pounds which formed the original capital was
quickly drained away by expenses attendant on the occupation.
The "Police Force," in actuality the company's standing army,
could be maintained at its original size of 480 men only with an
outlay which the company could not sustain[3]—within less than
two years, £200,000 was expended on it.[4] The pioneer column,
even though its core was volunteers who were paid in expectations, cost £90,000.[5] The costs of building railways and telegraph and of administering the chartered territories were also a
heavy drain. The Grand Scheme of the spring of 1889 when
faced with the hard realities of 1890 lost its glitter; the promoters who had talked of large expenditures for the expansion of
the British Empire became cost-conscious businessmen.

Development of Mashonaland, therefore, required the en-
listment of non-company capital. The pioneers quickly discovered that what gold there was in Mashonaland could not be
extracted by hand. Shortly after their arrival in Salisbury, most
of them had sold their farm and mining rights to money men
who bought them out for the going rate of £100 for each.
Prominent among the buyers were Frank Johnson, who had established a company to exploit whatever was exploitable in
Mashonaland, and Sir John Willoughby, who bought up large

2. Note by Fairfield, n.d., on BSAC to C.O., September 21, 1892, C.O.
417/89, P.R.O.
3. BSAC Minute Book, "Police Force General," LO 8/1/1, N.A.R.
4. Hole, *Making of Rhodesia*, p. 281.
5. Harris to Weatherley, March 24, 1890, LO 5/2/0, N.A.R.

numbers of claims which he intended to use to attract investors in England. The unavailability of surface gold, however, did not disillusion the pioneers who had sold out. Many of them reinvested their money in syndicates which were being formed to dig out the gold. The gold fever remained high, despite the lack of visual evidence of the existence of minerals. Gold must be there, though capital was required to exploit it. As one of the early settlers observed: ". . . such was the faith in the gold country that the officials thought that soon we would have several reefs eclipsing the Johannesburg main reef, and that next season the country would be swarming with a population and we— equally sanguine—were scouring the country in search of these reefs." [6]

As with other gold rushes, cupidity dominated reason. A. G. Leonard, one of the first arrivals after the pioneers, wrote that "My sole idea in coming out was to be of the first to see the ancient El Dorado under a new name." [7] But he did not travel merely to see a natural wonder; as he admitted, "The ruling passion is gold . . . Mashonaland is our Kilmansegg and its reefs of quartz are her golden legs." [8] The "second Rand" attracted attention from fortune hunters throughout South Africa. Within three months after the arrival of the pioneer column at the site of Fort Salisbury twenty-two syndicates had been formed in Kimberley alone for mining operations in Mashonaland. [9] Parties were organizing from throughout South Africa and the fever had touched investors in Britain.

The "Kaffir Circus," as the London market in South African gold shares was called, was in a particularly frenetic phase in the early 1890s. Its violent fluctuations were fed by rumors and "insiders' reports," which convinced investors that a gamble was a good one; stocks leaped to unprecedented heights or plummeted to new lows in response to factors which had little to do with the productivity of the mines to which they were presumably related. One particularly mercuric stock, that of the Oceana

6. Adrian Darter, *The Pioneers of Mashonaland*, p. 111.
7. A. G. Leonard, *How We Made Rhodesia*, p. 38.
8. *Ibid.*
9. Harris to London office, BSAC, December 14, 1890, LO 5/2/5, N.A.R.

Company, rose in a few weeks at the end of 1889 from £1 to £20, and other land and exploration stocks also rose substantially. Goldfields of South Africa rose to several times its par value.[10] With the founding of the South Africa Company, the fever rapidly spread to Mashonaland. One of the earliest syndicates to be formed, Matabele Concessions, Ltd., was organized in October 1889, almost a year before the pioneer column reached Mashonaland and, indeed, before the charter of the South Africa Company was formally ratified. The promoters appealed to the gullibility of the public with advertisements lavish with adjectives about the Mashonaland goldfields, and were handsomely rewarded. The stock, which had a par value of £1, soared to £8 within a month of the issuance of the first prospectus.[11] The urge to be "in on a good thing" extended even to Lobengula, who despite his animus toward the company sent an agent to mark out 40 gold claims for himself.[12]

As with other gold rushes, the fortune hunters at first were so bedazzled that they were blinded to hard realities. There was as yet no evidence in the form of actual gold mines that Mauch and Baines had reported facts rather than fancies. Even if the gold was there, its conversion into wealth involved formidable problems. The fields were over 800 miles from the railway terminus at Kimberley. Supplies had to be carted by wagon across the veld. In the best of times prices were several times those at Kimberley, and when the summer rains descended, as they did in torrents in the first year of occupation, the wagon tracks became impassable, and the residents were threatened with starvation. Mashonaland, it soon became evident, contained little alluvial gold, and mining required heavy machinery the transport of which by wagon was an arduous and expensive undertaking.[13] The continued tranquillity of the region was in doubt —pessimists predicted that an attack by the Ndebele was imminent, while optimists maintained that a collision would not occur for at least a year or two. Yet by February 1891, 7,000 claims had been marked off in Mashonaland, and applications

10. *Economist,* October 26, 1889.
11. *Financial News,* October 18, 1889; *Truth,* November 7, 1889.
12. *Financial News,* January 22, 1891.
13. Lewis H. Gann, *A History of Southern Rhodesia,* p. 95.

had been made for water rights for 2,000 head of ore-crushing stamps.[14]

During the first rainy season the settlement had come close to disaster despite the strenuous efforts of Rhodes and other company officials to provide relief. The experience was an emphatic documentation of the need for greatly improved transport facilities, and it was generally recognized that relief must come through Mozambique, for railway communication from the south was at best years away. Rhodes's effort to open an Indian Ocean route by the seizure of Beira was frustrated by Salisbury and the Portuguese, and Frank Johnson's company to supply Mashonaland through Mozambique by coaches and wagons expired quickly, done to death by incompetence and the tsetse fly. Johnson in 1891 had announced his intention to open a road from the Pungwe River, which would transport passengers and goods at much lower rates than were charged on the route from Kimberley, and many people took passage to Beira with the intention of riding into Mashonaland on Johnson's coaches. On arrival they found that the service had been discontinued. The reasons were emphatically in evidence in the rotting bodies of draft animals, victims of the tsetse fly. Johnson's "road" was littered with abandoned wagons and goods, the debris of a failed enterprise.[15] Johnson's failure underscored the urgency of railway communication through the fly belt; in the meantime the Mashonaland prospectors had to continue to depend on the route from Kimberley with all its risks and expense. Alfred Beit, who visited the gold regions in August 1891, was more impressed with the richness of the soil of Mashonaland than with its auriferous wealth. In any event, he concluded, little revenue could be expected from mining until a rail route to the Indian Ocean was established.[16]

The problems of transportation accentuated the speculative character of the British South Africa Company. The development of Mashonaland required great infusions of capital. If

14. *Financial News*, February 4, 1891. A "stamp" was a machine used for crushing ore.
15. James Johnston, *Reality versus Romance in South Central Africa*, p. 278ff.; J.E.S. Green, *Rhodes Goes North*, pp. 271–274.
16. Extract, Beit to BSAC board, August ——, 1891, in Notebook of the fourth Earl Grey, Grey Papers, Durham.

gold were found in abundance money would be readily available for mining operations; if rich strikes eluded the prospectors, investors could be attracted only by descriptions of Mashonaland which ranged from optimism to deceit. During the
early years of the chartered company, the paucity of gold discovered was obscured by glowing reports of sample assays and
of impending mining operations expected to produce handsome
returns. This dependence on illusion rather than reality attracted to Mashonaland syndicates which specialized in paper
rather than in gold.

The speculative emphasis of these syndicates illustrates the
uselessness of policy without enforcement machinery. The intentions of the company had been to use large land and mineral
concessions as the bait to attract capital into Mashonaland to
develop the mining-agricultural economy. With such a base,
more capital and more settlers would pour in without the
necessity of such lavish inducements. The mining regulations
promulgated by the company required all prospectors to obtain
a license, which gave them the right to peg one alluvial and ten
quartz claims.[17] Anyone could get a license for a small fee but
the claim holder was required to show evidence that he had
worked the mine within four months and to obtain an inspection certificate. If he intended to exploit his claim further he
was required to organize a company in which the chartered
company should have the right to a half interest.[18] The result
of these regulations was far different than the company had
anticipated. License holders sold their claims to companies
which in turn floated stock on the London market. The only
requirement they had to meet was that they had performed the
necessary amount of work to receive an inspection certificate.
Whether the mine was producing payable gold or not, the promoters could advertise their companies in a manner suggesting
the likelihood of rich returns. In most instances the riches came
to the promoters at the expense of a gullible public, and when
disillusionment set in, they could sell out to other interests who
were amalgamating mining companies with the intention of

17. An alluvial claim was 150 feet square and a quartz reef was 150 feet
by 400.
18. Percy F. Hone, *Southern Rhodesia*, pp. 242–251.

milking investors still further. Eventually, this orgy ended with a reaction against investment in Mashonaland mining and exploitation ventures, but the effects continued long afterwards to the detriment of the character and reputation of the Rhodesian economy.[19]

In large part these malpractices were a product of the total inadequacy of the administration in Mashonaland to perform more than the minimum duties required for the maintenance of law and order. Until new revenue sources became available beyond the company's own capital, the emphasis had to be on rigorous economy. After the resignation of A. R. Colquhoun in August 1891, local responsibility was vested in Dr. Jameson who was quite unequipped by experience or temperament to oversee an efficient administration. But even if he had been a paragon of administrative virtues he would have been unable to develop a strong efficient government, for the board's mandate of rigorous economy reduced the administrative staff to a level officials who with a few clerks were required to act as magistrates and mining commissioners and in a variety of other roles that made effective company government impossible. In 1893 Jameson's staff consisted of less than twenty administrative in a territory of approximately 110,000 square miles.[20]

By the beginning of 1890 the first mutterings from the London board with regard to the need for retrenchment reached South Africa. It had become evident to the London directors that there was no immediate prospect of large returns, and the financial accounts which Rhodes submitted seemed to reflect no awareness that resources were being eaten up at a rate that threatened imminent bankruptcy. Confidence in Rhodes's managerial ability was shaken. His estimates of expenditure were invariably far lower than the actual outlay; large liabilities such as a debt to De Beers for £35,000 were not included in the balance sheets he submitted to the London headquarters. The board had been willing to confide plenary authority on Rhodes because of his record of success in the diamond fields and his readiness to spend his own money. But as evidence mounted of

19. *Ibid.*, p. 240.
20. Robert Shenton, "The Chartered Company, 1889–1898," doctoral dissertation, p. 241.

sloppy business methods in the South African administration, they concluded that more rigorous control from London was necessary if the company was to be saved from ruin. The benign tone of their communications became acerbic. Two voracious consumers of capital caused particular concern—the police force and the commissary system. The police force had risen by the end of 1890 to 650 men, each of whom cost approximately £300 per year,[21] or a total outlay of £195,000. The senior commissariat and transport officer, Major Tye, made requisitions for food supplies and transport which the board considered far in excess of the company's ability to sustain. Rhodes was put on notice by the beginning of 1891 that there must be general retrenchment. Rhodes did not immediately respond to the board's mandate. Expenditures continued at a high level. By July 1891 the cash available to the company had dwindled to only £280,000; Rhodes had spent £700,000 in less than a year; yet, the board complained, there was no evidence that he was heeding their injunction to cut back expenditures.[22]

Rhodes was not accustomed to take orders, but he was eventually forced to follow the board's counsel. His independence of action could be maintained only if new sources of revenue were forthcoming, and none was in sight. Reports from Mashonaland continued bleak, and the South African backers on whom he relied for assistance began to show signs of revolt. The board of Consolidated Gold Fields, increasingly fractious because of Rhodes's and Rudd's vast profits from the company, made it clear that they disapproved of any further levies in support of what they considered to be Rhodes's folly. The De Beers board also was manifesting unwonted independence, and even the loyal Alfred Beit was opposed to any further expenditure either from De Beers or from his own personal fortune to shore up the collapsing chartered company. This incipient rebellion could be quelled by Rhodes if he chose to exercise his power, but the opposition was formidable enough to give even him pause.[23] He gave orders that the police force must be drastically reduced,

21. Currey to Jameson, December 11, 1891, A 1/2/2, N.A.R.
22. Currey to Harris, July 11, 1891; same to same, July 31, 1891, both in *ibid.*
23. Currey to Jameson, December 11, 1891, A 1/2/2, N.A.R.

with greater reliance being placed upon volunteer forces. Accordingly, the police establishment was reduced to 100 by the end of 1891[24] and to 40 a year later.[25] A burgher system along Boer lines was developed which made every able-bodied man subject to call, and the company organized a volunteer force of about 500 men, the Mashonaland Horse.[26] These drastic measures substantially reduced expenditures but the outflow continued to be substantially greater than the company's resources could sustain. Communications from London became increasingly testy. The board avoided a direct attack on Rhodes, concentrating instead on the alleged incompetence of his subordinates. Major Tye was a particular target because of his large expenditures for supplies. The London secretary communicated the board's displeasure. In January 1892 he wrote, "The board cannot understand without further explanation how the affairs of the Company could have been allowed to drift into their present condition."[27] By then the bank balances of the company in London had been reduced to £12,000. Another £205,000 could be raised by calls on the holders of shares which were not fully paid, but without additional assistance it was clear that the company could no longer pay its bills. Rhodes was forced to use his power to whip the recalcitrant boards of De Beers and Consolidated Gold Fields into sanctioning further financial assistance. In this pressure on De Beers he gained a powerful ally in Barnato. With Barnato's support the board of the diamond company in February 1893 agreed to lend £3,500 per month in addition to the £70,000 they had already advanced. Rudd went to Kimberley and induced Beit to contribute £500 per month, and the Gold Fields board, confronted with a threat that Rhodes might resign, sullenly agreed to advance £500 per month, and Rhodes pledged the same amount.[28] These guarantees provided £60,000 per year, and with the economy measures that had been put into effect the chartered company was saved.

24. Currey to London office, BSAC, December 9, 1891, LO 5/2/15, N.A.R.
25. Shenton, "Chartered Company," p. 243.
26. Hole, *Rhodesia*, 281.
27. Weatherley to Secretary, BSAC, Cape Town, January 23, 1892, A 1/3/3, N.A.R.
28. Currey to [Hawksley], February 11, 1892, A 1/2/2, N.A.R.

The subsidies continued in 1893 and 1894, but the company had to pay a price for this relief. On the renewal of the De Beers guarantee in 1893 the chartered company conceded the exclusive right to work any diamondiferous ground in any area under chartered control.[29] When Consolidated Gold Fields renewed its subsidy for 1894, it received the right to peg out 250 claims in Matabeleland without any requirement to spend any money on their development and an additional right to select 51,000 morgen in farms of not more than 3,000 morgen each at a cost not to exceed £50 per farm.[30]

With these various expedients, Rhodes subdued the complaints of the London board, but the condition of the company continued to be highly anemic. Rhodes and the board worked assiduously to keep the bleak outlook from the knowledge of the investing public. Rhodes and the other directors pumped into the public press and, in particular, the financial journals, optimistic accounts of the present and future of Mashonaland. Some articles were written by journalists subsidized by the company—notably Verschoyle of the *Fortnightly Review* and F. Scott Keltie, a prominent writer on imperial affairs.[31] The *Financial News* regularly published articles extolling the wealth of Mashonaland. It persisted in describing it as the "New Eldorado"[32] in the face of mounting evidence to the contrary. Witnesses friendly to the company were cited favorably; testimony of a discouraging nature was discounted. M. D. C. de Waal, a member of the Cape legislative assembly who accompanied Rhodes on a tour of the territory at the end of 1891, was quoted as saying, "Mashonaland is the finest country God ever made."[33] The journal's enthusiastic advocacy of Mashonaland contrasted strangely with its critical evaluation of land and exploration companies outside the company's jurisdiction.[34] *South Africa* was almost as laudatory. It quoted approvingly from a "promi-

29. Harris to Secretary, De Beers, February 2, 1893, CT 1/24/2, N.A.R.
30. Harris to Rudd, February 17, 1894, in *ibid.*
31. See, for example, Cawston to Keltie, March 15, 1890, BSAC II Misc., Rhodes House.
32. This is the title of a major article in the journal of July 3, 1891.
33. *Financial News*, February 17, 1892.
34. See, for example, "The Zambezi Rig," in *ibid.*, January 7, 1891.

nent provincial paper" that "it was always expected that Mashonaland was rich in auriferous deposit, but it now appears that the reality exceeds the expectations."[35] Sir Sidney Shippard, hardly an objective witness, was quoted by the journal in July 1892 as saying that "the wealth of Mashonaland is inconceivable; it is impossible to exaggerate it."[36] Another paper which consistently published favorable accounts of the company's territories was the *Pall Mall Gazette*. An essay in April 1890, reached the heights of ecstasy:

> . . . Scratch the wilderness and you will find a garden. It is well-watered, a country of a hundred streams. Game ranges its hills and valleys, and there is grazing for a thousand herds of cattle. But these are only half the favours which boon nature has lavished on this fortunate region. She has also made it one of her rare storehouses of mineral wealth. She has glutted it with gold. The rocks sparkle with gold; gold peeps out from every hillside; in the bed of every stream the sand is clothed with it. . . .[37]

Not all of the British press was enamored of the company or Mashonaland. That inveterate gadfly of privilege and corruption, Henry Labouchere, made Rhodes and the chartered company a special target for his bites. In the columns of *Truth* he branded Rhodes as a pirate and the company as a swindle. He did so without malice, he said—he professed to like the man[38] but such sentiment did not affect the sharpness of his attacks, which frequently stung Rhodes to fury.[39] *Truth* was hostile to all chartered companies—"speculators in jungles and niggers,"[40] but its animus toward the South Africa Company was particularly strong:

> . . . The Charter of the British South Africa Company is unique in the history of such charters, and for this reason—that it was conferred, not upon a Company of bona-fide traders, with territories in their possession, but upon a gang of speculators and Company promoters, whose first object was, and is, to "boom"

35. *South Africa*, January 31, 1891.
36. *Ibid.*, July 2, 1892.
37. *Pall Mall Gazette*, quoted in *ibid.*, April 12, 1890.
38. Algar L. Thorold, *The Life of Henry Labouchere*, p. 393.
39. See, for example, Rhodes to Ripon, June 25, 1894, Ripon Papers, Addtl. MSS. 43637, British Museum.
40. *Truth*, December 6, 1894.

their shares upon the Stock Exchanges of Europe, and to sell for fifty shillings what cost them five—or less. . . .[41]

Truth had an attentive audience among officials in Whitehall and Downing Street, though it probably had little direct impact on the investing public in general. But there were other newspapers with greater circulation which published reports that the riches of Mashonaland were largely an illusion. One of the most important of these journals, the *Daily Chronicle*, in 1893 printed an exposé of the company's alleged stock manipulation and misrepresentation.[42] Some visitors to Mashonaland also made unfavorable assessments of the future of Mashonaland. Most prominent of these was Lord Randolph Churchill, whom the company had expected would be a useful witness since he was a shareholder and a friend of several of the directors. So confident were the promoters of Mashonaland that two of the exploring syndicates paid for the expenses of his expedition, which was to be publicized by his articles in the *Daily Graphic*.[43] Churchill's backers soon regretted their support. Instead of a land of promise, he saw a wilderness inhabited by a few hundred settlers surrounded by "savages," their energy sapped by malaria, their dreams of wealth turned to disillusionment. On his way from Victoria to Salisbury Churchill wrote, "having now travelled upwards of two hundred miles through Mashonaland, I have, as yet, seen no place suitable for prosperous European settlements."[44] The Salisbury area was somewhat better, but the cost of food and other necessities was exorbitant.[45] As for the celebrated gold discoveries he was advised by Henry C. Perkins, the American mining expert who accompanied him, that while there were some reefs with gold which might yield a small profit, there were no great deposits which would justify the attention of any large mining company.[46] Churchill concluded that Mashonaland was a poor field for investment and unpromising land for emigration, and these findings were widely circulated

41. *Ibid.*, August 27, 1891.
42. *Daily Chronicle*, October 26, October 30, November 4, 1893.
43. *South Africa*, April 28, 1891.
44. Randolph S. Churchill, *Men, Mines and Animals in South Africa*, p. 199.
45. *Ibid.*, p. 207.
46. *Ibid.*, p. 245.

in his newspaper stories, subsequently incorporated in a book. Such statements from a person of Churchill's renown had a depressing effect on investors. Chartered shares, which had already been adversely affected by the tribulations of the pioneers in the first wet season, dropped still further. Shares which had sold for approximately £2.1.2 when first offered on the market at the beginning of 1891,[47] dropped by June to £1.1.2,[48] and by February 1892, after Churchill's assessments had their effect, had plummeted to 12/6.[49] The company's protagonists in the press attempted to discredit Churchill's credentials. *South Africa* discovered belatedly that he was incompetent, to be unfavorably compared with genuine experts such as E. A. Maund, whose description of Mashonaland was in as great contrast to Churchill's as was Dante's *Paradiso* to his *Inferno.*[50] But with all the company's efforts to buoy the market by optimistic reports, it remained depressed.

The low level of chartered shares in 1891 and 1892 produced gloom among the directors, and meetings of the board were dominated by the issue of the market. If golden promises from Mashonaland were not enough to excite potential investors, other expedients had to be considered. At a meeting of the board in July 1891, Farquhar and Cawston presented a proposal from some London financiers "to make a pool" for the purpose of raising the price of the stock. For their services these would-be manipulators asked compensation of £5,000. Their plan was to "work the Press" and control the market. Essential to the plan was an agreement from holders of large blocks of shares not to sell for a specified period. The riggers, in addition to their payment of £5,000, would have the option to buy shares at a price to be agreed upon. The agent of the pool was William C. Watson who a few years before had been the principal figure in a scandal involving the Hyderabad Mining Company, an enterprise which was far more active in extracting money from sales of stock than in the prosecution of its avowed objects.[51]

47. *Financial News*, February 2, 1891.
48. *Ibid.*, June 1, 1891.
49. *Ibid.*, February 2, 1891.
50. *South Africa*, January 9, 1892.
51. The Hyderabad Mining Company was the vehicle for a cleverly

268   CROWN AND CHARTER

The immediate response of most of the board to this proposal was favorable. Only one director, Grey, rejected the plan on moral grounds; Grey's position was that he could not be a party to a conspiracy to rig the market and that the board would be compromising its integrity if it were to agree.[52] But he did not presume to impose his ethics on other directors, who were free to respond individually as their consciences dictated, and he stipulated that he had no intention of parting with his shares in any event. Some other members of the board, after consideration, agreed with Grey, though not necessarily on moral grounds. Cawston thought the scheme dangerous, and Abercorn was moved by the argument that he, Fife, and Grey as appointees to the board to represent the public interest, had a special obligation not to be involved in transactions which could expose them to charges of unethical conduct.[53]

Farquhar resented Grey's lofty moralizing which had the flavor of the pulpit rather than the marketplace. This display of virtue he thought particularly galling because it reflected no understanding of the desperate financial condition of the company whose interests Grey was supposed to represent. Capital was rapidly running out; it would be necessary to raise more if the company were to avoid ruin, and it would be much easier to attract investors if shares were selling at $2\frac{1}{2}$ rather than at $1\frac{1}{2}$. But Grey's refusal to compromise on principle had wrecked the project and Cawston notified Watson that the company could not cooperate.[54]

This aborted effort to rig the market is the only documented instance of directors' involvement with an outside group with

manipulated swindle involving collusion between Watson and the Hyderabad director of mines to achieve profits for themselves by the sale of shares. Watson realized a net return of about £190,000. His activities were the focus of an investigation by the Select Committee on East India. The Hyderabad government decided not to prosecute because litigation would be prolonged and expensive. Great Britain, *Parliamentary Papers* (Accounts and Papers), 1888, First and Second Reports, xiii–xvi.

52. Memorandum by Grey, n.d. [1891], File 184/6, Grey Papers, Durham.
53. *Ibid.*
54. *Ibid.*

the object of manipulating the price of shares, but thereafter, there were reports in the press of the influence of outside pools in close touch with the company's management in pushing up the price of shares,[55] and the incident involving Watson suggests that several of the directors were not averse to such dealings provided that they were kept secret.

As Farquhar maintained, stock market transactions had some effect on the company's ability to attract capital, but the primary benefit accrued to those insiders who disposed of their large blocks of shares at prices that gave them substantial profits. The company continued a precarious existence, and the development of Mashonaland depended on investments by syndicates which would undertake to expend their capital in return for liberal grants of land and mining rights. Such policy required that the company have these rights to concede. So far as mining rights were concerned the imperial government had conceded their legitimacy despite Lobengula's repudiation of the Rudd concession. But not even the most complaisant government officials could maintain that the concession had conferred land rights on the company, and until Lobengula conferred rights to land, no bona fide titles could be assigned. Lobengula could hardly be expected to grant further concessions to men whom he regarded as thieves and frauds; consequently the company was forced to seek other expedients.

One line which was briefly considered and quickly discarded was to reject Lobengula's authority over Mashonaland. In terms of the realities of power, this position had considerable justification. Though the Ndebele raided sections of the Shona country, their control over the Shona people was hardly sufficient to justify their being considered "sovereign." The Shona at the time the company arrived were fragmented into a large number of independent chiefdoms, ranging in size from a few hundred to several thousand, with no central authority. Some paid tribute to Lobengula, some did not, some did not, some lived in fear of his impis; some, such as the Chivi chieftainship between the Lundi and Tokwe rivers, were well equipped with guns and

55. *Financial News*, April 15, April 22, 1893.

sufficiently proficient to be able to repel a strong Ndebele impi provided they could fight from the cover of the hills.[56]

The company might have exploited the tenuousness of Ndebele influence over the Shona if there had been a recognized central authority, but given the fractionation of the people such a course would undermine whatever legal status the company enjoyed from the Rudd concession and open up Mashonaland to rivals who could negotiate a concession from a Shona chief. This threat indeed materialized in 1890 when a party of Afrikaners negotiated a treaty with a chief whom they claimed to be the Chivi and pronounced their intention of settling a tract of about 200 miles by 100 miles. The lands they claimed were not under Chivi's control, and the chief with whom they negotiated was not Chivi,[57] but the company was as ignorant of Shona society as were the Boers and the prospect of a Boer trek caused the company great alarm.

The "Adendorff trek," so called from Louis Adendorff, one of the concessionaires, was avowedly organized to establish the Banyailand republic. It may have been a scheme to blackmail the company into buying the concessionaires out. But the company saw this movement as a great threat to its position. Rhodes used his influence with the Afrikaner Bond to work against the trekkers, and the board in London appealed to Salisbury to intervene. Salisbury responded by asserting that the territory in question was under British protection by the terms of the Moffat treaty with Lobengula, whose jurisdiction extended over Banyailand, and calling upon Kruger to prevent any movement to establish an independent republic. As a hostage for Kruger's compliance, Salisbury indicated that there would be no further negotiations with the Transvaal over Swaziland and Kosi Bay until the trek issue was resolved.[58] The imperial government, however, had no objections to the trekkers settling in the area as private individuals.[59] These pressures had their effect. The trek melted away from a projected size of 200 to a mere 112.

56. D. N. Beach, "The Adendorff Trek in Shona History," Henderson Paper No. 14, October 2, 1971, University of Rhodesia.
57. *Ibid.*
58. Gann, *Southern Rhodesia*, p. 97.
59. Telegram, Knutsford to Loch, confidential, April 25, 1891, F.O. 84/2164, P.R.O.

Confronted by a force of the company's police commanded by Jameson, they made only a token show of defiance. Some accepted the offer to settle in Mashonaland under the company's rules and the remainder dispersed.[60]

The Foreign Office in its response to the Adendorff trek had conveniently ignored the issue of land titles. It, however, had asserted Lobengula's rights to all of Mashonaland, and when the danger of the trek had subsided, the imperial government reasserted its position that the company had no power to grant valid titles to land. To secure this right, the company felt compelled to resort to devious means which involved it with one of the most unsavory financiers in South Africa, Edouard Lippert. Wherever money was to be made, Lippert was attracted. His best-known coup was acquisition of the exclusive right to manufacture dynamite for the Transvaal, but his ventures extended over a wide spectrum including cement factories, railways, and banking, and in Mashonaland, land speculation. Lippert was a cousin of Albert Beit but in the early 1890s their relationship was distinctly frosty. In part Beit's distaste for Lippert must have been motivated by his cousin's prosecution of schemes which were against the interest of the chartered company. Rhodes's assertion that there had been a German menace which the company had forestalled by the charter, usually assumed to be baseless, may well have been directed at Lippert, for Lippert, a native of Hamburg, had employed Edward Renny-Tailyour to seek a concession from Lobengula at the same time as Rhodes was dispatching Rudd and his party to Matabeleland. When Rudd was successful, Rhodes offered Lippert through his agent a considerable subconcession if he would use his influence with Lobengula in support of the Rudd concession. The company subsequently refused to reward Lippert, alleging, with justification, that Renny-Tailyour had not acted in the company's behalf, but Lippert maintained that he had been cheated.[61]

This incident undoubtedly added to Lippert's zeal in embarrassing the company, though he constantly made clear that his opposition could be transformed into friendship for an appro-

60. Gann, *Southern Rhodesia*, p. 97; confidential telegram, Loch to Knutsford, June 29, 1891, F.O. 84/2169, P.R.O.
61. The *Times*, January 25, 1897.

priate price. After the Rudd Concession, Lippert and his
brother William purchased from F. C. Selous rights which Selous had acquired from two Shona chiefs whom he described as
independent.[62] The Lipperts offered to sell the concession to the
chartered company and when it refused Edouard threatened to
appeal to the German government to support the concession.
The permanent undersecretary in the Colonial Office, Sir Robert Herbert, took the threat sufficiently seriously to advise Cawston to settle with Lippert,[63] but the Foreign Office, confident
that Germany would do nothing to blight developing Anglo-
German harmony, saw no cause for alarm. "Mr. Lippert is playing a game of brag," noted Sir Percy Anderson.[64] Strengthened
by the support of the Foreign Office, Rhodes offered Lippert a
mere 100 gold claims on halves "for the sake of peace,"[65] which
Lippert angrily refused.

Lippert, however, was a tenacious adversary and despite the
combined efforts of the company's agents and local imperial
officials to frustrate him, he continued to persevere. In April
1891 his agent Renny-Tailyour triumphantly announced that
he had acquired a concession from Lobengula granting exclusive rights to grant lands, establish banks, coin money, and
conduct trade in the territory of the chartered company on payment of £1,000 sterling and yearly contributions of £500. The
only witnesses to the document besides the induna Mtshete were
Renny-Tailyour's colleagues, a fact that made the validity of
the document doubtful.[66] But Lobengula undoubtedly gave his
consent to some sort of concession, acting on the basis of the assumption that Lippert was an enemy of the chartered company
and that the concession was supported by Theophilus (Offy)
Shepstone, adviser to Umbanzeni of Swaziland. Through his
contacts with the Swazi, Lobengula had developed a misplaced

62. Robertson to Salisbury, October 16, 1890, F.O. 84/2092, P.R.O.
63. Herbert to Cawston, March 22, 1890, BSAC II Misc., Rhodes
House.
64. Note by Anderson on C.O. to F.O., March 24, 1890, F.O. 84/2077,
P.R.O.
65. Telegram, Cawston to C.O., rec. April 1, 1890, F.O. 84/2078,
P.R.O.
66. Concession, April 22, 1891, LO 1/1, N.A.R.

regard for "Offy" Shepstone and Shepstone's father, the great Theophilus. One of Renny-Tailyour's party averred that Lobengula believed he was granting the concession to "Offy" Shepstone, whose agent was Lippert, and that the Lippert interests would not have succeeded had they not represented themselves to be acting on Shepstone's behalf.[67] The concession thus was both defective and fraudulent. But other dubious agreements with African chiefs—the Rudd concession among them—had been recognized, and Lippert was confident that he could force the company to buy him out at a substantial price: he indicated that £250,000 in cash or in shares at par, preferably cash, would be acceptable.[68]

The initial reaction of Rhodes, supported by Loch, was to brand the concession a fraud and to treat Lippert's agents as a threat to the peace of Matabeleland and Mashonaland. Loch issued a proclamation that all concessions which had not received the sanction of the high commissioner or the Colonial Office were invalid.[69] Further he promised Rhodes that if Lippert attempted to publish his concession, he would issue another proclamation warning that the document infringed on the company's charter and the Rudd concession, and that anyone associating with Lippert in attempting to exercise rights under the concession risked legal action.[70] The Colonial Office backed Loch's position that the claims of Lippert infringed on the Rudd concession and on the charter.[71] Assured of governmental support Rhodes decided to defy Lippert—he vowed that he would pay no more blackmail.[72]

Loch carried out his promise to take a hard line with Lippert. When Renny-Tailyour attempted to return to Matabeleland he and a companion were arrested at Tati by the imperial authorities on the charge that their presence was dangerous to the peace of the country, and were kept in custody despite Lobengula's protest to Loch that they were friends of his, that he considered

67. Ogilvie to Moffat, June 12, 1895, MO 1/1/4, in *ibid.*
68. Telegram, Dormer to Currey, May 29, 1891, LO 5/2/9, in *ibid.*
69. Currey to London office, June 10, 1891, LO 5/2/9, in *ibid.*
70. Telegram, Rhodes to Beit, May 30, 1891, in *ibid.*
71. Knutsford to Loch, confidential, July 1, 1891, S1428/17/7, N.A.R.
72. Telegram, Rhodes to Beit, May 30, 1891, LO 5/2/9, N.A.R.

them no threat to the peace of Matabeleland, and that he as its ruler had the right to decide who he would admit into his domain.[73]

Soon, however, doubts began to intrude as to the wisdom of challenging Lippert. Alfred Beit, on whom Rhodes placed great reliance in business matters, offered his opinion that the concession was genuine and reported that Lippert's legal adviser was confident that its legality would be upheld in the English courts.[74] Rhodes's determination not to give in to blackmail began to waver—perhaps it would be better to settle if Lippert would accept "reasonable" compensation. Beit was authorized to negotiate.[75] Bargaining went on for several weeks, with each side periodically accusing the other of bad faith. Lippert secretly offered to sell farms to Colonel J. P. Ferreira, a leader of the Adendorff trek who had been arrested by the company. Ferreira turned Lippert's letter over to Jameson, and Rhodes and Beit threatened to break off discussion because of Lippert's duplicity.[76]

This spasm of principle quickly passed. The company had to face the fact that it had no rights to land and that the imperial government would not recognize any titles unless they were based on a concession from Lobengula. Lippert might be disreputable, but he had been successful in acquiring a document from Lobengula granting land rights. The company could not long defer a resolution of the land issue. Settlers expected to get titles, and the company could neither grant titles nor charge quit rents. The London board, Rhodes, and Loch all concluded that it was desirable to use Lippert's services. The original concession was clouded, but if Lippert could induce Lobengula to ratify another concession, he was entitled to generous compensation.[77] Consequently, Rudd on behalf of the company nego-

73. Lobengula to Loch, August 14, 1891, S1428/17/9, in ibid.
74. Telegrams (2), Beit to Rhodes, May 30, 1891, LO 5/2/9, in ibid.
75. Telegram, Rhodes to Beit, June 12, 1891, confidential, in ibid.
76. Telegrams, Jameson to BSAC, Cape Town, July 1, 1891, S1428/17/7; same to same, July 1, 1891, LO 5/2/10; Beit to Currey, July 3, 1891, LO 5/2/10, all in N.A.R.
77. Currey to London office, July 8, 1891, LO 5/2/10; Loch to Moffat, August 4, 1891, confidential, MO 1/1/4; Currey to London office, August 12, 1891, LO 5/2/11; all in N.A.R.

tiated an agreement with Lippert. If Lippert could deliver a concession from Lobengula which the Colonial Office would sanction, he would receive the right to select an area of 75 square miles in Matabeleland with all land and mineral rights and would receive 20,000 shares of £1 each in the United Concessions Company and 30,000 fully paid £1 shares in the chartered company,[78] in addition to £5,000 in cash. Lippert agreed to spend £25,000 within one year in the development of the area he selected.[79]

The terms of the agreement forecast the future of Lobengula. At a time when the chartered company professed to be content to develop only Mashonaland, leaving Matabeleland outside the scope of its operations, its spokesman had conceded 75 square miles in Matabeleland, with the selection to be made by Lippert or his assignees.

The terms of the contract, of course, were not revealed to Lobengula, for Lippert's hopes for success in renegotiating a concession depended on the Ndebele chief's continuing belief that Lippert was an enemy of the chartered company, and all the parties concerned agreed to participate in the deception. Sir Henry Loch ordered John Moffat to cooperate. The son of the great missionary was told that he must not give Lobengula any cause for suspicion. "Your attitude toward Messrs. Lippert and Renny-Tailyour should not change too abruptly, though if consulted by the King you might profess indifference on the subject." Loch would assist in this deceit by writing a letter to Lobengula explaining in plausible terms his reasons for lifting his ban on the entry of Lippert and Renny-Tailyour into Matabeleland.[80]

Moffat was deeply troubled by the "palpable immorality" of the arrangement with Lippert, but he did not refuse to cooperate. His role, after all, was a limited one. He was merely re-

78. In order to provide the 30,000 shares for Lippert, the chartered company had to borrow 23,000 shares from De Beers and to cancel allotments to those persons in South Africa who had not paid for their shares. Currey to London, January 6, 1892, LO 5/2/16, N.A.R.
79. Currey to London, October 14, 1891, LO 5/2/13, N.A.R., Lippert-Rudd agreement, September 12, 1891, C.O. 417/89, P.R.O.
80. Loch to Moffat, September 12, 1891, confidential, MO 1/1/4, N.A.R.

quired to keep silent and to assure that the concession granted
by Lobengula was valid. He rationalized that Lobengula was
just as deceitful as Lippert, but his conscience still nagged him.
He wrote to Rhodes that he would perform the role assigned to
him, but "I feel bound to tell you I look on the whole plan as
detestable, whether viewed in the light of policy or morality."[81]

With the unwilling connivance of Moffat, Lippert and
Renny-Tailyour were successful. In Moffat's presence, Lobengula in November 1891, granted to Lippert sole right for a
hundred years to lay out farms and townships and to levy rents
in the territories of the chartered company's operations. For
these rights, which superseded those granted to Renny-Tailyour,
Lippert agreed to pay £500 per year.[82]

The concession was quickly approved by Loch, who expressed
satisfaction at the elimination of a vexing problem.[83] Loch advised Moffat to take "a well-earned holiday."[84] The Colonial
Office noted with approval that a serious obstacle to the company's administration in Mashonaland had been removed.[85]
Except for Moffat's impotent anguishing, there was no evidence
of concern that the representatives of Her Majesty's government had been an accessory to a transaction which at best was
unethical. Nor was there any examination of the legalities of
the arrangement. Almost thirty years later the judicial committee of the Privy Council found that the concession merely made
Lippert the agent of Lobengula in land transactions and that
the concessionaire had no right to use the land or to take its usufruct.[86] Also, in African law there could be no alienation to a
third party as was the case with Lippert's sale of his rights to
Rhodes.[87] The Privy Council's judgment decided that the land

81. Moffat to Rhodes, October 9, 1891, quoted in Robert U. Moffat,
John Smith Moffat, p. 258.
82. Concession, November 17, 1891, LO 1/1, N.A.R.
83. Loch to Moffat, November 22, 1891, MO 1/1/4; Loch to Knutsford, December 2, 1891, S1428/17/7; Bower to Rudd, December 21,
1891, LO 5/2/15; all in N.A.R.
84. Loch to Moffat, December 4, 1891, confidential, MO 1/1/4, N.A.R.
85. C.O. to F.O., December 4, 1891, F.O. 84/2180, P.R.O.
86. John H. Harris, *The Chartered Millions*, pp. 143–144.
87. Ian Henderson and Philip Warhurst, "Revisions in Central African History to 1953," Central Africa Historical Association, Local

belonged to the Crown rather than the company. But the decision was of no moment to Africans. Lobengula was long dead, and the Shona whose land had been bargained away gained cold comfort from the fact that the sale was illegal.

The imperial government's response to the Lippert concession reflected neither a concern for African rights nor a disposition to exercise the controls over the company embodied in the charter. Sir Henry Loch wished to involve the high commissioner more intimately in the government of Mashonaland, with the top administrator being appointed by the government with the concurrence of the company but only removable by the government,[88] but the Colonial Office rejected his recommendation.[89] The company's officers were thus free to act with virtually no control from the imperial government so long as their actions did not produce international complications. The consequences were that vast discretion was vested in the local administrator. Rhodes as managing director was responsible for the actions of his subordinate Jameson, but Rhodes in Cape Town was 1,600 miles away from Salisbury, and he was too involved in his multifarious activities in politics and finance to devote much attention to the details of Jameson's administration even had he been so inclined. Rhodes reposed great confidence in Jameson. At the time of Jameson's negotiations with Lobengula in 1890 over the right of the pioneers to enter Mashonaland, Rhodes had remarked that "Jameson never makes a mistake." He believed that Jameson understood the objects and the means to their attainment almost as well as Rhodes himself. In this conviction he was undoubtedly justified. Jameson was devoted to the execution of Rhodes's plans, and Rhodes gave him great discretionary authority. They discussed plans during occasional visits and through telegraphic communication, but it was left to Jameson to use his judgment in carrying out the details. As Rhodes said to Jameson in one of these telegraphic

Series 15 (Salisbury, 1965), pp. 11–12; Terence O. Ranger, *Revolt in Southern Rhodesia*, p. 83.
88. Loch to Knutsford, May 25, 1891, encl. in C.O. to F.O., pressing, June 20, 1891, F.O. 84/2168, P.R.O.
89. Stafford Glass, *The Matabele War*, pp. 20–23.

interchanges, "Your business is to administer the country as to which I have nothing to do but merely say 'yes' if you take the trouble to ask me." [90]

Jameson conceived his mission to be the encouragement of maximum development in a minimum time. In advancing that object he was required to recognize the precarious financial condition of the company and to restrict his administrative staff to the barest minimum. This limitation of funds also imposed the necessity of using the resources of the country rather than money as a means of rewarding services. And these same resources were used as the lure to attract outside capital. The award to Lippert of vast land and mineral rights on the condition he spend an agreed amount of capital was typical of the terms offered to other syndicates, though the extent of the grant was more generous than most.

The standard condition for the flotation of a syndicate was that the chartered company would receive a half interest in the enterprise, but the terms varied at the discretion of the chartered company, and groups that promised to invest large amounts of capital or who were represented by favored individuals received much more liberal terms. Other syndicates were founded on grants made by the chartered company in partial payment for the transfer of claims. For example, Henry Moore received over 45,000 acres for his claims and for other services during the amalgamation, and he then proceeded to form a syndicate with a nominal capital of £150,000, of which a little more than half was actually paid up.[91] A syndicate in which Albert Grey was interested acquired about 35,000 acres and 40 gold claims on the condition that the chartered company receive one-third of the net profit rather than half the vendors' scrip.[92] The Anglo-French Exploration Company received the right to acquire 100 gold claims on payment of forty percent if £90,000 was spent in exploration within two years. Edward Maund's Mazoe Syndicate was granted over 2000 acres for every ore-

90. T. Fuller, *Cecil John Rhodes,* p. 7.
91. Moore's Rhodesia Concession records, B.T. 31/6080/43034, P.R.O. The company was liquidated in 1899.
92. Currey to London office, BSAC, January 13, 1892, LO 5/2/16.

crushing stamp (of 600 pounds) erected up to thirty stamps.[93] Alexander Fraser of the firm of Messrs. Fraser Brothers of Basutoland was granted 25,000 acres at an annual quitrent of £25 if he brought out twenty families within a year.[94]

The requirement of developing the country as a condition of a grant was a legitimate and indeed necessary policy for the chartered company if it was to realize profits from Mashonaland. But the condition was not enforced. Promises of providing capital were not fulfilled, and the company's administrators took no action to revoke the grants. One of the most lavish grants had been made to Sir John Willoughby in gratitude for his acts of valor in the company's encounters with the Portuguese. In addition to mining claims, he had been assigned 600,000 acres of Mashonaland on the condition that he raise £50,000 capital for the development of his property.[95] Willoughby and his associates were unable to fulfill the terms of the contract, but they were allowed to retain possession of their land. Company officials shied away from forfeitures which might compromise the already doubtful future of their territories. But the practice continued of granting large concessions to syndicates which did little or nothing to develop them. The London board in 1893, before the Matabele War, expressed its concern to Rhodes about the lavish manner in which land was being assigned. They cited among others the following examples:[96]

Northern Territories Exploring Company Ltd.
    300 square miles north of Zambezi,
    600 acres coal grant north or south of Zambezi
Copenhagen (Mashonaland) Company Ltd.
    100,000 acres Mashonaland
Chartered Gold Fields Ltd.
    100 square miles north of the Zambezi,
    6000 acres coal grant north or south of Zambezi,
    200,000 acres Mashonaland
J. W. Dore
    30,000 morgen (c. 60,000 acres) north of Zambezi

93. Grey's Notebook, Grey Papers, Durham.
94. *Ibid.*; Harris to Administrator, May 18, 1893, CT 2/1/5, N.A.R.
95. London office to Cape Town, April 14, 1893, LO 3/1/13, N.A.R.
96. London office to Cape Town, May 25, 1893, LO 3/1/28, N.A.R.

Mashonaland Agency Ltd.
   30,000 acres
Moore's Rhodesia Concession
   75,000 square miles Mashonaland
North Charterland Exploration Company Ltd.
   10,000 square miles north of Zambezi

Rhodes after reading through the list of large land grants concluded that the board was right. "We must make no more of these land grants," he told Jameson. "They will close up the country. We must have occupation by individual farmers."[97] The board on hearing of this decision expressed pleasure that Rhodes's views were "absolutely identical" with its own.[98]

The new policy, however, was not introduced until mid-1893 and many large grants had already been made. Furthermore, even after this belated decision, Rhodes continued to make large grants as exceptions to the general policy. The ineffectuality of the board is nowhere more evident than in its failure to control the allocation of land by its South African representative.

William H. Milton who in 1896 was sent by the board to reorganize the administration of Rhodesia placed the entire blame for the fiasco in land-grant policy on Jameson who, he said, had "given nearly the whole country to the Willoughby's, White's and others of that class so that there is absolutely no land left of any value for the settlement of Immigrants by the Government." Jameson, he suggested, "must have been off his head for some time before the Raid. The worst is that Rhodes will not clear himself at Jameson's expense."[99]

Rhodes as Milton portrayed him was a noble leader who refused to censure an erring subordinate. But Jameson was carrying out land policy in accordance with what he thought were Rhodes's wishes. Rhodes frequently instructed Jameson to make lavish land grants and occasionally Jameson was moved to express a mild caveat about giving away so much of the arable and

97. Rhodes to ————, n.d., encl. in Secretary, Cape Town, to Canning, June 14, 1893, CT 2/3/1, N.A.R.
98. Canning to Harris, July 7, 1893, CT 1/11/4/1, N.A.R.
99. Milton to his wife, September 18, 1896, MI 1/1/1, N.A.R.

pastoral land of the high veld to individuals who could not develop it effectively.[100]

From the standpoint of the company's interests, Jameson's great deficiency was not that he did not act in accordance with Rhodes's intentions but that he was an incompetent administrator. When he was removed from office, his successors found appalling acts of misfeasance during his tenure. The surveyor-general, for example, had been awarded, allegedly with Jameson's sanction, 1,000 square miles for relinquishing his private practice. This same surveyor had left the land descriptions in a shambles. H. Wilson Fox of the London office wrote to Milton: "More of the Augean stable of the past to sweep up I suppose you will say. It certainly is hard that the cleaning of all the dirty corners left by Jameson should fall on your shoulders."[101]

The failure of the company to attract settlers and capital gave an unintended reprieve to the Shona people. By the company's own estimates, which were probably generous, only about 300 farms were occupied by the end of 1892. Most of Mashonaland was left in the possession of its inhabitants, though "legal titles" to the land had been transferred to Europeans.[102]

Gold, not land, had been the great lure of Mashonaland. And the attraction continued to be illusory, despite frequent reports of great new strikes. By the end of July 1894 a total of 34,560 claims were registered,[103] but few produced gold in quantities sufficient to warrant investment in equipment to exploit them. This condition continued until after the Boer War, when the mining regulations were changed to allow individuals to engage in mining and the company changed the terms of its contracts to provide for payment of a share of the royalties rather than fifty percent of the vendor's scrip.[104] In the early years, however, much more money was made from sales of stock and from amal-

100. Telegrams, Jameson to Rhodes, March 10, 12, 1892, LO 5/2/17, N.A.R.
101. Fox to Milton, October 14, 1898, A1/5/1, in *ibid.*
102. Robin H. Palmer, "War and Land in Rhodesia," *Transafrican Journal of History*, I, 2 (July 1971), 48–49.
103. Walter H. Wills and L. T. Collingridge, *The Downfall of Lobengula*, p. 312.
104. Gann, *Southern Rhodesia*, p. 158.

gamations and re-amalgamations of syndicates than from the gold itself.

Most of the gold claims pegged out could have been proved to be worthless with a little investigation, but the boom rode not on reality but on hope and illusion. Any claim with surface gold could be sold to London capitalists even though there was no evidence that the veins extended for any depth. All the companies were greatly overcapitalized. Promoters allotted the largest proportion of the shares to themselves, and the chartered company received up to half of the vendor's scrip; consequently little money was available for working capital. This milking of companies by insiders was common on the Rand, but Mashonaland was no Rand. Rich mines could sustain such a company, but those of Rhodesia were generally low yielding. Speculators and directors who did not "know a mine from a railway cutting" controlled the companies in the early years, and the preoccupation on stock exchange transactions rather than on mining was abetted by the chartered company policy which imposed no requirement of serious development. Jameson in 1907, after the policies were changed, admitted that "even up to the death of Queen Victoria we never had any real prospecting. All the prospecting done was then pegging old workings."[105]

In the Alice-in-Wonderland world of the stock exchange in a bullish market, the facts of production and profit bore little relationship to the rise and fall of shares; indeed chartered shares for a time seemed to be rising in direct proportion to the depletion of the company's resources. While the company floundered, consequently, the directors and other insiders enjoyed large returns from the sale of their holdings. After the early vicissitudes which had caused such concern to the board, chartered shares were caught up in the great boom on the "Kaffir circus" which gripped the stock market in 1893. The stock which had sold for as low as ten shillings in 1892 soared to £2.10 by April 1893—as the *Economist* noted—for no evident reason.[106] The shares fluctuated considerably thereafter, drop-

105. J. W. McCarty, "British Investment in Overseas Mining, 1880–1914," doctoral dissertation, pp. 104–109.
106. *Economist*, April 29, 1893.

ping briefly below par but in the fall of 1895 they rose sharply again to over £8.10.2.[107] Each director was entitled to an allotment of 9,000 shares at par, and thus was in a position to make substantial profits for himself.[108] In addition, some directors profited from participation in related or subsidiary companies. In the Central Search Association, the following shares were assigned to beneficiaries of the Rudd Concession:[109]

Gold Fields of		Nathan Rothschild	3,000
South Africa	25,000	Maguire	3,000
Exploring Company	22,500	Rhodes, Rudd,	
Rhodes	9,750	and Beit	9,000
C. D. Rudd	9,000	Austral Africa	
Beit	8,250	Exploration	
		Company	24,000

When Central Search was transformed into United Concessions Company with a nominal capital of £4,000,000 the holdings of these participants also ballooned. In 1892 the principal shareholders in United Concessions were:[110]

Thomas Rudd and		Jameson	25,000
H. D. Boyle	840,000	BSAC	75,000
Beit	324,816	J. Wernher	10,000
Rhodes	338,567	Donald Currie	10,000
Rothschild	98,000	Farquhar	24,500
Maguire	123,976	S. Neumann	53,698
Rhodes, C. D. Rudd,		Goldfields of South	
and Beit	60,400	Africa	35,400
Exploring Company	734,700		

The Exploring Company, which had substantial holdings in both the chartered company and in United Concessions, had the following major shareholders after its reorganization in June 1889 as part of the amalgamation leading to the chartered company:[111]

107. *Financial News*, October 11, 1895.
108. Testimony of Beit in Matabeleland Co. v. BSAC, *Truth*, January 4, 1894.
109. Memorandum of Agreement, May 30, 1889, B.T. 31/4451/28988, P.R.O.
110. List of Shareholders, United Concessions, November 4, 1892, Rhodes Papers 9, Finance, Rhodes House.
111. Schedule Exploring Co., December 7, 1889, B.T. 31/4468/29152, P.R.O.

Bechuanaland		E. A. Maund	5,000
Exploration		Ricarde-Seaver	1,250
Company	4,725	Cawston and T.	
Cawston	4,625	Gladstanes	499
Gifford	601		
Mrs. G. Cawston	1,000		

The principal participants in the formation of the chartered company were also involved in related and subsidiary companies. Rhodes was a substantial shareholder in the Austral Africa Exploration Company, Mashonaland (Central) Gold Mining Company, Victoria District (Mashonaland) Gold Mining Company, and Goldfields of Mashonaland. Beit was involved with the same companies. Grey was the principal promoter of the Northumberland Mining Syndicate. Gifford and Cawston were shareholders in Goldfields of Mashonaland, Maguire held shares in Mashonaland (Central) Gold Mining Company and Goldfields of Mashonaland.

Individual and corporate holdings were enmeshed in a complicated financial network. Precisely how much the various directors profited from their involvement is impossible to determine. The chartered company was not subject to the provisions of the Limited Liability Acts with regard to disclosure and large investors could be protected by the use of dummy holders. The company, however, did publish a list of its shareholders in 1889 which indicated that the main promoters held about 70 percent of the shares. By November 1893 this proportion had declined to about 15 percent.[112] Sales at favorable times could have produced substantial profits.

One who certainly gained was Alfred Beit, perhaps the shrewdest operator in the stock market. In 1895 The *Mining World* published a list of South African millionaires, with comments on the way each had acquired his fortune. Beit led the list with £10,000,000 which the journal indicated he had amassed by "taking good things and sticking to them, or by purchasing for his partner to sell." His partner, Julius Wernher, was credited with £7,000,000, allegedly acquired "by selling things bought by his Partner Beit."[113] These estimates might have been some-

112. Shenton, "Chartered Company," p. 104.
113. *The Mining World*, November 16, 1895.

what exaggerated, though Beit at his death left an estate of about £7½ million.[114] Rhodes in 1895 was estimated to have a fortune of £5,000,000, acquired largely from Consolidated Goldfields and De Beers,[115] but the difference between his ambitions and those of Beit was reflected in the way they invested. Rhodes did not always invest in "good things" as defined by Beit; he poured much of his fortune into projects related to the advancement of his imperial ambitions and the returns were psychic rather than financial. When his will was probated, with a net worth after taxes of £3,432,000, his stock holdings reflected this emphasis. He had made large investments in companies related to Rhodesia and northern expansion, most of which with the exception of his chartered shares had a market value far below par, as illustrated by the following:[116]

	No. shares	Nominal amt. per share	Market price	Total value
African Transcon-tinental Telegraph	84,354	£1	1/–	£ 427.14
BSAC	19,337	£1	£3.10	£67,679.10
Charter Trust and Agency, Ltd.	7,500	£1	6/10½	£ 2,578.2.6
Mashonaland Consolidated	5,812	£1	10/7½	£ 3,087.12.6

Rhodes's fortune, then, unlike those of Beit and the other directors, derived from the companies he had founded prior to his commitment to creating his empire north of the Limpopo, and these companies fed this expansion which was so voracious of his money. This distinction between Rhodes and his fellow directors is a reason why he is remembered and they are in oblivion. But whether the object was Rhodes's passion for empire or his associates' passion for wealth, there was a problem which they had in common. The chartered company flirted with bankruptcy, and might well collapse if public confidence was shaken in the economic future of Mashonaland. If that confidence were destroyed, the fabulous paper capital which had been created would collapse.

114. A. P. Cartwright, *The Corner House* (Cape Town: [1965]), p. 260.
115. *The Mining World*, November 16, 1895.
116. "C. J. Rhodes, deceased, Liabilities, Statement as far as can be ascertained at July 23, 1904," Grey Papers, unnumbered, Durham.

Mashonaland, it was more and more evident to the insiders, had poor prospects, and the public could not be deluded indefinitely. During the winter of 1893 two American mining engineers, H. C. Perkins and John Hays Hammond, inspected the reefs of Mashonaland at the behest of the chartered company. Hammond was circumspect, but Perkins flatly stated that though small operators might make a living from mining in Mashonaland, there were no gold reefs of such extent as to attract big companies. Perkins's report was smothered, but censorship could not be depended upon indefinitely.[117]

Rhodes had been willing to confine the company's area of mining operations to Mashonaland because he was confident that here was the new Rand. That illusion was now shattered. In mid-1893 the realities of the company's position as seen by the directors bore no relationship to the optimistic reports which continued to appear in the financial pages of British and South African newspapers. How long the investing public could be kept deluded was a serious question. Once confidence was lost, not even Rhodes's fortune could prevent the early demise of the South Africa Company. This slide into dissolution was arrested with the outbreak of the Matabele War.

117. McCarty, "British Investment," p. 105.

9
The Matabele War

THE BRITISH SOUTH AFRICA COMPANY DID NOT GO TO
war with the Ndebele in 1893 merely because it sought to exploit the resources of Matabeleland. War did not come as the
result of a plan conceived by Rhodes and Jameson. A variety of
factors, some of which could not have been anticipated, created
the environment for war. But when Jameson had the choice of
peace or war, his decision was certainly influenced by the fact
that Mashonaland had been a great disappointment and the
hope that Matabeleland would be a more lucrative source of
revenue. There had never been any doubt that sooner or later
the Ndebele power must be crushed. Their military system was
incompatible with the economic objectives of the company.
But until the summer of 1893 the disposition of both Rhodes
and Jameson had been to postpone a collision. War would tax
the slender resources of the company and there was always the
possibility that Lobengula might decide to emulate his ancestor
Mzilikazi and lead his people north away from the area coveted
by white men.[1] Barring that eventuality, the policy was to keep
Lobengula in "good humour" until "next year," when the company was ready to deal with him.[2] Rutherfoord Harris, less dis-
creet than most in putting his thoughts on paper, in commiserat-
ing with Johannes Colenbrander who had been assaulted by
an Ndebele, wrote at the beginning of 1892:

1. Grey to Rhodes, July 29, 1893, Grey Papers, File 181/1, Durham.
2. The expressions are Harris's in a letter to Moffat, September 20,
1890, private, MO 1/1/4, N.A.R. But this was the general line before
the outbreak of war.

. . . mentally when they knocked me in the eye the 2nd day I was there I made the same resolution as no doubt you did, that when the bell really rang for their disappearance from the stage, that I wd. be there to help them leave—but that day is still 2 years at least distant—possibly it will never come or they may accommodate themselves to their environment as the Swazies have. . . .[3]

Lobengula might have postponed his fate by forfeiting all claims to control over the Shona but in so doing he would have produced pressures within his own society which could have destroyed him. With all his dedication to restraint he could not fulfill the specifications necessary to maintain peace. The company required unchallenged control over the resources of Mashonaland and its people and the availability of a docile labor force to work the mines. The proximity of the Ndebele military state was a threat to these interests, and the company would undoubtedly have seen the necessity of destroying that threat even if Mashonaland had been prosperous and there was nothing in Matabeleland to covet. The financial straits of the company and the possibility that the wealth that had eluded it in Mashonaland awaited it in Matabeleland certainly predisposed Rhodes and Jameson to action against the Ndebele, but they hoped that such action would come at a time most favorable to quick and decisive victory, for the finances of the company were too anemic to support a prolonged campaign.

Neither Lobengula nor Jameson, however, was entirely a free agent. The settlers and miners of Mashonaland were under very lax control from the paid officers of the company. With the disbandment of most of the police force, the company depended upon the settler community for military defense and for the policing of the districts that they inhabited. The de facto government of Mashonaland was largely in the hands of farmers and prospectors, with field cornets appointed from their number being vested with the powers of magistrates and guardians of order. Without legal authority the settlers intervened in African disputes, punished Africans for alleged offenses, and forced Africans to work on the farms and in the mines. The actions of the settlers usually went unnoticed by the company

3. Harris to Colenbrander, February 9, 1892, CO 4/1/1, N.A.R.

administration, and when clashes between Africans and whites
occurred which necessitated intervention by the company, its
officers invariably took the side of the settlers.[4] After one particularly flagrant instance of arbitrary police action, Jameson
justified the conduct of his subordinates on the basis that leniency would be suicidal in a country in which there were a few
hundred whites and more than a hundred thousand blacks.[5]

Despite the laissez-faire policy of the company, the white
population was restive. There were always ample opportunities
for grumbling—shortages of supplies and exorbitant prices were
a constant grievance. But fundamental to settler unrest was
disillusionment. The promised land had not fulfilled its promise—there were no fortunes to be made from gold, and the life
of the farmer was hard and unrewarding. The company was
naturally blamed for these tribulations, and a particular focus
of distcontent was its mining regulations. In mid–1892 the
Mashonaland Claimholders' Protection Association was formed
to protest against and, if possible, abolish the requirement that
the company receive half the vendor's scrip.[6] James Johnston
who was visiting Mashonaland at the time reported that business was stagnant, bankruptcies frequent, and indignation at
the company's deception at a fever pitch. The lush farmlands
of the advertising brochures were "dreary wastes" where no
one could hope to earn even a bare living.[7] Earlier, when
Rhodes had visited "his North" in 1891, he had been barraged
with complaints about the mining regulations and the poverty
of the country about which the company had boasted so much.[8]

As it became more evident that mining in Mashonaland was
not highly profitable, pressure increased on the company's officers to expand the area in which mining operations would be
conducted. Jameson maintained that he and Lobengula had
come to an understanding that the company would be left un-
disturbed in the exploitation of Mashonaland. The border with

4. Terence O. Ranger, *Revolt in Southern Rhodesia*, pp. 60–66.
5. Harris to London office, BSAC, LO 5/2/20, N.A.R.
6. *South Africa*, September 3, 1892.
7. James Johnston, *Reality versus Romance in South Central Africa*,
pp. 262–263.
8. Sarah Gertrude Millin, *Rhodes*, (London, 1933), pp. 163–164.

Matabeleland as defined by Jameson was the Umniati and Shashi rivers and a line drawn between the two.[9] While Lobengula did not explicitly avow that such an agreement existed, he acted as if he accepted a de facto partition. But Lobengula's understanding of what this modus vivendi involved was quite different from Jameson's. The Ndebele ruler insisted that the powers of the company extended only to Europeans and that the line represented a boundary for gold prospecting rather than limiting his powers over the Shona.[10] Jameson at first did not challenge Lobengula's right to levy tribute and punish his vassals. When Lobengula in 1891 sent an impi to chastise the Shona chief Lomagundi for his refusal to recognize Ndebele supremacy or to pay his tribute, Jameson acknowledged that Lobengula was acting within his authority and in accordance with Ndebele laws and customs. And he expressed pleasant surprise that only Lomagundi and three of his followers had been killed.[11] But Jameson notified Lobengula that he was sending a party of police to investigate the incident and suggesting that if there were any other occasions in which a subsidiary chief refused to pay tribute, the "proper course" would be to ask the company to intervene, since its "laws were framed for black as well as white."[12] This half-way position Jameson maintained until after the company acquired the Lippert concession. For the time being he chose not to make an issue of Lobengula's right to tribute, but at the same time he asserted the company's right to exercise control over the Shona as well as the whites.

It was of little consequence that such authority was legitimized only by its assertion. The settler attitude was that as white men they were justified in disciplining Africans and that if they did not do so with firmnesss and resolution they risked loss of the aura of power and invincibility which enabled them to overawe a vastly more numerous African population. Summary justice as meted out by settlers was thus both right and expedi-

9. Stafford Glass, *The Matabele War*, p. 32ff. and map on p. 295.
10. Harris to London office, BSAC, August 9, 1893, LO 5/2/28, N.A.R.
11. Ranger, *Revolt in Southern Rhodesia*, p. 28; Jameson to BSAC, Cape Town, December 2, 1891, LO 5/2/16, N.A.R.
12. Jameson to BSAC, Cape Town, December 2, 1891, LO 5/2/16, N.A.R.

ent, and Jameson's police carried out their responsibilities to maintain order without regard for the niceties of English law. In February 1892, for example, the police intervened in a dispute between two chiefs in the Victoria district. One, Moghabi, had raided another chief who appealed to the company for assistance. Moghabi refused to recognize the right of the company to interfere. Jameson ordered a contingent of police to "give Moghabi a lesson." The lesson cost Moghabi his life, and his kraal was burned.[13] In the same month, another patrol under Captains Graham and Lendy was ordered to apprehend the murderer of a European trader. The murderer was unknown, but Graham and Lendy held the chief of the district responsible. Several kraals were burned, and the chief was taken prisoner. Then, on its way to Salisbury, the patrol "chastized" another chief some of whose men had been guides to the trader; further, there had been complaints by whites that these people were thieves. The kraal of the offending chief was burned and in the assault several Africans were killed or wounded. Jameson justified this action on the basis that there were numerous complaints of "the impertinent and threatening attitudes of the natives in that district."[14]

During 1892 there were many instances of such "salutary punishment." James Johnston saw a large Shona kraal which had been deserted by its inhabitants who had fled after a police raid leaving their belongings in their haste.[15] Most of the actions went unnoticed outside of Mashonaland, except for approving comments from Rhodes who congratulated Jameson on "maintaining the dignity of the law."[16] The only dissenting voice from within the company's administration came from Johannes Colenbrander who since he was stationed at Lobengula's capital looked on events from a different perspective. Colenbrander, on hearing of the death of Moghabi, expressed great apprehension as to the consequences of intervention in African disputes:

13. Telegram, Jameson to BSAC, Cape Town, February 29, 1892, LO 5/2/17, in ibid.
14. Ranger, Revolt in Southern Rhodesia, p. 64.
15. Johnston, Reality versus Romance, p. 260.
16. Rhodes to Jameson, February 12, 1892, CT 1/15/4, N.A.R.

"Small matters like this will bring on difficulties and cause us both endless trouble and lengthy palavers. The Doctor was wrong to mix himself up in the matter."[17] But the raids continued, much to the satisfaction of the settler population.

One incident, however, did attract attention. Captain Lendy, one of the most ardent practitioners of the policy of rule by terror, was sent to the kraal of Ngomo, a headman subject to chief Mangwende. Ngomo allegedly had been involved in a dispute with a trader who claimed his goods had been stolen and the trader and his son had been struck by some of Ngomo's people. Lendy in his first visit to Ngomo found him insolent and Mangwende professed to be unable to take any action. Lendy thereupon returned to headquarters for further instructions and Jameson directed him "to take summary measures." Lendy carried out these orders zealously. His force, equipped with Maxim guns and a seven pounder cannon, surrounded Ngomo's kraal. "A well-directed shot from the seven pounder" opened up firing on both sides, at the end of which twenty-one Africans including Ngomo had been killed. Lendy's men suffered no casualties and captured forty-seven head of cattle and several goats.[18] The result was highly gratifying to Lendy; he concluded his report with the observation that "I am sure a very wholesome lesson has been given to all the chiefs of the district."[19]

Lendy's severity came to the attention of the imperial authorities in Cape Town and London. The high commissioner's office had already expressed displeasure over the burning of kraals, and the punishment of the innocent as well as the guilty;[20] and the killings of Ngomo and his people produced still more emphatic protest. Graham Bower, the imperial secretary in Cape Town, condemned Lendy's severity as "utterly disproportionate to the original case."[21] In London, Knutsford, the colonial secretary, privately communicated to the company's board his displeasure at Lendy's "outrageous act," and reminded the company that if the "outside world" heard of it, the

17. Colenbrander to Currey, May 1, 1892, LO 5/2/19, in *ibid.*
18. Ranger, *Revolt in Southern Rhodesia*, p. 65.
19. Lendy to Magistrate, Salisbury, A1/9/1, N.A.R.
20. Ranger, *Revolt in Southern Rhodesia*, p. 65–66.
21. *Ibid.*, p. 66.

company would be severely attacked and pressure put on the government to annul the company's charter.[22] But the board was so much subservient to Rhodes that its chairman confined himself to a mild comment that it would "have been better if the attack and slaughter had not been made."[23] Jameson's response, transmitted through Rhodes, was that the Colonial Office and, by implication, the London board should recognize that such fastidiousness was all very well from the distance of London but that the whites in Mashonaland could survive only by a strong line.[24]

The local administration in Mashonaland was thus asserting, with only a feeble challenge from the London board and the imperial government and with the full support of Rhodes, that decisions on "native policy" must be made by those who were closest to the problem and that criticism from afar was not only unwelcome but dangerous.

In effect, therefore, Jameson had asserted his autonomy of any control but that of Rhodes, and Rhodes had given Jameson carte blanche to act as he saw fit, subject only to general advice from Rhodes. That advice when offered was in support of Jameson's assertion of company authority over all the peoples of Mashonaland, black and white. Inevitably this line led to a confrontation with Lobengula.

In July 1892 an Ndebele impi raided a Shona district where the chief had not paid tribute. Jameson telegraphed Rhodes that the impi had not only seized cattle but had killed six men and carried off women and girls. The report was inaccurate—there had been no casualties and no abductions—but the incident gave Rhodes and Jameson the occasion to make an issue of Lobengula's right to raid into Mashonaland. Jameson suggested to Rhodes that Lobengula should be informed that he should no longer collect tribute within Mashonaland. The Shona could hardly be expected to pay taxes to both the Ndebele and the company, and Jameson planned to institute taxation of the

22. Knutsford to Abercorn, confidential, n.d., encl. in Abercorn to Rhodes, May 25, 1892, A1/3/10, N.A.R.
23. Abercorn to Rhodes, May 25, 1892, A1/3/10, N.A.R.
24. Harris to London office, BSAC, June 22, 1892, LO 5/2/20, in *ibid.*

Shona as a means of raising necessary revenue and as an encouragement to their young men to work.[25]

Jameson sent Lord Henry Paulet to interrogate the induna in charge of the impi. Paulet reported that the induna maintained he was collecting tribute due Lobengula before the company's occupation, but that he and his men were "most humble and civil."[26] This restrained conduct reflected Lobengula's policy of avoiding any collision with the company short of the abdication of his authority over the Shona. But restraint was not enough. Jameson's position was incompatible with Lobengula's, as was manifested on the occasion of the election of a successor to the ill-fated Lomagundi. The new chief gave his allegiance to the company, which had acted as his overlord, Jameson asserted, "at the request of the tribe." Rhodes considered this action as symbolic recognition that the company was now master of Mashonaland, and that Lobengula no longer had any authority over the Shona people.[27]

In 1892 Jameson was not yet ready for a showdown with Lobengula. His communications with the chief did not directly challenge Ndebele rights, but concentrated on the disruptive effects of Ndebele raids and the importance of keeping impis away from white settlements.[28]

Lobengula made every effort to comply with what he understood to be the company's requirements. He was dominated by the fear that the whites were seeking an excuse to invade Matabeleland. In March 1893, in response to a rumor that whites were on their way from the south to attack him, he ordered out an impi, and in April he sent another impi to the border of the Ngwato country in response to a report that the Bechuanaland Border Police were about to invade his country.[29]

25. Extract of telegraph conversation between Jameson and Rhodes, printed in *Cape Times*, July 26, 1892. The newspaper did not indicate how it had acquired the transcript.
26. Harris to London office, BSAC, August 3, 1892, LO 5/2/21, N.A.R.
27. Harris to London office, BSAC, September 14, 1892, LO 5/2/22, in *ibid*.
28. Glass, *Matabele War*, p. 37.
29. Harris to London office, BSAC, April 12, 1893, and encl., Colenbrander to Harris, March 9, 1893, LO 5/2/26, N.A.R.

Lobengula tried to insure that there should be no incident which could be used as an excuse to justify a war. His impis were under strict instructions not to molest white people, and they generally obeyed with perfect discipline. Some prospectors who crossed into Matabeleland despite Jameson's orders complained that their goods had been seized, but no whites were killed. Furthermore, in the case of one party, only the belongings of the bearers were taken and in another, goods seized from two traders were returned to them.[30] Lobengula, however, had not given up his claims to mastery over the Shona nor had the company's officials insisted that he do so. In this shadowy area there lurked the danger of a collision which could lead to war.

In the early part of 1893, however, there seemed to be little basis for apprehension on either side. There had been a little flurry over the cutting of the telegraph wire by persons unknown in an area on the border of Matabeleland and Mashonaland. The Shona people in the vicinity blamed the Ndebele, and Jameson suspected the Shona. But Jameson sent Captain Lendy to Bulawayo to demand that Lobengula punish the offenders if they should prove to be Ndebele. Lobengula promised to do so, but he asked Jameson to tell the whites to stop shooting hippopotami and he requested the payment of another 1,000 guns which he said had been guaranteed him if the white people discovered gold in Mashonaland.[31] The offenders were later identified as Shona who had fled to avoid punishment. Jameson promised to use his best efforts with regard to the hippos, and to inquire into the matter of the guns. In May 1893 there was another and more serious incident involving alleged wire cutting. A party of company police seized cattle belonging to Lobengula which were being herded for him by a Shona chief. Lobengula was angered by this action of the company's police. He called upon both Loch and Jameson for an explanation of why they had allowed such an outrage, and he emphasized to Jameson that only his forbearance had kept his people from marching to take back his cattle by force if necessary. The im-

30. Glass, *Matabele War*, pp. 33–35.
31. *Ibid.*, pp. 61–63; Lendy to Jameson, February 1, 1893, A1/9/1, N.A.R.

mediate crisis passed away when Jameson gave assurance that the cattle would be returned.[32]

This relationship of mutual restraint did not long continue. In June Lobengula sent an impi into Mashonaland to punish a chief in the vicinity of Fort Victoria whose people had stolen some of Lobengula's cattle. The impi's instructions were to confine themselves to punishing the Shona and to stay away from the white people. The immediate reaction of Jameson and Rhodes was relaxed. Jameson noted that though some Shona had been killed, Lobengula had assured the Europeans that they had nothing to fear and that the impi had acted accordingly. There was no cause for anxiety, he telegraphed Rhodes.[33] Rhodes professed satisfaction at Lobengula's pacific policy toward whites, but he told Jameson to "intimate plainly and distinctly" to Lobengula that while the company could not object to his punishing his own subjects, he must not allow his impis to cross the border; rather, he should ask the company to bring the offenders to justice.[34]

The issue, Rhodes insisted, had to be faced squarely because Ndebele raids not only called into question the company's authority over the Shona and its ability to protect them but disrupted the economy of Mashonaland. Mining and agriculture depended on stability and the availability of labor. The company was planning to impose a hut tax on the justification that it provided peace and order in Mashonaland. Lobengula's raids consequently must cease.[35]

After receiving Rhodes's message Jameson became more militant; the pacific tone he had taken with Lobengula disappeared. Rhodes's advice undoubtedly contributed to this shift, but Jameson was subject to powerful pressure from the settlers to smash the Ndebele. As late as July 17, 1893, Jameson still seemed to be hesitating as to whether he should force the issue,

32. Glass, *Matabele War*, pp. 64–65. The cattle never were regained by Lobengula. They were sent to Tuli to be reclaimed, but for a variety of reasons they were not yet in Lobengula's possession when war broke out.
33. Cable, Harris to London board, BSAC, July 11, 1893, encl. in Harris to London board, July 12, 1893, LO 5/2/28, N.A.R.
34. Harris to London board, July 12, 1893, LO 5/2/28, N.A.R.
35. *Ibid.*

but he was leaning toward war. The labor question, he tele-graphed Harris, was the serious problem. There was no danger to the white population, but "unless something is done," it would be difficult to induce the Shona to return to the mines even after the present panic had passed.[36] This message was dis-patched the day he arrived in Salisbury. He found awaiting him an outraged settler population. A mass meeting had been held two days before when resolutions had been drawn up demand-ing that he end the reprehensible policy of temporizing with savages. If he did not give satisfactory assurance that he would take resolute action, the settlers vowed to deal with the Ndebele themselves, supported by 500 Boers whom they would invite in from the Transvaal.[37] Caught up with the passions of the com-munity, Jameson abandoned restraint. Later in the day of July 17 he wired Rhodes that the company must make a show of force and drive the Ndebele away, and he received a reply expressing support, with the further admonition that "if you do strike, strike hard."[38]

Jameson consequently had already decided on direct action when on July 18 he met the Ndebele indunas outside Fort Vic-toria. After delivering them a fiery harangue he gave them an ultimatum to depart for Matabeleland within one hour. The impi was on its way back when it was overtaken by a patrol un-der Captain Lendy which had been sent out by Jameson less than two hours after the ultimatum. Lendy's orders were, "If they resist, shoot them" and he interpreted his mission in the same spirit he had shown against the Shona. He came upon a party of the Ndebele a few miles away from Fort Victoria and, though they offered no resistance, ordered his men to fire. About thirty Ndebele were killed. Lendy led his troopers back to Vic-toria. An eyewitness reported that cheer after cheer went up as the patrol was seen to be carrying shields and assegais as memen-tos of their encounter. One of the troopers exulted that their ride had been "as good as partridge shooting" and another said that "fox hunting couldn't hold a candle to it."[39]

36. Telegram, Jameson to Harris, July 17, 1893, LO 5/2/28, N.A.R.
37. C. H. Rattray diary, July 15, 17, 1893, RA 8/2, N.A.R.
38. Telegram, Harris to Jameson, July 17, 1893, LO 5/2/28, in *ibid.*; Glass, *Matabele War*, p. 96.
39. Rattray's diary, July 18, 1893, RA 8/2, N.A.R.

If there had been any lingering hesitation in Jameson's mind, Lendy's action removed it. Jameson considered himself at war with the Ndebele. His problem now was to convince the imperial authorities in Cape Town and London that that war was just. To accomplish this end, he began a campaign of carefully calculated deception. Just as the avowed reason for the Jameson raid was humanitarian—the rescue of helpless victims of tyranny —the shooting of the Ndebele was justified because they were savages who had slaughtered helpless Shona, including women and children, and burned their kraals. These killers had not restricted themselves to African areas but had pursued their intended victims into the very streets of Fort Victoria. Servants of white people had been murdered before the eyes of their horrified masters. Confronted by such outrages against humanity, the company's officers had nevertheless attempted to effect the withdrawal of the Ndebele without violence. But the indunas had rejected Jameson's demand that they withdraw their men beyond the demarcation line. They had retired slowly and had shown their contempt for the company by burning other kraals as they went. The party which Lendy overtook was engaged in burning a kraal. When he ordered them to disperse the Ndebele had opened fire, and Lendy had no alternative but to respond. This was the version which Jameson gave to the imperial authorities, and which they initially accepted.[40] Jameson pressed the humanitarian issue which he expected to be sufficient justification not only for Lendy's action but for war. Failure to protect the helpless Shona would not only be craven but it would weaken the whole position of the white community in Mashonaland, whose ability to maintain order and to develop the country would be undermined. Jameson's private communications to Rhodes were not so exalted. On July 19, the day after he had resolved to force a war, he wired to Harris: "We have the excuse for a row over murdered women and children now and the getting Matabeleland open would give us a tremendous lift in shares, and everything else. The fact of its being shut up gives it an immense value both here and outside."[41]

40. Telegram, Loch to Ripon, July 19, 1893, C.O. 879/39/454, P.R.O.
41. Jameson to Harris, July 17, 1893, MSS Afr. s. 228, C 3B, Rhodes

Jameson had to manufacture a *casus belli* which would not only justify war but would give the company full authority to wage it without interference from imperial officials. He believed that Sir Henry Loch wholeheartedly supported war, but that the high commissioner had to be cautious until the groundwork had been adequately laid. Jameson telegraphed Maund on July 24:

> ... You understand the position with the High Commissioner and one must go gently. He is backing us in every way. I cable carefully and the truth occasionally and Capetown does the same. The whole gist is that we must settle the affair ourselves and I mean to go the whole hog—as to cables "all quiet and people at work."[42]

Jameson sought to ensure that all information coming out of Mashonaland conformed to the line he had adopted. It was essential that the press and public officials in South Africa and Britain be given the impression that the Ndebele had forced war upon the company. Any conflicting reports might "bust the show."[43] Telegraph operators were instructed to submit to company officials any telegrams containing statements bearing on relations with the Ndebele. A message written by a Wesleyan minister at the end of August was returned to him because he mentioned that he had accepted the chaplaincy of the Matabele expedition. This information, the minister was told, might "hinder us in what we are doing," since "the people down below," in Cape Town might conclude that the company was planning on war.[44] Jameson was determined to have his war, and the scenario he wrote was widely accepted as being true. Not all politicians and newspapermen were convinced; suspicions were expressed in Parliament and in some papers that the company had forced war on Lobengula, but there was little hard evidence to back such opinions until after the war had begun.

Amidst the welter of conflicting interpretations of the causes

House, quoted in T. O. Ranger, "The Last Word on Rhodes?" *Past and Present*, 28, 117.

42. Telegram, Jameson to Maund, July 24, 1893, Maund Papers, Witwatersrand.

43. Duncan to Borrow, August 24, 1893, A 2/14/1, N.A.R.

44. Duncan to Shimmio, August 26, 1893, A 2/14/7, N.A.R.

of the Matabele War, the conclusion seems beyond argument that the men who decided company policy entertained no doubts that sooner or later Ndebele power must be destroyed. The collision, they hoped, would come at a time when there would be little doubt that the Ndebele would be smashed quickly, with as little drain on the company's resources as possible, and with minimum risks of imperial intervention. Such decisive action was necessitated in the first instance by the requirement of a stable labor supply but as the company resources flowed away and the realities of Mashonaland remained bleak, attention shifted to Matabeleland. Perhaps the golden bounty which had eluded the company in Mashonaland would be found there. The first consideration was more powerful in precipitating the war in 1893. Pressed by the settlers' community, Jameson decided to "strike hard." He was assured by eager police and volunteer officers that their cavalry would destroy the Ndebele even more easily than the mounted Boers had dealt with other African peoples. Having made his decision, he found additional justification in the prospective benefits to the company in the occupation of Matabeleland.

Rhodes, while backing Jameson, had made it clear that he would have preferred that the crisis come at a more propitious time. In London, Grey expressed the same theme. He wrote to Rhodes, "I had hoped it might have been avoided as our resources though abundant are hardly liquid enough to enable us to contemplate any large tax on our finance without misgiving unless you like Moses can again tap water from the rock, but it would have been much more satisfactory if the work of peaceful development had been allowed to continue unchecked for another year. . . ."[45]

As Grey's emphasis indicated, the board was concerned about finances, but they had to rely on Rhodes's judgment, and perhaps he would again "tap water from the rock." Rhodes allayed their apprehension by guaranteeing £50,000 from his private funds, and he argued that it would be cheaper to destroy the Ndebele power immediately rather than to patch up a peace, since a complete cessation of Ndebele raids could only be guar-

45. Grey to Rhodes, July 29, 1893, 181, File 1, Grey Papers, Durham.

anteed by the maintenance of a force of 700 to 800 men at a cost of £120,000 per year.[46] This combination of assurance and argument apparently convinced the board, for it expressed no further reservations.

Jameson, then, had the satisfaction of knowing that he had full power to act and the realization that this authority carried with it responsibility for failure. His prospects for success were materially enhanced when a large impi returned from a campaign against the Lozi riddled with smallpox and the infection spread rapidly throughout the Ndebele. And the necessity for economy was met by offering to volunteers shares in the loot of Matabeleland rather than monetary wages. By the celebrated Victoria agreement of August 14, 1893, which Jameson made with Allan Wilson as the representative of the volunteers, each enlistee would receive 3,000 morgen (over 6,000 acres) in Matabeleland and the right to 15 reef gold claims and 5 alluvial claims. All "loot," principally cattle, which would be collected would be divided one half to the company and the other half to the officers and men in equal shares.[47] With the combined appeal of avarice and adventure, there was no difficulty in recruitment. The reaction of one young recruit is probably typical. George Graham wrote on August 18 that he was on "the war path" and expected to fight the Ndebele, "the best fighting men in South Africa," in about a fortnight. He had intended to go elephant hunting; now he had more exciting game. "Yesterday I was at the range with my express practicing how to bowl over the niggers and made very good shooting indeed."[48]

Recruitment was not confined to Mashonaland. An agent of the company was sent to the Transvaal to enlist 250 volunteers and to purchase 740 horses. Permission was not sought from either the government of the South African republic or the British high commissioner, and the recruiter activities went on unnoticed by these authorities until some of the more unruly recruits ran afoul of the law. The state secretary at Pretoria no-

46. Harris to London office, BSAC, September 6, 1893, LO 5/2/29, N.A.R.
47. Glass, *Matabele War*, p. 149.
48. Graham to "My Dear Jim," August 18, 1893, GR 7/1/1, N.A.R.

tified Loch at the beginning of September that "a troop of persons in the service of the Chartered Company are trekking through the Republic, stealing and robbing along the road" and that a warrant had been issued for their arrest. Subsequently the president of the Transvaal prohibited any burghers from enlisting in the volunteer forces.[49] But the proclamation came too late to prevent a contingent of burghers from crossing into Mashonaland to participate with the volunteer forces.[50]

Imperial officials in Cape Town and London were concerned that when war came the company would have the force to defeat the Ndebele without involving the imperial government. Few disputed the assumption that the Ndebele faced only two alternatives—peaceful submission, which was highly unlikely, or war, which should come at a moment most favorable to the company's fortunes. One official with a disturbed conscience, Sydney Olivier, a junior official in the Colonial Office, suggested a possible third alternative—that the company buy out Lobengula's raiding rights as it had purchased mining and land concessions. His proposal was treated as an imaginative but impractical idea by a bright young man.[51] Ripon, the colonial secretary, and his parliamentary undersecretary feared that the company would not be able to overpower the Ndebele and would have to call for aid from the imperial government.[52] Loch was instructed to make clear to Rhodes that the company should not begin hostilities without Loch's permission unless the Ndebele attacked and that cutting telegraph wires alone would probably not be sufficient cause for war.[53] But Loch was almost as militant as Rhodes in his posture toward the Ndebele, their basic difference being as to the involvement of the high commissioner in the critical decision as to when to strike. Loch feared that a war might spread to other African peoples in

49. Telegram, State Secretary to Loch, September 2, 1893, HM agent, Pretoria to Loch, September 8, 1893, both in C.O. 879/39/454, P.R.O.
50. Glass, *Matabele War*, pp. 148–149.
51. Notes on BSAC to C.O., September 13, 1893, C.O. 417/110, P.R.O.
52. There is considerable correspondence on this subject in the Ripon Papers, Addtl. MSS. 43561, British Museum. For further elaboration on discussions within the imperial government, see chapter 10.
53. Telegram, Ripon to Loch, August 28, 1893, C.O. 879/38/452, P.R.O.

South Africa, particularly if the company suffered reverses.[54]

The imperial government, Loch maintained, would have no alternative but to support any actions taken by the company against the Ndebele, for "the natives would never understand that the English might be fired on and attacked on one side of a river while the English on the other side quietly looked on." The high commissioner sought to restrain the company until it was sufficiently prepared to ensure a quick victory. Jameson and his lighthearted associates seemed cocksure. Loch pointed out that they did not have enough horses at their disposal to maintain a mounted force. Until sufficient horses were available from the Transvaal and elsewhere for a highly mobile campaign Loch thought it unwise that the company take the offensive.[55] Beyond this cautionary advice to the company was his determination that the high commissioner be involved in decisions regarding future policy in the chartered territories. Loch was jealous of his authority and sought to curb Rhodes's habit of acting independently. But he had no more sympathy or understanding for the Ndebele than had the company. A peace mission sent by Lobengula to the queen was given short shrift by the high commissioner. Rutherfoord Harris predicted that Loch would send the mission back to Bulawayo three days after it arrived in Cape Town,[56] and Loch almost vindicated the prophecy. The delegation was in Cape Town for about ten days, between September 26 and October 5, 1893, but the Ndebele delegation headed by Mshete, who had accompanied Maund to England, was essentially given an ultimatum to stop raiding the Shona and was sent back to Matabeleland rather than being permitted to proceed to England.[57]

Graham Bower, the imperial secretary, cautioned Rhodes against precipitate action, but Bower's concern was strictly pragmatic. The temptation to strike while a large impi was absent in

54. Loch to Ripon, private, July 26, 1893, Ripon Papers, Addtl. MSS. 43561, British Museum.
55. Telegram, Loch to Ripon, October 2, 1893, C.O. 879/38/454, P.R.O.; Loch to Ripon, private, October 4, 1893, Ripon Papers, Addtl. MSS. 43562, British Museum.
56. P.S. by Harris on telegram, Colenbrander to Harris, September 1, 1893, LO 5/2/29, N.A.R.; Glass, *Matabele War*, p. 160.
57. Glass, *Matabele War*, p. 161.

Barotseland, he advised, had to be restrained by the prospect that if Lobengula's authority was destroyed the country would be overrun by small bands of marauding Ndebele subject to no control but that of force. In addition a considerable police establishment would have to be maintained to await the return of the Barotseland impi.[58]

The effect of these injunctions from London and Cape Town to be cautious was to encourage Rhodes and Jameson to be bold. They correctly interpreted the position of imperial officials to be that the company must take full responsibility for military operations and that war must appear to be provoked by the Ndebele. Jameson had no doubts about quick and easy victory, and it was easy to manufacture evidence that the Ndebele were the aggressors, particularly since there were no independent observers in Mashonaland to provide testimony to the contrary. Moffat, the nearest imperial official, was far away in Palapye, Bechuanaland, and Lobengula had no means of rebuttal. Indeed, Europeans at Bulawayo whom Lobengula trusted contributed to Jameson's fabrications. Johannes Colenbrander who represented the king in negotiations with the company even though he was paid by the company, described the Ndebele as being "up in arms and anxious for the fray." Lobengula, he said, professed to want peace, but he would undoubtedly unleash his warriors when the large impi returned from Barotseland.[59] Colenbrander's loyalty in 1893 was entirely given to the company which he served and from which he hoped to derive benefits. He was approaching forty and he felt that he had not achieved the recognition that his talents deserved. The chartered company had appointed him as an interpreter, a position in which he was particularly useful because Lobengula trusted him as he did few other white men,[60] and the chief was unaware that his confidant was in fact an agent of the company which was the Ndebele nemesis. This service, however, did not immediately win Colenbrander the advancement he sought. Later

58. Bower to Rhodes, July 21, 1893, C.O. 879/39/454, P.R.O.
59. Colenbrander to Harris, August 14, 1893, LO 5/2/9, N.A.R.
60. Hugh M. Hole, Lobengula. Colenbrander's wife also was a skilled linguist.

in 1890 he had complained to Harris: "Kindly remember that I am anxious to become something more than an interpreter. I have the will and the experience to be in a more responsible position."[61]

With the departure of Moffat in 1892, Colenbrander became not only the company's agent but the principal source of the imperial government's information on events in Matabeleland. Colenbrander was a valuable asset in the company's campaign to justify war. As a resident of Bulawayo he was presumed to be peculiarly well placed to report movements of the Ndebele regiments, and his communications were treated as authentic by the imperial authorities. It was not until after the war had begun that the extent of his deception was known by the high commissioner and the Colonial Office. Colenbrander knew that Lobengula did not want war; he sought to force war upon him. He told Lobengula that troops were on the way toward Matabeleland at the same time as he was warning whites in the vicinity of Matabeleland that impis were on the way and that they should flee. The general manager of the Tati Concession on receiving word from Colenbrander that an impi would descend on his mining community called on the high commissioner for protection. The impi did not appear, and the Tati manager realized that he had been duped. He correctly concluded that the chartered company through Colenbrander was trying to produce a crisis. The panic which had been created by Colenbrander's false reports contributed to that end.[62] Colenbrander's misrepresentations conformed nicely to Jameson's and Rhodes's specifications, and he undoubtedly propagated them on their instructions.[63]

Jameson needed an incident to provide the justification for war and he found it in a report of a skirmish on September 30 involving a contingent of the company's police. The commander of the unit reported that he had investigated a report

61. Colenbrander to Harris, August 20, 1890, CT 1/13/3, N.A.R.
62. Kirby to Moffat, August 3, 1893; Kirby to Girdlestone, October 1, 1893, both in TA 1/1/1, N.A.R.
63. For a detailed account of Colenbrander's duplicity, see Glass, *Matabele War*, pp. 168–172.

that an Ndebele impi had crossed the Shashi River, captured cattle, and returned across the border. He stated that he had sent two policemen to follow the spoor, which led to a kraal eight miles beyond the river. The police demanded to see the induna, whereupon a large body of Ndebele appeared among the rocks and fired on the police. The police returned the fire and rode back to the patrol. Those who shot at the police must have been part of an Ndebele impi, the commander asserted, because no Africans would have fired even on two policemen unless a large body of Ndebele were in the vicinity.[64] At the same time, Jameson reported that an Ndebele impi estimated at 7,000 had passed northeast of Victoria—he first indicated that his scouts had encountered this force and later that the size of the impi had been determined by the number of footpaths across the veld.[65] Furthermore, Lobengula had stationed his men in every Shona kraal along the border.[66] Jameson's "impi" of 7000 was a phantom of his imagination, as Moffat suggested,[67] but Sir Henry Loch was sufficiently impressed with the evidence that he authorized Jameson to adopt any measures necessary to ensure the safety of the company's posts.[68] Loch's response was not in itself an authorization for war, but if liberally interpreted gave Jameson the opportunity for offensive action. The last feeble restraint was soon removed. Loch on receiving further reports from other sources of Ndebele aggressive action, gave Jameson discretion to use whatever means were requisite to force the Ndebele impis to retire.[69] This authority was all that Jameson needed to act. The company's columns were set in motion. The war had begun. Lobengula's pathetic protest to the high commissioner arrived after he had abandoned his capital and he was a fugitive in a flight which ended with his death: "Every day I hear from you reports which are nothing but lies.

64. Jameson to high commissioner, October 2, 1893, LO 5/2/30, N.A.R.; Glass, *Matabele War*, p. 173.
65. Telegrams, Cape Town office, BSAC, to London, October 2, October 4, 1893, LO 5/2/30, N.A.R.
66. Jameson to high commissioner, October 4, 1893, LO 5/2/30, in *ibid.*
67. Moffat to high commissioner, October 3, 1893. in *ibid.*
68. High commissioner to Jameson, October 2, 1893, in *ibid.*
69. Glass, *Matabele War*, p. 176.

I am tired hearing nothing but lies. What Impi of mine have your people seen and where do they come from? I know nothing of them."[70]

The Reverend Mr. Helm who considered the Ndebele to be an obstacle to progress, could not bring himself to defend the company's methods of removing them: "As you know it is my opinion that we shall never do much good in Matabeleland until the Matabeles have had a lesson. And their treatment of the Mashona and other tribes deserve punishment. But I wish we entered on a war with clean hands."[71]

Helm's world was alien to that of Rhodes. In anticipation of war, Rhodes had left Cape Town in mid-September for Mashonaland. At first he was in great haste to reach Salisbury from Beira, but after Loch's ambiguous authorization to Jameson, Rhodes halted at an out-of-the-way place removed from any communication with the high commissioner. He did not resume his journey until he heard that the forces had left for Matabeleland and were beyond recall by the high commissioner.[72] His precautions were unnecessary; no countermanding telegram was sent.

Rhodes and Jameson had gambled and won. In the face of warnings from imperial officials to be cautious, they "struck hard," and the hammer blows destroyed the Ndebele in a brief campaign which involved few casualties on the company's side except for the celebrated Shangani patrol under Major Alan Wilson, whose deaths became a heroic legend.

For most of the troopers the war was almost without risk; they pursued the Ndebele as the hunter chases his quarry. Maurice Gifford, one of the most respected officers, confided in Cawston that "I should like to lay out about 2,000 more Matabele as we have not killed enough of them. The only way with these swaggering warriors is to leave your mark behind, they cannot understand leniency, they take it as weakness."[73] Ndebele tactics

70. Lobengula to high commissioner, October 12, 1893, US 1/1/1, N.A.R.
71. Helm to Thompson, October 9, 1893, LO 6/1/5, in *ibid*.
72. George H. Tanser, *A Scantling of Time*, p. 121; Hans Sauer, *Ex Africa*, pp. 226, 228.
73. M. Gifford to Cawston, January 14, 1893[4], BSAC IV Misc., Rhodes House.

would have made it easy for Gifford to achieve his wish, for they fought in the open and were slaughtered rather than employing the hit and run maneuvers which characterized the uprising three years later. The consequences of a prolonged campaign for the company can be assessed by the fact that this short easy war fought by volunteers cost £66,000 in direct expense. Most of the money to pay for it came from Consolidated Goldfields, Rhodes, and Beit.[74] Had operations been prolonged, as would have been the case if Ndebele had not chosen to fight with tactics ideal for their early annihilation, and had paid troops been required, the burden would have quickly exhausted the resources of the chartered company. But Rhodes and Jameson relied on their intuition and on their stars, and the auspices were favorable.

Several years later John S. Moffat branded the company as "clearly the aggressors" who had manufactured the evidence to justify their assault upon an African chief who had pursued a policy of peace.[75] Moffat's verdict was essentially just; but the Matabele War had no relation to justice.

Lady Florence Dixie, writing on "The Long and Short of the Matabele Trouble," interpreted the war in Social Darwinian terms: "I will not attempt to argue out the justice or injustice of attacking Lobengula. I cannot find that either has even been much considered in the great struggle for the survival of the fittest. . . ."[76] This was in accord with Rhodes's view of life. He and his associates had concluded that the Ndebele had to be subjugated because they disrupted the mining-agricultural economy of Mashonaland and because they occupied a territory which might contain the riches that had thus far eluded the company. With the news of the company's victory, the price of chartered shares rose substantially in the London and Johannesburg markets.[77] Investors expected the spoils of Matabeleland would redeem the disappointments of Mashonaland. The lands

74. Notebook of the Fourth Earl Grey, Grey Papers, Durham. Rhodes offered to provide up to £50,000 from his private fortune, but apparently his actual contribution was less. Harris to London office, BSAC, September 6, 1893, LO 5/2/29, N.A.R.
75. Paper by Moffat, May 6, 1898, MO 2/1/2, N.A.R.
76. *Pall Mall Gazette*, September 23, 1893.
77. *Financial News*, November 4, 1893.

of the Ndebele were forfeit, and the people were reduced to working for the white landowners and miners. Matabeleland had now been united with Mashonaland under company rule, and the official designation of these united provinces as Rhodesia was appropriate recognition of the force which had brought this about.[78]

78. The name "Rhodesia" had been employed unofficially earlier but was adopted by the company in May 1895, and by the imperial government in 1898.

10

Crown and Charter

"IMPERIALISM ON THE CHEAP" CHARACTERIZED BRITISH colonial policy long before the scramble for Africa. The conquest and control of India was at the expense of Indians; the breach with the American colonies had been occasioned in large part by British efforts to compel them to pay for imperial forces stationed among them. In these policies Britain was acting in accordance with the universal principle that dependencies should pay for their own protection. But after the American Revolution and particularly after the Canadian rebellions, British policy toward the "colonies of settlement" evolved to acceptance of a more relaxed relationship. Free association, imperial statesmen came to recognize, was not only more enlightened but less expensive. Those on the scene should make decisions for themselves and assume the financial burdens involved. These principles made it possible for the aspirations of the settlement colonies to be realized within the Empire-Commonwealth rather than their following the precedent of the United States.

Nineteenth-century Britons, however, did not look upon the empire solely in terms of power and wealth (indeed, there were doubts that, with the exception of India, it contributed to either). They had a sense of mission. Britain, they had no doubt, was peculiarly fitted to rule. British law, British morality, and British religion were priceless gifts to the peoples fortunate enough to come under imperial rule. Under the protection of the great queen the benighted of the earth would enjoy peace, order, and justice, and they would learn useful employments which would enable them to develop whatever capacities they possessed. This evangelical strain affected British policy throughout the century. But these ideals were always subject to the overriding consideration that colonies should not be costly. The treasury rigorously evaluated all expenditures, and the surest way to produce an eruption in Parliament was to bring in bills for supplementary colonial expenditures. The consequences were disastrous in those dependencies where white settlers were a privileged minority. Humanitarianism at a distance is rarely effective; when it was coupled with penury it contributed to turmoil. In Cape Colony before responsible government, great pretensions and little means led to a succession of "native wars" which were costly to Britons in money and to Africans in life and land. Eventually the imperial factor, disillusioned with the manifest failure of its well-intentioned intervention, pressed self-government on the white settlers. Authorities on the spot, responsible to the settler population, formulated their own native policy, with little substantive restriction from London so long as they did not act in a way too blatantly offensive to British principles of justice.

The authorization of the British South Africa Company, like the creation of other chartered enterprises, was a product of the imperial government's desire to lay claim to territories without accepting the financial burdens of administration. The chartered company was seen as a means not only of filling a vacuum but of developing the resources of new lands for the benefit of British society.

The promoters of the company, like their counterparts in East and West Africa and in Borneo, avowed their objects to be economic development to the mutual benefit of Britons and indigenous peoples. They indicated in their application that they would build railways and telegraphs, develop commerce, encourage British immigration, and exploit mineral resources. They would do so while respecting the rights of African peoples, whose interests would be advanced by the protection afforded them against unscrupulous adventurers. All of these laudable purposes would be achieved without any calls upon the imperial exchequer. Lord Knutsford, the colonial secretary, saw in the company a means of relieving the government of diplomatic complications and of heavy expenditures. It would occupy a territory containing valuable resources, thus reducing the temptation of foreign states to intrude. It would carry on an administration at its own expense; and once it was firmly established, its jurisdiction might be further extended. Administration of the Bechuanaland Protectorate entailed large outlays from the exchequer to support civilian officials and a semimilitary police force. Transfer of control to a private company would relieve the taxpayers of a burden. Governmental receptivity to the promoters' application thus developed primarily from powerful negative considerations. The controls incorporated in the charter became little more than a façade.[1]

The charter paid conventional lip-service to such noble purposes as the abolition of the slave trade and the advancement of African welfare, and it contained provisions which reserved to the government powers of review of the company's policies. All concessions and treaties were subject to approval by the Colonial Office. The government had the right to intervene in any dispute with an African chief, and the company was bound to accept the government's decision. The charter conferred no administrative authority on the company; any such rights had to be acquired by agreement with the appropriate African chief —in the case of Matabeleland and Mashonaland it was assumed that Lobengula held governmental power.[2]

Within this framework, the Colonial Office was assigned powers of surveillance over a wide range of matters including land policy and the administration of justice, and provision was made for repeal of the charter if the company would be a responsible agent of government; all that was lacking was commitment on the part of imperial officials either in South Africa or in London.

Both by omission and commission, the imperial government contributed to an illusion on the part not only of African chiefs but of its own representatives in Africa that the chartered com-

1. "Memorandum on the Origin and Operations of the British South Africa Chartered Company," n.d., African (South) No. 439, C.O. 417/89, P.R.O.
2. For the charter, see John H. Harris, *The Chartered Millions*, pp. 301–312.

pany not only enjoyed the queen's blessings but acted on her behalf. Spurred by Rhodes and the London board, the Colonial Office sought to rectify the damage done to the company by the "Queen's advice" to Lobengula not to surrender his "whole herd" to any concessionaire, by sending out two royal emissaries with the message that Lobengula had been wise to grant the monopoly to this company which enjoyed the queen's favor. Lobengula grumbled that the queen spoke with "two tongues" but he was led to believe that the company had the full support of the imperial government. That impression was strengthened by the cordial support of the company by the British resident, John S. Moffat. That support, unknown to Lobengula, even extended to allowing Jameson to edit the queen's message in the company's interests. Moffat, exulted Jameson, was "a brick, and as always willing to do anything for the advancement of the Company."[3]

Moffat did not act in this way because he had been suborned. He did so because he believed that the company was indeed acting with the sanction and support of the imperial authorities. Moffat had no doubt that this powerfully backed enterprise was the most expedient means of advancing British interests beyond the Limpopo and that he should use the powers of his office to back the company's representatives. His identification with the company became so intimate that he almost seemed an alter ego for Jameson; until the high commissioner felt compelled to remind him that he was a representative of the queen, not of the company.[4] Before that salutary reminder, however, and on occasion thereafter, Moffat justified Rhodes's and Jameson's confidence that he was a man upon whom they could rely.

Moffat's confusion as to the distinction between imperial and company interests was in large measure attributable to lack of guidance from his superiors. In the years before the Jameson Raid, the Colonial Office showed no inclination to exercise effective supervision over the actions of the company. This reluctance to intervene has usually been explained in terms of the government's fear of offending Rhodes, who might be pro-

3. Jameson to Harris, January 17, 1890, CT 1/13/6, N.A.R.
4. Imperial secretary to Currey, December 11, 1890; Moffat to Shippard, January 10, 1891, S1428/16, N.A.R.

voked to drastic actions if he were thwarted. But long before the power of Rhodes had been made manifest, the prospects of effective imperial surveillance had already disappeared. The supervision for which the charter made provision could only be effectuated if the imperial government had accurate information on the company's activities from its independent representatives in South Africa and was prepared to act on this intelligence to restrain the company. Neither condition was in evidence in the early years of the chartered company.

Consistent with the policy that chartered companies should pay their own way, the British resident on the spot in the company's territories received his salary from the company rather than from the government. The company paid Moffat £1,200 and an additional £300 for a secretary, as well as providing funds for other expenses.[5] The consequence was that he acted as much as possible in the company's interests. When possible conflicts developed between the roles, Moffat could not be relied upon to take a line which might be embarrassing to the company.

Moffat was no mere hireling of the company. He on occasion expressed misgivings about the actions of the company, as he did when he warned Rhodes that the entry of a large body of armed men with the pioneer column was a provocation to Lobengula and was unnecessary in terms of the avowed purposes of the expedition. But he was not a completely independent reporter on the state of affairs in Matabeleland and Mashonaland.

The assurance of full support from the resident, on the other hand, benefited the company greatly. The cordial cooperation between the company and the resident and repeated assurances from the high commissioner and the imperial government that the resident was the queen's mouthpiece convinced Lobengula that the company was in fact the agent of the queen, and this assumption undoubtedly made the Ndebele chief more cautious in his reactions to company initiatives. When the pioneer column went into Mashonaland, Lobengula was deterred from thoughts of attack by the belief that should he order his impis

5. Knutsford to Loch, April 5, 1890, in African (South) No. 32, December 1890.

against the company he would have to face the full force of the imperial government. This belief was reinforced by a message from Sir Henry Loch and from the Colonial Office assuring Lobengula of the column's peaceful intention and of the friendship of the chartered company for the Ndebele.[6] Colonel Pennefather, in charge of the police accompanying the pioneers, was also cast by the company in the role of the "Queen's Induna."[7] The distinction between company and government was never made clear to Lobengula by any imperial representative, and until his death he continued to be guided by the belief that they were manifestations of the same power.

To a considerable extent, of course, this belief was correct. Imperial officials in South Africa were not neutral arbiters between the company and the Ndebele. Some, such as Sir Sidney Shippard, were "company men," on whom Rhodes could rely.[8] Others, notably Sir Henry Loch, had reservations about the autonomy permitted the company. But all believed that the lands between the Limpopo and the Zambezi must be opened to European industry and were eager to advance that end, though they differed in fastidiousness as to how this was to be accomplished.

Without an independent observer on the spot, the imperial government had to rely on information filtered through the company or on press reports largely derived from the same source. But instead of attempting to correct this deficiency, the government further reduced the effectiveness of its local intelligence. Impelled by continued pressure from the treasury to reduce expenses in the Bechuanaland Protectorate, the Colonial Office on the recommendation of Loch decided in 1892 to shift Moffat to Palapye in Kgama's Ngwato territory. Loch argued that since the land question had been settled with the company's acquisition of the Lippert concession, there was no

6. Telegrams, Loch to Knutsford, rec'd. July 31, 1890, Knutsford to Loch, August 2, 1890, both in *ibid.*
7. Jameson to Pennefather, July 4, 1890, A 1/2/1, N.A.R.
8. H. C. Moore told Sam Edwards in 1888 that Rhodes had said he could make Shippard and Sir Hercules Robinson "do whatever he told [them] to." Edwards to Dawson, December 13, 1888, DA 1/1/1, N.A.R. The quotation may not have been accurate but it certainly reflected Rhodes's assumption.

longer need for the continued presence of a highly paid official
in Bulawayo. Moffat could make occasional visits to Lobengula
to keep informed on the political climate, and an assistant could
be stationed at the Ndebele capital to report on any events
worthy of notice. The immediate occasion for Loch's recommendation was the company's notice that it wished to reduce
its subsidy for Moffat's maintenance. With Moffat in a dual
role, half of his salary could be paid for his Bechuanaland responsibilities and the company could supply the remainder.[9]
The decision to shift Moffat's headquarters was symbolic of the
imperial government's apathetic stance toward the company's
activities. In Mashonaland there was no independent official to
provide information, much less to control.

In Matabeleland after Moffat's departure the imperial government derived much of its intelligence from a company em-
ployee, Johannes Colenbrander. In the strategic position he
occupied, Colenbrander was able to serve his masters well. Imperial officials when they found that Colenbrander had been
guilty of providing false information, were indignant at his
duplicity, but the government itself had made this deception
possible by its penuriousness.

Among key imperial officials in South Africa there were only
two who were not unqualified advocates of the company. Moffat's moral training made him uneasy in his relations with an
enterprise which, like the juggernaut, crushed those who stood
in its way. Late in 1891 he rebelled when Rhodes demanded
that he rewrite a report not sufficiently favorable to the company's claims in the disputed territory. "I cannot do it even if
they sack me," he wrote. "They must find tools for such work
elsewhere."[10]

Sir Henry Loch, the high commissioner, supported the company to the extent that it served his own objectives. Like Harry
Johnston, Loch was an imperialist; like Johnston, his imperialism was not entirely compatible with that of Rhodes. When he
succeeded Sir Hercules Robinson, Loch was in the last years of

9. Loch to Knutsford, January 26, 1892, in African (South) 426, October 1892.
10. Moffat to ———, September 27, 1891, in Robert U. Moffat, *John
Smith Moffat*, p. 236.

a career dedicated to the service of the queen. He had served with Elgin in China, where he had been imprisoned and tortured. In 1884, after a variety of appointments in Britain, he was made governor of Victoria, where he had served five years. His superiors agreed that Loch was a highly capable and conscientious pro-consul. They also agreed that he set his judgment on matters within his jurisdiction higher than that of officials in Downing Street and that he lacked any appreciation for the wider problems of government which they had to face. Sir Robert Meade expressed this vexation: "It is heart-breaking work dealing with Loch as a diplomatist. He passes over his instructions, and our political difficulties at home, with a sublime indifference which would be amusing were it not so disastrous."[11]

Loch had accepted the position in Cape Colony on the understanding that he would be consulted on all questions regarding South Africa,[12] and both Conservative and Liberal governments sought his views and were deferential to his judgments,[13] particularly with regard to problems involving the Transvaal. Loch, with his insistence on exercising power as the imperial presence, would have seemed to be a natural antagonist for Rhodes in the latter's determination to be the dominant factor in southern Africa. Rhodes and Jameson were sometimes annoyed at Loch's emphasis on his prerogatives. Jameson once castigated him as "possessed of egotism and vainglory."[14] But the relationship of Rhodes and Loch, if not cordial, was usually cooperative. Loch fully supported the company in its aggressiveness toward Portugal, and the Duke of Abercorn was delighted to observe that the thorny governor was on such good terms with the dynamic managing director.[15] Even after Rhodes

11. Meade to Ripon, April 3, 1893, Ripon Papers, Addtl. MSS. 43556, British Museum.
12. Draft, Ponsonby to Knutsford, August 1, 1889, Knutsford to Ponsonby, August 8, 1899, both in George E. Buckle, ed., *The Letters of Queen Victoria*, 1:519.
13. Buxton to Ripon, December 17, 1892, Ripon Papers, Addtl. MSS. 43553, British Museum.
14. Oliver Ransford, *The Rulers of Rhodesia*, p. 22.
15. Abercorn to Cawston, January 23, 1890, BSAC II Misc., Rhodes House.

became prime minister, he and Loch were usually able to work harmoniously. But the fundamental conflict in their views on the ultimate locus of power could not be resolved. Loch believed it essential that chartered company policy be controlled by the imperial representative; Rhodes would brook no restraints. Loch seemed to have his way when he insisted on approving the detailed arrangements of the pioneer force before he permitted its entry into Mashonaland, but this stipulation involved no real check to Rhodes's plans. The first test of strength between the two came in 1891, and Rhodes won, in large part because Loch's desires contravened imperial policy. Loch had backed the company against the Portuguese but the filibustering character of the company's operations seemed to him to underscore the necessity of strengthening the supervisory powers of the high commissioner. Britain, he argued, could be drawn into a war with any of three opponents—Portugal, the Transvaal, or the Ndebele—as the result of actions of a body over which it exercised little control. Turbulence in the company's territories could affect the rest of southern Africa. He knew that his superiors would not authorize additional expenditures, and he sought a means by which authority could be asserted without responsibility. The model he suggested to the Colonial Office was that of the East India Company. The South Africa Company in London might be subject to the counterpart of the board of control, and the chief officer of the company's territories, like the governor general, should be appointed concurrently by the imperial government and the directors but would be removable only by the government.[16] The response of the Colonial Office was emphatically negative. "The existing arrangements," Loch was informed, were "not only most correct in principle," but most consistent with the interests both of the company and of the government.[17]

The Colonial Office in essence had asserted that the company must accept responsibility for the chartered territories subject to imperial supervision but declined to adopt any measures

16. Loch to Knutsford, May 24, 1891, confidential, printed in African (South) No. 414, February 1892.
17. Knutsford to Loch, confidential, June 26, 1891, in ibid.

which would make such supervision effective. The consequence of this policy was that the imperial government became involved in legalities rather than substance. Before the Matabele War of 1893 the review mechanisms incorporated in the charter, with few exceptions, operated only when questions of law arose regarding the adoption of proposed ordinances in Mashonaland. On such occasions there were impressive displays of erudition by Crown lawyers on the applicability of Roman-Dutch law and Ndebele customs, the precise meaning of a protectorate, and other issues so intriguing to the legal mind. But these briefs touched only lightly the relations of the company with Africans and settlers or the policies it employed in the exploitation of land and minerals. The main effect of Crown review was to make necessary the redrafting of some ordinances and the acquisition of additional instruments to buttress the Rudd concession in giving the color of legality to the administration in Mashonaland. An order in council of June 1890 authorized the high commissioner to give effect to any power which the imperial government wished to exert, provided that this authorization did not abridge any treaties or native laws.[18] But what powers had Lobengula granted the company? The legal counsel of the Crown advised that the Rudd concession provided no basis for administrative authority over either whites or Africans, and the Colonial Office insisted that the company must secure such authorization from Lobengula. Given the chief's conviction that he had been duped by the company's agents and his belief that the settlers sent in to Mashonaland were a mortal threat to his people, such action on his part seemed highly unlikely. The company nevertheless sought Moffat's help in extracting a document from Lobengula. Moffat's approaches to the chief, however, were met by evasion and temporizing: "He is getting more and more disinclined to sign anything."[19] Lobengula's resistance caused great concern among the company's directors. A draft of proposed mining laws was rejected by the Colonial Office on the basis that no authority had been granted

18. Order in Council, June 30, 1890, in Morgan O. Evans, *The Statute Law of Southern Rhodesia*, pp. 13–15.
19. Moffat to Harris, October 22, 1890, CT 1/13/10, N.A.R.

by Lobengula to exercise such jurisdiction.[20] Appeals to Moffat became more and more importunate, but still the chief resisted making any commitment. Why, asked Lobengula, should the company ask him for power to punish whites in Mashonaland when they had sent these men into his country without his consent and against his protests?[21] The question was not answered.

Lobengula's uncooperativeness created a crisis. As Loch pointed out, if the mining population learned that they were not subject to any lawful authority, "the place will become an Alsatia and a disgrace to civilisation."[22] Knutsford and Salisbury agreed that delay was dangerous,[23] and the government in May 1891 issued an order in council recognizing the territory as under British protection and authorizing the appointment of officials to exercise jurisdiction over the white population.[24] Loch assumed that the problem was now resolved. He published a proclamation announcing that jurisdiction over whites north of the Limpopo would be exercised by officers of the chartered company appointed by the high commissioner.[25] But again the Crown lawyers intervened. They held that the company could not issue a draft code of laws it had drawn up for Mashonaland without some document from Lobengula indicating that he had delegated such power. Rhodes was furious with the pedantic legalists who insisted on dotting i's and crossing t's when it was imperative that the company assert its authority, but there was no alternative but to seek to comply. Harris wrote to Moffat: "I need not say what a great service you would be rendering Mr. Rhodes & the Charter, but also Christianity & Civilisation if you cd. obtain us some simple written form, with Colenbrander's assistance from Lobengula."[26]

Moffat was unable to secure the desired document. The most he was able to deliver was a reported oral admission by Lobengula of the company's right to deal with Europeans "even up

20. C.O. to BSAC, September 16, 1890, A 1/2/4, N.A.R.
21. Lobengula to Loch, January 1, 1891, HO 1/3/1, N.A.R.
22. Loch to Knutsford, November 20, 1890, African (South) No. 414, February 1892.
23. F.O. to C.O., March 5, 1891, in *ibid.*
24. Morgan, *Statute Law*, pp. 15–18.
25. Loch to Moffat, June 20, 1891, MO 1/1/4, N.A.R.
26. Harris to Moffat, November 1, 1891, in *ibid.*

here" which Moffat interpreted to mean Matabeleland.[27] Another remark of the chief was also cited as indicating consent: "I hear that the white men have laws in Mashonaland."[28] These assertions were far from explicit recognition of the company's rights, but the government professed to be satisfied.

There can be no better illustration of the barrenness of the letter of the law when unrelated to its application. The hours of research into legal precedents had little to do with the state of society between the Limpopo and the Zambezi. And the erudition of the review of the company's code of laws was not in evidence in the government's response to the sale of the Lippert Concession to the company. Many years later, legal experts held that the concession did not convey title to land and that the transfer of a concession to a third party was contrary to native law. But in 1891 and 1892 the high commissioner and the Colonial Office quickly accepted the validity of a transaction which they believed solved the problem of land ownership in Mashonaland.

Virtually the whole range of company administration in Mashonaland was beyond the scrutiny of imperial officials. Before 1892 the only representative was in Bulawayo, and after Moffat's departure for Palapye, the high commissioner and his London superiors relied for information on a man whose sole responsibility was to the company. The language of the May 1891 order in council was explicit that there should be no interference with native laws and customs, and the instructions from the Colonial Office and the high commissioner reaffirmed this principle. But there was no means to ensure that the company acted in accordance with this mandate. Contrary to imperial instructions company officials did intervene in strictly African disputes, and their assertions of authority were challenged only when some particularly flagrant misuse of power came to the attention of the government.

The company had no legal right to intervene in the dispute between Moghabi, a chief of the Victoria district, and another

27. Telegram, Moffat to Loch, September 11, 1891, in African (South) No. 414, February 1892.
28. Jameson to Acting Secretary, BSAC, Cape Town, December 2, 1891, LO 5/2/16, N.A.R.

chief, but Jameson nevertheless responded to the other chief's appeal for protection. When Moghabi refused to submit to the company's "authority," a police unit attacked him, killed him, and burned his kraal.[29] The response of the high commissioner to this illegal exercise of force was a communication through his military secretary that he had "read with interest" Jameson's account of the affair.[30] On this and other occasions the company without protest from imperial officials established a de facto power to exercise control over Africans. On the installation by the company of a chief in succession of Lomaghundi, killed by the Ndebele, Rhodes stated that the event demonstrated that the company was now "overlord" in Mashonaland.[31] That assertion also went unchallenged.

Within very broad limits, the administrator of Mashonaland made his own law and his own policy. Rhodes and Jameson were profligate; their land policies compromised the future welfare of Rhodesian society. They were able to act in this way only because they were literally irresponsible. Their discretion was checked neither by the London board of the company nor by the Colonial Office, which by their inaction contributed to the conditions they were later to deplore.

This passivity was also in evidence with regard to policy on the involvement of African labor. Colonial Office, board, and local administration were agreed that indolence as defined in English terms was a vice and that honest labor by Africans in a cash economy benefited not only the white employers but the African workers themselves. As early as the 1840s, imperial officials had sanctioned taxation as a means of forcing Africans into paid labor. If the Crown had been in control of Mashonaland it probably would have imposed taxes like those assessed by the company. But the decisions made by the company were not made in consultation with the Crown, except on the narrow questions of the legality of ordinances. With the labor problem, as with other issues, the administrator used his discretion.

From the early days of mining operations, the attention of

29. Jameson to Acting Secretary, Cape Town, January 15, 1892, CT 1/15/5, N.A.R.
30. Sapte to Harris, July 18, 1892, CT 1/15/1/2, N.A.R.
31. Harris to London office, September 14, 1892, LO 5/2/22, N.A.R.

the company administration was engaged in the assurance of an adequate and reliable labor supply. Shona men were not always available to work in the mines, and when hired they did not always stay. The attitude of the employers was typified by one young English miner:

> We have a great trouble in getting native labour up here, the only way we can do it is to go and catch them at dawn and compel them to work, and it is strange that when they do begin they work well, cause no trouble whatever, we pay them a blanket and a shirt a month, and this satisfies them. The blanket costs 7/ up here, they are the ordinary cotton blanket, and the shirts are 24/ a dozen. It is not the pay that they won't work for, but because they are lazy.[32]

This "catch them at dawn" policy, however, was not a satisfactory means of ensuring a reliable work force. In 1892 the company began to consider imposing a poll tax or a hut tax for the double purpose of raising revenue to support the administration and forcing able-bodied men to offer their labor. Major Forbes made a tour of Mashonaland warning the people that they must plant more grain because the tax would be levied some time after the harvest.[33] The company anticipated no difficulties in introducing a hut tax because such levies had been in effect for half a century in Cape Colony. But again the lawyers blocked the path. W. P. Schreiner, Loch's legal adviser, pointed out that the colonial acts cited as precedents were inapplicable to Mashonaland. In Cape Colony and British Bechuanaland, hut taxes were imposed on dwellings situated either on Crown land or on private land alienated from the Crown. But in Mashonaland no concession or treaty vested in the company ownership as against the African occupiers.[34] As Graham Bower, the imperial secretary, commented, since the Africans were probably the legal owners of the land they occupied, the company had no right to levy a tax on the dwellings they had erected on it.[35] There was some doubt whether this conclusion

32. Mallett to his father, July 3, 1892, MA 9/1/1, N.A.R.
33. Notes, in CT 1/15/1, N.A.R.
34. Opinion by W. P. Schreiner, August 29, 1892, printed in African (South) No. 441, July 1893.
35. Imperial Secretary to Secretary, BSAC, Cape Town, August 29, 1892, in *ibid.*

applied equally to the Ndebele and the Shona;[36] if Lobengula was the overlord of the Shona, presumably he would have the right to impose taxes just as he levied tribute. But the company had been delegated no such power by Lobengula.

Loch was not impressed with the legal argument but he was concerned at the political effect of the company's asserting the right to tax a people who had previously been considered Lobengula's vassals, and he desired to avoid antagonizing the Ndebele chief. He therefore proposed that if the tax were authorized it be levied only on people living either east of the telegraph line or east of the 30th meridian. In effect Loch was suggesting that those areas most remote from Bulawayo be detached from Lobengula's domain. If this division were made, however, Loch emphasized, the company would have to assume full responsibility for the consequences. Any trouble with Lobengula would be the company's problem, and the imperial government could not be expected to provide any assistance.[37]

Several months had elapsed while the hut tax was considered in South Africa, and the issue reached London almost a year after the company had asked for approval. The reaction of the Colonial Office was mixed. Sydney Olivier pointed out that the company had entered Mashonaland to make money from gold and land and that the profits from these sources were expected to pay for administration. But now, with the first optimistic expectations blighted, they were asking for the right to levy tribute:

> The further concession they desire is a concession of forced labour. They employ the Pecksniffian argument with which we are so familiar in South Africa, that it is the holy mission of the white man to teach the native habits of settled industry, the industry, *bien entendu*, being always contemplated under the form of wage labour for the white man in the mines or the land which he cannot work for himself.[38]

Not all of the permanent staff agreed with Olivier with regard to the issue of principle. Edward Fairfield, who by his years of

36. Harris to Imperial Secretary, CT 2/4/2, N.A.R.
37. Imperial secretary to secretary, BSAC, Cape Town, May 23, 1893, African (South) No. 441, July, 1893.
38. Minute by Olivier, July 13, 1893, on BSAC to C.O., July 7, 1893, in C.O. 417/110, P.R.O.

experience with colonial policy had become a cynic, brushed aside his young colleague's moral strictures. The issue, he said, had little to do with morality; what was important was the practical consequence of the imposition of the tax. In view of the heightening tension between Lobengula and the company, it was unwise to authorize an additional provocation. The decision on the hut tax should be deferred until the current crisis had been resolved. Fairfield's position was adopted; the Colonial Office suspended action on the hut tax.[39]

This ponderous deliberation was not related to events in Mashonaland. The company's South African office had interpreted Loch's suggestion of a demarcation line as approval, and Jameson thereupon proceeded to introduce the hut tax gradually into Mashonaland without waiting for the formalities of Colonial Office assent. The administration in Mashonaland had developed the practice of taking action in the absence of explicit prohibition. In 1892 Jameson had prescribed regulations for migrant labor in the Salisbury area without referring them to the high commissioner and these rules were in effect for three years before they were transmitted to the Colonial Office.[40]

The hut tax did not receive final approval from the imperial government until July 1894,[41] and the proclamation of the high commissioner giving final authorization was issued a month later.[42] When Jameson received notification that he could now legally proceed, hut tax collections had been going on for at least fifteen months. The fact that the company was collecting the tax was public knowledge as early as May 1893. In that month the *Financial News* reported that the tax, "recently imposed," was bringing in larger returns than expected. In consequence, the journal predicted, there would likely be a sharp rise in chartered shares, and knowledgeable insiders were buying on every decline.[43]

This flouting of legality and disregard of imperial authority

39. Note by Rosebery, on *ibid.*
40. J. M. Mackenzie, "African Labour in the Chartered Company Period," *Rhodesian History*, vol. 1, 1970, p. 48.
41. By Order in Council of July 18, 1894, printed in Morgan, *Statute Law*, pp. 21–31.
42. Harris to Administrator, August 16, 1894, CT 2/1/6, N.A.R.
43. *Financial News*, May 20, 1893.

went unrebuked by the Colonial Office, though the staff had been aware of the violation. In the opinion of Fairfield, it seemed unwise to antagonize the company, particularly since the issue was a legal technicality rather than a substantive conflict.[44] The Colonial Office did not disagree with the desirability of the introduction of the levy which after all was modeled on taxation in British colonies in southern Africa.

This reluctance to challenge the company involved an abdication of responsibility. The rationalization that "small offenses" could be ignored encouraged Rhodes and Jameson in their belief that they could act much as they pleased so long as they did not insist on formal governmental approval. At worst the Colonial Office would request information if a particularly flagrant misuse of power was brought to its attention, but the only official sources who could provide the information were the company's officers themselves. There seemed little reason to fear governmental intervention unless the actions of the company produced a major issue with another power or resulted in a war which would necessitate an appeal for imperial military assistance. The validity of their assumptions was amply demonstrated in the Matabele War.

Before the "Victoria Incident" which provided the spark for a war, Loch, acting on instructions from the Colonial Office, had emphasized to Rhodes that the company alone was responsible for money and men if a war broke out and that it should not expect imperial help.[45] Bower, the imperial secretary, underscored this warning. He advised Rhodes that any advantage the company might gain from attacking Lobengula while a large impi was fighting in Barotseland would be overbalanced by the anarchy which would result when Lobengula's authority was destroyed. The company would have to contend with small bands of Ndebele roaming about the country, and a large police force would have to be maintained to check these marauders and to await the returning impi.[46] A reasonable interpretation

44. Minute by Fairfield, June 29, 1892, in C.O. 417/136, P.R.O.
45. Telegram, Loch to Ripon, July 26, 1893, C.O. 879/39/452, P.R.O.
46. Imperial Secretary to Rhodes, July 21, 1893, C.O. 879/39/454, P.R.O.

of these messages was that the issue of war and peace should be decided on the basis of the company's ability to smash the Ndebele without imperial assistance and that indeed seems to have been Loch's intention. "It is essential," Loch wrote Ripon in July 1893, "that the Company should not be allowed to rush lightly into a war unless there is a fair prospect of their being able to bring it to a rapid and successful issue."[47]

In these messages there was no suggestion of concern for considerations of justice. Loch welcomed the prospect of the destruction of the Ndebele military system. But while he had little sentiment for the Ndebele, the high commissioner was much concerned with his authority in relation to the chartered company. Despite his failure in 1891 to win the backing of the Colonial Office for his plan to bring the company's local administration under his control such regulation was essential. The imminence of war gave him the opportunity to reassert himself. Loch and his superiors in London were convinced that Jameson and the settler population were using the "Victoria Incident" as an opportunity to provoke a war with Lobengula. The Colonial Office feared that despite explicit warnings "Jameson and Company" would force the issue in the expectation that the imperial government would be forced to come to their assistance. The danger was that their calculations might be correct, for if the white population were unable to cope with the Ndebele, imperial troops would almost certainly have to be sent to their aid. The consequence would be another of the miserable little wars which were anathema to every government, Liberal or Conservative. Buxton, the parliamentary undersecretary, reminded Ripon that it was "the small wars" of the 1880s which had been the undoing of the last Liberal government.[48] The colonial secretary needed no reminding, nor did the cabinet.[49] Loch was instructed to inform the company that its forces were to make no "aggressive" movement without

47. Loch to Ripon, private, July 26, 1893, Ripon Papers, Addtl. MSS. Addtl. MSS. 44648, British Museum.
48. Letters, Buxton to Ripon, August 14, 16, 24, 27, 1893, in Ripon 43561, British Museum.
49. Notes of cabinet meeting, August 31, 1893, Gladstone Papers, Papers, Addtl. MSS. 43553, British Museum.

his previous approval unless they were attacked.[50] Buxton also told Grey and Maguire who came to see him with word that war was inevitable, that if this was the case it must be fought entirely at company expense.[51] The effect of Buxton's warning was not what he had intended, for Grey and Maguire had come to their meeting with him after receiving a cable from Rhodes that no imperial help was needed or desired and that he would guarantee any additional outlays that might be required beyond the company's resources.[52]

The government had assumed that the denial of its help would be a deterrent to the company's aggressiveness. The Colonial Office did not understand that such intervention was precisely what Rhodes was determined to avoid. If the government became involved, he recognized, control of policy toward the Ndebele would pass out of the company's hands. Jameson had assured him that the volunteer forces could defeat the Ndebele without outside assistance and he backed his lieutenant's judgment that "the Matabele question" should be settled immediately. Rhodes's assurances in turn, were all the board required. Grey wrote him on September 1:

> We are in the dark here, at least I am, as to your plans but I have the fullest confidence in the wisdom of any move agreed on by you and Jameson and if you do go ahead shall know you have sufficient resources within reach to make the move right and prudent so only do whatever you think right and we will support you whatever the issue but keep us as fully informed as you can for our guidance with Government and the Public.[53]

Rhodes's fears that the imperial government intended to fetter his freedom of action were reflected in attacks on "Downing Street pusillanimity" in the press which he controlled. The *Cape Argus* called Ripon's counsel of caution "a most disgraceful exhibition," unparalleled since Lord Derby's "shilly-shally

50. Telegram, Ripon to Loch, August 28, 1893, C.O. 879/39/452, P.R.O.
51. Buxton to Ripon, August 25, 1893, Ripon Papers, Addtl. MSS. 43553, British Museum.
52. Grey to Rhodes, September 1, 1893, File 181/1, Grey Papers, Durham.
53. *Ibid.*

over Sir Charles Warren."[54] The *Cape Times* denounced the "peculiar intellectual and moral activity" which denied the company the right to just compensation for the atrocities of the Ndebele.[55] The campaign was unnecessary. There was no iron in the Colonial Office's injunctions, and backed by Colenbrander's inventions, Rhodes and Jameson had little difficulty in securing Loch's approval for the commencement of hostilities.

With regard to the prosecution of the war there was no dispute between government and company. The government did not wish to intervene in military operations, since such involvement would bring a measure of responsibility; the company did not want government participation for essentially the same reason. Both the Colonial Office and the company therefore, agreed that this was and must continue to be the company's war. The governmental position involved a corollary which the government did not accept—that the outcome of military operations would shape the character of the peace settlement. The inducements offered volunteers in land and booty evoked some moralizing in the Colonial Office. A nearly bankrupt company, unable to pay its forces directly, was offering "dirty money" in the form of plunder. This rapacity must be restrained, but beyond that the government must assert its prerogative to determine the terms of peace. This was the Colonial Office position. As expressed by Buxton, "The interest of the Company is to drive out Lobengula and possess his land—ours is to keep him there with his claws clipped and his teeth drawn—to become a sort of second Khama."[56] In the first weeks of the war, the Colonial Office had apparently firmly decided that the company would be brought under the control of the Crown, with Lobengula remaining as titular chief to do the bidding of his British advisers. The company would be expected to contribute at least part of the costs of administration.[57]

54. *Cape Argus*, September 19, 1893.
55. *Cape Times*, September 20, 1893.
56. Minute by Buxton, October 28, 1893, on Loch to Ripon, October 17, 1893, C.O. 537/127, P.R.O. The Foreign Minister, Lord Rosebery, noted that Buxton's minute was one with which he essentially agreed.
57. These conclusions are indicated in notes on Loch to Ripon, October 17, 1893, C.O. 537/127, P.R.O.

These conclusions were in accordance with the recommendations of Sir Henry Loch. He had not changed his view that the
company must be brought into the harness of the high commissioner, and he could not resist reminding Ripon of his advice
in 1891 that it was highly dangerous to allow the chartered
company such a high degree of independence. He did not explicitly indicate that war might have been avoided if his counsel
had been heeded, but this was strongly implied. The wisdom
of 1891 was documented by the lesson of 1893, "that the execu-
tive of a country should not be personally interested in the
acquisition of the lands and property of those they are called
upon to govern." [58] Ripon's instruction to Loch in October 1893
that all negotiations with Lobengula must be conducted by the
high commissioner[59] were highly gratifying to Loch.

While the government debated its position on the terms of
the peace, the company's administrators in South Africa were
exerting their energies to ensure that the government had no
more part in the peace settlement than it had in the war.
Rhodes, who had arrived in Salisbury after the departure of the
columns had put them out of reach of recall by telegraph from
Cape Town, sent a special messenger after Jameson to be certain
that when he took Bulawayo the entire management of postwar
Matabeleland was retained in company hands.[60]

The government and the company had taken apparently ir-
reconcilable positions. The nature of the resolution of the conflict provided further commentary on the ineffectuality of the
mechanisms regulating the chartered company. Lord Ripon
considered it poor policy to use chartered companies as an instrument of government. He wrote to Gladstone in November
1893:

> I regard the system of administration by Chartered Companies
> as essentially bad. These companies are really speculative, got up
> mainly for Stock Exchange purposes, and a good deal blown up
> in that aspect of their existence. The B.S.A. Coy has been very
> near bankruptcy—from which probably their success in Mata-

58. Loch to Ripon, secret and confidential, October 18, 1893, C.O.
879/39/459, P.R.O., printed in African (South) No. 459, January 1894.
59. Telegram, Ripon to Loch, October 22, 1893, African (South) No.
454, December 1893.
60. Telegram, Rhodes to Harris, October 21, 1893, LO 5/2/30; N.A.R.

beleland will save them for a time. But anyhow they are not pleasant instruments of administration. . . .[61]

Most of Ripon's colleagues in the Colonial Office and the government shared his opinion in varying degrees. But government is not carried on by moral maxims, and given the disinclination of Parliament to vote money, and the desire of administration to assert British claims to vast territories, no alternative to chartered rule seemed feasible. Privately the "buccaneering" propensities of Rhodes were condemned, but this distaste was not much in evidence among the British public or in most of the influential newspapers. Labouchere's *Truth* and the *Daily Chronicle* applauded the government's decision to control the peace settlement, but "public opinion" as assessed by the politicians did not seem to be much aroused. Fairfield, whose minutes in the Colonial Office often had the flavor of soured idealism, commented that "John Bull's Sunday-School conscience" seemed to have fallen asleep and that "there never was a time when principles of brutality were so strongly represented in the press." [62] The one eventuality which would produce certain outrage was the involvement of the government in expenditure for the war, but the prospect diminished as the company's forces confounded the predictions of imperial military authorities by destroying the Ndebele regiments who so conveniently had attacked in crowded masses mounted riflemen, Maxim guns, and artillery. Under these circumstances the government lacked the will to defend its position resolutely against an irate Rhodes. Within four days of Loch's communication to Rhodes that the high commissioner would decide the terms of peace, the government's retreat had begun. On October 24, 1893, the company's board forwarded with their endorsement a telegram from Rhodes that the company if victorious must be allowed to settle the peace, subject only to the approval of the Colonial Office.[63] Two days later, the Colonial Office responded that it had not

61. Ripon to Gladstone, confidential, November 4, 1893, Ripon Papers, Addtl. MSS. 43515, British Museum.
62. Minute by Fairfield, October 25, 1893, on Loch to Ripon, October 17, 1893, C.O. 537/127/ P.R.O.
63. BSAC to C.O., October 24, 1893, African (South) No. 459, January 1894.

contemplated any interference with military operations and
that in coming to any decision on the postwar settlement Loch
would consult with Rhodes and give his views "due weight."[64]
This strategic withdrawal merely intensified the barrage from
the Rhodes-influenced press in South Africa and from his backers in Britain. Albert Grey told Ripon that the government's
position in effect set aside the powers of the company under the
charter and that the announcement without prior consultation
with the board and with Rhodes was a "slap in the face."[65]
Ripon protested that the government was acting strictly within
the terms of the charter and that the settlement affected not
only the welfare of the company but the peace of South Africa.[66]
Ripon's initial inclination was to defend this position. "It is a
point on which we cannot give way," he wrote to Loch. But, he
added, the high commissioner should work as much as possible
in cooperation with Rhodes and "let him have his full way in
all matters affecting the Company." Despite his avowals, Ripon
had no stomach for a dispute with Rhodes. He concluded: "I
have a personal liking for Rhodes; his boldness & resource attract me; & if he quarrels with me it will be his fault not mine.
Therefore don't you get wrong with him if you can help it. I am
inclined to suspect that the present trouble is stirred up by Dr.
Harris rather than by Rhodes."[67]

This rationalization that the problem was not Rhodes but
overly militant subordinates was a theme which frequently was
played when officials sought to avoid a direct encounter. Fairfield provided his own variation when he suggested that if
Rhodes went to the front personally he might be authorized to
conduct negotiations with Lobengula under the supervision of
Loch. Rhodes, Fairfield observed, had no ill-will toward Lobengula, but Jameson under no circumstances should be allowed
to carry on negotiations. He was "wanting in coolness, and he is

64. C.O. to BSAC, October 26, 1893, in *ibid.*
65. Grey to Ripon, confidential, October 26, 1893, in File 184/13,
Grey Papers, Durham; and LO 3/1/17, N.A.R.
66. Ripon to Grey, private, October 26, 1893, File 184/13, Grey
Papers.
67. Ripon to Loch, confidential, October 27, 1893, Ripon Papers,
Addtl. MSS. 43562, British Museum.

gravely implicated in the charge against Captain Lendy of having fired on the retiring Matabele without provocation."[68]

Resistance to Rhodes's insistence on "a free hand" rapidly
crumbled with news from Matabeleland at the beginning of
November that the Ndebele had been crushed and Lobengula
had fled.[69] The cabinet on November 4 concluded over Ripon's
opposition that the collapse of the Ndebele power had made the
argument with Rhodes unnecessary and that the government
should adopt a more conciliatory line. This decision, protested
Loch, was based on pure expediency, and the cabinet had been
motivated primarily by a desire to avoid a clash with the Cape
government which Rhodes dominated.[70] Even discounting the
rumors that Rhodes might decide to lead a secession movement
in Cape Colony if he did not have his way,[71] the issues of Matabeleland did not seem sufficiently important to warrant a breach
with the most powerful man in South Africa.

Ripon, though he considered chartered companies to be inherently a bad means of government,[72] was sufficiently a pragmatic politician that he wished to avoid a clash with Rhodes
which could subject the Liberal government to strong opposition attacks. It was best to accept the fact that the company's
success had given it a strong position to demand a greater share
in the administration of Matabeleland than he had wished to
assign to it. The government, he believed, must now fall back
on the powers reserved to it in the charter to ensure that the
company's administration acted with due regard for native
rights and customs.[73] This was also the judgment of his
colleagues.

Parliament received with general placidity a statement by the
parliamentary undersecretary which in effect was a declaration

68. Minute by Fairfield, October 28, 1893, BSAC to C.O. October 27,
1893, C.O. 417/110, P.R.O.
69. BSAC to C.O., November 2, 1893, C.O. 417/110, P.R.O.
70. Ripon to Gladstone, confidential, November 4, 1893, Gladstone
Papers, Addtl. MSS. 44287, and Ripon Papers, Addtl. MSS. 43515, both
in British Museum.
71. The *Daily Chronicle*, November 4, 1893.
72. Ripon to Gladstone, confidential, November 4, 1893, Ripon Papers, Addtl. MSS. 43515, British Museum.
73. Ripon to West, November 12, 1893, in *ibid.*

Fig. 1. A cartoon by Edward Fairfield. Copyright Public Record Office, London, England.

that imperial policy on Matabeleland was being reconsidered and that the company rather than the Crown would be assigned the administration.[74] Ripon was required to make as graceful a transition as possible to acceptance of Rhodes's having the principal control over the peace settlement. Loch gave him some assistance in this distasteful task when he wired that the great success of the company made it impossible to adopt the recommendations he had made at the outbreak of the war, and that it now seemed necessary to treat Matabeleland and Mashonaland as being one country under the administration of the company, with safeguards for the protection of imperial and African interests.[75]

Rhodes had triumphed not only over the Ndebele but over the imperial government. The capitulation of the Gladstone cabinet had been almost unconditional; the experience fed his contempt for the politicians of Whitehall who, he thought, lacked both understanding and courage. He believed in his stars. The outcome of the Matabele War was yet another demonstration of the power of his audacity to achieve great objects. At a banquet in Cape Town to celebrate his victory over the Ndebele, Rhodes told an enthusiastic audience that he had pursued expansion for the benefit of Cape Colony, which he hoped would be the nucleus of a United South Africa. He had "no objections to the Crown, if the Crown would recognise its duties," but he would brook no interference from "meddling functionaries in Whitehall."[76]

Such remarks on various occasions were highly irritating to the imperial government. Though Rhodes protested that his meaning had been misinterpreted, there was no doubt that he meant what he said when he attacked the "Imperial factor." He was particularly contemptuous of the Liberal government. Gladstone and his followers he considered both shortsighted and spineless. If they had their way, Britain would cease to be a great power; it would sink to insignificance in world affairs. Such men did not represent the true England. The people of

74. The *Times*, November 10, 1893.
75. Telegram, Loch to Ripon, November 12, 1893, African (South) No. 459, January 1894.
76. *Financial News*, January 29, 1894.

Britain, like those of Cape Colony, supported the ideals for which he strove, and the Liberals would not dare to make a test of strength with him because they would be turned out of office. This view of British society was to a considerable extent colored by manifestations of support from members of the Conservative opposition. Rhodes undoubtedly overemphasized his support and underestimated the actual potential opposition to his policies. As Ripon wrote to Loch:

> ... I hope Rhodes will not mistake public opinion here. If he is as wise a man as I suppose him to be he will feel the necessity of considering it. It will not do for him to rely on the support of the Opposition. They hate the Govt much more than they love him or the Chartered Coy: & if they saw a chance of beating us they would vote for Labouchere, or stay away without a moment's compunction.[77]

This statement had considerable validity. There were limits to what Rhodes could do without incurring strong opposition in Britain, and he did not recognize those limits. But in his insistence that the company must have the right to administer Matabeleland he did not evoke powerful protest. The high commissioner was generally accommodating in his response to Rhodes's proposals, and the order in council of 1894 for the government of Matabeleland and Mashonaland was essentially based on Rhodes's and Loch's draft. The company was accorded the right to appoint administrators, subject to approval by the secretary of state. The order in council prohibited exceptional legislation for Africans except with regard to liquor and arms, but the hut tax was specifically exempted from this restriction.[78]

In only two areas were Rhodes and the South Africa Company seriously inhibited by the imperial government. He sought to incorporate a clause in the ordinance providing that all South African goods should be admitted free of duty in the company's territories south of the Zambezi and that British goods would be admitted for all time at the existing tariff of Cape Colony. Imports from foreign countries, however, might be taxed at

77. Ripon to Loch, confidential, December 15, 1893, Ripon Papers, Addtl. MSS. 43562, British Museum.
78. Matabeleland Order in Council, July 18, 1894, Morgan, *Statute Law*, pp. 21–31.

higher rates. This three-tiered system was related to a far larger objective than the regulation of trade in the chartered territories, the value of which was of no great moment in the 1890s. Rhodes sought to promote South African unification by any feasible means. Political union could be advanced by common economic interests, and to this end he desired a free trade community within southern Africa behind a protectionist tariff wall against foreign competitors. The imperial government saw Rhodes's proposed clause as the "thin edge of the wedge" for the introduction of protectionist policy and refused to approve.[79] Ripon was willing to accept a policy by which both foreign and British goods were subject to the Cape tariff,[80] but this did not accord with Rhodes's desires. On this occasion the imperial government did not give way, and the clause was deleted.[81]

The other area in which the company was checked involved the spoils of conquest, and here the imperial government demonstrated that its professions of concern for the welfare of the defeated Ndebele were not mere rhetoric. With the Ndebele subjugated, the company proceeded not only to fulfill the terms of Jameson's contract with the volunteers but to compensate itself for the expenditure it had incurred. Large quantities of Ndebele cattle were seized on the ground that they had belonged to the king and now were the company's by right of conquest, and Jameson began the process of awarding farms and marking out townships. In this disposition of Ndebele land and cattle there was little evidence of concern that the people be left sufficient land and cattle to maintain themselves. Loch concurred with the company's position that it had a right to seize all cattle belonging to Lobengula. Indeed, he thought the wholesale rounding up of the cattle was salutary since it was the "best evidence to Matabele that they have been beaten as they are the symbol of the chief's authority."[82] But the distinction

79. Confidential memo for board, March 1, 1894, CT 1/11/3/2, N.A.R.

80. Ripon to Rosebery, May 5, 1894, Ripon Papers, Addtl. MSS. 43516, British Museum, Grey to Edward Grey, May 8, 1894, File 211/5, Grey Papers, Durham.

81. *Financial News*, June 21, 1894.

82. Telegram, Loch to Ripon, rec'd. December 11, 1893, in African (South), 459, January 1894.

between the king's and the people's cattle the Colonial Office rejected as "fallacious."[83] In Ndebele as in other African societies, Ripon wrote Loch, all cattle in a sense belonged to the chief. Beyond the issue of ownership, however, there were humanitarian considerations. The government made it clear to Rhodes through Loch that it could not sanction the distribution of cattle and land without regard to the needs of the African population. In this insistence the government had the backing of the press and of humanitarian groups in Britain.[84] This intervention by the imperial government undoubtedly had the effect of increasing the number of cattle left to the Ndebele, though Rhodes insisted that the company had been sensitive to the needs of the Ndebele and had needed no imperial reminder.[85] As a result of the government's insistence on reservation of adequate land for Africans, the order in council provided for the appointment of a land commission charged with the responsibility of making a survey of needs for grazing and agricultural lands and the demarcation of reserves for Africans. This decision was probably unwise. Whatever the definition of "adequate," the reserves were not sufficient to sustain the increase in population, and necessity forced an outflow to work in the "white areas." Furthermore, the preservation of reserved areas with communal tenure inhibited the development of an efficient agriculture and the integration of Africans into the Rhodesian economy. These effects document the lack of understanding of nineteenth-century policy makers of the complicated social problems with which they contended, but the intent of the imperial government was benign, and it acted on behalf of its professions rather than allowing the company a free hand.

Such manifestations, however, were infrequent. When a commission headed by Francis J. Newton exonerated Jameson from any wrongdoing in Captain Lendy's attack on the Ndebele impi on July 18, 1897, Ripon expressed his pleasure that the imperial government could now proceed to honor him for his services to the empire, and Jameson was made a Companion of the Bath, a

83. Ripon to Loch, December 13, 1893, in *ibid.*
84. *Financial News*, June 21, 1894, the *Economist*, June 23, 1894.
85. Telegram, Rhodes to high commissioner, December 25, 1893, LO 5/2/32, N.A.R.

recognition, noted Ripon, on which Jameson had "set his heart."[86] This distinction was awarded largely because of the success of the company's forces in subjugating the Ndebele without involving the imperial government.

After the Matabele War, as before, the imperial government was not willing to exercise a substantial supervisory role over the British South Africa Company, and the provisions in the charter for such regulation remained inactive. At the same time the London board of the company did not exercise control over their managing director. Rather, they became on most occasions a vehicle for the justification of Rhodes's policies. The only occasions in which the board reproved Rhodes related to the company's finances. When it appeared that Rhodes was guilty of mismanagement and excessive spending and that the company faced ruin, the board expressed itself with authority. But, with that exception, in the years before the Jameson Raid Rhodes was subject to little control either from the London board or from the imperial government. By their abdication of responsibility, the board and the government became accessories to Rhodes. Between 1889 and 1896 the chartered company was an engine without a governor.

86. Ripon to Rosebery, private, August 21, 1894, same to same, September 29, 1894, both in Ripon Papers, Addtl. MSS. 43516, British Museum.

Bibliography

Manuscript Sources

THE PRINCIPAL SOURCES FOR THE STUDY OF THE EARLY years of the British South Africa Company are the manuscript collections of the National Archives of Rhodesia. Virtually all of the official correspondence of the company is preserved there, as well as many private letters which throw additional light on the company's operations. The materials are well organized and the indexes are excellent. The following sources have also been useful in the preparation of this work:

British Museum
  Dilke Papers
  Gladstone Papers
  Ripon Papers
Christ Church College, Oxford
  Salisbury Papers
University of Durham
  Papers of Fourth Earl Grey
Public Record Office
  Series C.O. 417, 537, 879
      F.O. 83, 84, 179, 343
      B.T. 31

Rhodes House, Oxford
  British South Africa Company
    Papers
  Maund Papers
  Rhodes Papers
University of Witwatersrand
  Maund Papers
Royal Commonwealth Society
  Harry Johnston Papers
West Register House, Edinburgh
  Records of African Lakes
    Company,
    Scottish Exploration Company

Unpublished Theses

McCarty, J. W. "British Investment in Overseas Mining, 1880–1914." Ph.D. thesis, Cambridge, 1961.

Macmillan, Hugh W. "The Origins and Development of the African Lakes Company, 1878–1908." Ph.D. thesis, Edinburgh, 1970.

Shenton, Robert. "The Chartered Company, 1889–1898." Ph.D. thesis, Harvard, 1961.

Government Publications

Great Britain, Admiralty, I.D. 1889. *A Manual of Portuguese East Africa*. London, 1920.

Great Britain, Colonial Office. *North Charterland Concession Inquiry*. Colonial No. 73. London, 1932.

Great Britain. *Parliamentary Debates*.

Great Britain. *Parliamentary Papers*: C. 5918 (1890), C. 7171 (1893), C.1790 (1893), C.7196 (1893), C.7290 (1894), C.7637 (1895), C.8117 (1896), Cmd. 1129 (1921), Cmd. 1129B (1921), Cmd. 1273 (1921).

Books

Axelson, Eric. *Portugal and the Scramble for Africa, 1875–1891*. Johannesburg, 1967.

Aydelotte, William O. *Bismarck and British Colonial Policy. The Problem of South West Africa*. Philadelphia, 1937.

Baines, Thomas. *The Gold Regions of South Eastern Africa*. London, 1877.

Baker, Ernest. *The Life and Explorations of Frederick Stanley Arnot*. New York, 1920.

Baker, Herbert. *Cecil Rhodes by His Architect*. London, 1934.

Buckle, George E., ed. *The Letters of Queen Victoria*. 3rd series, 3 vols. New York, 1952.

Caplan, Gerald. *The Elites of Barotseland, 1878–1969*. Berkeley, 1970.

Cartwright, A. P. *Gold Paved the Way*. London, 1967.

————. *The Corner House*. Cape Town, [1965].

Cary, Robert. *Charter Royal*. Cape Town, 1970.

Chesterton, G. K. *A Miscellany of Men*. London, 1912.

Churchill, Randolph H. S. *Men, Mines, and Animals in South Africa*. New York, 1892.

Clay, Gervas. *Your Friend, Lewanika*. London, 1968.

Coillard, François. *On the Threshold of Central Africa*. London, 1897.

Colvin, Ian. *The Life of Jameson*. 2 vols. London, 1922.

Consolidated Gold Fields of South Africa, Limited. *"The Gold Fields," 1887–1937*. London, 1937.

Cook, E. T. *Edmund Garrett*. London, 1909.

Cornet, René J. *Katanga*. Brussels, 1946.

D'Andrada, J. C. Paiva. *Report and Protest of the Affairs Occurred at Manica.* Cape Town, 1891.

Darter, Adrian. *The Pioneers of Mashonaland.* London, 1914.

Duff, H. L. *Nyasaland Under the Foreign Office.* London, 1903.

Duffy, James. *Portuguese Africa.* Cambridge, Mass., 1959.

Dugdale, E. T. S., ed. *German Diplomatic Documents, 1871–1914.* 4 vols. New York, 1928–1931.

Emden, Paul H. *Money Powers of Europe in the Nineteenth and Twentieth Centuries.* London, 1938.

————. *Randlords.* London, 1935.

Evans, Morgan O. *The Statute Law of Southern Rhodesia.* Salisbury, 1899.

Fitzpatrick, James Percy. *South African Memories.* London [1932].

Frankel, S. H. *Capital Investment in Africa.* London, 1938.

Fripp, Constance E., and Hiller, V. W. eds. *Gold and the Gospel in Mashonaland.* London, 1949.

Fuller, T. *Cecil John Rhodes.* London, 1910.

Galbraith, John S. *Mackinnon and East Africa, 1878–95.* Cambridge, 1972.

Gann, Lewis H. *A History of Northern Rhodesia.* London, 1964.

————. *A History of Southern Rhodesia: Early Days to 1934.* London, 1965.

Garson, Noel. *The Swaziland Question and the Road to the Sea, 1887–1895.* Cape Town, 1957.

Glass, Stafford. *The Matabele War.* London, 1968.

Goldmann, Charles Sydney. *The Financial, Statistical, and General History of the Gold & Other Companies of Witwatersrand, South Africa.* London, 1892.

Green, J. E. S. *Rhodes Goes North.* London, 1936.

Gross, Felix. *Rhodes of Africa.* London, 1956.

Hammond, R. J. *Portugal and Africa.* Stanford, 1966.

Hanna, A. J. *The Beginnings of Nyasaland and North-Eastern Rhodesia, 1859–95.* Oxford, 1956.

Harris, John H. *The Chartered Millions.* London, [1920?].

Hind, R. J. *Henry Labouchere and the Empire, 1880–1905.* London, 1972.

Hintrager, Oskar. *Südwestafrika in der deutschen Zeit.* Munich, 1955.

Hole, Hugh Marshall. *Lobengula.* London, 1929.

————. *The Making of Rhodesia.* London, 1926.

Holmberg, Ake, *African Tribes and European Agencies.* Göteberg, 1966.

Hone, Percy F. *Southern Rhodesia.* London, 1909.

Hughes, A. J. B. *Kin, Caste, and Nation Among the Rhodesian Ndebele.* Manchester, 1956.

Isaacman, Allen F. *Mozambique. The Africanization of a European Institution.* Madison, 1972.

344 BIBLIOGRAPHY

Johnson, Frank. *Great Days*. London, 1940.
Johnston, Harry H. *The Story of My Life*. New York, 1923.
Johnston, James. *Reality versus Romance in South Central Africa*. London, 1969.
Knight, E. F. *Rhodesia of To-Day*. London, 1895.
Knight-Bruce, G. W. H. *Memories of Mashonaland*. London, 1895.
Kuper, Hilda, Hughes, A.J.B., and van Velsen J. *The Shona and the Ndebele of Southern Rhodesia*. London, 1954.
Leonard, A. G. *How We Made Rhodesia*. London, 1896.
Lockhart, J. G., and Woodhouse, C. M. *Cecil Rhodes*. New York, 1963.
Mackenzie, John. *Austral Africa, Losing It or Ruling It*. 2 vols. London, 1887.
Mackenzie, W. D. *John Mackenzie, South African Missionary and Statesman*. London, 1902.
McIntosh, Duncan. *South Africa*. Glasgow, 1876.
Michell, Lewis. *Cecil John Rhodes*. 2 vols. London, 1910.
Moffat, Robert U. *John Smith Moffat*. London, 1921.
Oliver, Roland. *Sir Harry Johnston and the Scramble for Africa*. London, 1957.
Olivier, Lord. *The Anatomy of African Misery*. London, 1927.
Pearson, Hesketh. *Labby*. London, 1936.
Perham, Margery. *Lugard, The Years of Adventure, 1858–1898*. London, 1956.
Plomer, William. *Cecil Rhodes*. Edinburgh, 1933.
Rademeyer, J. L. *Die Land Noord van die Limpopo in die Ekspansie Beleid van die Suid-Afrikaanse Republiek*. Cape Town, 1949.
Ramm, Agatha. *The Political Correspondence of Mr. Gladstone and Lord Granville, 1876–1886*. 2 vols. Oxford, 1962.
Ranger, Terence O. *Revolt in Southern Rhodesia*. London, 1967.
Ransford, Oliver. *The Rulers of Rhodesia*. London, 1968.
Raphael, Lois A. C. *The Cape-to-Cairo Dream*. New York, 1936.
Robinson, Ronald, and Gallagher, John. *Africa and the Victorians*. London, 1966.
Rotberg, Robert I. *Joseph Thomson and the Exploration of Africa*. London, 1971.
Rouillard, Nancy, ed. *Matabele Thompson, an Autobiography*. London, 1936.
Samkange, Stanlake. *Origins of Rhodesia*. London, 1968.
Sauer, Hans, *Ex Africa*. London, [1937].
Selous, Frederick C. *Travel and Adventure in South East Africa*. London, 1893.
Stokes, Eric, and Brown, Richard, eds. *The Zambesian Past*. Manchester, 1966.
Tabler, Edward C. *The Far Interior*. Cape Town, 1955.
Tanser, George H. *A Scantling of Time*. Salisbury, 1965.

Thomson, James B. *Joseph Thomson*. London, 1897.

Thorold, Algar L. *The Life of Henry Labouchere*. London, 1913.

Tilsley, G. E. *Dan Crawford, Missionary and Pioneer in Central Africa*. London, 1929.

Twain, Mark. *Following the Equator*. 2 vols. New York, 1899.

Vambe, Lawrence. *An Ill-Fated People*. London, 1972.

Verdick, Edgar. *Les premiers jours au Katanga (1890–1903)*. Brussels, 1952.

Verschoyle, F. (Vindex). *Cecil Rhodes, His Political Life and Speeches, 1881–1900*. London, 1900.

Wallis, J. P. R., ed. *The Northern Goldfields Diaries of Thomas Baines*. 3 vols. London, 1946.

Warhurst, Philip R. *Anglo-Portuguese Relations in South-Central Africa, 1890–1900*. London, 1962.

Weinthal, Leo, ed. *The Story of the Cape to Cairo Railway and River Route*, 4 vols. London [1923–27].

Williams, Basil. *Cecil Rhodes*. New York, 1921.

Williams, Ralph. *How I Became a Governor*. London. 1913.

Wills, Walter H., and Hall, J. *Bulawayo Up-to-Date*. London, 1899.

————, and Collingridge, L. T. *The Downfall of Lobengula*. New York, 1969.

Wilson, A. J. *An Empire in Pawn*. London, 1909.

Wilson, Monica, and Thompson, Leonard. *The Oxford History of South Africa*, II, Oxford, 1971.

Articles and Pamphlets

Ashton, Ford. "Mr. Rhodes as Capitalist Conspirator," *Progressive Review*, II, 7, April 1897, 57–68.

Beach, David N. "The Adendorff Trek in Shona History," Henderson Paper No. 14, 1971, University of Rhodesia.

Bull, Mutumba M. "Lewanika's Achievement." *Journal of African History*, XIII, 3 (1972), 463–472.

Caplan, Gerald. "Barotseland's Scramble for Protection," *Journal of African History*, X, 2 (1969), 277–294.

Ferris, N. S. "Draft History of the British South Africa Company." Part One. For Office Use Only. Typescript, National Archives of Rhodesia, n.d.

Fox, H. Wilson. "Memorandum on the Position, Policy and Prospects of the Company." Printed for the information of the Board, 1897. Strictly Private and Confidential. Supplemented to 1907.

Henderson, Ian, and Warhurst, Philip. "Revisions in Central African History to 1953," Central Africa Historical Association, Local Series 15. Salisbury, 1965.

Mackenzie, John M. "African Labour in the Chartered Company Period." *Rhodesian History*, I, 1970, 43–58.

Miers, Suzanne. "The Brussels Conference of 1889–1890: The Place of the Slave Trade in the Policies of Great Britain and Germany," in Gifford, Prosser, and Louis, W. Roger, *Britain and Germany in Africa*, New Haven, 1967.

Palmer, Robin H. "War and Land in Rhodesia," *Transafrican Journal of History*, I, 2, July 1971, 44–62.

Shaw, Flora L. "The British South Africa Company," *Fortnightly Review*, XLVI, New Series, November 1889, 662–668.

Sims, Graham. "Paladin of Empire, Earl Grey and Rhodesia," Local Series Pamphlet No. 26, Central Africa Historical Association, Salisbury, 1970.

Turner, Henry Ashby. "Bismarck's Imperialist Venture: Anti-British in Origin," in Gifford, Prosser, and Louis, W. Roger, *Britain and Germany in Africa*, New Haven, 1967.

Wheeler, Douglas L. "Gungunyana the Negotiator: a Study in African Diplomacy," *Journal of African History*, IX, 4 (1968), 585–602.

Periodicals

Cape Argus
Cape Times
Daily Chronicle (London)
Financial News (London)
The *Economist*
Pall Mall Gazette

St. James's Gazette
South Africa
South African Telegraph
The *Times* (London)
Truth

Index

Countess of Carnarvon (ship), 191–192
Currie, Sir Donald, refuses membership on chartered company board, 114
Currie, Sir Philip, 139

D'Andrada, Paiva, 38, 178; promotes companies, 184
Delagoa Bay Railway, 94–95
de Waal, M. D. C., praises Mashonaland, 264
Dilke, Sir Charles, buys shares in chartered company, 124
Dixie, Lady Florence, 308
Doyle, Denis, 134
Durban Gold Mining Company, 32

Edwards, Sam, 43, 66
Euan Smith, Sir Charles, role in forming chartered company board, 113–114; agent for Rhodes, 123
Exploring Company, founded (1888), 54; backers, 56; seeks Imperial support, 60; sends Maund to Lobengula, 60; participates in Central Search Association, 84; liquidated, succeeded by company of same name, 86

Fairfield, Edward, 74, 80; appraises Rhodes, 23
Farquhar, Horace P., on board of chartered company, 117; supports rigging stock, 268
Ferreira, Major J. J., action at Maçequeçe, 199
Fife, Duke of, accepts vice-chairmanship of chartered company board, 114; lack of interest in company affairs, 115
Forbes, Patrick W.: engagement at Maçequeçe, 178–179; refuses to march on Beira, 182; assignment to Barotseland, 222
Francis, Daniel, 32
Francis, William C., 50
Frere, Sir Bartle, supports expansion, 34–35
Fox, H. Wilson, criticizes Jameson, 281
Fry, Ivon, 66
Fry, John, 43, 61

"Garaganze country." See Katanga
Gazas, origins, leadership, 166–167
Gifford, Lord: first interest in Matabeland, Mashonaland, 39; renews

interest in gold, 53; and Exploring Company, 55–56; amalgamation with Rhodes, 79ff.; on board of chartered company, 116; plans for great African trading, transport company, 239–240
Gifford, Maurice, 307
Gladstone, W. E.: reacts to German expansion, 11–13; imperial policy, 35–36
Gold Fields of South Africa. See also Consolidated Gold Fields, 58; interest in Rudd concession, 84
Gouveia. See Sousa, Manoel António da
Grant, James A., 245
Great Britain Colonial Office, policy toward Ndebele, 74–75; backs Rhodes-Gifford-Cawston amalgamation, 80ff.; indifference to Barotseland, 102; rejects Lobengula's appeals against Rudd concession, 106–107, 120; indifference to Africans, 107, 113, 134; suggests Lobengula accept resident, 112; sends mission to Lobengula, 121; fails to control chartered company, 133, 277, 312, 313; questions armed force into Mashonaland, 149; overridden by Salisbury, 149; deference to Rhodes, 157–158; misapprehensions about chartered company finances, 256; approves Lippert land concession, 276; rejects company mining laws, 319–320; approves mining laws, 320–321; suspends action on hut tax, 322–325; accepts fait accompli, 325; insists on role in peace settlement, 328–333; surrenders to Rhodes, 333–334; rejects Rhode's tariff policy, 336–337
Great Britain, imperial policy, 3–4, 14, 36–37, 310–311; public views of Africa, 130–131
Great Northern Gold Fields Exploration Company, 49–50; sells concession to Caisse des Mines, 53
Grey, Albert (fourth Earl), 79, 92, 156; on board of chartered company, 116; dominated by Rhodes, 116; opposes stock rigging, 268
Grey, third Earl, 79
Grobler, Pieter, 64; treaty with Lobengula, 42
Gungunyana, chief of Gazaland, 166; dispute over status, 167ff.; his